To    Elizabeth & Herman

Best Wishes for Xmas 86

Lyn

# THE ARCHJOCKEY OF CANTERBURY
# AND OTHER TALES

# The Archjockey of Canterbury

## of

## Canterbury

## and other tales

by Kent Hollingsworth

1986
THE BLOOD-HORSE, INC.
LEXINGTON, KENTUCKY

Articles in this book were published originally
in The Blood-Horse Magazine during the years 1964-1972.

Text printing: Johnson and Hardin Company, Cincinnati, Ohio
Binding: C. J. Krehbiel Company, Cincinnati, Ohio
Dust jacket color separations: Magna Graphic, Inc., Lexington, Kentucky
Dust jacket printing: Jones Printing Company, Chattanooga, Tennessee
ISBN 0-939049-10-4

*Thumbing through the dictionary, the way one does when possessed with only a vague notion of spelling, we found just below archbishop a fine word new to us, archjockey, which we tucked away to lighten a heavy sentence some day. Soon thereafter, Michael Hole, an English rider, reversed the field on Chaucer, journeying from his native Canterbury to ride in the United States. Hole did well here, winning more than 2,000 races. Thus we found Big Spruce in winning the Marlboro Cup, and Dearly Precious in her championship season—ridden by the archjockey of Canterbury. Fleshing out this bare comment, New York artist Susan McHugh sent us her conception of this rider as he might appear before the Clerk of Scales, a joyous piece of work which after 20 years has been removed from its spot on our office wall to a dust jacket.* K.H.

# PREFACE

Before getting into this thing, readers should be forewarned about the time warp. Unlike your usual narrative that begins at a specific point in time and proceeds through successive events to a subsequent conclusion, this is a collection of contemporary comment, in no chronological order whatever, written some 20 years ago for *The Blood-Horse* magazine under an ambiguous column heading, "What's Going On Here..."

Readers hereby are put on notice that suggestions hereinafter to the effect that something happened only "last week" refer to matters that were topical in the 1960s or early 1970s. This is in conformance with the racing rule that permits a man to say, "I win it last week." Triumph in racing, whether experienced today, yesterday, or expected tomorrow, ever is now, and always is expressed in the present tense.

Such is the game of racing. In essence, racing is much the same today as it was 20 years ago, or a century ago—only the names and numbers have changed. There are more Thoroughbreds racing in North America now, some 85,000 where only about 35,000 raced 20 years ago; a stallion share in Seattle Slew was sold for $3 million recently, compared to the record $170,000 for a share in Nijinsky II. True, Col. Phil T. Chinn was unique, and Eddie Neloy had no peer, but there are racing men today cut from the same cloth.

Thus, this book has no beginning or end in the normal sense of time; readers may start anywhere, cut a pole, start again farther down the course, and still be among racing men, talking horses, of races won, and promise unfulfilled.

# INTRODUCTION

In 1945 we had Jimmy Brynes and no racing in the United States. Mexico had racing, but also had Don Meade, so it was hard to tell where racing was getting the worst of it.

It was during the racing blackout in the U. S. that a Kentucky breeder looked out his living room window and saw one of his 2-year-old colts had broken into a field that already had been plowed for tobacco. The colt galloped the fence line once around, then cut across the middle, running easily over the rough ground.

"Look at that!" the breeder exclaimed. "He's going at a 1:40 clip over plowed ground! That's my Derby horse next year." Prescience is a wonderful thing, handy for a horse breeder or player, but difficult to come by.

Actually the Kentucky breeder knew long before that he was going to get a Derby horse. The idea came to him when he paid Col. W. V. Thraves $3,000 for a half-interest in two fillies and a colt "with a stifle" that John Goode was training for $6 a day. Bucked shins and one thing or another, and neither of the fillies started at two; the colt was just coming up to a race when he threw a stifle. A knee here, ankle there, that stifle again, and none of them did anything at three.

The best of the trio was a filly named Little Sissie, by Longridge—Granddaughter, by Harry Shaw, a pedigree that defies comparison. She did not start until she was four, then ran 17 times. A good deal of money was bet on this filly, but she never won a race. She did get as close as third once, in a $1,000 claiming race at Thistledown, and was retired with earnings of $50.

The Kentucky breeder, reluctant to spring for more training bills, begged out of the deal, and Col. Thraves grandly presented him with Little Sissie as a broodmare. This was all right, for she was an outcross to any stallion in

Kentucky, and, if all the money spent on training, veterinary bills, black-smiths, shipping, jockey fees, and losing bets for the three horses were to be credited against the one, she amounted to a high-priced—if not valuable—broodmare.

Mr. Tom Piatt was standing Maedic at the time. Maedic was the best 2-year-old in Saratoga in 1937, but he had only three 2-year-old winners in his first crop when the Kentucky breeder asked about booking to the horse, and Mr. Piatt was glad to get any kind of mare.

The result of this mating was the 1943 foaling of a "nice colt." This is a descriptive term the Kentucky breeder had picked up from Arthur Hancock Sr., who described every foal ever dropped at Claiborne Farm—no matter the conformation, no matter the breeding—as a "nice filly" or "nice colt."

Inasmuch as the nice colt was by a sire with a double name, the breeder announced to his son: "I'm going to name him after you and your sister, Dorcas. We'll call him Kendor."

Charley Kingsland broke the breeder's yearlings in the fall of 1944 at Keeneland and he picked out the sleepy Maedic colt as a good one. When Byrnes suggested that the race tracks close to help the war effort, Kendor came home and showed his lick over plowed ground.

Byrnes resigned as head of the War Mobilization Board, the Germans gave up in Europe, racing returned, Fred Hooper won a June 9 Kentucky Derby with the first horse he ever owned, and the Kentucky breeder started his 2-year-old toward the 1946 Kentucky Derby. The route was devious.

It started at the old Fair Grounds in Detroit. This in itself was not an unusual starting place for a Derby horse. Dixiana Farm had a Balladier colt on the grounds which was said to have been clocked three furlongs in :33, pulled up, but nobody really believed a 2-year-old could run that fast in Detroit. The colt's name was Spy Song.

Gas ration stamps were pooled and the car trip from Lexington to Detroit to see Kendor's first race was made by the breeder and his son along with John Stanley (who spent the entire trip explaining how smart he was to breed Double Jay), and E. Gay Drake (who spent the entire trip saying nothing). Kendor finished third.

He did not win until his eighth start, then with a $4,000 claiming tag. Marion H. Van Berg claimed the third horse in the race. Time for the six furlongs was five seconds off the track record and it seemed the Derby was a long way off. Six days later, however, ridden by Canadian Pat Remillard, Kendor won again, this time in a 1 1/16-mile allowance race; he was on again for the Derby.

In his next start Kendor finished sixth, but ahead of David Ferguson's Bob

Murphy, which was duly noted. Shipped to Churchill Downs, he finished sixth to Jimmy Brink's Lookout Dice, but ahead of Lucas Combs' Dark Jungle, and that also was duly noted.

Shipped to New Orleans, Kendor finished dead last at 5½ furlongs. In his next start, ridden by Len Stroud, he was second to Bank Balance, ridden by Nick Jemas (subsequently the managing director of the Jockeys' Guild).

Thus as a 2-year-old Kendor had started 17 times, won three, and earned $3,500. To the objective student of form, Kendor was a $4,000 claimer which had improved to be an allowance horse and seemed to do his running at the end. No one, except the owner and his son, knew Kendor at this time was a Derby horse—not even the trainer, Bobby Young.

In his first four starts at three Kendor won two Class C allowance races. His fifth start was in the $3,000-added Gulf Coast Handicap at a mile and 70 yards over a heavy track. Eric Guerin brought Kendor from sixth place after the first half-mile, swooshed by Jemas on William Helis Sr.'s Honeytown at the stretch turn, and drew out to win by seven lengths. Jemas claimed that he had been bothered. Kendor's number came down.

By this time it was conceded, at least in Louisiana, that Kendor was a Derby horse, and under the conditions of the Louisiana Derby he drew top weight of 120 pounds. Hal Price Headley shipped in with Pellicle which, with 117 pounds, won by two lengths; Helis' Earshot, with 115 pounds, was second; Kendor third, "closing well." Back home to Keeneland.

Now to most people in this country Mrs. Elizabeth N. Graham had all the real Derby horses—four or five of them, a band finally pared to Lord Boswell, Knockdown, and Perfect Bahram. Oh, Willie du Pont was galloping a horse called Hampden he was planning to send to Louisville, and Max Hirsch thought he might have something for King Ranch when his club-footed colt won the Wood Memorial, and everybody knew Spy Song would be in front the first part of it. But nobody—nobody except the Kentucky breeder and his son—thought Kendor was a Derby candidate.

Eddie Arcaro flew into Keeneland to ride Lord Boswell in the Blue Grass Stakes. Gordon Hettinger had the mount on Pellicle, Doug Dodson was up on Calumet Farm's In Earnest, and Art Craig had the mount on Bob Murphy, which had won the Arkansas Derby since he had last seen Kendor. Al Bodiou rode the sleeper horse.

As expected, Arcaro brought Lord Boswell down at odds-on to beat Pellicle by a neck. Bodiou brought Kendor back seventh, 7½ lengths behind Lord Boswell. Not everyone reads a chart of a race the same way. Many people may have thought Kendor was soundly beaten in the Blue Grass Stakes, but when Kendor's owner studied that chart he decided that inasmuch as

Kendor was 16 lengths off the pace after going a half-mile his colt had closed 8½ lengths in the last five furlongs on the leaders, "Lord Boswell, Pellicle, and those kind of horses. And I say any time you can pick up eight lengths in the stretch on the Derby favorite—you've got yourself a shot at the Derby. No telling what he'll do with another furlong."

There was telling, a lot of it—by his trainer, his wife, his family, his friends. Look at your horse: He's won two allowance races in New Orleans this year.

"Three! And he's a come-from-behind horse!"

At Churchill Downs, superintendent Tom Young did not take Kendor's candidacy seriously and stabled him virtually off the grounds, near the mile chute in the big old brick Waggoner barn.

A gaggle of reporters flocked around the barns of real Derby horses and reams of copy were turned out on the Maine Chance horses. Occasional stories were worked up on Hampden, Spy Song, Assault, and Rippey. By midweek virtually all the odd angles had been explored. Col. Matt Winn was exhausted, every groom had been interviewed, Lord Boswell had written his last column.

Then on Wednesday a photographer from the Louisville *Courier-Journal* wandered aimlessly over to the Waggoner barn. Kendor was asleep, but when his stall door was opened, he raised his head and peered at the photographer.

That night the Kentucky breeder discussed the matter of Kendor's Derby chances for the 5,000th time with his family and numerous house guests, and late in the evening, an odd time and place for such a thing to happen, logic began to prevail. Kendor should not be entered.

With the morning, however, came the *Courier-Journal*, and there it was on the front page: Six columns of Kendor sacked out in the straw. Rain was predicted for the 72nd Derby. "Mud's My Dish," said the picture caption.

"We're gonna run! See there? They think we've got a chance! Everybody knows we won the Gulf Coast Handicap by seven on a heavy track! They're scared to death of us." At Louisville, $250 and Kendor's name went into the entry box. The sky was dark. It rained.

On Friday it stopped raining, but remained overcast, and the track was muddy all day. First Page won the Kentucky Oaks in 1:51⅖, more than seven seconds off the track record. Rain was predicted again for Saturday.

Early Saturday morning the owner and his wife drove from Lexington to Louisville. For 25 cents he bought the most expensive *Daily Racing Form* in his life. "Sweep" picked Kendor fourth.

With brisk step and light heart the breeder entered the racing secretary's office and grandly parted with a $1,000 starting fee. As he stepped outside the sun broke through the clouds. Tom Young and his mules went to work harrowing the track.

At noon the first race was run on a muddy track and a 2-year-old Maine Chance colt making his first start won by nine lengths. His name was Jet Pilot.

By 3:20 p.m. the track had dried out considerably and was classified slow, the fifth race being won by Busyridge, he by Longridge ("Now I told you he was a sire").

When the band started playing "My Old Kentucky Home," there were only a few dark spots on the track. Spy Song led for the first mile, then Assault went past him easily and won by eight lengths. Hampden was third, Lord Boswell fourth, Bob Murphy seventh, Pellicle eighth, Rippey 10th, Dark Jungle 12th, With Pleasure 14th, Kendor 17th—"last, as expected," concluded radio announcer Clem McCarthy.

"Well, son," my father said to me as we walked back to the barn, "we've had a Derby horse."

Kent Hollingsworth

# Northern Dancer, By A Long Neck

It was an exciting, record-breaking 90th Kentucky Derby in which a good little horse beat a good big horse. It was 7 (Northern Dancer) and come 11 (Hill Rise), but No. 11 did not come soon enough in one of the fastest final quarters in the fastest Kentucky Derby ever run.

"We were getting to him," said Bill Shoemaker immediately after dismounting from Hill Rise, "but we ran out of ground. Maybe we'll catch him next time."

Hill Rise's venerable trainer, Bill Finnegan, who had said before taking the favorite over to the paddock that he would rather any day have a 10-1 shot than a 6-5 chance, watched his charge cool out after the race. "Well, he looks like he's all right, so I guess we've got another shot at it."

Thus the Derby issue, which seemed clearly decided in the stretch run at Churchill Downs, will be tried again in Baltimore May 16. Northern Dancer, Hill Rise, The Scoundrel, and perhaps Roman Brother, Quadrangle, Mr. Brick, and Mr. Moonlight, which finished in that order in the Derby, will go at it again in the 88th Preakness.

Last winter, few dared predict such an exciting 90th Kentucky Derby. The best of last year's 2-year-olds, Raise a Native, was retired in August and the survivors took turns beating each other thereafter. Hurry to Market, Garden State Stakes winner, and Golden Ruler, Arlington-Washington Futurity winner, suffered quarter cracks and were counted out for the 3-year-old classics. That left Chieftain, Roman Brother, and Northern Dancer among those ranked at 123 pounds or more on the Experimental Free Handicap. Quadrangle was ranked at 118, Hill Rise at 115, and The Scoundrel at 110, and one usually does not think of looking that far down among the 2-year-olds to find the Kentucky Derby contenders.

1

Chieftain looked like something on Feb. 10 when Bill Hartack rode him and he beat Northern Dancer by two lengths in a six-furlong allowance race at Hialeah. Two weeks later in an exhibition race, Northern Dancer beat Chieftain by seven lengths and the latter's connections began thinking of things other than the classics.

In his first race of the season, Northern Dancer was ridden by Bobby Ussery. Northern Dancer was knocked sideways leaving the gate and Ussery rushed the little colt into contention, whipping him soundly, but could get no better than third to Chieftain and Mom's Request.

Trainer Horatio Luro was distressed by Ussery's whipping of the little Canadian colt. Luro said he had to play the violin to settle his horse. Shoemaker was called in to ride the colt in the exhibition and never raised his stick.

"His need is encouragement, never punishment," said Luro. "When he is hit as he was the other day, it can turn him sour. He could stop training kind and it could have been the first step for a year of disappointments. I happen to know both the sire (Nearctic) and the dam (Natalma), which I trained, and neither of them was a stick horse, especially the dam. You could get nothing out of them by punishing them. They were very much the same kind as Northern Dancer."

Shoemaker did not hit Northern Dancer in winning the Flamingo in excellent time of 1:47⅘ for nine furlongs. Shoemaker did hit the colt in the Florida Derby when The Scoundrel closed strongly in the stretch, "but he didn't like it much," Shoemaker said.

Meanwhile in California, Hill Rise was running over and away from his rivals and there were those who said he was the best since Swaps. After finishing third in his first two starts in May as a 2-year-old, Hill Rise was one of the many horses hit by the coughing epidemic last year and did not start again for six months.

He came back on Nov. 22, won a maiden allowance race by nine lengths, another allowance, than the 1¹/₁₆-mile Freshman Handicap, and the seven-furlong California Breeders' Champion Stakes on Dec. 28.

In his first start at three, he won the 1¹/₁₆-mile San Felipe Stakes in 1:41⅖, the fastest time ever recorded by a 3-year-old at the distance in California. Then he won the Santa Anita Derby by an impressive six lengths.

Shoemaker could have ridden either Northern Dancer or Hill Rise. He chose the latter. Why? "Because I thought he was the better horse, that's all." Hartack was secured for Northern Dancer. Both horses were shipped to Keeneland.

Hill Rise was sent in the seven-furlong Forerunner Purse, and with indif-

2

ferent opposition was unimpressive in winning by three-quarters of a length. Shoemaker, after his first ride on the colt, felt he had made the right decision.

Northern Dancer was sent in the nine-furlong Blue Grass Stakes, and after being held to a half in :50²⁄₅, won with a last eighth in :11²⁄₅. This also was Hartack's first ride on the colt and he apparently was happy to have the mount, remarking that he could not understand why Shoemaker "got off him, unless it was because The Scoundrel got within a length of him in the Florida Derby."

Both horses were shipped to Louisville for final preparations. Hill Rise was worked a mile in 1:40¹⁄₅ on April 21 and four days later went another mile in 1:39²⁄₅. Then he ran a smashing race in the Derby Trial, winning as Shoemaker chose, going the mile over a track labeled good in 1:35¹⁄₅. Northern Dancer was worked five furlongs in 1:00²⁄₅ on April 30. Both horses seemed ready to run the race of their lives. They did.

Hill Rise, at 16.2 hands a full four inches taller than Northern Dancer, was installed the favorite for the Derby at odds of 1.40-1, with Northern Dancer at 3.40-1. Quadrangle went off at 5.30-1 and The Scoundrel at 6-1. Churchill Downs handicapper Allan Lavin, in an informal handicap before the race, said he would weight Hill Rise at 128 pounds, Northern Dancer 125, Quadrangle 124, The Scoundrel and Roman Brother at 119.

On the day of the race, George A. Pope Jr. leaned on a rail outside Hill Rise's stall and said to trainer Bill Finnegan: "We're lucky to have the horse come up to the race in such good shape. At this distance, with a good track, the best horse should win. I feel we have the best horse, but you never know until you see the number put up there."

At the start of the 90th Kentucky Derby, Mr. Brick broke quickly from his No. 1 post position and veered sharply to his right, interfering with Quadrangle breaking from No. 2. Wil Rad also broke quickly from No. 3 and Quadrangle was squeezed back, causing his trainer Elliott Burch to say he believed Quadrangle's chances were compromised at the start. Royal Shuck, cutting over from the No. 10 position, rushed to the early lead, vying with Mr. Brick for the dubious honor of calls at the first polls.

Passing the finish line for the first time with a mile yet to go, Hill Rise was sixth, 1½ lengths in front of Northern Dancer. Rounding the upper turn, it was Mr. Brick and Royal Shuck running the first half in 46 seconds, then a gap of two lengths to Wil Rad, which was a half-length in front of The Scoundrel and Quadrangle. Northern Dancer hugged the rail with Hill Rise running along beside him on the outside.

During the run down the backstretch, Hartack made the first of two im-

3

portant decisions for Northern Dancer. Hartack said that if he had felt his mount did not have a lot of run in him, he would have saved ground on the rail and hoped for an opening and something left to get through when it came, but he decided he had ample reserve in Northern Dancer and started to ease off the rail and away from a possible pocket.

He moved decisively with Northern Dancer at the five-furlong pole, taking Shoemaker and Hill Rise by surprise. The two horses had been running side by side behind a wall of three horses. Hartack eased his horse away from the rail and Northern Dancer spurted in front of Hill Rise and to the outside of Quadrangle, Royal Shuck, and Wil Rad. Shoemaker said later that he had intended to keep Northern Dancer sealed in behind the trio, but could not get his bigger horse moving in time to prevent Northern Dancer's nimble escape.

At the half-mile pole, The Scoundrel took the lead from Mr. Brick. Royal Shuck began his fadeout, and Northern Dancer was running easily on the outside in fourth place with Hill Rise tracking him two lengths back. The Scoundrel held the lead going around the turn as Hartack conserved his horse for the final drive. Mr. Brick hung on in third place. Roman Brother ("He's just a little banty rooster going up against big gamecocks," said trainer Burley Parke) had moved up along the rail from far back and was even with Quadrangle and Hill Rise as the first six came to the head of the stretch only three lengths apart.

Here Hartack made another decision. He tapped Northern Dancer lightly and the colt responded, bounding into the lead. Shoemaker got into Hill Rise and the big colt started his long drive. Delighted with Northern Dancer's response to the whip, Hartack hit the little colt harder, on the left side. Northern Dancer surged ahead. Hill Rise, too, responded to the whip and the real race was on, between two horses and two riders.

Hartack hit the "no-stick" horse 10 times from the three-sixteenths pole home. Shoemaker asked for and received a tremendous effort from Hill Rise. With powerful strides, the big California horse gained on the little Canadian colt. Little by little, the gap was closed as the two raced through probably the biggest Derby crowd which ever screamed from both sides of the stretch. Hill Rise inched closer. He reached Northern Dancer, his flank, his girth, his shoulder.

Northern Dancer met the challenge with courage and valor. Responding gamely to Hartack's fierce whipping, he raced the final quarter in 24 seconds. Hill Rise ran the same distance in :23⅗, equaling Whirlaway's famous final Derby quarter of 23 years ago, but it was not fast enough.

At the finish it was Northern Dancer, by a long neck. He had run the 1¼

4

miles in two minutes flat, a track record and the fastest of the 69 Kentucky Derbys run at 10 furlongs. Three and one-quarter lengths behind Hill Rise came The Scoundrel, Roman Brother, and Quadrangle, which the camera separated by a nose and neck. Then came Mr. Brick, Mr. Moonlight, Dandy K., Ishkoodah, Wil Rad, Extra Swell, and, 14 lengths later, Royal Shuck.

It was a victory from which even the defeated could claim honor—no one could ask for a finer last quarter than Hill Rise's—but special acclaim was due the winner. Weighing only 950 pounds and standing but 15.2 hands tall, Northern Dancer is not yet three years of age. Foaled on May 27, he became the first "2-year-old" Kentucky Derby winner since 1939, when Johnstown wore roses 16 days before his actual third birthday.

For owner-breeder Edward P. Taylor, Northern Dancer's victory was of special significance, adding a new dimension to an already-extensive Canadian breeding and racing operation. The most prominent racing man in Canada, Taylor has been the leading breeder in North America for the last four years in point of races won, and horses bred at Taylor's Windfields Farm and National Stud earned more than a million dollars last season. His best horse to race in the United States in previous years was Victoria Park, which, also trained by Luro, finished third in the 1960 Kentucky Derby.

While Northern Dancer became the first Canadian-bred to win America's most famous race, the second and third finishers were bred in California, the fourth in Florida, the fifth in Virginia, the next three in Kentucky. It gives rise to the thought that there are no geographical restrictions for combining in a Thoroughbred bone, muscle, and stoutness of heart.

## A Beaten Favorite

NEARLY everyone wanted Canonero II to win the Triple Crown. He was the storybook horse, the cheap yearling with a crooked leg, shipped unnoticed to another country and returned with the same fanfare, only to drop out of the clouds and win the Kentucky Derby, confirming his excellence by a track-record performance in the Preakness.

He had overcome all manner of adversities that would have been valid excuses for other classic candidates. He became a symbol of anti-establishment challenging The Jockey Club (whose members now have won eight of the

5

last 10 Belmont Stakes), owned, ridden, and trained by two Indians and a black who do not speak English.

He attracted the attention of New Yorkers as no horse since Kelso. A record New York race crowd turned out to see him, cheer him, and bet that he could overcome the latest adversities that had beset him. Few thought the $1\frac{1}{2}$ miles in deep going, or any of his 12 rivals, could bother him—if he were right. But the loss of conditioning, resulting from the temporary setbacks of a skin disease and foot infection, was too great. He tired after a mile. He did not quit. But heart alone was not enough.

Canonero II is a good horse. He is worth at least $2,000,000 as a stallion right now. It is hoped, however, that he will continue racing, for he is a star, one not likely to be forsaken by his new following, no less a hero for the Belmont Stakes, a horse of class.

## Program Error

HRUMPH. Man o' War beaten. Indeed. One day, shortly after Man o' War was retired to stud, Miss Elizabeth Daingerfield looked out her office window and saw him running in his paddock with the majestic, unrestrained power that was intrinsically his. She called to John Buckner, a wise old stud groom who had handled the fire of Peter Pan when he managed the James R. Keene stallions—Kingston, Colin, Commando, Ben Brush, Sweep, Disguise, Celt, and such:

"Buck! Don't you see him ripping and running in that paddock? Stop him before he gets hurt!"

"Why, Miss Lizbeth, iffn all the good horses in New York couldn't ketchim, how'n you expect *me* to stop Man o' War?"

If legend serves, the task was too great for mere man or beast. So a computer was engaged. Not one with some native American calculating ability would do. It was necessary to leave the country to find, in the computational and statistical science department at the University of Liverpool, a machine that could digest figures in such a way as to print out a suggestion that Man o' War could be beaten carrying a feathery 126 pounds at a mile and a quarter.

No racing man would propose—as did Miami radio station WIOD's call of a computerized Race of the Century last week—that Buckpasser could take the track (two lengths on top after a half-mile) from such as Man o' War or, for that matter, War Admiral, Swaps, and Count Fleet. This is as outrageous as suggesting that Babe Ruth would get only singles off Christy Mathewson, that Bill Tilden would move up two steps on Pancho Gonzales' serve.

For Buckpasser (which ran best when a stablemate took care of the early speed) and Citation (which usually came from just off the pace) to be knocking heads on the lead from the start, Man o' War had to be facing the other way at the break, Count Fleet had to go to his knees, and little War Admiral had to be knocked sideways. As for Eddie Arcaro having Nashua 10th after a quarter-mile, the name of a substitute rider must have been inadvertently omitted by the computer.

The machine figured (without an opportunity to assess Colin's unbeaten record, or that of Sysonby, whose sole defeat came when he was drugged by a groom) that Citation could have beaten Man o' War by a neck with Buckpasser third by three-quarters of a length, followed by Exterminator, Kelso, Swaps, Nashua, Tom Fool, War Admiral, Native Dancer, Equipoise, and Count Fleet.

We figured that if Man o' War were to be beaten again, it might be by Jim Dandy, but, barring that chance, Man o' War would remain the classic shoo-in, Citation a driving second, and an extraordinary dead heat would find 10 horses stretched across the track for show.

Further, we figure that computer was administered LSD, should have been sent to the spit box, and ruled off the Turf.


## It's Who's Up Front That Counts


"YOU just cannot put a horse on the lead early in a classic race and expect him to stay there all the way around." Virtually every year this flat statement is issued by disgruntled trainers of pace setters which faded in the 1½-mile Belmont Stakes. It is repeated by writers. It is accepted as axiom.

Last Saturday, however, champion rider Lester Piggott sent Athens Wood to the front at the start of England's oldest classic, the $85,780 St. Leger, and led throughout the mile, six furlongs, and 127 yards.

Athens Wood is by Celtic Ash, which won the Belmont Stakes of 1960. After that Belmont, trainer Vic Sovinski announced that second-finisher Venetian Way could not be expected to hold on after forcing the pace and taking the lead so early in such a long race. A few weeks earlier, Sovinski had taken Bill Hartack off Venetian Way because he said Hartack had let Bally Ache run off from Venetian Way in the Preakness and steal the Baltimore classic by running easily on the front end all the way. So Hartack was up on Celtic Ash in the Belmont, kept him dead last for the first mile, then hustled up on the outside to win by 5½ lengths.

From these contradictions, we offer a new axiom: A good rider can bring home a good horse in a classic by going to the lead at once, or by coming from dead last, or even by coming from just off the pace.

Pace makes the race, all right, but it is nice to have a good rider and a good horse.

## No Place To Hide

BIDDING for a client, Dr. Bill Lockridge thought he might get a Damascus filly at Keeneland for about $100,000, but gave up when the count went over $130,000.

"You know, you just can't hide a good-looking yearling in that ring."

## Hardboot Advice

MIGHTY CITATION left two legacies: (1) A standard by which we can judge the merit of a real race horse, and (2) Silver Spoon.

Bred and owned by C. V. Whitney, Silver Spoon was kicked as a suckling and ran thereafter with a hitch in her gait. But run she did. In California she beat Preakness winner Royal Orbit in the Santa Anita Derby, Kentucky Derby winner Tomy Lee in the Cinema Handicap. At four in California, she carried 130 pounds to win the Santa Margarita and the Vanity. If she had been able to bring the Santa Anita or Hollywood track along with her when she was shipped east, Silver Spoon might have surpassed the exploits of earlier Whitney fillies Artful, Regret, and Top Flight.

As it was, despite her disappointing races in the East, Silver Spoon was voted champion 3-year-old filly of 1959 in one poll and was retired to stud as the best of Citation's racing progeny.

Silver Spoon's first foal, by champion Warfare, was unplaced. Then she was barren to Natallah and slipped her foal by Tudor Minstrel. Next came Silver Coin, by champion Never Bend, which won two races at two. Her next foal, by Bold Ruler, was killed before he got to the races. Under the Bold Ruler breeding agreement, Ogden Phipps got Silver Spoon's next foal, Inheritance, which won one race last year at two. At that point, Silver Spoon must have been regarded by Whitney as something of a disappointment as a broodmare.

On Monday, Silver Spoon's fifth foal, Inca Queen, a filly by champion Hail to Reason, won the Demoiselle Stakes at Aqueduct. She became the 148th stakes winner bred by Whitney, and no man around today has bred more.

The late Tom Piatt was asked one time how a man should get started in the breeding business: "Get some of those Whitney mares."


# No More Seeing Stars

AFTER a long illness, as distinguished from the other cause listed in most obituaries—the short illness, the Asterisk, aged 65, died this week in *The Blood-Horse* pedigree *department.

The Asterisk was not just born *and developed into maturity over a period of years, but sprang full blown—as the goddess of wisdom, Athena, emerged from one of Zeus' splitting headaches—from the head *of The Jockey Club registrar in 1906.

In *the preface to Volume 9 of the *American Stud Book*, an explanation appears: "While the general features of this Volume remain the same as Volume 8, it has been found necessary, in order to avoid a two Volume work, to condense the subject matter in every way possible, the most radical change being the substitution of a * in place of the word Imported wherever possible."

This "wherever possible" aspect has been a continuing source of trouble by virtue of its *inconsistency and was part of the complications contributing to the demise of the Asterisk.

There was a time during the early development of American racing and breeding when the addition of (Imp) to a horse's name added a touch of *class. The Asterisk, nee (Imp), immediately implied that the subject animal was indeed a Thoroughbred race horse duly registered in the *General Stud Book* in England and not just an ordinary American blood-horse which, although by *Glencoe, might be out of an unnamed mare by Col. Elsworth's Boston (a horse of a different color from champion four-miler Boston). Further, the Asterisk implied additional value, trans-Atlantic shipping costs, and a high *esteem of the horse's stallion prospects to warrant such expenditure.

The Asterisk was thought a happy thing for students of pedigrees because it signaled a junction ahead and the need to turn from the *American Stud Book* to another country's registry, usually the *General Stud Book* of England, to trace a *pedigree farther back to the Darley Arabian or to Tragonwell's Natural Barb mare (Bruce Lowe's tap-root mare for the No. 1 Family).

Then, 25 years ago, a *horse got on an airplane. Then a plane exeeded the speed of sound. The Asterisk began spinning as horses were shipped in and out of the United States, to and from England, France, Italy, Germany, Holland, Belgium, Argentina, Chile, Venezuela, New Zealand, Australia, Japan—not to mention traffic to and from Mexico, Canada, Puerto Rico, and Cuba. Horses were *imported and exported for a few breeding seasons, for one breeding season, for racing only, for one race—here and gone almost on the hour.

With the registrar of The Jockey Club (the official Asterisk fixer of the United States) lagging eight years or so behind these *importations with publication of the stud book, proper use or non-use of an Asterisk became a matter of expediency or personal taste.

Significance of the Asterisk has become shifted from class to *vagueness. It is of little help to the pedigree searcher now, for it does not suggest in which of the 20 or so foreign stud books the pedigree can be traced. It means *horse was foaled abroad, but not that it has a foreign pedigree, e.g., *Malicious (by American-bred Helioscope, out of American-bred Blackball, by American-bred Shut Out); it means a *horse was imported, but not that it remained here, e.g., *Zucchero (which raced in England, finished third in the first *Washington, D. C., International, was exported without siring an American foal, stood in Ireland, and now is in Japan).

The cluster of Asterisks around Gyr signify nothing. Bred and owned by an American, foaled at Claiborne Farm in Kentucky, Gyr is considered a French-bred in France because he was physically present there at the age of five months with his dam. Gyr, which raced only in France and England, is by French-bred *Sea-Bird, now standing in Kentucky, out of Italian-bred

10

*Feria II, now in France, she by Italian-bred *Toulouse Lautrec, now in Kentucky. *Sea-Bird is by American-bred Dan Cupid (by Native Dancer), now in France. Gyr is standing in *England.

It would be erroneous to infer an Asterisk means a horse was raced abroad (*Gallant Man and *Princequillo raced only here), or that its absence means a horse was raced here (American-owned-and-bred Nijinsky II and now Mill Reef have raced only abroad), or that its presence means a *stallion stands here (*Epinard, *Our Babu, *Norseman were returned to stand in Europe) or ever did (*Ballymoss), or that its absence means a stallion does stand here (of 1970 American-bred stakes winners, To The Man was sired by no-asterisked Counsel, an English-bred standing in England; My Dad George was sired by no-asterisked Dark Star, a Kentucky Derby winner standing in France).

Application of the Asterisk is inconsistent among *American publications, and has no connection with the Asterisk in foreign publications. Newspapers here never did fool with the thing, either because of its doubtful significance or the inability to place a footnote at the bottom of a story explaining it. *Daily Racing Form* and *Morning Telegraph* do not use the Asterisk in stories, but began a few years ago to use *it in the past-performances section, yet not in pedigrees, nor in race charts.

At any rate, we lost an Asterisk here not long ago, one meant to be affixed to English Derby winner *Papyrus (because he was a foreign-bred imported for a 1923 race); later it was found cluttering the name of champion Top Bid's American-bred sire, published as *Olympia. The sick-and-tiredness here reached epizootic proportions.

And then the Asterisk succumbed. *Over-exposure. Right in our pedigree department. We will miss the sight of *it—like Sam Snead's hat—for a while, but we cannot truthfully say we are sorry to see *it go. We buried *it, from whence *it came, in the *American Stud Book*.


## It's Oil In The Name

NEXT YEAR'S car models are due soon. These dramatic unveilings seem to come earlier each fall. We have regarded always the unveiling of 2-year-olds at Saratoga as something of a first-showing of next year's classic models. A model that has stolen the march on the others this season is Chevron

11

Flight, whose victory in the Sapling on July 31 before the curtain was raised at Saratoga established him as the leading 2-year-old in the East.

Bred by Ocala Stud, Chevron Flight is by I'm For More—Flying Fable, and was named by Ocala Stud manager Joe O'Farrell's daughter, Nancy. Standard Oil-man Terry Trovato naturally was fascinated by the colt's name and asked Nancy how she happened to select the brand:

"There's a folk-rock singer named Joni Mitchell who wrote a song entitled 'The Urge for Going.' In the song there's a phrase '. . . see the geese in chevron flight, flapping and racing on before the snow,' and since his dam was Flying Fable . . ?"

## Are We Seeing Things?

AMONG things that give us pause: The shimmering reflection of a full moon across an undulating, ice-crusted pasture; empty glasses raised high down at Mory's since its liquor license was revoked; Johnny Sellers being set down at Santa Anita for failing to keep a sraight course while on Lost at Sea.

## $40,000 Embarrassment

IN 1888, James Ben Ali Haggin became America's leading owner, displacing the Dwyer Brothers' stable which had topped the list for almost a decade. That year the Haggin stable included 2-year-old Salvator, 4-year-old Firenze, and 42 others which won 67 races and earned $125,666. That year Haggin also shipped 64 yearlings from his vast Rancho del Paso in California to William Easton's sale at the old Madison Square Garden in New York; the consignment brought $112,775 and included America's first high-priced yearling bum.

One of Haggin's partners in acquiring a goodly portion of the gold, silver, and copper in this hemisphere was George Hearst. While Haggin had been investing in Thoroughbreds, Hearst plunged into politics, eventually purchasing a seat in the United States Senate.

12

(Addressing the 1882 California Democratic Convention in San Jose, "My opponents say that I haven't the book learning that they possess," Sen. Hearst grumbled. "They say I can't spell. They say I spell bird b-u-r-d. If b-u-r-d doesn't spell bird, what in hell does it spell?")

Armed with such logic and enough money to make it persuasive, Sen. Hearst attended the June 25 yearling sale at Madison Square Garden determined to purchase the best Haggin had to offer to begin a horse operation at San Simeon Ranch. The most-publicized yearling was a full brother to proven horses Ban Fox and King Fox. There was talk that it would bring a record price (the highest price ever paid for a yearling in America was $8,200, which the Dwyer Brothers had bid to get a full brother to Hanover).

Bidding on the Haggin colt, by King Ban—Maud Hampton, by Hunter's Lexington, began at $5,000. Phil Dwyer entered the bidding at $15,000 and Lucien O. Appleby raised to $16,000. Dwyer finally dropped out, leaving the contest to Sen. Hearst and Appleby (breeder of Harry Bassett and part owner, with Davy Johnson, of Roseben). Sen. Hearst stopped at $37,500 and Appleby got the colt for a record $38,000. Immediately after the hammer fell, Sen. Hearst caught Appleby's arm, offered him a $2,000 profit, and for $40,000 acquired an embarrassment.

Named King Thomas, the $40,000 yearling earned $500 at two and three for Sen. Hearst, placing in the Bowling Brook Handicap; he raced on for successive owners and finally as a 5-year-old won a $500 purse, his only victory in 24 starts.

Well, you win some and you lose some at yearling sales. From the same consignment that he got King Thomas, Sen. Hearst paid $3,300 for Tournament, about the best of several thousand horses Haggin bred, winner of the Lawrence Realization, Jerome, Choice, Omnium, Holly, and Great Eastern Handicaps, one of the first half-dozen horses in America to earn as much as $100,000.

## Thirty Eight Skidoo

STEVE CADY of the New York *Times* figured out that if 20,000 horse players took $10 each to a track and were required to bet the whole bundle, $200,000, on the first race, and further were required to bet back everything they had on each successive race on a nine-race card—those 20,000 players would walk away from the last race with $32,797 of change between them. (This was figured with a 17 per cent takeout, plus 1.2 per cent breakage, with the 18.2 per cent subtracted each time the same money was turned over for each of nine races.)

If the takeout lightens a player so dramatically after nine races, what happens to the stout producer who hangs in there all day and all night for one of those doubleheaders at Charles Town and Shenandoah Downs?

"Well, I'll tell you," Bill McDonald explained. "Over the Fourth of July weekend, we had two doubleheaders: Nine races Saturday afternoon, another 10 that night, another 10 Monday afternoon, followed by nine more on Monday night. Our daily average handle is about $430,000, but on those two days we averaged $1,124,207, very big days for us. So after the 38th race, the last one on Monday night, as everybody was leaving one big guy stands up in the clubhouse and yells, 'Just one more time!' "

Ye cannot find the depth of the heart or pocket of the horse player, neither can ye perceive the things that he thinketh.


## Vive!


CANONERO II has captured the attention of the general public as has no other race horse in recent times. Persons whose interest in racing heretofore spanned no more than the 10 days during which memory faded of the name of the Kentucky Derby candidate drawn in the office pot are still talking about Canonero II.

Cocktail party chit-chat, seasonally concerned with Dan Issel's shot from the corner, or Johnny Bench's batting average, or Greg Cook's arm, is bubbling with uncommon knowledge of and interest in the Kentucky Derby-Preakness winner.

From women and men who do not recall having heard of Bold Ruler or Fort Marcy, we are confronted with such questions as: Who can beat him in the Belmont? Why did he sell for only $1,200 as a yearling? Is Pretendre (with varying pronunciations) to be brought back from New Zealand? What is Canonero II worth as a stud prospect?

Such interest in racing, evoked by the sudden stardom of Canonero II, is a stimulus for the industry. It came when needed. Some racing men were prepared to dismiss this year as a bore when the promising, and exciting, 3-

year-olds His Majesty and Hoist the Flag went wrong, for the pro-tem leaders of the handicap division could not seem to win a race. To insiders, Shuvee was a saver, but a season is seldom counted a good one when a mare is the best around.

So Canonero II, living proof that a man can pick a good one from the yearling sales at less than the cost of a green hunter, has inserted a new and vital enthusiasm for racing which more than offsets the public wrangling over Howard Samuels' off-track betting schemes, union disputes, and horse owners' pleas for purse money to equal training costs. Vive Canonero II.

## Inquiry!

COLONEL ELSWORTH happened by the office with a book under his arm. We had not seen him since Jim French won the Santa Anita Derby last April.

"I told you he was a solid horse," he reminded. Colonel, where have you been between the Santa Anita Derby and the Dwyer?

"Oh, moseying around, trying to learn something. For example, I found out they had a big horse race here in Kentucky a little while ago won by a bull. What do you know about that?"

Sounds like a lot of bull, Colonel.

"Yes. The obvious aside for a moment, I would direct your attention to this text here, the *History of Jessamine County, Kentucky*, by Bennett Young, on page 18 of which is stated that in 1802 . . ."

A little while ago?

"Please. Everything is relative; to a younger man. 1802 is just a little while ago. Now I have brought along my authority and I am prepared to let you in on something if you will give me a little racing room.

"Heretofore you probably thought Jimmy Nichols was the only bull rider to make it on the race track and that Don Brumfield was the only jockey of note to come out of Jessamine County. Let me introduce to you an old-time rider named Mike Arnspiger. But first, the Ted Bassett of his day, a Revolutionary War officer described by Mr. Young as:

" 'Major Netherland who wore a cut-a-way coat, short breeches with knee buckles, and low shoes with silk laces and silver buckles. His pants were always fastened with red bands, and his long queue was tied with a red rib-

15

bon. From his entrance into Nicholasville early in 1791 for 40 years he was prominent as a leader in all its affairs. He was postmaster for about 23 years and always dispensed the village hospitality with a lavish hand. He was passionately fond of horse racing and owned some of the great race horses of Kentucky in the early part of the century. He was a fair and just man in his dealings and not averse to a good time, as people call it. He opened a race track on the Willoughby place near Sulphur Well and maintained it for many years. In 1802 in the hearing of the crowd, Major Netherland announced that there would be a race on a certain day for a purse of $50, one mile heats, which was "Free for anything with four legs and hair on."

" 'At that time there was working on a farm a young man named Michael Arnspiger who had broken a bull to the saddle, which he rode to the mill. He immediately put the bull in training and for several days gave him turns around the race track. He used spurs on the bull and when these were dug into his sides, he was accustomed to bellow.

" 'On the day of the race, Arnspiger appeared on the ground with his bull. He had placed a dried hide of an ox on the bull's rump, and he carried a tin horn in his hands. He demanded of the judges the right to enter his animal, to which the owners of the horses vehemently objected, but Arnspiger answered by appealing to Major Netherland if he had not said that the race was free to "anything with four legs and hair on." Major Netherland admitted that he had and that the bull had a right to enter.

" 'When the drum was tapped, Arnspiger blew his horn, planted his spurs in the sides of the bull, and the bull bounded off with a dreadful bellow, the ox-hide flapping on his sides. This spectacle, combined with the noise, had never been seen on the race track before. The horses immediately flew the track and Arnspiger galloped home a winner.

" 'The losers contended that they had been swindled out of their money, that Arnspiger should not have been allowed to blow the tin horn or use the ox-hide. Thereupon Arnspiger offered to take off the ox-hide and leave his tin horn at the stand and run them from end to end.

" 'Mr. Willoughby and Mr. Netherland were the judges for the next heat. Arnspiger planted his spurs into the sides of the bull with redoubled fury. The loud bellow that followed again drove the horses from the track despite the exertions of the riders, and Arnspiger pulled in the second $50.' "

How come we never read about this Arnspiger boy bringing down something in the Phoenix Hotel Stakes at the Kentucky Association track?

"Well, I think he must have had a weight problem. According to Mr. Young, 'With the money thus obtained, Arnspiger purchased a black-smithing outfit and worked for many years at this trade near Wilmore where he died in the sixties, in the 85th year of his age.' "

Colonel Elsworth closed his book and rose in triumph. "So there you are, a matter of historical record, an open race in Kentucky won by a bull. And when Jim French wins the Monmouth Invitational," he said over his shoulder, "remember where you got it."

## Weight And See

TARTAN STABLE'S grand filly Ta Wee has run six furlongs five times this year, has won the Correction Handicap with 131 pounds, the Hempstead Handicap with 132 pounds, the Regret Handicap with 136 pounds, and on Monday took the Fall Highweight Handicap carrying 140 pounds, conceding her five-pound sex allowance and six to 24 actual pounds to colts.

Ta Wee is approaching the Pan Zareta class—which is some class, indeed. Bred in Texas by J. F. Newman in 1910, Pan Zareta carried 140 pounds or more seven times; she won with 140 pounds at Juarez, at New Orleans, and at Empire City, she won with 142 at Oaklawn Park, and she won with 146 at Juarez. She was some mare: Pan Zareta set or equaled 11 track records at five furlongs to a mile, won 76 races, and earned only $39,082. Rewards for gameness and valor were smaller in those days.

## Americans In Paris

BETTER than Nijinsky II, Englishmen were saying. Four days before the race, one player felt so strong about this that he was able to carry 14,000 pounds into William Hill's betting shop and place the whole bundle on Mill Reef at 2-3 odds to beat the best horses in the world.

Five million Frenchmen—how could they be wrong?—held the same conviction in varying degrees of strength and, as a consequence, Paul Mellon's Virginia-bred 3-year-old was odds-on to become the first American-owned-and-bred horse in 50 runnings to win the Prix de l'Arc de Triomphe in Paris on Oct. 3, 1971.

17

He was the nap, they said; he figured. Since finishing second in the English Two Thousand Guineas, Mill Reef had swept all before him, winning the 1½-mile English Derby in easy fashion, defeating France's best 4-year-old, Caro, in the 1¼-mile Eclipse Stakes, and running off from Italy's best 4-year-old, Ortis, in the 1½-mile King George VI and Queen Elizabeth Stakes in July.

Last year coming up to the Arc, Nijinsky II had a more impressive record. He never had been beaten and, in addition to becoming the first English Triple Crown (Two Thousand Guineas, Derby, St. Leger) winner in 35 years, he had won the Irish Derby and King George VI and Queen Elizabeth Stakes. Nijinsky II, as did his sire, Northern Dancer, had a burst of speed that could be turned on at any point in a race; it was a two-furlong burst which swamped his fields and permitted Nijinsky II to coast home alone.

Now, every racing man longs for a horse with a good turn of speed, but there are times when reliance on a burst of speed in a crucial point of a race can be misplaced. In last year's Arc, Nijinsky II was blocked and had to check in the middle of his charge to the front and, quite possibly, this momentary stopping, and starting again when a hole opened, accounted for Nijinsky II's loss by a head to Sassafras.

Mill Reef has a different style. His races have not been marked by the sudden acceleration which dramatized Nijinsky II's triumphs. Mill Reef has speed, of course, being by champion 2-year-old Never Bend, but he has been deftly trained by 32-year-old Ian Balding so as to produce a sustained, steady run that seems to gain in momentum at the end. Mill Reef gallops along at a steady rate, never far off the early pace, and about a half-mile out he just seems to get stronger, gradually going to the front and then drawing away. He overpowers his fields.

It is this power, rather than a quick burst of speed, which captured the fancy of Europeans and made Mill Reef a heavy favorite to capture the record first prize of $251,847 in the $403,047 Arc.

Whatever doubt preceded the Arc was based on Pistol Packer, a 3-year-old filly by Gun Bow—George's Girl II, by Ossian, bred in Pennsylvania by Mrs. John R. H. Thouron and sold as a yearling at Saratoga for $15,000 to French trainer Alec Head.

This year, Pistol Packer had won the Prix Chloe and the Saint-Alary, then beat Cambrizzia (Cambremont—Alizian, by Alizier) by a scant lip in the 1¼-mile French Oaks in June, by 2½ lengths in the 1¼-mile Prix de la Nonette on Sept. 5, and by one length in the 1½-mile Prix Vermeille on Sept. 19.

French trainers were saying that Pistol Packer might be the best filly seen in France in the last 30 years. Jack Cunnington Sr., who with Alec Head's 84-year-old father, Willie, has been training horses in the Chantilly forests for a half-century, said she was "Oh, a very good filly indeed, exceptional. We must remember Corrida, which twice beat colts in the Arc in 1936 and 1937, and Nikellora, and Pola Bella, Hula Dancer, Roseliere—I would say Pistol Packer must rank in the top seven of the best fillies we have had here."

Pistol Packer had yet to prove herself against colts, however, particularly one of the power of Mill Reef, and she was installed a 4-1 second choice for the Arc.

In the absence of Rheffic, a son of American-bred Traffic which had broken down after winning the French Derby and Grand Prix de Paris, the only other colt counted a serious challenger to Mill Reef was Ramsin (Le Haar—Maritchia, by La Varende).

Ramsin's owner, Baron Thierry de Zuylen de Nyevelt, was openly confident he had a stayer that could do what Sassafras had done to Nijinsky II. Ramsin, like Sassafras, had shown he could run from here to the Pyrenees. This year, he had finished first in the 1⅞-mile Prix Jean Prat, but was disqualified and placed second, and had won the 1⅞-mile Prix de Barbeville, the 2½-mile Prix du Cadran, and the 1⁹⁄₁₆-mile Grand Prix de Saint-Cloud.

To insure that something would go with Mill Reef during the early part and set up the thing for Ramsin to amble along at the end, Baron de Zuylen also entered Ossian, which had not won a stakes this year. The entry was installed third choice at 7-1, with none of the others less than 20-1.

LONGCHAMP has the Seine at its back and, from a high point in the sparkling new stand constructed in 1966, racegoers can look over the 2,500-acre Bois de Boulogne and see the Eiffel Tower, which serves as something of a 1¼-mile pole, marking the spot on the Arc course where the field has gone the first quarter-mile from the start. The gate is located on the north end of the course in front of the Moulin which survived several centuries of storms, but was damaged by World War II bombs.

From the gate, the Arc field races a straight six furlongs, the first two of which (to the Eiffel Tower) are flat; then begins a half-mile, up-hill run, to a point 33 feet above the level of the finishing point. At the top of the hill, the course turns right, and down, for two furlongs, then levels off for a furlong of straight to the final, slight, right turn into the three-furlong straight path to the finish. It is a demanding course which has tested the stamina, and courage, and luck, of Europe's best horses and riders since 1920.

As a usual thing, very few people go to the races in France. Players place their off-course bets in tobacco shops all over France in the morning and

19

concern themselves with something else in the afternoon. Owners, breeders, trainers, and a few others genuinely interested in watching horses race make up the small crowds in attendance.

Arc day is something else entirely. An estimated 65,000 filled the Longchamp stands and crowded the centerfield tribunes to see the spectacle of the Arc. Part of the spectacle, of course, is the crowd. There is nothing so chic as a chic French woman, and Longchamp on Arc day is a high-fashion showing for Paris designers. Men in dark suits, with some bowlers here and there (no morning suits as is the custom for Royal Ascot), fade into the background as style and femininity lend to the Arc day crowd a grace uncommon to assemblages for American classic races.

Fewer Americans attended the Arc this year than did last year. James P. Mills was on hand and reported that Tyson Gilpin was in the process of syndicating Limit to Reason to stand next spring at Mr. and Mrs. Mills' Hickory Tree Farm near Middleburg, Va.

Trainer John Jacobs revealed that Our Beloved, the full sister to Personality which he had purchased out of the Bieber-Jacobs Stable dispersal last year at Saratoga for a record $256,000, had contracted a staph infection and died at the University of Pennsylvania last June.

Peter Fuller of Boston said Daniel Wildenstein had told him that a Dancer's Image colt was the best of 90 yearlings he had training in France.

Artist Richard Stone Reeves of New Jersey accompanied Mrs. E. H. Augustus and her daughter Betty of Virginia.

Jimmy Drymon of Kentucky, who with his father raised at Gallaher Farm near Lexington most of the horses Mrs. P. A. B. Widener II raced in France, scanned the pedigrees of horses listed on the day's program and noted the names of Kentucky-raised Widener horses which had become sires: Spy Well, Blue Tom, Dan Cupid, Neptunus, Timmy Lad. "You know, we never sent over more than three of four yearlings each year, and none of these were very fashionably bred—mostly $500 stud fees—except, of course, Dan Cupid, which is by Native Dancer."

Also on hand were Jimmy Stewart of Hollywood Park, Charles Cella of Oaklawn Park, Spencer Drayton of the TRPB, and John F. Kennedy of The Jockey Club.

In the Ritz bar one night, Ogden Mills (Dinny) Phipps looked around and saw Mr. and Mrs. Howard B. Keck, Adm. and Mrs. Gene Markey, Mr. and Mrs. Gerard Smith, Mr. and Mrs. John Schapiro, Maj. and Mrs. C. C. Moseley, Mr. and Mrs. Paul Hexter, Reginald N. Webster, Robert Coleman, Mr. and Mrs. Horatio Luro, and Mr. and Mrs. Whitney Tower. It is a relatively small bar; no Frenchman could get in. "This place looks like Paris, Ky.,"

Phipps said.

The entry of Kentucky-bred One for All in the Arc accounted for the presence of most of the Alls in the One for All syndicate: Mr. and Mrs. John A. Bell III and their four children; Mr. and Mrs. E. V. Benjamin III, Mr. and Mrs. Jacques D. Wimpfheimer, Webster, Coleman, Luro, and W. R. (Fritz) Hawn.

Two years ago at the Newmarket sales, Hawn happened to notice that an 11-year-old mare by Hyperion was being offered. Six-time leading English sire Hyperion was 27 years old when he sired the mare and Hawn figured there might not be too many Hyperion mares around; he had Keith Freeman buy her for $8,800. She had a weanling filly by the Irish Bold Lad at the time and was in foal to the same sire. Last week, that weanling filly, now named Waterloo, added the Cheveley Park Stakes to her previous victory in the Queen Mary Stakes and appeared to be the best 2-year-old filly in England. At Longchamp, five English bloodstock agents approached Hawn from different angles to see about buying Waterloo's yearling full sister.

Hawn is from Dallas, is a member of the board at Del Mar, has a foal by Buckpasser out of his good mare Blue Norther in Kentucky, had seen the Cheveley Park Stakes at Newmarket, had imported Colorado King from South Africa to race in California, had sold his Keeneland yearling purchase Poleax to stand in France, had won this year's French Two Thousand Guineas with a Deauville yearling purchase, Zug, by American-bred Nasram and out of a Bolero mare. A racing man today is not bounded by national borders.

Paul Mellon said as much when, as a steward of The Jockey Club from the United States, he was called upon to speak at Marcel Boussac's annual dinner at Maxim's the night before the Arc. Mellon emphasized the one-worldness of the sport of racing which had brought racing men from England, Ireland, Italy, Belgium, Germany, Sweden, Spain, Mexico, and the United States to Paris. Mellon said he looked forward to the day when President Pompidou not only would attend the races (the French president made his first appearance at Longchamp, where he was to present gold champagne buckets to Mellon the following afternoon), but would have a horse in the race; and he observed what a wonderful thing it would be if other heads of government would have their racing colors represented in international races in England, the United States, and Russia.

No. 1 in the post parade for the Arc was another American-bred horse, John A. Bell III's syndicated One for All, a 5-year-old by America's current leading sire, Northern Dancer, out of champion Quill, by Princequillo. A

21

turf specialist in North America, where he had won the 1⅜-mile Niagara Handicap, 1½-mile Laurel Turf Cup, 1½-mile Pan American Handicap, and the $100,000 Sunsest Handicap over two miles of grass, One for All had been trained for distance, not quick starts.

When the gates opened for the Arc, One for All was away as usual. In the United States, where ordinary horses can get the first quarter from the gate in 22 seconds, One for All was never known as a fast breaker. In France, the game is played quite differently; fields come away from the gate quite leisurely and gradually set about the task of running, which comes at the end.

The first quarter-mile of the Arc was run in 27.6 seconds; One for All, at 39-1 odds, suddenly found himself in the unaccustomed position of being on the lead. Willie Carson, England's second-leading rider, took a good hold on One for All and allowed 31-1 shot Sharapour (Tanerko—Paola II, by Palestine), winner of the Prix La Rochette, to take the lead as the field began the half-mile ascent to the first turn. Ramsin, breaking along-side One for All, had been startled into going to the front early, neglecting to wait for his scheduled pacemaker, Ossian, which was scrambling up from the rear to assume his role. Then came 28-1 Irish Ball (Baldric—Irish Lass, by Sayajirao), winner of the Irish Derby, followed by Mill Reef, with 21-1 Hallez (La Fabuleux—Haguenau, by Krakatao). Dead last beginning the ascent was 39-1 Cambrizzia; third from last was Pistol Packer, which had broken from the outside post position and remained on the outside during the entire race.

Halfway up the hill, the field disappeared from view from the stands as the horses raced behind a small wood, which is the point where jockeys were said to have drawn knives prior to the advent of film patrol.

Review of the films showed that behind the trees, Ossian, Ramsin, and Sharapour vied for the lead with the Italian Ortis (Tissot—Orientale, by Nagami), which had set the pace in last year's Arc, ranging up on the outside. Mill Reef had moved over to the rail in fifth place with One for All right beside him and Hallez on the outside. Miss Dan II (Dan Cupid—Miraloma, by Clarion), which had run a courageous third in last year's Arc and a game second to Fort Marcy in the Washington, D. C., International, was up on the outside of the second flight, with Pistol Packer running in her tracks two lengths behind in ninth place.

At the top of the hill, with the first six furlongs raced in 1:19.5, the field turned right and started the descent—that is, all of the field except One for All, in his first clockwise race. Like Tom Rolfe in the 1965 Arc, One for All did not change leads in trying to make the unfamiliar right turn; a neck off Mill Reef at the top of the hill, One for All was shuffled back to be next to

22

last as Sharapour, Ortis, Hallez, Miss Dan II, Ramsin, and Mill Reef raced down the hill with a quarter-mile in 21.7 seconds.

Leveling off with a straight run to the final, slight bend, Geoff Lewis began to ease Mill Reef off the rail to get around Sharapour, and Ortis, which had about finished their racing for the day. Hallez, with Lester Piggott up, took the lead with Miss Dan II closest to him, she still tracked by Pistol Packer.

As the field swung wide into the final, straight three furlongs, Mill Reef and Pistol Packer were about even, Lewis wondering whether he should try to get through between Sharapour and Ortis, or go around Ortis and inside of Hallez; Freddy Head meanwhile decided that, since he had been on the outside all the way around the downhill turn, he may as well stay on the outside of Miss Dan II. Mill Reef and Pistol Packer made their moves at the same time, both passing tired horses that would not finish in the first 10.

Lewis sent Mill Reef on the outside of Ortis and then dropped in on the rail, taking aim on Hallez; Pistol Packer rounded Miss Dan II. The power of Mill Reef began to tell. He gradually gained on Hallez and, as his momentum built, went by him with no apparent change in acceleration and two furlongs from home had a lead he was to lengthen. Pistol Packer could not match the colt's move. She was not to be caught by Caro, which had followed essentially the same outside path taken by the daughter of Gun Bow, and she was never to know that her old rival, Cambrizzia, was coming through the middle of the pack to get within 1½ lengths of her at the finish. One for All, next to last at the final right turn, began to run again, too late, passing tired horses at the end to finish ninth, seven lengths behind the best 3-year-old in the world, Mill Reef.

As Mill Reef drove relentlessly toward the finish of the 1½ miles in record time of 2:28.3, bettering Levmoss' 1969 Arc time by seven-tenths of a second, a wave of applause rolled down the Longchamp stand. Three lengths separated the two American-breds at the finish, with Pistol Packer 1½ lengths in front of Cambrizzia. A neck back in fourth was Caro, by three-quarters over Hallez. A half-length back came Royalty, by a neck over Bourbon, a nose in front of Arlequino, then One for All, Irish Ball, Oarsman, and Mr. Sic Top, with the other early leaders far back.

First money of $251,847 raised Mill Reef's career earnings to $652,654, placing him second only to Nijinsky II ($677,117) on the list of Europe's all-time leading money earners. Mill Reef is scheduled to be raced again next year. Second money of $86,400 raised Pistol Packer's career earnings to $474,346; she is the first filly ever to earn as much as $400,000 in Europe.

Thus, the 50th running of the Prix de l'Arc was run to form. Mill Reef, which had beaten Caro by four lengths in the Eclipse, finished about five lengths in front of Caro; Pistol Packer finished ahead of Cambrizzia for the fourth time this year and, racing many lengths further than the winner on the outside, confirmed that she was indeed an exceptional filly.

And thus it was in France, American-bred horses one-two, in the richest Prix de l'Arc de Triomphe.

## And That She Does Well

AT Oaklawn Park last week, a 9-year-old Royal Note mare which had started 15 times, won five races, and finished in the money seven times last season, turned in a surprisingly poor race. Last year she always was on top for the first two or three calls, but in her first start this season she was sixth after a quarter-mile and was pulled up on the stretch turn. Two nights later she produced a colt, by an unknown sire. Her name is Keep Quiet.

## Skip It

FORTY years ago at Saratoga, Mrs. Payne Whitney's Greentree Stable paid $1,000 for a yearling by Supremus out of Hal Price Headley's champion mare, Chacolet, and named it Dynastic. He developed into a nice 2-year-old, winning the Champagne Stakes and placing in the Futurity, Tremont, Hudson, and Kentucky Jockey Club. Over the winter a good deal of study was put to Dynastic's pedigree to determine whether he would stay the route for the Kentucky Derby. True, he came from a male line of speed (Supremus, Ultimus, Commando, Domino), but Supremus was a half-brother to Headley's grand mare, Handy Mandy, which had set the American record for $1\frac{1}{2}$ miles in winning the Latonia Derby and had won the two-mile Tijuana Cup; Chacolet, of course, had won the $2\frac{1}{4}$-mile Latonia Cup and had beaten In Memoriam in the $1\frac{3}{16}$-mile Kentucky Special.

Such study of pedigree and published comments thereon came to nothing. Dynastic did not run in the 1933 Kentucky Derby. He made his first start at three in the Suburban, giving weight by scale to everything in the field except the winner, 5-year-old Equipoise, which was about 20 pounds better than anything in training that year. Dynastic finished last in the Suburban, was gelded, did nothing more in stakes, and died the next year. Nothing more was thought of him until Greentree showed up with another Dynastic this year in Florida.

The way the current Dynastic fought back after his long lead in the Flamingo evaporated, the way he ran the last eighth to finish second by a head to Executioner, led many to pick him for the 1971 Kentucky Derby. His pedigree had speed through Bold Ruler on the top and stamina through Track Medal on the bottom side. In the Blue Grass, Dynastic went to the lead and easily turned back challengers running down the backstretch, but after a mile faded out of the Kentucky Derby picture. The Greentree Dynastics, traditionally, skip the Derby. The current one is going for the Withers.

## Seeing Double

TWINS are double trouble. They cause mares to abort, breeders to cry. Some years ago, twins were reported once in every 53 pregnancies; since palpating follicles has become more or less a common practice, the incidence of twins probably is less frequent. Still, twins are troublesome. If they die, the breeder has lost a year's production from a mare; if either twin lives, the breeder is stuck with a sub-normal physical specimen and unlikely racing prospect.

Few twins are placed in training and it is rare indeed for a twin to amount to anything as a runner. Thus it was a surprise to find the winner of the Dover Stakes at Delaware Park last July, Walter Fletcher's 2-year-old Spouting Horn, registered in the foal supplement as a twin. This prompted search for other stakes-winning twins.

Two stakes-placed twins were discovered: Galedo (1945 colt by Gallahadion—Torpedo, by Man o' War) finished third in the 1948 Select Handicap, started 62 times, won 13 races, and earned $30,840; Duke K. (1950 colt by Whirlaway—Anchors Ahead, by Man o' War) finished third in the 1955 Magic City Handicap, started 57 times, won four races, and earned $19,235. Another twin out of a Man o' War mare was Transatlantic (1945 gelding by

25

Blenheim II—Firetop) which did nothing in stakes, started 166 times, won 31 races, and earned $57,545.

In England, however, stakes-winning twins show up regularly, every century: Nicolo (1820 colt by Selim out of a mare by Walton) won the classic Two Thousand Guineas and four other races in nine starts; Orum Blaze (1944 filly by Umidwar—Gold Race, by Colorado) won the 1946 Princess Margaret Stakes at Ascot and finished second in the Hopeful Stakes at Newmarket in six starts.

Stakes-winning twins being so rare, we regret to report the loss of one. The last issue of the *Racing Calendar* listed Spouting Horn, as "Not a twin. (Error in supplement.)"

## One For The Vets

REMEMBER Creme dela Creme? Following victory in the 1966 Jersey Derby, his seventh in eight starts, he finished second by 1¾ lengths in the Arlington Classic when Buckpasser lowered the world record for a mile to 1:32⅗; he was quickly syndicated by Leslie Combs II for $40,000 a share.

Favored for the Quaker City Handicap at Garden State Park on Oct. 12, Creme dela Creme suffered a fracture in his right knee during the race. Bwamazon Farm manager Bill O'Neill recalls that seven veterinarians pronounced the colt as suffering such pain as would dictate destruction, and collection of his $1,200,000 insurance value. The Bwamazon homebred was taken to New Bolton Center at the University of Pennsylvania, however, and a series of operations resulted in Creme dela Creme's recuperation and shipment to Combs' Spendthrift Farm near Lexington in the late spring of 1967.

O'Neill says lots were drawn by syndicate members and 10 mares were bred to Creme dela Creme that year, resulting in four live foals. (Registration applications have been entered for 18 foals in his second crop.) The first winner from Creme dela Creme's first small crop was Combs' homebred filly, Silent Beauty, which won at first asking at Florida Downs on Jan. 28 of this year. Still unbeaten, Silent Beauty in her third start at Florida Downs finished in a dead heat with First Bloom in the $5,000-added Miss Suwannee Stakes on March 25 to become Creme dela Creme's first stakes winner.

At this point, with 25 per cent stakes winners in his first crop and his

26

yearlings averaging $23,700, the decision to try to save Creme dela Creme appears wise. The saving of Your Host for stud duty, and the advances in veterinary orthopedics evidenced in the work on Hoist the Flag, suggest that insurance carriers may be more reluctant in the future to permit destruction of a good race horse on grounds of suffering pain from a bone fracture.

## The Key To Success

AMONG other things discovered in Paris is The Key to unlimited wealth. According to the New York *Times'* report of the dismissal of 50 pari-mutuel clerks in Paris, The Key was used by ticket sellers to turn back a manual validating machine to a previous race, thus permitting the punching out of as many winning tickets as desired.

The Key apparently had been in use for many years and police were unable to estimate how many millions of francs had been stolen. One of the discharged clerks said he learned of the system when he was given The Key by an elderly colleague, who was retiring.

The comment which passed with The Key challenges imagination as to how often it was used: "Take it, I don't need it anymore."

## Strings Unraveled

BUCKPASSER'S third-place finish in the Bowling Green Handicap last week concluded his string of consecutive victories after 15. We wondered what horses had put more together, started checking records of good horses which came to mind, and were surprised by the inconsistency of horses which win a large number of races.

Kingston, winner of more races than any horse in America—89, never won more than 13 in a row; Bankrupt, which won 86, never extended a string beyond seven; King Crab, which won 85, never put more than four victories together.

Citation won 16 in a row, 15 of these as a 3-year-old and another in his first start at five. Miss Woodford won 16 consecutive races in 1883-85. Hanover won 17 in a row in 1886-87. His sire, Hindoo, won 18 consecutive races before Crickmore beat him in 1881; the year before as a 2-year-old, Hindoo had a string of seven going when Crickmore beat him.

Old White Nose, James Long's Boston, perhaps dominated racing the longest of all. He lost his first start, then won 17 consecutive races from 1836 through 1838. He was brought out half fit for his first start of 1839 and lost to an indifferent horse named Portsmouth, then proceeded to win 19 in a row. During a five-year period, Boston won 36 of 37 races, most of them at four-mile heats.

Boston's string of 19 was terminated by William Gibbons' 4-year-old filly, Fashion, described by historian John Hervey as the greatest race mare ever produced in America. Fashion beat Boston in four-mile heats at Camden on Oct. 28, 1841. Nobody believed this at the time, of course, and America's second great North vs. South Match Race was set up at the old Union Course on Long Island the following spring, the mare again turning back the aging champion at four-mile heats. Fashion raced on, winning or receiving forfeit in 20 consecutive races from 1841 through 1844, winning her 32nd race in her 36th start at the age of 11 in 1848.

In those days a race mare raced.


## But We Thought . . .


EARLIER THIS month here, we noted that more than a few shareholders in the Governors Stable had gone out of the governing business as a result of the elections. This week the entire Governors Stable was claimed out of the racing business.

Last spring, the Thoroughbred Breeders of Kentucky presented a Chateaugay colt to 28 Republican governors attending a conference in Lexington. The Thoroughbred Breeders of Kentucky bought the colt for $10,000 and agreed to pay the training expenses with profits, if any, to go to the Grayson Foundation for equine research, and with knowledge of the progress, problems, costs, and pleasure of owning a horse in training going to the governors.

Named Chief Exec, the Governors Stable's property made its first start at Keeneland on Oct. 22 and finished fifth. Eight days later, Chief Exec finished third and earned $350. At Churchill Downs on Nov. 16, Chief Exec was the betting favorite in his third start, for maiden 2-year-olds with a $6,000 claiming tag. In a field of 12, he saved ground while racing just off the pace, "moved willingly to the leader in the drive, then proved best at the wire," winning $1,755 first money by a half-length.

The winner promptly was transferred to trainer Clarence Breedlove, who had claimed him for owner Charles Ginsberg Jr. This may or may not be a new experience for some governors: winning a race and losing all.

## You All Should Know

DECEIT, a daughter of Double Agent, came in out of the cold for her first start this year at Keeneland. We liked her. She looked beautiful and ran wonderfully to the eighth pole, where she held a length lead, then finished second by three lengths to You All in a prep for the Ashland Stakes. Well, she needed that one.

A week later for the Ashland, she looked beautiful and ran wonderfully to the eighth pole, where this time she held a commanding three-length lead, but she chucked it and You All beat her again. That did it. We had seen with our own eyes uncontrovertable evidence that she would not go seven furlongs. She had convinced us.

So she wins the mile Acorn, then the 1⅛-mile Mother Goose, and is the early choice for the 1½-mile CCA Oaks. Best named filly in America.

## In The Black

WHEN the Thoroughbred Breeders of Kentucky, Inc., presented Republican governors with a Thoroughbred yearling last year, it seemed a great opportunity to educate some chief executives on racing.

Monthly reports from a trainer have been known to educate an owner where university courses in economics, history, sociology, veterinary science, and philosophy were inadequate.

Unfortunately, the Governors Stable was in action only a short while. Its horse, named Chief Exec, started only three times before he was claimed last month. Educational opportunities, normally spanning the humanities, social and physical sciences, were limited to a short course in mathematics.

We have at hand the final statement of cash receipts and disbursements of the Governors Stable showing a net profit of $206.26. Income is shown as $2,105 from Chief Exec's purse earnings and $6,000 from his being claimed. Expenses are shown as $5,890 for training, $456 for trainer and jockey commissions, $95 for veterinary work, $74 for vanning, $120.50 for blacksmith work, $167 for pictures (sent to the owners of the Governors Stable), $1,064.30 for insurance, and $31.94 miscellaneous. Thus, income of $8,105 exceeded expenses of $7,898.74 for a net of $206.26.

Like most new owners, the governors decided at the onset how profits would be distributed. They decided last year profits would go to the Grayson Foundation for equine research. This donation amounted to $5,300.06.

This is where the education starts. Now, as a usual thing, an owner buying a horse for $10,500, losing him for $6,000, earnings $2,105, and footing expenses of $7,898.74, would figure he dropped $10,294.74 on the deal, rather than having $5,300.06 in his pocket.

A footnote to the Governors Stable Final Statement of Cash etc. explains that donations from Kentuckians covered Chief Exec's $10,500 purchase price, $1,566.20 in legal and accounting fees, and $5,093.80 of the "profits" distributed to the Grayson Foundation.

It can be learned from this, then, an owner receiving $17,160 as a gift can buy a yearling, can meet his training expenses if the horse wins and places in three starts before he is claimed, and can have some $5,300 left over to give to research. The trick here is learning how to get that $17,160 stake.

## About Restricted Races

As we were saying here, before being gang-tackled by Dick Butkus and a bunch of other guys with I-Like-State-Restricted Races painted on their helmets:

To restrict a race to state-bred horses is to stipulate or admit as true that state-bred horses are inferior, that state-bred horses would not have an opportunity to win a purse if the race were open to all comers on the grounds.

While this is true, mention of it tends to irritate state breeder organizations and infuriate individual owners and breeders who have picked up some money from state-bred restricted races.

To say that races restricted to state-breds reward mediocrity, allocating money for horses not good enough to win against all comers, touches the heart. State breeder organizations have worked long and hard to wrest any kind of breeders fund from state mutuel handles; as with a daughter's piano recital, compliments are expected for the good parts of the program. Comments on sour notes and casual suggestions for improvement are not happily received.

Be that as it may, the time has come to review state breeding fund programs as they now exist, to determine their purposes, and assess their methods of accomplishing their purposes.

The time has come in that off-track betting literally is just around the corner. Right now, off-track betting is being considered by legislatures in California, Kentucky, and Maryland; off-track betting bills are pending in Delaware, Florida, Illinois, Massachusetts, Michigan, New Jersey, Ohio, Pennsylvania, and Rhode Island; off-track betting laws have been passed in Connecticut and New York.

Wherever in the world off-track betting has been established successfully, money therefrom is channeled back into the horse industry—in bigger purses for owners, better training facilities, improved racing plants, more equine research, and breeder awards.

Off-track betting as established in New York has not helped the horse industry. Yet. There is a strong possibility the off-track betting law in New York will be amended; it is hoped that the amendments will cause more money to be channeled back into the horse industry.

Traditionally, drafters of laws follow, often verbatim, provisions of laws enacted elsewhere. It is hoped that the New York off-track betting law will be amended to provide revenue to the horse industry before the dozen other states considering off-track betting legislation lift the New York language and adopt it as their own.

In the meantime, state breeder organizations might send knowledgeable representatives down to the capitol to insure some provision is made in state off-track betting legislation to protect, nurture, foster, and improve the horse-breeding industry within the state.

Viewing the future affirmatively, or optimistically, it may be presumed that state breeder organizations active enough to have a breeders fund from on-track betting now, can get some funding from off-track betting. Presume again that the breeders fund will be increased. (In France, after 40 years of

31

off-track betting, 85.6 per cent of the total handle is bet off track; in Japan, after 24 years, 48 per cent of the total handle is bet in 14 off-track betting shops; in New South Wales, after 20 years, 60 per cent of the total handle is bet off track.)

How best can these increased breeders funds be distributed so as to protect, nurture, foster, and improve the horse-breeding industry within a state?

Presently, most state breeders funds are distributed by giving a majority of the fund in purses for state-bred horses, and a small portion in breeders awards.

For example, last year the Maryland-Bred Race Fund amounted to $943,700, of which 87.8 per cent went to purses for races restricted to Maryland-breds, 8.8 per cent to Maryland breeder awards, and 3.4 per cent to Maryland stallion awards. (Additionally, Maryland tracks put up $466,741 for state-restricted races and breeder awards in "open" races. Of the combined $1,510,441, 80 per cent went to purses for races restricted to Maryland-breds, 18 per cent to breeder awards, two per cent to stallion awards.) Last year, the Ohio Thoroughbred Race Fund amounted to $1,215,348, of which 62.6 per cent went to purses for races restricted to Ohio-breds, 5.7 per cent to Ohio breeder awards, and 9.9 per cent for equine research.

The segue from improving the state breeding industry to improving the state racing program is difficult to follow, in respect to purse money for races restricted to state-breds. It has been argued that such restricted races keep state-breds racing within a state (rather than shipping out of state to competitive tracks) and thus protect state racing.

It is implausible to presume a bettor goes to a track because the day's program includes a race restricted to state-bred horses. It is unreasonable to presume a player will bet more on a restricted race than on an open race, particulary if the restricted race draws only six horses (races restricted to Ohio-breds and restricted to Illinois-breds have been very difficult to fill this year), and if these have horses of less ability than those in an open race.

The most important factors in determining the amount of handle on a race are (1) size of field or number of betting interest, (2) quality of the field, and (3) whether the race is started in front of the stands. If restricted races can draw 12 horses of good and relatively even ability, they can help the racing industry within a state.

The suggestion here, however, is that a state breeders fund would better reward small breeders and big breeders, and would serve as a greater stimulant to breeding better horses if: A greater percentage of state breeder funds went for breeders awards; that breeders awards should equal 10 per cent of

32

whatever a state-bred earns—in or out of state. A man fortunate enough to breed a filly good enough to go out of state and win the CCA Oaks and Alabama, for example, could be rewarded by $10,425 from the state breeders fund.

We are prepared to predict that the first state setting up a program which allocates a state breeders a sum equal to 10 per cent of a horse's career earnings, no matter in what state earned, will be flooded with top broodmares bred to top stallions. And that state's breeding industry will be improved. By the production of more good horses.

That is where the money should go. For something better.


## Pleasant Dream


A DREAM dreamed a thousand times by racing men the world over became a reality for Australian trainer Bob Hoysted. He reportedly bought a horse "not worth 20 cents" for that amount, patched him up, and on Jan. 15 at Newcastle sent his purchase, Port Tudor, six furlongs for a $450 purse. Port Tudor led every step of the way.


## Room For All Comers


RACING has become a very complex business in recent years, entangled in tax, legal, labor, and cost problems like all businesses, but in essence it remains a game. It is not the free-wheeling game played by the Lorillards and Dwyers a century ago, but it is still a wonderful, exciting, unpredictable game played with horses.

The rich man still can buy a good horse and a degree of success, but he cannot wrap up the game. A little man still can come along with one horse and take down a big pot.

On June 27, Charles W. Engelhard, who has spent more in the yearling market trying to buy a good horse than any man in history, realized yet

33

another return on a $84,000 investment when unbeaten Nijinsky won the Irish Sweeps Derby. That same afternoon in California, breeder-owner-trainer-groom-hotwalker Robert K. Miller sent his entire stable, Hanalei Bay, after the $100,000-added Hollywood Derby and he got it, by a neck. He also got a $7,320 breeder's award. He bred his $400 mare, Miss Ali, on a free season to Grounded II, and she died shortly after foaling Hanalei Bay, leaving Miller with the task of raising the orphan on a formula.

Now there is a real game.


## An Alarming Trend


WITh the first major yearling auction of the year coming up at Keeneland July 19-20, we are reminded that the last three Kentucky Derby winners were bought out of that ring as yearlings for an average of $85,900.

Horse seller John Finney, president of Fasig-Tipton Company, observed that the average was satisfactory, but the trend worried him—$250,000 for Majestic Prince, $6,500 for Dust Commander, $1,200 for Canonero II.


## Blatantly The Best


BUCKPASSER is back. The best horse of last year, away from the races since Jan. 14 growing a new right fore hoof, returned with style in the Metropolitan Mile on Memorial Day.

In any horse race there is some doubt the expected will transpire, and for a moment there around the five-furlong pole, when Advocator and Buckpasser were head and head for third place and Advocator made a little move, we admit to having had some doubt. In retrospect, it seems foolish.

When Buckpasser began to roll at the half-mile pole, and with Braulio Baeza just sitting there with no more use for a whip than an after-burner, there was no possible doubt of his winning. His was not a devastating sweep to the front, just a strong, blatant assertion of superiority.

Buckpasser's performances suggest he has an untapped reserve that will be

34

called upon only when absolutely necessary to win. Memories of his last-jump thrust in the Flamingo and his 1:32⅗ Arlington Classic linger.

It is hoped that he can measure the French horses as well when, or if, he is sent after the Grand Prix de Saint-Cloud on July 2. Here is a horse all the world should see.


## Doomed To Repeat

ODYSSEUS had been racing for some years at the Little A, as Asia Minor then was called, winning a few but getting outnodded for important money. For him the sport had palled and he was looking for shipping money back to Ithaca. The days had gone from six to nine, with 10 on Saturdays, and the seasons were getting longer—Agamemnon was talking about starting up next year in February and closing out the third week in December. The stable's breadwinner, Achilles, who already had a suspicious tendon, had bolted in his last out and now could not be dragged onto the track in the morning. And a good spear-thrower could not be hired any more; some organizers from Crete were stirring unrest among the troops, pointing out the poor facilities (gotta walk 20 tents down and turn to the left to find a shower) and bad food (greasy wild boar, day in, day out). Why, the organizers were saying, the good life just beyond the sea had gold bathtubs, a 32-hour week and topless dresses.

Anyway, Odysseus was looking for something to pay the feedman and he could not win a race. Everybody on the grounds had nothing but nonwinners of two other than maiden or claiming, and Menelaus was giving out stars for races he was just thinking about writing. Finally, an extra was put on, but Ajax dropped in not one but two young bold rulers and took all the prizes. So, there was only one way out for Odysseus—a horses-of-racing-age sale.

Now Odysseus had nothing he wanted to cull at the time; he had some cheap fillies, but they were bred right and might do as broodmares, and the others could run a little and would more than earn their keep after freshening.

So he made a horse. Out of wood. This had its advantages, for Odysseus could shape the horse to any conformation he chose. Knowing the Trojans were knowledgeable horsemen, the cunning Odysseus shaped a big stomach

35

on the horse, so they would know it was not a poor doer, and placed a small a small splint below the near front knee, small enough not to be considered a serious defect, but prominent enough to attract attention, possibly away from the more obvious point that the horse was of wood.

There were disadvantages, too, for even the wiliest hardboot cannot bring a wooden horse into a sale cold. Odysseus rumaged through a trunk in his tack room, brought out a vase of oil squeezed from lotus. As he was administering this substance to the horse, a member of Agamemnon's honor guard happened by the tent and inquired what was going on.

"Oh, just using some old-time all-purpose linament Macedonia Sam Hildreth told me about. He swore by it, called it butazolidin," Odysseus said. "This thing hasn't even been schooled from the gate and we don't plan on running for some time." The guard nodded and walked on, thinking, Boy, those old-timers really had a lot of remedies, especially Macedonia Sam, who made his own and always used the same label-Butazolidin.

The horses-of-racing-age sale was widely advertised and the next morning the Trojans crowded their battlements to inspect the stock. There was this horse, with no hip number, handled by a man who had just been employed to bring it to the sale and consequently knew nothing about it. The king of Troy was Priam, sire of Troilus, winner of the Flamingo Stakes in Sword Dancer's year, and also sire of Paris, reputed to be the best man in the world with fillies.

Priam sent Troilus and Paris around to look at the horse for him. Troilus said it was a shame it was so fat and asked the handler how it happened to get that splint. The handler said it popped the splint while unloading that morning from the boat. Paris noted the horse had no past performances and wished he had known where the horse was before the morning of the sale so he could have inspected it more closely. He told a hundred Trojans to grab some lines and pull the horse away from him, then pull him back toward him so he could see how it moved.

Troilus said it rolled good and Paris said it had good depth through the heart; Troilus said the knees were not the best, but that they matched, and Paris said it looked like it toed in a mite, but a good blacksmith could fix that.

Meanwhile, Laocoon had been inspecting the horse also and he finally said, "Why, for all we know, that might be a wooden horse rolling in here on butazolidin." Laocoon promptly picked up a spear and threw it into the horse's belly. The horse remained placid, but a Greek soldier inside with a spear in his neck gurgled.

"I tell you," Laocoon insisted, "that horse is on Butazolidin and can't feel

36

anything! We don't know anything about this horse at all. We ought to have a saliva test made down at the lab in Babylonia."

"That's ridiculous," Priam retorted. "You can't ask for a saliva test at a horses-of-racing-age sale. Nobody's supposed to look this kind of horse in the mouth, anyway, and who would pay for a saliva test?"

"The consignor, or the sales company, or both," Laocoon asserted. "And that's no gift horse; you're buying it and what you're buying is trouble!" About that time, two serpents came up out of the water, snatched Laocoon and his two sons who happened to be close, and spirited them out to sea.

"Well, I guess we've heard enough about Butazolidin and saliva tests for horses-of-racing-age sales," Priam said. "Knock out that wall there. We're taking the horse."

Less than 48 hours later, the Butazolidin wore off and the bottom fell out of the horse. Greek soldiers descended therefrom, ravished and plundered around, and generally reduced the place to rubble. Odysseus shipped out the next day with everything Priam had owned that was negotiable, set up a breeding center in the sunny climes of Carthage, made all the bush meetings, finally arrived home 10 years later in time to save Penelope by running all the turf consultants out of the house, and lived happily ever after.

This is more or less a myth that passed from lyre to lyre for a thousand or so years until one day a Roman heard it and gave it a title: "Caveat Emptor."

Virgil subsequently picked it up and, twisting the story line a bit, had the horse come up as the winner of the inaugural Roman Derby. Which makes it very difficult to draw a clear lesson from the past and get anything done about horses-of-racing-age sales.

## Head Count

In COLD blood, Truman Capote deliberately unnerved academicians by introducing a new literary classification—the non-fiction novel. This is just a variation of an old Turf journalistic form—the non-novel fictional race-crowd estimate.

This form was introduced by Cadwallader R. Colden, who for some reason preferred to use the pen name of "An Old Turfman" when writing for the *American Turf Register*. An Old Turfman is credited with having penned one of the classics of Turf journalism in describing the famous American

Eclipse vs. Sir Henry match of May 27, 1823, and the attendant crowd at Union Course, Long Island.

"The stands on the ground, for the reception of spectators, were crowded to excess at an early hour, and the club house, and balcony extending along its whole front, was filled by ladies; the whole track, or nearly so, for a mile distance in circuit, was lined on the inside by carriages and horsemen, and the throng of pedestrians surpassed all belief—not less than sixty thousand spectators were computed to be in the field."

For incredulous readers cognizant that only 123,706 persons resided in New York City, according to the 1820 census, An Old Turfman noted that about 20,000 came up from the South to bet on Sir Henry.

Crowd estimates continued to spice race accounts through the ensuing century, but it was not until Assault's year (1946) that a crowd for the Kentucky Derby was estimated at 100,000.

We now have a report from Kozo Nakamura on the 56th running of the Grand Steeplechase at Nakayama race course near Tokyo, won by Admiral (Admiral Byrd—Sandar) on April 24. "A crowd of about 350,000 watched this biggest and most popular biannual event at the rain-drenched course."


## Rejected Cribber


LAST year, Hollywood movieman Irving Allen, now a successful film producer and distributor in London, agreed to buy Cragwood Stable's Halo for $600,000 to stand at his Derisley Wood Stud at Newmarket along with My Swallow, Double Jump, and Jolly Jet.

Halo had won the Lawrence Realization, earned $127,309, and had a high-fashion pedigree: By leading sire Hail to Reason, Halo is out of Cosmah, a half-sister to the dam of Northern Dancer; Cosmah produced champion Tosmah, stakes-winning sires Maribeau and Father's Image, and the dam of Kentucky Derby winner Cannonade.

Upon learning that Helo was a cribber, however, Allen refused to take the horse, sued the seller and agents involved, and in turn was countersued for the purchase price, commission, and board, these cases still pending.

Personally, we never have cared for cribbers. Once had a mare which dutifully taught each of her foals to crib; they ate more fences than grass. Lined her stall ledge with a metal strip, which stopped her cribbing in the barn,

38

but when she was turned out with a cribbing strap, it only reminded her of what she had missed all night and she would rush out to grab a gate or top plank. Would not have put up with her—if her foals had not run so well.

Then, too, Kelso was a cribber, so cribbers can have saving graces.

At any rate, Halo was returned to trainer MacKenzie Miller this year. He tried him twice on grass, and Halo won both times, including last week's Tidal Handicap, raising his pre-trial earnings as a 5-year-old this season to $51,710 and raising his value as a stallion prospect considerably.

Mark Twain advised against being too particular: It is better to have old second-hand diamonds, his Puddin'head Wilson observed, than none at all.

## The Kleberg Principle

ROBERT J. Kleberg Jr. has bred 69 stakes winners in the last 30 years and he can dazzle you with footwork as he skips around pedigrees explaining how he did it. He leads with St. Simon-Galopin and follows up with Man o' War-Fair Play, then jabs with some nicks and finally lands a roundhouse of line breeding. If a listener is still standing, Kleberg finishes him off with Domino inbreeding.

Take Buffle, the first 3-year-old to win the Suburban in 40 years. Kleberg bred him in a considerable part of southern Texas known as King Ranch, where Zenith stands. Zenith, according to his owner-breeder and his trainer, Max Hirsch, had everything it takes to make a good horse—pedigree, looks, heart—everything except a good race record. He won three races in 16 starts; in his two stakes appearances he finished 50 lengths back in Francis S.'s Wood Memorial and 24 lengths back when Harmonizing beat Bald Eagle and Sword Dancer in the 1960 Man o' War.

Zenith is out of Timed, which started four times and never got part of a purse. Timed is by Beau Max, which Kleberg and Hirsch also considered a better horse than his race record indicated—three wins in 14 starts. Timed is out of Stop Watch, which started four times and never got part of a purse. Lest one be misled by these poor race records, it might be noted that Beau Max ranks in the top four per cent of all active stallions with an Average-Earnings Index of 2.33, along with Eight Thirty, Count Fleet, War Admiral and such, while Stop Watch produced Stymie.

To get Zenith, Kleberg sent Timed to England and bred her to six-time

39

leading sire Hyperion. Hyperion, of course, is one of the world's great sires; Kleberg indicates, however, he was not so much interested in Hyperion as he was in Hyperion's pedigree in that it contains three crosses of Galopin. Hyperion is inbred to Galopin's great son, St. Simon, with three free generations.

If you carry Timed's pedigree out far enough, you can find St. Simon's name twice within seven free generations. Kleberg says none of the Man o' War-Fair Play horses was first class without a double cross of St. Simon-Galopin. Timed is inbred to Man o' War with three free generations. Zenith, then, has two crosses of Man o' War four and five generations away through his dam and has four crosses of St. Simon four, five, six, and seven generations away. Buffle's dam, Refurbish, also has St. Simon in her pedigree, so Buffle has five crosses of St. Simon, five, six, seven, seven, and eight generations away.

For those who would like to account for Zenith's siring a Suburban winner from his first nine foals because of a nick, Kleberg has one. Timed's second dam is Sunset Gun, second dam also of champion High Gun, the latter sired by a son of Hyperion, as was Buffle.

Kleberg said some years ago one of the reasons his Middleground was good enough to win the Kentucky Derby and Belmont was because he was inbred to Domino. As a usual thing, more than three generations free of the same name is not considered inbreeding; Middleground had seven free generations of Domino, but he did have four crosses, Domino's name appearing four, four, six, and eight generations back.

Buffle has nine crosses of Domino in his pedigree. We found this by extending his pedigree 10 generations, which involved 2,046 names. The closest Domino appears is in the sixth generation, twice through Buffle's dam.

There are other ways to view Buffle's pedigree. He is by an allowance horse which was out of an unplaced filly, she in turn being by an allowance horse and out of an unplaced filly. On the bottom half of his pedigree, Buffle is out of a filly which won once in seven tries, his second dam was a stakes winner which produced only three moderate winners, his third dam was unplaced in two starts (yet produced in addition to Renew, champion filly But Why Not and champion steeplechaser Oedipus).

Off hand, one could say Buffle has—apart from his grandsires Hyperion and Bold Venture—a want of racing class close up in his pedigree while St. Simon, Man o' War, and Domino are too far back to be of any significance.

This is the breeding pattern, however, which has produced a Stymie, High Gun, But Why Not, and now Buffle. If not the breeding pattern, then what did?

Mr. Kleberg, breeder of 69 stakes winners, including two Kentucky Derby winners, two Belmont winners, two CCA Oaks winners, two Suburban winners, we are dazzled.

## Bingo

PREDICTING the auction price of a yearling generally valued at more than $50,000 requires the sagacity, keen eye, and years of experience necessary to win at bingo. Anybody can play—it is pure guesswork. Auction prices of the top yearlings do not always reflect with precision relative value—it is difficult to believe that Personality's yearling full sister is $166,000 better than the daughter of champion Buckpasser out of champion Lady Pitt.

Prices for top yearlings more often reflect a momentary demand by two or more people for a particular prospect considered likely to join the top three per cent of the breed as a stakes winner.

For example, when Bunker Hunt stopped on the Buckpasser—Lady Pitt filly at Saratoga last week, Charles W. Engelhard got her for only $90,000. Now it may seem flippant to refer to another man's expenditure as "only $90,000," but we had fixed in our mind that the auctioneer would not draw a breath before bidding on this filly passed the $100,000 mark. Minutes later, the Ribot—Natashka filly was led into the ring and Engelhard had to go to $140,000 to top the persistent bidding of insurance man Ken Opstein of South Souix City, Neb. The thought here is that Engelhard got two top fillies, one at a bargain price.

## Waiting In The Wings

ON May 4, as Dancer's Image roared through an opening along the rail and ran past Forward Pass in the Kentucky Derby, Greentree Stable trainer John Gaver was occupied with other things, among them a big green colt which had never won a race.

41

On May 18, when Dancer's Image tried to bull his way through too small an opening and Forward Pass scampered away to win the Preakness, Gaver was studying his colt, which seemed to be a brighter chestnut with less greenness about him. While the big names among the 3-year-olds were contesting the first two classics, the Greentree colt had broken his maiden in a mile race at Aqueduct—and he had shown some ability. Slow to settle into stride, as had been his way in his three previous starts at two and three, he was taken from seventh place around the outside of his rivals and with brisk urging drew off to win by six lengths; time for the mile was 1:35⅕, a full second faster than the distance was run by older horses in a $20,000 claiming race the same day.

On May 23, the Greentree colt of some ability was tested for class against seasoned stakes horses in a nine-furlong allowance race. In the field were Verbatim, winner of the Gotham, Bahamas, and a division of the Bay Shore; T. V. Commercial, fifth-ranked 2-year-old of last season which had placed in the Kentucky Derby and Blue Grass Stakes, and had finished fourth in the San Felipe; and Draft Card, Ardoise, and Chompion, each prepping for the Belmont Stakes.

The Greentree colt took command after five furlongs, settled in the stretch with a good lead and crossed under the wire four lengths in front. Jockey Heliodoro Gustines had no pre-race instructions to work the colt farther, so his mount was more or less being pulled up when clockers caught the colt in 2:01⅕ for 10 furlongs, 2:16 for 11 furlongs.

On May 24, nine days before the 100th running of the Belmont Stakes, Greentree suddenly had an announced classic candidate in a chestnut colt with a classic-situation name of Stage Door Johnny, by Prince John out of Peroxide Blonde.

In less than three weeks this chestnut colt had emerged from the obscurity of the maiden ranks with a name well known to and respected by Henry Forrest, trainer of Belmont favorite Forward Pass, and by venerable Max Hirsch, trainer of the second-choice entry of Draft Card and Call Me Prince (Draft Card, of course, was classified 1A).

While this seemed sudden, the development of another classic horse in the Greentree stable was not surprising. For more than a half-century the Greentree racing and breeding operation, founded by Mrs. W. Payne Whitney and continued after her death in 1944 under the corporate direction of her children, John Hay Whitney and Mrs. Charles Shipman Payson, has been designed to produce classic horses. Since 1923, 10 horses had carried the watermelon pink with black-striped sleeves in renewals of the Belmont Stakes; Twenty Grand had won in 1931, Shut Out in 1942, Capot in 1949.

42

The development of Stage Door Johnny into a serious Belmont candidate was considerably more than a three-week proposition. It may be said to have been in the making 10 years ago when Bob Green moved across the pike from Elmendorf Farm to become manager of Greentree Stud. As manager of Elmendorf, Green was quite familiar with Nuit de Folies, a French mare by Tornado which at Elmendorf had produced $145,409-earner My Night Out and in 1958 had a colt which was to be named Speak John (winner of the Del Mar Derby and sire of Verbatim).

One of Green's first assignments at Greentree was a trip to Europe to buy some mares. Study of the 1958 Newmarket December sale catalogue by Whitney, Gaver, and Green resulted in pedigree approval of 3-year-old Mother Goose, by Escamillo out of Folie Douce, the latter a half-sister to Nuit de Folies. Green flew to England and almost immediately took off again for France; he had seen in a French publication that Folie Douce was advertised for private sale by the estate of Auguste Daubin.

"I got a car in Paris—I couldn't speak French, had a crazy damn driver, but we missed every cart along the way—drove up to a farm in Normandy to see Folie Douce," Green recalled. "She was nine then, small but clean, and she was in foal to Sica Boy. Greentree bought her for about $42,000, I believe. Then I went back to Newmarket and we bought her daughter, Mother Goose, for $51,800. The next year we bought another filly out of Folie Douce, Mi Carina, just after she won the 1½-mile Prix Vermeille."

Folie Douce was shipped to England (where Whitney served as U. S. ambassador to the Court of St. James), her Sica Boy foal died, she was bred to Ballymoss and then shipped to Greentree Stud near Lexington, where she foaled a light chestnut filly with flaxen mane and tail inevitably named Peroxide Blonde.

A big, rangy filly with a fiery temperament, Peroxide Blonde was broken at Keeneland by John T. Ward, then shipped with the other Greentree yearlings to Gaver in Aiken, S. C. There she kicked a shedrow post and split a pastern. When the Greentree stable headed out of Aiken for New York, Peroxide Blonde was sent back to Keeneland. Ward walked her under the shed for a month, put her back in training, and at the Keeneland fall meeting started her once. The chart footnotes: "Steadied when seeking racing room nearing the first turn, Peroxide Blonde worked her way between horses when moving strongly on the final turn and quickly drew out as much the best," coming from seventh place to win by five lengths. Thus undefeated at two, Peroxide Blonde was shipped to winter quarters in Aiken. At three she raced only once, in May finishing far back in an allowance race in which Rare Exchange finished second to Nautical Miss. Her temperament was against her, but there was a liking for the family (in addition to stakes winners Mother Goose and Mi Carina and stakes-placed Old England, Folie Douce in 1964 produced Sweet Folly, last year's winner of the Gazelle and Ladies Handicaps) and Peroxide Blonde was retired to the Greentree brood-mare ranks.

"We were at Saratoga when Prince John was being syndicated and moved from Elmendorf to Spendthrift Farm," Green recalled. "Walter Kelley, who has this long memory, comes up to me and asks do I remember how high I was on Prince John as a sire? 'Well, Max Gluck has given me a share in the horse for training him, and the share's for sale for $10,000.' So, in about 10 minutes, Greentree bought the share. Peroxide Blonde was bred to Prince John and her first foal was Stage Door Johnny."

He was a chestnut, of course, as were his sire and dam. Shipped to the Greentree Florida Annex at Ocala with the other weanlings, Stage Door Johnny was returned to Kentucky as a yearling and turned over to Ward for breaking at Keeneland. "Only notes I made on him," Ward reported, "was that he was big and strong, especially through the shoulders; I breezed him four or five times. The first time he went a quarter in :23³⁄₅, which is faster than we like to have them go; then he went an eighth in :12²⁄₅ and bucked his shins in September. We fired him in October, sent him to Aiken in December, and I have noted here, 'Clean and sound.' "

Gaver remembered Stage Door Johnny at two as being a "big, dumb colt, had beefy joints." By dumb, he said he meant that the colt was slow in learning what a race horse is supposed to do, that he appeared awkward while other colts were quicker to learn.

"He was very green and when we got him to the races at Saratoga, he ran all over the track, but did finish second. We thought then he had tremendous ability, but he was so slow in catching on." Footnotes to the chart of Stage Door Johnny's first race stated: "Racing greenly and outrun away from the gate, drifted out at the stretch turn, but finished fast after being straightened up and was easily second best."

Gaver said: "Then we started him one more time, at Aqueduct; he started slow, got caught in behind a lot of horses, finally got through and finished second again. We stopped on him then, fired his ankles, and went on down to Aiken."

On the morning before the 100th Belmont Stakes, Gaver worked Stage Door Johnny a half-mile in sparkling time of :47³⁄₅, five furlongs in two ticks less than a minute. Watching the colt cool out beside the Belmont barn where Greentree classics candidates have been walked since 1923, Gaver said:

**44**

"Two weeks ago I didn't know we had a Belmont horse. We did think this horse had a great deal of ability. When he broke his maiden, we knew he could run, but he is still green. He's getting smarter. We're not sure yet about his class, although he ran awfully well there last week when we sent him against some nice horses."

The day was overcast and it had been a rainy week. Was Gaver worried about the weather and what kind of track there would be for the Belmont?

"Well, I'm always worried about the weather. But, then, I always worry about everything else, too."

Max Hirsch, trainer of Mrs. Frank Rand's Call Me Prince and King Ranch's Draft Card, was not worried about the condition of his two Belmont candidates. On the morning before the race the pair had worked together, going a half-mile in exceptionally fast time of :45⅗; Call Me Prince went out five furlongs in :58⅕ and Draft Card was timed five furlongs in :59⅖. Hirsch said both the horses had "trained beautifully for the race; only wish it was being run today, because my horses are ready right now."

Call Me Prince, winner of the mile Withers Stakes for his fourth victory in as many starts this year, was considered the better half of the Hirsch entry. Call Me Prince is by Princequillo (the 63rd stakes winner sired by the two-time leading sire which died in 1964) which suggests an inherited ability to go a distance. Draft Card is by Gallant Man, the best stayer in the Bold Ruler and Round Table crop, and is out of Dotted Line, which beat Bald Eagle at a distance, and she is by Princequillo.

Hirsch had two horses with pedigrees that might be associated with 1½ miles. He thought Forward Pass was a very good horse up to a mile. "Down there at Pimlico it looked like all the others fell in a hole after a mile and Forward Pass went on and finished by himself.

"Gaver has a good horse; looks like he can go a mile and a half. Beat Draft Card at a mile and an eighth last week...awful good race."

Henry Forrest shrugged off suggestions that Forward Pass would not go the Belmont distance. No 3-year-old had proven this season it could race 1½ miles, and Forrest figured the son of On-and-On out of Princess Turia had as much right to be a distance horse as did any of his rivals.

The Calumet Farm colt had been in top condition when he won the Hibiscus Stakes on Jan. 20, and it is a tribute to a master's hand that Forward Pass in winning the Everglades on Feb. 21, the Florida Derby on March 30, and the Blue Grass on April 25 seemed to look better and run better with every effort. The day before the Belmont, Forrest sent the early favorite for a short gallop, and the big bay, in full bloom, came back looking for his feed tub.

"Oh, he's a good doer; never has backed up from his feed the way some horses do when they run a lot," Forrest said. "Who am I worried about in this race? Well, John Gaver's horse ran real good the other day, and Max Hirsch is high on his horses—you know he thinks they're better than Out of the Way, and he ran second to us in the Preakness and won the Jersey Derby yesterday." Forrest was confident, but he did not view the 100th Belmont Stakes as a walkover.

The most beautiful saddling paddock and walking ring in America was crowded well before the nine Belmont candidates were led in from the barn area. There were Paul Mellon, George Widener, the Alfred Vanderbilts, the C. V. Whitneys, Leslie Combs II, A. B. Hancock Jr., James Cox Brady, James P. Mills, the John Galbreaths, John A. Morris, Thomas Bancroft, John A. Bell III, Cortright Wetherill and a hundred more representing racing's most distinguished names.

On a circle of benches surrounding the great white pine which has shaded owners of Belmont Stakes horses since 1905, Mrs. Charles Shipman Payson sat with her trainer as Stage Door Johnny was led in. The chestnut colt had a figure 8 over his head, but he still managed to get his tongue out of a corner of his mouth.

"He runs with his tongue out," Gaver said. "We tried him last year with a tongue strap, but he still got it out; then we tried a special bit, now we're going with the figure 8; it seems to keep his mouth closed pretty well."

So it came about, the 100th running of the Belmont, with Calumet Farm's Forward Pass a solid, even-money favorite, with the best record, his coat glistening condition; Mrs. Frank Rand's Call Me Prince, considered the most likely to challenge Forward Pass in the testing 12th furlong, readied to run by a man who had saddled four Belmont winners in the last 40 years and installed with Draft Card as second choice at 9-5; Greentree Stable's Stage Door Johnny, still green, racing in his first stakes, third choice at 4-1; and five others whose chances were figured at no better than 20-1.

Forward Pass took the lead from the start, and he took it easily, Milo Valenzuela saying later that "I took all the hold on him I could take; we were going real easy the first part of it."

Bill Boland on Call Me Prince waited to see if any of the others would go after the expected leader, and when no one did, he hustled the Withers winner into second place, less than two lengths behind the Calumet colt. Stage Door Johnny came away from the gate without undue hurrying and was seventh going into the first turn.

Although Valenzuela was trying to conserve something for the last, testing furlongs of the classic, Forward Pass clicked off early fractions identical to those of Citation when, 20 year ago, the Calumet great led all the way in completing the last Triple Crown. Both Citation and Forward Pass ran the first half-mile of their Belmonts in :48$\frac{2}{5}$, the first six furlongs in 1:12$\frac{3}{5}$, the first mile in 1:37 flat.

Forward Pass, however, was not running evenly. The margin between the pacesetter and Call Me Prince opened and closed three times going down the backstretch and around the far turn. Boland said his horse did not make any challenges then; Boland contended that Forward Pass was running in spurts.

"My horse would hear that No. 1 horse coming up behind him," Valenzuela said, "and then he would draw away and then I would settle on him, and then he would hear him again and my horse would take off; but I was saving something for the stretch."

Meanwhile, Stage Door Johnny began picking up horses after leaving the seven-furlong pole. He did not really begin his drive that far back, for he was running easily.

"All of us were running easily the first part of it," Boland said, "but I began to make a move at the half-mile pole. Around the turn, I looked over and Gustines was lapped on me; there I was trying to go somewhere and he wasn't even driving yet with his horse."

The race began, really, when Forward Pass and Stage Door Johnny straightened for the last quarter-mile, and it obviously was between these two. Forward Pass had raced 1¼ miles in 2:02$\frac{2}{5}$, a tick faster than Citation had, and Valenzuela felt he had a lot of horse left.

"When the winner came up to me, I thought we could do it," Valenzuela said, but the big chestnut on the outside, reaching out with ground-devouring strides, was not to be denied. Slowly he gained on the pacesetter.

"I thought he would stop when I get to him," Gustines said, "but he no stop." This was not the case of a one-run horse running past a tired pacesetter. Forward Pass dug in, valiantly meeting the challenge.

At the eighth pole the two were even, and then Stage Door Johnny wrested the lead. Forward Pass did not quit. Valenzuela switched the whip to his left hand, struck, and Forward Pass dug in again. Stage Door Johnny began to draw ahead. Forward Pass was losing ground, and he was beaten, but he would not concede it.

"I thought Forward Pass never was going to give up," Gaver said after the race. "Every time Milo hit him left-handed, it seemed to me he came again."

Stage Door Johnny moved ahead by more than a length, but he could not draw away. Forward Pass left no doubt that he was a 1½-mile horse, still driving at the end, but a better 1½-mile horse beat him in the second-fastest Belmont ever run—2:27$\frac{1}{5}$, only three-fifths of a second slower than Gallant

Man's stakes and track record.

Call Me Prince finished 12 lengths behind Forward Pass, five lengths in front of stablemate Draft Card.

In the Trustees Room after the race, a beaming owner, John Hay Whitney, accepted congratulations on the 127th stakes winner bred by Greentree (additionally, Whitney has bred 24 stakes winners in his own name, his mother two, and his sister three, for a two-generation Whitney total of 156 stakes winners).

"I think this is a real good horse," Whitney said happily, "It's not as though he went by a lot of bad horses with one run. Forward Pass is a very good colt who never quit, and was driving right to the finish. I think I would like to go to the barn and check the winner."

A waiter came by with a tray of filled champagne glasses.

"May I take one for my horse?"

"Sir, with a horse like that, I'd take the whole tray."


## Probable, But Not Predictable

WITH the Keeneland summer yearling sale upon us, a considerable amount of conversation around here is devoted to breeding. This may be expected, but it is tiresome, inasmuch as the most emphatic pronouncements on this subject usually are made by persons who have yet to breed a good horse.

It is refreshing, therefore, to hear from a breeder who has done the job; in last week's Rockingham Special, Sense of Rhythm became the 50th stakes winner bred by Alfred G. Vanderbilt.

"All I know about breeding can be said in a minute or two," Vanderbilt has said. "If you breed a mare of ability to a stallion of ability, you've got a better chance of getting a horse of ability than if you don't.

"Breeding is probabilities, not predictabilities, and certainly not certainties. The fact that a good horse pops up once in a while from pretty strange parents keeps a lot of mediocre stock in production that doesn't belong. That is all I know about breeding."

When Vanderbilt was honored at the 1953 Thoroughbred Club testimonial dinner, he gave a classic explanation of how he happened to breed Native Dancer: "Well, I gave the mating of Geisha to Polynesian a great deal of thought and a great deal of study and the somewhat nebulous value of 20 years of breeding experience, and lo and behold, here comes Native Dancer. Of course, I also gave the same amount of thought, study, and experience to a lot of other horses that couldn't get out of their own way."

## Ho Ho Ho

SOME practical jokes are near felonies.

Letters, telegrams, and telephone calls have deluged the Louisville home and office of Dr. Hoyt D. Gardner, all messages graciously accepting his invitation to the big "fox hunt on his estate," the gala Derby-eve mint julep festival in his "spacious gardens," and clubhouse tickets for the Kentucky Derby. At latest count, about 125 adults and 40 children—"My dogs are going to love the fox hunt"—had accepted an offer to spend Derby Week with the Gardners.

But Dr. Gardner never issued such a preposterous invitation. His Derby guest of last year, Dr. Rex Kenyon, president of the Oklahoma Medical Association, did for him, by way of publishing Dr. Gardner's picture on the first page of *Oklahoma Medical Journal* and inviting every doctor and his family in Oklahoma.

Dr. Gardner and his family have been writing letters for two weeks trying to reach Oklahomans, before they reach them, to explain it all is a practical joke. He also is responding to doctors in 10 other states who have reproved him for confining his guest list to Oklahoma.

## Lightening In a Bottle

"This filly is parrot-mouthed, but she can run a little bit. Some day, I believe she'll throw a good horse," said the late Hal Price Headley in 1957 when he presented his daughter, Alice Headley Bell, with a 4-year-old filly by Mr. Trouble. The filly was Attica, dam of Sir Ivor.

49

Right now Sir Ivor appears to be the best 3-year-old in the world. Jockey Lester Piggott, who has brought home four English Derby winners, declared Sir Ivor to be the best horse he ever has ridden. Trainer Vincent O'Brien, who has saddled winners of all the English and Irish classics, said Sir Ivor was the best horse he ever has trained. In becoming the first odds-on winner of the English Derby since 1905, Sir Ivor caused Hill's, the London book-makers, "a net loss of £400,000, our worst day in memory."

On June 10, Ladies Night at the Thoroughbred Club of America, Mrs. Bell was presented with a julep cup by TCA President Humphrey S. Finney as a memento of her contribution to American breeding.

In accepting the cup, Mrs. Bell explained how she happened to breed Sir Ivor: "Caught lightning in a bottle; it will never happen again." Seeking greater detail on the old lightning-in-a-bottle trick, we drove out the next morning to Mrs. Bell's Mill Ridge Farm, located about 10 furlongs down the Bowman's Mill Pike from our Lexington offices.

Mill Ridge Farm is a 400-acre section of Beaumont Farm, purchased in 1880 by George Washington Headley, enlarged by his son, Hal Petit Head-ley, and made famous by *his* son, Hal Price Headley. The entranceway at Mill Ridge is lined by wire fences, topped with a conrete rail and supported by concrete posts. A blacktop road points toward a 24-stall concrete barn which Hal Price Headley had designed and was building when he died in 1962.

One end of the 265-foot barn contains a breeding shed, laboratory, warm-ing room, blacksmith shop, and four-room farm office. Mrs. Bell sat at her desk with a window view of some of the 100 mares on the farm, one of these being Attica with a five-week-old full brother to Sir Ivor.

"Well," began Mrs. Bell, "I always thought Attica was more of a stayer type than sprinter. She is by Mr. Trouble, which I consider a mile-and-a-quarter horse because he killed off Your Host in the Kentucky Derby and still finished third to Middleground. He was a hot stallion, bred hot; you know he was hell bent on suicide every day of his life, the only horse I believe Daddy ever insured." Mr. Trouble had a tendency to pounce on unwary spar-rows which flew too low in his paddock, and there were times when a tree might irritate him for some reason—he would back up to it and kick it down.

"Attica had her quirks, but she was not what you would call hot. As a race mare she liked to come from far out of it and I always had it in my mind that she could go on. Anyway, I bred her to Sir Gaylord because he was a top race horse, had good speed, had good family, and was a good-dispositioned horse—I think of him as phlegmatic.

50

"The first time Attica was bred to Sir Gaylord, she had Young Noble, a bad-legged colt, but game; had one good leg and a lot of speed. Everything Attica's produced has had speed: Be Careful, I broke at Keeneland and she worked a quarter in :23 barefoot; McCoy had speed that would break your watch in the morning.

"The second time she was bred to Sir Gaylord, she had Sir Ivor, exceptionally big foal, May 5. He was a very sensible colt. I remember about a month before the Keeneland sale we had a terrible thunderstorm during the night, lightning and wind; I went out in the paddock and he walked right up to me, let me lead him into the barn without a shank.

"You know, he was raised on the concrete floors in this barn. Daddy had a lot of doubters when he poured concrete for the stall floors here, but they have worked out perfect for us.

"Just before the sale, he began to grow—taller, not out. Raymond Guest asked Bull Hancock to buy a colt at the sale and Bull picked out two—the full brother to Garwol, absolutely the best-looking colt in the sale, and my colt. Tommy Gentry consigned the other colt and Charles Engelhard bought him for $67,000, [I think named Pamir, he won two of his three starts last year and was ranked at 110 pounds on the Experimental Free Handicap], so Bull got my colt for $42,000. He went to Claiborne and then to Vincent O'Brien in Ireland. Vincent thought he was big and rangy and would not do at two, but he got him to the races in July. [Sir Ivor lost his first start, then won the Probationers' Stakes and National Stakes in Ireland; shipped to France, he won the Grand Criterium, earning a total of $100,514 and top weight on the Irish 2-year-old Free Handicap.]

"The first time he ran this year, in the Two Thousand Guineas Trial, Piggott got him to the front too soon and another horse almost sneaked up on him; it was thought then that he might not be the kind of horse to stay. In the Two Thousand Guineas, however, Piggott waited with him, shot him forward just at the end.

"My mother and I went over to see him run in the Derby. Humphrey Finney had tried to prepare me for what it would be like, but I really wasn't ready for Epsom. They bring the horses over from the barns down the middle of a blacktop road, with cars whipping by on both sides. They saddle them in a paddock, then bring them into the walking ring for about 15 minutes.

"Sir Ivor had not seen Epsom until the day before the race. Vincent never worked him more than a mile for the Derby, and the morning before the race he was blown out about three-eighths of a mile, from Tattenham Corner up the hill, at about a two-minute lick.

51

"Oh, he looked good. Stands about 16.2½ hands, very muscular—has a rear end on him like a miler. Vincent told Piggott before the race that he was not sure Sir Ivor wanted to go a mile and a half on that course and that he should save as much of him as he could. Piggott really did. He is ice—just out there hacking along the first part of it—never made a move until the last 100 yards.

"When they came around Tattenham Corner, Sir Ivor was eighth, in on the rail where it looked like he could not possibly get free. And he just sat there. Then, suddenly, he just shot forward—Piggott never laid a whip on him—he just moved around those horses with the most spectacular run you've ever seen. He was beaten—really—100 yards out, and then he was winning, going away, just like that."

Like that. Lightning. In a bottle.


## Jolly And Rich

YES, Virginia, there is a Santa Claus syndicate. The winner of the 1964 English Derby, Irish Derby, and Irish Two Thousand Guineas is being syndicated, 40 shares valued at $1,480,000.


## Getting Stoned

NOW when David chose five smooth stones from a brook with the idea of slinging them at somebody, he was regarded as a game and admirable fellow. Last week, however, when union pickets held up racing at Santa Anita and slung some smooth stones through trainers' car windows, they became the Philistines.

Which just goes to show how regard for rock throwers varies with the direction of the rock. Trainers do not mind, some have been known to enjoy, getting stoned on their own, but they do not like to have their car windows smashed.

At any rate, horsemen and track management united in opposition to union demands for another $2 a day and fringe benefits for pari-mutuel clerks in California. Negotiations disintegrated and Santa Anita's scheduled Dec. 26 opening was postponed.

Gus Ring leaned on the rail and watched his horses work for races that may never be run. He said it always was the way for him. The last time he shipped horses to Santa Anita, Pearl Harbor was attacked and the race meeting was canceled.

## Foul Play

ONE would have to think that with a four-horse field going nine furlongs, there would be room on the race track for everybody. In the second furlong of the Jersey Derby on Memorial Day, however, there was a jam.

Manual Ycaza, on his day of grace before starting a 20-day suspension imposed by New York stewards, was on the outside with Dr. Fager, unquestionably the best horse in the race, and going past the finish line the first time he squeezed the three horses inside of him, causing two distinct series of bumpings.

Earlie Fires on In Reality immediately next to Ycaza yelled for room and the patrol judge heard him. These bumpings really were not serious enough to affect the outcome of the race.

Between the 7½-furlong and seven-furlong pole, however, Ycaza believed he was far enough in front with Dr. Fager to cut over to the rail on the first turn.

"If Ycaza had maintained his position for perhaps only three more strides," said Keene Daingerfield, New Jersey state steward, "he would have been clear. But he did not. He was not clear and he did come in. Fires had to swerve to avoid hitting Dr. Fager's heels, and this caused Gallant Moment to hit the fence. I'm surprised Gallant Moment did not go down.

"I suppose we should have put up the inquiry sign, but Dr. Fager was so much the best (he won by 6½ lengths from In Reality) and I was hoping maybe there would be extenuating circumstancaes revealed by a close study of the films."

Ray Broussard, who finished fourth with Gallant Moment, claimed foul against Ycaza; Jacinto Vasquez, who finished third with Air Rights, in trainer Frank Martin's name claimed foul against Fires.

"I don't believe in taking a horse's number down when a foul is committed," Daingerfield said, "if the disqualification will not benefit the horse suffering from the infraction. If Gallant Moment had finished sixth and would have been moved up only to fifth, we might not have disqualified the winner. But in this instance, Gallant Moment, which definitely was fouled and which, according to the betting at least, could be expected to have finished third, was benefited by being moved up from fourth place to be awarded third money."

In response to the various claims entered, Ycaza claimed the innocence of an unborn babe and inquired if the stewards expected him to run his horse around the outside fence.

It is suspected here that Ycaza could have given his field six lengths at the start, have run all the way around on the outside fence, and still have won by a comfortable margin.

At any rate, the horse which had run the fastest Jersey Derby (1:48, three-fifths faster than Hail to All's previous stakes record) was placed last and In Reality, unquestionably the second-best horse, was declared the winner.

Ycaza was set down for 15 days, to begin at the expiration of his current suspension. According to NASRC records, this 81st suspension brings Ycaza's ground time since 1954 to 586 days.

## "Well Done My Friend"

On a dull, cold Nov. 11, suddenly there came the flash that was Sir Ivor. It was this brillance, a demonstration of sheer class, which lifted the 17th Washington, D. C., International above the ordinary show.

Sir Ivor, a Kentucky-bred son of Sir Gaylord—Attica, by Mr. Trouble, purchased as a Keeneland yearling for $42,000 by Raymond Guest, then United States ambassador to Ireland, had established himself as the best 3-year-old in England this season. As the first English Derby winner to race here in 45 years, he soundly whipped America's best grass horses and confirmed his class on two continents.

Sir Ivor, less than even money with London bookmakers, was installed at almost 2-1 odds, by the 30,183 on hand at Laurel. The night before the race there had been a rumor, as wispy and vague as any race track rumor, that Sir Ivor was not right ("oh, the bloody French must have started it"). The source was apocryphal, but the result was an overlay, for Sir Ivor was going to win this race, according to his rider, Lester Piggott, "by 10 lengths but for the going."

Rain and snow had rendered the Laurel track "muddy," the turf course officially "soft," but what Fort Marcy's rider Manuel Ycaza (who has ridden more International winners than any jockey—three) described as "very soggy, very deep." Sir Ivor's rider, Piggott (riding in his sixth International), mentioned the "patchy softness in places; he did not like it because he could not get a hold of it."

The condition of the course accounted for the extraordinarily slow time for the 1½ miles—2:37⅕, which was 13⅖ seconds slower than the American record set by Kelso when he beat Gun Bow on a surface labeled "hard" in the 1964 International. Sir Ivor's winning time was the slowest since Fisherman won the 1954 International on a "soft" surface in 2:47⅘.

Time, in this instance, is of no value in assaying the quality of Sir Ivor or in indicating the authority of his victory. Sir Ivor is an outstanding horse, in appearance and performance.

He is big, with massive hindquarters suggesting extraordinary driving power; he is deep through the heart and he has a not-unattractive head, characterized by alertness. He is, in short, what a good horse is supposed to look like.

At two, Sir Ivor finished sixth in his first start in Ireland (second in that race was Ballygoran, a stablemate sired by Guest's 1962 English Derby winner, Larkspur, which accompanied Sir Ivor to Laurel and is to be turned over to Frank Y. Whiteley Jr. to be trained for an American campaign). Sir Ivor then won the Probationers' Stakes and National Stakes, sufficient showings to be ranked at the top of Ireland's Free Handicap, and when shipped to France he won the Gran Criterium.

At three this year, Sir Ivor won the Two Thousand Guineas Trial Stakes at Ascot, the Two Thousand Guineas at Newmarket, and the Derby at Epsom for his sixth consecutive victory. He then was upset by Ribero in the Irish Sweeps Derby, was beaten three-quarters of a length by older Royal Palace in the Eclipse Stakes, and was put away for 11 weeks. Prepping for the Prix de l'Arc de Triomphe, he finished second in the Prix Henry Delamarre in France and on Oct. 6 finished second to Vaguely Noble in the Arc.

There were some plausible explanations for three of these defeats, but none for his second-place finish in the Arc other than that offered by his owner and jockey—he had met a better horse in Vaguely Noble. Returned to England two weeks after the Arc, Sir Ivor won the rich Champion Stakes in easy fashion, prompting Guest to seek a return meeting with Vaguely Noble.

The latter's owners, in the midst of solidifying a syndication for Vaguely Noble, declined an invitation to race in the International. [At midweek it was announced that Vaguely Noble would be shipped from France to arrive at John Gaines' Gainesway Farm near Lexington, Ky., on Nov. 20. Gaines has acquired an option to purchase a quarter interest in Vaguely Noble for $1,250,000, placing the Arc winner's value at a record $5,000,000.]

In the absence of Vaguely Noble, Sir Ivor's only serious competition for the International was to come from the United States representatives, Gus Ring's Irish-bred Czar Alexander and Paul Mellon's Fort Marcy.

Czar Alexander beat Fort Marcy, although in receipt of five pounds, by three lengths in last month's Man o' War Stakes over $1^{1}/_{2}$ miles of grass at Belmont Park. He was getting seven pounds from Fort Marcy in the International and was installed second favorite at 2.10-1 while Fort Marcy was available at 3.80-1.

Fort Marcy, which beat Damascus at level weights in last year's International, was voted America's best grass horse last season. On turf this year he had won the Stars and Stripes Handicap in Chicago and the $1^{1}/_{2}$-mile Sunset Handicap at Hollywood Park and he was brought up to the International in superb condition.

"Last year Fort Marcy was stabled in our barn," Whiteley commented as he stood outside the stall where Damascus, retired after the Jockey Club Gold Cup with a bowed tendon, nuzzled hay. "This year we're stabled in Fort Marcy's barn."

Fort Marcy ran the good race that it was thought he would run, forcing the pace all the way, taking the longest route on the outside, assuming the lead briefly in the early stretch. The 4-year-old Amerigo gelding, under the race conditions assigned 127 pounds, just could not give seven pounds to such 3-year-olds as Sir Ivor and Czar Alexander.

The betting public did not accord the others much consideration.

From Argentina came Azincourt II, a 5-year-old son of Rianco—Bataille, by Bahram, which young Bertram Firestone of Wilton, Conn., purchased from Pedro Bruno last month. In six starts this year, Azincourt II had won the Clasico Japon Handicap at San Isidro, the Clasico Mariano Moreno Handicap at San Isidro, the Gran Premio 25 de Mayo at San Isidro, and the Clasico Vicente L. Casares at Palermo. In his last start he finished second with 137 pounds in the $2^{3}/_{16}$-mile Gran Premio de Honor at Palermo.

From France came Carmarthen, a 4-year-old son of Devon—Kuwait, by Persian Gulf, bred and owned by Mrs. R. B. Strassburger. Her late husband, a Norristown, Pa., newspaper publisher, moved to France in 1923 and at his 400-acre Haras des Monceaux bred Worden II, which carried the Strass-

56

burger colors to victory in the 1953 International. Carmarthen had won only once in four starts this year, taking the Prix d'Harcourt, and had finished third in the Arc, seven lengths behind Vaguely Noble, four lengths behind Sir Ivor.

Also from France came Petrone, a 4-year-old son of Prince Taj—Wild Miss, by Wild Risk, owned by Daniel Wildenstein, art historian and head of the Wildenstein Galleries founded in Paris with branches in New York, London, and Buenos Aires. Author of several books and editor of "La Gazette des Beaux-Arts," Wildenstein is an American citizen who inherited the French stable and breeding farms of his father, George, in 1963. His stable, with some $600,000 in earnings, currently leads the French owners' list. He was at the Keeneland sale of broodmares the night of the International. Petrone had won two of eight starts this year, the Prix Henry Foy and Prix du Prince d'Orange, before finishing unplaced in the Arc.

From Japan came Takeshiba-O, a 3-year-old son of China Rock—Takatsunami, by Yashima Manna, owned by Masao Obata, president of a Japanese racing publication printing firm, who has owned horses for three years. Takeshiba-O had won two allowance races and the Tokyo Yonsai Stakes (on dirt) and had finished second in his six other starts this year, including the Japanese Derby and Two Thousand Guineas.

The lone filly in the field was La Lagune, a 3-year-old daughter of Val de Loir—Landerinette, by Sicambre, owned by Henri Berlin, a financier with a residence in Monaco and a breeding farm in Normandy. La Lagune was pronounced a wonder when she won this season's English Oaks by five lengths for her fourth victory without a defeat. She then was beaten by Roseliere in the French Oaks and Prix Vermeille and finished fifth, nine lengths back, in the Arc.

Thus it was an oddly classified field of Internatioinalists: Six of the eight are owned by Americans, one representing America having been bred in Ireland and raced in Germany before importation; the English Derby winner, an American-bred owned by an American, represented Ireland, where he had raced only once this season and lost; while the English Oaks winner represented France.

From the beginning, Sir Ivor was full of himself. Led calmly to his saddling place in the infield, he kicked off his International blanket and generally scattered casual observers. He cared nothing about being restrained by a shank and more or less shattered the decorum of the post parade by refusing to be led in front of the odds board. An outrider attempted to take his head, but this never worked out, and attendants finally placed the matter in the capable hands of champion rider Lester Piggott. Sir Ivor bolted in front of the stands for a few strides, then Piggott gathered him up and placed him in his proper position in the post parade.

Loaded into the gate, Sir Ivor promptly backed out and became the last to be put in. Starter Eddie Blind sent the field away immediately, all breaking evenly save for Carmarthen, which came away slowly and was quickly sent up into the middle of the closely bunched leaders.

Takeshiba-O took the lead at once, closely followed by Czar Alexander, with Fort Marcy third on the outside. These three set the pace for the first mile, with the others in close pursuit, no more than six lengths separating the entire field the first time around. Then the field bunched.

With a half-mile to go, Sir Ivor was last—but only two lengths behind the leader. Going into the far turn, six horses were abreast, forming a seemingly impenetrable barrier for Sir Ivor (which had raced on the rail throughout) and La Lagune.

Suddenly, on the turn, the knot dissolved as Takeshiba-O stopped badly and Azincourt II and Petrone faded. Sir Ivor, proceeding at his same steady rate, took over third position by default.

Czar Alexander, on the rail, took a head lead over Fort Marcy, but, straightening out for home Fort Marcy inched ahead. Sir Ivor was directly behind Fort Marcy, hemmed in by Carmarthen. For a moment it seemed that Piggott had eased into a pocket.

Then, with a sixteenth of a mile to go, Piggott struck Sir Ivor for the first time. The best 3-year-old in England spurted away from Carmarthen, pulled around Fort Marcy as though coming out of a parking place, and accelerated past the two leaders with consummate ease.

Both Czar Alexander and Fort Marcy drifted away from the rail in the final 70 yards, and Piggott swung his whip four more times ("I believe he was looking at the people standing on the Tote board there and I wanted to keep his mind on the business") to send Sir Ivor under the wire three-quarters of a length in front. Piggott, who stands 5 feet 7 and rides exceptionally high, immediately eased his mount after crossing the finish and both Czar Alexander and Fort Marcy passed him quickly in pulling up.

In adding the $100,000 first prize in the International to his earnings in Ireland, England, and France, Sir Ivor moved into second place on the list of Europe's greatest money winners with $561,243. Only Sea-Bird, winner of seven of eight starts, has earned more—$645,645. Sir Ivor was returned this week to Ireland, where he will stand the 1969 breeding season. He is to make his fourth trip across the Atlantic to stand at Claiborne Farm near Paris, Ky., in 1970.

In the excitement of the race finish, Raymond Guest was jostled, lost one

58

of his contact lenses, and had to be guided to the winner's circle. "This is my lucky day, though," said the former seven-goal polo player who served as a commando during World War II, "because a chap found the lens in a few minutes."

Now Guest's father was a first cousin to Winston Churchill who served in Parliament for 30 years and served as England's first Secretary for Air; Yale man Guest served in the Virginia legislature for six years before becoming an ambassador, so he comes by the grandiloquent phrase through inheritance and training.

From any other handsome millionaire, it may have been suspect, but Guest is a horseman and he has an intense, sincere enthusiasm and respect for a good horse. In accepting the International trophy from E. P. Taylor, Sir Ivor's owner chose to say:

"If I could talk to him as a human being I would say: 'Well done, thou good and faithful friend.' "

## Too Little, Too Late

WE are in receipt of a request for "1 dollar's worth of information on Swaps." This recalls the time shortly after pari-mutuels replaced bookmakers at Belmont Park when a bettor approached a $2 window with a single he wanted on the favorite; the seller advised that he could not accept a dollar bet.

"Awright, then, take any part of it you can handle."

## Best Race Story Ever Written

YEARS AGO Tom Sheehan would take time off from play—arguing with the mayor or PTA president in his role as owner-publisher of a New Hampshire weekly, and punching racing's Establishment in the ear as editor of the *Horsemen's Journal*—to attend Keeneland sales and try to smarten us up by providing titles to books we should read.

59

At the 1963 January sale, Sheehan directed us to William Faulkner's last book, *The Reivers*, with the flat declaration that it contained the best race story ever written. Numerous attempts to enjoy Faulkner previously had been thwarted by an inability to grasp his style of punctuation, a matter of small moment to others, obviously, inasmuch as Faulkner had won the 1949 Nobel Prize for literature and a 1955 Pulitzer Prize for *The Fable*.

We struggled through the first 100 pages of *The Reivers* and decided if Faulkner got a prize for those, the fix would have to be on. Then, abruptly, the story took off on a dead run. It is a dandy.

Ned William McCaslin Jefferson Mississippi trades a "borrowed" motor car for 3-year-old Forkid Lightning (nee Coppermine, also "borrowed") and a coup is planned in matching Lightning against a "Possam horse" which already had defeated Lightning twice at Parsham, Tenn. Faulkner obviously had loaded a horse on a box car at night for him to describe in such detail the loading of Lightning at Memphis. The preparation for the match and the running of the race are fascinating in their telling and are indeed worthy of the Pulitzer Prize Faulkner won for this story.

Now it is a movie. The race lost a couple of lengths in the adaptation, but the rest of the book was moved up considerably. The photography is marvelous (the fanciest fancy house since *Gone With The Wind* and the acting is superb.

You better see this movie. If the unions remain adamant at Santa Anita, it could be the last good thing in a racing way to come out of Los Angeles.

## Riders Up

IN Chicago, Circuit Court Judge Edward Egan issued an injunction last week prohibiting the Illinois Racing Board from enforcing its new rule setting minimum jockey fees. This decision followed a similar circuit court decision in Miami last summer which declared that the Florida State Racing Commission did not have the power to set jockey fees.

Judge Egan noted that the Illinois legislature specifically was prohibited from setting wages, that the racing board was created by the legislature, and that the board could not have greater power than the legislature.

On an ancillary point raised earlier in the case, Judge Egan determined that jockeys were track employes. Meanwhile, the New Jersey Supreme

Court determined, for workman's compensation purposes, that jockeys were employed not by the track or by trainers, but by owners of horses they rode. On the other hand, decisions in other jurisdictions have classified jockeys as independent contractors, employes of no one.

As Mr. Bumble poignantly remarked some time ago, the law is confused on this point.

## But Can He Run Clean?

FOR nearly 40 years now, Alfred Vanderbilt has been writing screen plays and short stories in 16 letters or less. A current work on display at Belmont Park is a homebred 3-year-old by Tom Fool out of Last Leg, named Dirty Old Man.

## Swift Shrift

CHARLEY HATTON, who "as a mere shaver saw George Smith beat Star Hawk by another of those proverbial whiskers on the post for the Kentucky Derby," probably has seen more good racing and reported it more entertainingly than any other man in a track pressbox today.

In his pre-Suburban column this past week, Hatton was perturbed by younger generations perpetuating and magnifying a question that Whisk Broom II's 1913 Suburban time was out of joint. "We happen to believe with Joe Notter, who was on him at the time," Hatton wrote in *Daily Racing Form*, "that Whisk Broom II actually carried 139 a mile and a quarter in 2:00 flat."

Lacking the stature of even a mere shaver in 1913, we have relied on historian John Hervey's summation of this controversy: "The moment the time went up—2:00 flat—there were cries of dissent, and large numbers of turfmen who had been holding their watches on the race, as well as the timer for *Daily Racing Form's* official charts, immediately registered protests. None of them had got anything within two seconds of 2:00, the majority of their watches showing 2:02⅗ to 2:02⅘, with a few slightly faster.

61

"The attention of the officials was at once called to this and it was pointed out that 2:00 was manifestly incorrect—and by a wide margin. The protestors also called to notice the fact that at the start the man with the flag had been unduly slow in dropping it and did not do so until the horses were past him. To their representations a deaf ear was turned. The official timer stuck to 2:00 and the stewards backed him up, despite the many watches shown them that registered a bit better than 2:03.

"Finally the matter was referred to the late August Belmont II, then the 'dictator of racing' in the Metropolitan terrain and ex-officio head of the American Turf. He gave the matter short shrift, in effect telling the dissidents to go tell their troubles to a policeman. The official time, he stated crisply, was 2:00. And that was that.

"Next morning all the New York dailies, as well as all other newspapers in the country of any prominence, headlined the affair and pronounced the new so-called record questionable. Whereupon Mr. Belmont, who believed that it was a dictator's function to dictate, gave out an interview in which the public was informed that to question the infallibility of the official timing at Belmont Park was equivalent to *lese-majeste*, as also was any imputation that the stewards did not know their business. And thus the incident was closed—officially."

Unofficially, it remained opened, for with the mile time recorded at 1:36⅘, the last quarter would have had to be run in :23⅕, and few thought that possible at the time. It further was noted that Lahore, an ordinary horse, was gaining on Whisk Broom II at the end and would have had to run the last quarter in less than 23 seconds. August Belmont, Charley Hatton, and Joe Notter notwithstanding, it would seem more reasonable to believe that Broomstick's 1¼-mile record of 2:02⅘ was first broken by Roamer in 1914 when he was timed in 2:02 over the trotting track at Syracuse.

## The Flag Is Down

AFTER Mrs. Stephen C. Clark Jr.'s Hoist the Flag had romped home seven lengths in front of the best 3-year-olds that could be mustered in the East for the Bay Shore Stakes on March 20, jockey Jean Cruguet exuberantly proclaimed:

"I don't think he'll ever get beat unless he falls down."

On the morning of March 31 at Belmont Park, Hoist the Flag figuratively fell down. Trainer Sidney Watters Jr. sent out the champion son of Tom Rolfe, with Cruguet up, for a five-furlong work in preparation for the Gotham. Hoist the Flag was sent away from the mile pole and passed the three-eighths pole in 1:02. Galloping out, the colt apparently twisted his right hind ankle nearing the quarter pole and Cruguet stopped him.

Strongest early Kentucky Derby favorite since Graustark, Hoist the Flag had a comminuted (shattered into minute particles) fracture of the first phalanx (long pastern bone) and a fracture of the distal end of the large metacarpal (cannon bone) extending obliquely up four inches from the fetlock joint. This type of fracture is not uncommon among barrel racers and cutting horses which twist or turn abruptly while weight is solidly planted on one hind foot. Attending veterinarian Dr. Michael Gerard said consultants in veterinary orthopedics and human surgery had been summoned on the case. Whether Hoist the Flag can be saved for stud duty depends upon how well he tolerates immobilization, how good a patient he proves to be.

Another real good one, lightly raced, unhurried, has been taken prematurely, by a misstep.

## Counting Heads

ACTUAL attendance at the Kentucky Derby has not been announced by Churchill Downs officials since a record crowd appeared in 1946 to see 15 horses finish between Assault and Kendor, and Col. Matt Winn issued the first "100,000 estimate."

Col. Winn was not such a promoter as to let an estimate down, so to speak, and the "100,000" crowd came to be part of Kentucky Derby tradition perpetuated by successive Churchill Downs presidents Bill Corum and Wathen Knebelkamp.

In 1963, a crowd of 82,131 saw Chateaugay swoosh by No Robbery, Candy Spots, and Never Bend, and Knebelkamp revealed that this was the first year the 1946 record had been exceeded. Actual attendance climbed with successive records to 98,357 in Kauai King's year, then dropped to 80,031 in 1967 when overcast skies and overtones of civil unrest brought rain, the National Guard with night sticks, and Darby Dan again with a 30-1 shot.

Twenty-three years after the first estimate of 100,000, President Nixon and 106,332 others saw Majestic Prince beat Arts and Letters by a neck in the greatest race in the history of the Kentucky Derby.

Actual attendance figures for Kentucky Derby Day filed by Churchill Downs with the Kentucky Department of Revenue include an average of about 4,000 complimentary and pass admissions in recent years:

| | | |
|---|---|---|
| 1960—66,874 | 1964—85,706 | 1968— 92,617 |
| 1961—70,373 | 1965—90,088 | 1969—106,333 |
| 1962—72,886 | 1966— 98,357 | 1970—105,087 |
| 1963—82,131 | 1967— 80,031 | |

## Legalesse

OHIO racing officials, embarrassed by a court decision reversing their suspension of rider Danny Weiler after his "altercation" with steward H. H. Battle, may be interested in a marvelously articulated—general yet specific—order issued by the Puerto Rico Racing Administration:

"The Racing Board declares Luis Ballester Albizu a racing nuisance, thus denying him the privilege of the grounds of any race track in Puerto Rico."

This rule is handy, but dangerous. If strictly enforced it could remove from racing many of our most prominent trainers, owners, and racing commissioners. And, we have been warned, some writers.

## Now Do You Get It?

FROM Milton R. Daniels Jr. of Baltimore comes a letter: "Re Dr. James R. Rooney—How about some photos in the next issue to demonstrate what the good doctor is trying to explain? I go to lots of local auctions and often find the 'sprinter' vs. 'router' theory of conformation to be an extremely subtle distinction, particularly among young horses. Specifically, some front leg and full body views would be a great assist."

From Dr. James Rooney, presently conducting research at the Equine Research Station at Newmarket, England: "There is no way to say at this time what a buyer should seek. The mechanics of the situation are clear, but the application would require measurements that I do not know how to make. In essence, a ratio of weight of horse, pastern length and angle, and speed of running is required. We may be able to do that some day, but not now. If I recommend, by word or picture, a certain shape of pastern, it may be dead wrong for the weight of the horse and the distances demanded of him. Therefore, I now can only define the problem, not solve it."

## Can't Quite . . .

AT Aqueduct on Monday, jockey Bill Boland was up on Bill Boland, a 2-year-old full brother to Beau Purple which finished fifth behind a son of Beau Purple. This would seem to involve inbreeding, or coupling in the betting, or something—unable to put a finger on it.

## A Star Is Made

JIMMY KILROE took a look at sagging daily average attendance, the Garden State Park survey and Stanford Research Report, and suggested that radio and television might be used to close an intelligibility gap, to let a potential public in on the secret of racing.

Last week *Sports Illustrated* took a look at Kilroe's case, seemed to agree with the diagnosis, but disagreed in part with the etiology: "While it's true that racing has failed to educate its patrons, there's more to it than that. Sport, like show biz, needs stars, and racing doesn't have them.

Standards for stardom vary with the classifier, of course, but it would seem to us that Buckpasser did everything Frank Robinson did last year and has a better percentage this season, that Manny Ycaza has more flash than Jimmy Piersall or Joe Don Looney or Rube Waddell, that Native Diver has an eye to match Whitey Ford's elbow, that a match between Damascus and Dr. Fager would command as great an interest as one between Arnold Palmer and Jack Nicklaus, that Forli is more exciting than Gary Player, that Alfred Vanderbilt is better copy than Vince Lombardi.

65

*Sports Illustrated* suggests racing lacks stars because as soon as a horse becomes a name [as distinguished from a star] it breaks down or is retired for breeding, its hour upon the stage too brief for stardom. This brevity—putting aside for the moment Kelso's five years—we must bear; apparently we cannot prevent all good horses from breaking down and we must of necessity retire good fillies and colts to stud to ensure crops from which stars may emerge in ensuing years.

The time element may not be as critical as supposed. Short tenure does not preclude or lessen the stardom of the annual crop of college football all-Americans. We are not sure what precisely makes a star. We suppose that all superb athletes are potential stars—and racing has these crop after crop—but we suspect stars are made, not born; that stars are fashioned by the amount of attention focused upon them by radio, television, newspapers, and magazines.

Undeniably, the appeal of spectator sports is enhanced by individual stars and racing could use some more of them. We call now upon the man hiding another Citation and waiting for a spot. We have the spot.

## Seminole Is Down

SEMINOLE DOWNS, the ill-conceived racing venture near Orlando has canceled the last 12 programs of its scheduled 57-card summer meeting in Florida because it was losing about $12,000 a night. Such is free enterprise—if you haven't got it, you can't sell it.

## If You Say So

COMES a stewards' ruling from the Fair Grounds: "Groom Walter J. Mahogany is suspended for causing a disturbance in the barn area in the nature of armed robbery."

Well, almost anything can cause a ruckus in the barn area. The cause of this particular disturbance, however, is tantalizingly vague. "In the nature of" suggests something less or, possibly, more complex than a simple holdup.

66

It might refer to a man playing sharp poker in the tack room with a menacing bottle of bourbon at hand, or a man asking to borrow a five-spot while carrying a twitch.

We would appreciate steward Francis Dunne and his colleagues' spelling out their rulings with greater particularity.

Now, when stewards Clay Puett, Vasco Parke, and Noel Chilcutt hand down a decision at Arizona Downs, the complete story is told: "Jockey Paul Peter Frey is fined $50 for allowing his horse Hold Me to drift during the stretch run of the eighth race Dec. 31, causing the rider on Double Double to shorten his stride."

Any time you notice a jockey running down the stretch and suddenly shortening his stride, you can be assured something is wrong.

## The Duyvil Made Her Do It

ACTUALLY, we never have wandered too far from Baker Street in search of mystery reading—oh, a stop here with Agatha Christie or a stop there with Mary Roberts Rinehart, just hit and run—and as a consequence we were not familiar with the monthly mystery publication, *Saint*, until the Saratoga sale.

A man is subject to being touted at Saratoga when he might not be susceptible elsewhere, and only causal suggestion was needed to send us scurrying for the October issue of *Saint*.

It has a short murder mystery entitled "In Spite of the Devil" written by Leighla Whipper, daughter of the Spuyten Duyvil's owner. This dimly lit oasis fronting on George Street and bordered on three sides by the Fasig-Tipton Company's sales yards in Saratoga at once serves as the locale of the story and provides its title when the piece is reprinted in Dutch.

The cast of characters includes: Fasig-Tipton auctioneer Milton Dance, John Finney, and "a benign white-haired man who comes to the microphone with tears in his voice, 'Ladies and gentlemen, I beg you to consider the blood of this extra-ordinary colt..' "

Other characters include Lou Doherty, his wife Jane, and "the famous California trainer, Charlie Whittingham," who were thought to own the Spuyten Duyvil because of their ardent patronage of the place.

"Big Jim Wiley, the original Virginian, good looking, good natured, 6-5

67

and 220 pounds, rarely seen without a felt hat pushed back at a precise angle."

"L. Clay Camp, another big consignor with a matchless sense of humor, rarely seen without his pretty wife who knows as much about horses as any horseman in Saratoga."

Then there are other characters whose similarity, if any, to persons living or dead must be considered coincidental: H. T. (Catfish) Jones, millionaire ex-football star; Robbie Scallie, veddy British despite his many years of horse breeding in Kentucky; Liz Whitley, who wears dungarees, drives her own Rolls, and is known to pay as high as $100,000 for a yearling such as Rise and Fly; Vick Travers, big, spoiled, puffy-faced from constant drinking, member of a proud old Virginia racing family, and Shelby Franklin, Virginia breeder who sells well even though his ex-wife, Sandra, puts the knock on his yearlings.

No disrespect for the late Sir Arthur Conan Doyle is here intended, but Holmes' pinning the trainer's murder on Silver Blaze, just as Silver Blaze is winning the Sussex Plate by six, must be rated as least 10 pounds below Leighla Whipper's "In Spite of the Devil."


## Measure For Measure

"PLEASE advise as to the exact linear measurement of a 'length'."
There is none.

For some two centuries now, racing men have been stipulating that the length of a length is the length of a horse—from nose to hindquarters—and leaving it at that.

A "length" is not subject to precise measurement by another standard. No more than is "good" when used to describe a horse. These are relative terms, generally understood and accepted by horsemen as constant inconstants.

The distance between a horse's nose and his hindquarters varies, of course, with his size and the way he holds his head. A reasonably good guess, not an exact linear constant, but a guess based on some measurements is that a "length" averages about 100 inches.

As a relative unit of measure to relate distances between horses in a race, a "length" may be used with some precision. Still photographs taken from the grandstand roof of horses racing by the five-furlong pole permit a studied

68

measurement by ruler of comparative distances which race observers can only quickly estimate by eye.

The "length" of a horse photographed while racing varies with his manner of running and the moment in his stride that the photograph records. The variance is small on a ruler and an average may be taken to measure in "lengths" the comparative distance between horses at the point of the race photographed.

There is a thought, stoutly held by students of speed ratings, that a length may be expressed in time, specifically, that one length equals one-fifth of a second. This is all right, but should not be used with confidence in discussing Thoroughbreds.

A mile amounts to 63,360 inches. Buckpasser ran a mile in 1:32⅗, which averages out to 137 inches for one-fifth of a second. Impressive ran the first half of that race in :43⅗, which averages out to 145 inches for one-fifth of a second.

For 100 inches to equal one-fifth of a second, we would have to be talking about a mile in 2:06⅘, and trotting horse men avoid that kind of discussion.

At Buckpasser's mile rate, a time-length is 1.37 times greater than the estimated linear-length; Buckpasser ran four linear-lengths in three-fifths of a second. This lends alternative authority to the common expression, "He win by three or four lengths."

## Up Tight

THERE are 997 other ways to lose a race, of course, but two recently came to our attention: At the Iroquois Hunt Club point-to-point meeting near Lexington, young riders Mason Lampton and Gregg Morris were racing head and head in a two-horse brush event when Lampton was unseated at the fourth jump. Morris gallantly pulled up his mount (Cabelery, winner of seven races and $32,510 on the flat) caught the loose horse, led him back to Lampton, and the race was resumed. Morris finished second.

Colonel Elsworth suggested that Cabelery's tail may have been braided too tight. His authority for this cause of defeat was the late John D. Hertz, quite possibly the only man in the world who felt he knew why his Reigh Count lost the 1928 Travers Midsummer Derby. Champion at two, Reigh Count won seven of eight starts at three—the Kentucky Derby, Jockey Club Gold

Cup, Saratoga Cup, Lawrence Realization, Miller Stakes, and Huron Handicap—but at 3-2 he finished dead last in the Travers to Petee-Wrack, Victorian, and Sun Edwin.

Reigh Count's trainer B. S. Mitchell, rider Chick Lang, and a sizeable crowd of chalk players could not fathom an explanation for Reigh Count's singular reversal of form. Hertz said the braid was too tight.

## Horsepower

HENRY FORD II is said to have spent nine million dollars to run 1-2-3 in the 24-hour endurance race at Le Mans last month. Ah, but in Missouri, the show-me land, he came up short. In a challenge race at Missouri Meadows race track recently, a Quarter Horse named Double Q Leo literally ran off and left a souped-up GT Mustang in a 100-yard dash from the starting gate. Jockey Johnny Grizzard said he would have won easily if he had to go 300 yards. Mr. Ford, you might as well forget about those distance races in France; you are being sprinted to death in Missouri.

## Killjoys

A headline writer for the Louisville *Courier-Journal* last week summarized a wire story from Middleburg, Va.:

"IRS Joins the Hunt, Bars Steeplechase Bets," "5 Bookies Fleece and Flee."

Bookmakers, or their occupational forebears, have been working the races in Virginia since the Rev. James Blair founded William and Mary College and the Williamsburg race path near by. As Col. Phil T. Chinn once explained the practice of owning horses and a spot in the betting ring at the same time: "There's nothing really wrong with this; it just happened to be against the law."

Nine bookmakers from Philadelphia popped down for the Middleburg Hunt last week, set up their easels and blackboards, and the action was brisk on the first three races. Then some Internal Revenue Service agents elbowed (non-leather-patched) their way toward the layers and inquired about $50 federal betting stamps—in effect raiding the place.

The agents ordered all betting halted after the third race, and reportedly precipitated the sudden disappearance of five bookies—before settling up. This just goes to show how too much government corrupts. Before this sad turn of events, who ever heard of a welching bookmaker? Damon Runyon declared the term a paradox.


## In His Image

NEVER name a horse after a close friend, shoeman David Shaer counseled Triangle Publications columnist Joe Hirsch. One of Shaer's best customers was Lester Pincus, a "wonderful man; when I told him I was going to name a horse for him, he was delighted. Unfortunately, the horse wasn't worth a half-smoked cigarette. My friend kept calling me and asking when Lester Pincus would make his first start."

The horse started, finished last, and the friend was on the telephone, "I gave him a story—the horse was blocked, the jockey wasn't too good, the track was off. That held him for a while, but when Lester Pincus ran a second time, then a third time, my friend called in a state of agitation, 'Shoot him!'

"Why? He tells me that all his customers all over the country have been betting on Lester Pincus. Now whenever they order shoes from him their checks are a few dollars shy to cover betting losses."


## Appetite Supressant

SEVERAL years ago, the late Tom B. Young, son of Col. Milton Young, showed us through his apartment; its walls seemed constructed of goldleaf frames which broke up a virtual mural of McGrathiana's famous stallions and mares painted by Stull.

"Now here's a picture of Strathmore. Stull was a heavy drinker, you know;

71

would come down to the farm and sketch some of the horses, then go back to his New York studio and paint," Young said. "My father always kept this picture in a back room at McGrathiana. See, Stull painted Strathmore black. He was a bay.

"There's Hanover when he was in training. There's Onondaga; see the dapples? He was the meanest horse we ever had. My father had him blinded, which raised quite a furor in the press, but Onondaga would eat a man alive, rather eat man than hay. Couldn't get rid of him, though he was the leading sire of 2-year-olds for many years."

## Hi Ho Silver

EUGENE CONSTANTIN JR.'S 2-year-old Nashua colt, Silver, won at Gulfstream Park last week. Hi ho. Behind him came, not Tonto, of watcha-mean-we-whiteman fame, but something called Drawbakanub, by Retreat.

## Big Government Lessons

ONCE upon a time New York realized nothing in state tax revenue from horse racing. At the same time, Gov. Charles Hughes and the state assembly determined it to be a sinful sport of non-church going kings and outlawed racing for two years.

It returned, however, for racing is a good game and cannot be put down for long. It returned to Rockaway at Hewlett Bay Park on April 23, 1913, for a one-day hunt meeting, memorable at this point by the six-length triumph of gentleman rider Skiddy von Stade aboard Pall Mall in the two-mile Hewlett Plate. Major racing returned to Belmont Park on May 30 with H. P. Whitney's Whisk Broom II winning the Metropolitan.

By 1939, New York was getting $25 a day in track license fees and 15 per cent of the admissions from Thoroughbred racing. The following year, pari-mutuel machines were introduced; to give these legal sanction, the assembly decided the state needed half the take, that is, half the 10 per cent commission retained on wagers made through the machines, plus half the breakage on the nickel.

Well, by 1942, management was so embarrassed by the new riches which previously had been keeping bookmakers in Pierce Arrows and Packards that it graciously said, "We only need four per cent—you take the rest." The state did, of course, because betting on horses did not appear to be unholy as in Gov. Hughes' day and, besides, separation of church and state was a consitutional safeguard. The following year, just to keep the books neat, the breakage split was altered, 60 per cent to the state, 40 per cent to the tracks.

In 1947, New York City Mayor William O'Dwyer bit. He took five per cent off the top, raising the take from the mutuels to 15 per cent plus breakage (which amounted to another 1.2 per cent of the total handle in New York last year). Management complained. The state assembly agreed that the O'Dwyer Bite was unjust: "The city has no right to that five per cent. We'll take it." The city and county were given 15 per cent of the admissions instead.

So by 1956, New York was getting 11 per cent of the handle and 60 per cent of the breakage while the tracks were keeping four per cent and going on the rocks. Unable to meet competition of race tracks in other states, New York track management agreed to give up all possible future profits, sold out to a non-profit corporation which obtained a franchise, for $1,000 a day, and a one per cent reduction of the state's mutuels cut so the non-profit corporation could pay off the loan necessary to rebuild Aqueduct.

Remember now—in 1939, New York was getting $25 a day in license fees and 15 per cent of the admissions. Last year, New York took $67,495,862 in pari-mutuel commissions, $6,628,541 in breakage, $1,827,026 in admissions, $332,450 in track suprvisory fees, $702,000 in franchise fees, $12,525 in track license fees, $53,769 in occupational licensing fees, $141,606 in laboratory fees, an estimated $374,181 left from uncashed mutuel tickets, plus $1,079 in fines and miscellaneous. Total: $77,569,039.

Last April, after Assembly Speaker Anthony J. Travia personally stopped promised legislation which would have reduced the state's take from pari-mutuels to 9.5 per cent, shifting .5 per cent of the handle to purses, horsemen refused to enter horses and New York racing was canceled for five days.

Based on attendance and betting figures for the same five days in 1966, New York appeared to have lost $2,159,982 in tax revenue by the five-day racing blackout.

The state came out of this tiff without a glove being laid on it. Racing was resumed when the NYRA borrowed a sum equal to the expected half per cent and boosted purses with the loan. The state still takes 10 per cent of the handle—promising to take less next year—plus 80 per cent of the breakage, and now has a chance of getting back its five-day loss.

Last week the New York Racing Commission announced approval of an NYRA request to extend the racing season five days to Dec. 15; that leaves New York players seven shopping days until Christmas.

From this, it may be seen that New York racing acquired a bad partner 27 years ago. It should be noted, however, that the partner was given more than it took. Surely, there is a lesson here that owners and breeders interested in getting a healthy statute in new jurisdictions should study.

## Sacrificial Cow

As jockey demands go, it did not seem much. All they wanted was to sacrifice a cow, and they even offered $112 to cover the cost. One rider and two horses had been killed at one spot on the track and 55 jockeys refused to ride until a cow was sacrificed in a purification and pacification ceremony to appease angry gods and dispel evil spirits from the trouble spot. The stewards did not think much of the idea, and last week the Accra Turf Club of Gold Coast, Africa, fined each rider $70 and suspended all 55 for the meeting.

## Who's Kidding Who?

A lie repeated often enough can be believed by anyone. A trainer complaining about excess ice in a Scotch-on-the-rocks on the Reading Room lawn at Saratoga related an example:

"I was trying to get this filly claimed, see, so I send her out one morning for a half-mile work. She goes in :51 and change, and I run up to the clockers' stand. 'I caught her in :48$^{1}/_{5}$, but I think my watch is on the bum; what'd you catch her?' Mac says, 'You had her in :48$^{1}/_{5}$? I think I caught her in :48 and three. Who was that?' So I tell him, figuring that will get around pretty good.

"Then I enter her for $4,500, and outside the secretary's office I give three jocks agents $20 apiece to bet on her, provided they 'say nothing; we just keep this one ourselves.'

"Well, next morning, Frank comes around the barn, says he has a top filly in the race, she can handle everything in it but my filly, and he wants to know about my filly before he puts his money down. 'This the bay filly that broke from the half-mile pole the other morning, Bobby was up on her?' and I say yeah, and then Frank tells me he caught her in :48$^1$/$_5$!

" 'You had :48$^1$/$_5$? Clockers had :48$^3$/$_5$ on the tab.' But he describes this filly again, breaking from the half-mile pole, and all, and he says that if she is the one he timed, his filly can't beat her.

"Well, you know what happened. Kept hearing over at the kitchen about this hideout horse, parking guys give her to me, and before long I get to thinking maybe my watch *is* busted. Sure enough, I reached down and put a hundred on her myself. She did get claimed though, had to shake for her."

## I'll Drink To That

KEENELAND has a happy practice of giving julep cups to winning owners, gold for stakes and silver for allowance races. A man who has been breeding horses of high promise for as long as we can remember was hurrying down to the winner's circle and casually remarked, "Ho, hum, won another one."

A smart-alec son reminded that, irrespective of adventures at Gulfstream, Delaware Park, and elsewhere, the man had not won a race at Keeneland since the spring meeting of 1946.

"Yes, it's been a long time between drinks around here."

E. K. Thomas won the next race, a smashing performance by his and Mrs. Thomas' top filly, Furl Sail, which killed off Lady Swaps with a half-mile in :44$^3$/$_5$ and drew off to win by five lengths, indicating that she would be going into the Spinster Stakes fit for the task.

"Wasn't that a nice race?" Thomas was asked. Thomas smiled and nodded before he knew what race was under discussion. "My colt climbed coming away from the gate in his first start here last Saturday, and didn't get to running until the head of the stretch and then, of course, he was running over horses and although he finished sixth I was satisfied he could do something, so when he broke on top today, I knew the race was over—oh, the boy snugged him back a little to save ground and when they go by me here at the sixteenth pole with five horses heads apart, I knew we had it because..."

Thomas continued to nod although Furl Sail did not happen to be mentioned and, after shifting his weight from one leg to another several times, he finally was rewarded with the observation, "Say, your filly ran pretty good, too."

The man has a large family. One son in the headmaster and preacher line of work lamely offered that problems at school had caused him to miss the race, another in the doctoring business admitted he had not checked the entries, a son-in-law merchant prince felt the day's racing would be reported adequately by his wife, and another son who builds things happened to see the race, but missed the important element of racing triumphs—the rehash.

So there was a family gathering that evening at the place where this latest colt of high promise was foaled, ostensibly to view the telecast of the patrol films, but primarily devoted to an explanation of the study and deliberations involved in selecting the sire of this colt, the various field expedients necessary to transport the mare to the stallion, the foaling, the look in the eye, the weaning, the breaking, the first breeze of an eighth of a mile, the bucked shins, the depth through the heart, the cough, the stifle that was nothing.

There was an interruption of 1:26 while the film of the race was televised, followed by congratulations, comments on the ride, instructions therefor, and so on until some champagne appeared and a toast was raised, not so much to the winning colt, but to continue riding of the tiger.

And these are the shared pleasures racing affords; be they occasioned by victory in a maiden race at Keeneland, a stakes at Aqueduct, or a claiming event at Centennial, these are the winnings.

## Blue Hens

ONLY 14 per cent of all broodmares produce stakes winners. About four per cent produce two stakes winners, one per cent produce three, and .1 per cent produce five or more.

Suffice it to say a small percentage of mares produce as many as eight stakes winners. We know of only two: Lady Juror (1919-41), by Son-in Law—Lady Josephine, by Sundridge, and Grey Flight (1945-1974), by Mahmoud—Planetoid, by Ariel.

76

Grey Flight just had her ninth from her first 12 foals, What a Pleasure's victory in the National Stallion Stakes last week raising his dam's progeny earnings to $1,001,095.

Lady Juror had 12 foals, her eight stakes winners being leading sire Fair Trial, top 2-year-old The Black Abbot, Jurisdiction, The Recorder, Riot, Sansonnet, Giftlaw, and Dispenser.

Figuring the pre-war pound at $5, these eight winners earned $140,028 in first money, which may not appear to be much today in this country but gave Lady Juror a progeny Average-Earnings Index for 21 year-starters of 7.88.

Grey Flight's progeny Average-Earnings Index through last year for 43 year-starters was 7.30. This means that all her foals earned an average of more than seven times the average earnings of all other runners in the years they raced, while Lady Juror's foals earned an average of almost eight times that of their contemporaries.

We have been asked many times for the formula to success in breeding horses. Now we have it: Pick up a couple of young stakes-winning fillies like Lady Juror and Grey Flight.

## The Vagaries Of Racing

TWO years ago a young Greek shipping magnate, Capt. Marco Lemos, became emotionally involved in the bidding while attending his first yearling auction at Newmarket and wound up with a Never Say Die colt for 27,000 guineas ($79,380). The price was only 1,000 guineas less than the then-record bid which got Sayajirao in 1945 and it startled the audience, stunned his trainer, and rather surprised Lemos:

"The figure I had in mind was something in the region of four or five thousand, but I had to have him. My trainer thought I had gone mad; he stopped at 10, and when I went on, he kept warning me. 'He may not be worth that. You could be taking a tremendous risk. He needn't ever win a race, you know,' but my heart was set on having him.

"As a newcomer to racing I'm willing to pay for experience. To me the colt represented an investment, not a passing fancy. This colt, I believed, would give me excitement, and pleasure, and fun, something—how can I put it?— something to look forward to."

The colt broke its neck last year before racing.

Last week, one of England's most important 2-year-old fixtures, the historic Gimcrack Stakes, was won with trifling ease by Petingo (Petition—Alcazar, by Alycidon). Undefeated and now favored for next spring's Two Thousand Guineas, Petingo was purchased as a yearling for $22,932 by a young Greek shipping magnate, Capt. Marco Lemos.

## Good Point

NEW YORK steward Francis Dunne, whom the late Tom Piatt identified as Pat Dunne's boy, was talking to no one in particular about the high costs of sleeping in Saratoga:

"It has always been my fondest hope that someone prominent—like yourself, or Tommy Trotter—will get elected president; then I can be appointed Secretary of the Navy. First thing I would do is order me a cruiser up the river—you know, you can get a pretty big ship past Albany—and then I'd tell them to throw some shells into this nest of pirates here. Charge you $900 for a $250 house during the month of August. Been holding people up here for years."

## The Teney Touch

Meshach Tenney was right. He was right about his horse and he was right about the track. He won the richest race in the country for 3-year-olds, the $150,000-added Preakness, an uncommon reward for being right.

Tenney is a horseman, an appellation encompassing perhaps more than horse trainer. He probably has worked with more horses, different types of horses, for longer periods during a day, for more years, than any other Thoroughbred trainer in the country.

His methods of training Thoroughbreds were developed by him from experience with many horses and often vary sharply from what other horse trainers consider normal methods. For this, Tenney has been criticized—when he loses.

Tenney shrugs off such comment on his training methods. He long since has accepted that what seems normal to him does not seem so to others. He hears the beat of another drummer. Last year, he was America's leading trainer when horses he saddled for Rex Ellsworth earned $1,099,474, raising some question as to who is out of step.

The Ellsworth-Tenney racing stable (Tenney has a 25 per cent interest in the racing stock; Ellsworth pays all the bills and reassumes complete ownership when the horses leave the track for breeding) numbers about 90 head and is one of the biggest in racing. It is easy to lose track of a good 2-year-old in such a large stable, but then, easy to find one, too.

Candy Spots did not show up publicly until August of last year, at Chicago, where he won his first start by two lengths. Three weeks later, he won a division of the Futurity Trial Stakes by a half-length from Petro Tim and Delta Judge. Thirty-seven days after his first start, he won the richest race in the world, the $357,250 Arlington-Washington Futurity, defeating Never Bend by a half-length.

Ellsworth and Tenney then closed up shop and went home to round up cattle.

Rated at 125 pounds on the Experimental Handicap, a pound below Never Bend and even with Crewman, Candy Spots was brought along slowly by Tenney in California. Tenney said he was hoping an allowance race might be written for Candy Spots' first start as a 3-year-old. The soft spot was not found. Candy Spots was entered for the San Vicente Stakes on January 31, but it rained, which is against the rules of racing in California, and Tenney scratched his colt.

"I wasn't afraid of a sloppy track; I just didn't want him to have to race over one in his first start. Might take too much out of him." Tenney waited again for a race. He finally started him on February 19 in a six-furlong allowance that also drew Bonjour. Candy Spots just did beat Bonjour, by the dirt on his nose.

Eleven days later, Candy Spots was running along with the pack into the first turn of the Santa Anita Derby. Win-Em-All went down and three other horses tumbled over him. Country Squire (which was to win the Preakness Prep) slammed Candy Spots, knocking him right out of the pile-up. Recovering, Candy Spots settled back into stride, picked up his horses on the last turn and won by 1½ lengths.

Four weeks later, Candy Spots won the Florida Derby by an easy 4½ lengths from Sky Wonder. Tenney shipped his horse to Louisville and Candy Spots did not race again for five weeks.

For the first seven furlongs of the Kentucky Derby, Candy Spots appeared

79

to be in perfect position, a close third to pace-setting Never Bend and No Robbery. Then he ran into a pocket and was checked.

For the last quarter of the Derby, Candy Spots did not have a straw in his path. He also did not have any gas. He picked up a little ground, but could get no closer than 1½ lengths to Chateaugay and lost second money to Never Bend by a neck. Tenney was not overly concerned by Candy Spots' suffering his first defeat. Any good horse, raced often enough, will be beaten.

If Candy Spots was short, the Derby's 10 furlongs helped him. Tenney shipped his horse to Pimlico, worked him a mile in 1:38²⁄₅ on May 11, and seven furlongs in 1:25²⁄₅ on May 15, three days before the Preakness.

The day before the race, Tenney brought Candy Spots on the track three times. He was galloped in the morning, schooled in the afternoon, and breezed after the ninth race.

Pimlico's management decided to have the Preakness horses saddled this year on the centerfield grass course in front of the stands rather than in the enclosed paddock which had been hot and the subject of heated discussion last year. During the afternoon's races, Tenney stood Candy Spots near the grass course hedge and saddled him. After the last race, Candy Spots was galloped around the track, opened up briefly on the final turn for a good eighth of a mile, then eased up, going three-eighths in more or less an extended gallop.

In the foggy drizzle of Preakness morning, Candy Spots went to the track again. Tenney had said before the night's heavy rain that he did not believe the track at race time would be in a shape to hurt any of the horses' chances. He seemed more worried over whether Ellsworth's plane would be able to land. It did.

The wind blew, the sun shone, and the track was fast by the time the Preakness candidates were led from the barn to the centerfield saddling area. The picnic air was absent from this year's Preakness, no lunch baskets or bettors being allowed in the infield as in the past. It was just as well; a $5,000 camera inadvertenly was dropped from the 50-foot TV tower in the centerfield Friday and the thought of that happening again was a greater deterrent for picnics than ants.

While saddling in front of the stands was new to Pimlico, it was old hat to Candy Spots, older to Tenney and Ellsworth, who had saddled Swaps in the centerfield for his 1955 match with Nashua at Washington Park. Horses, owners and the crowd of 35,263 seemed to like the idea. Chateaugay was the only horse in the field that appeared skittish, but he was not as troublesome about his saddling as he had been in the close paddock at Churchill Downs.

80

Pony boys all wore bright yellow jackets with "Preakness" lettered on the back. The horses were given black saddle cloths with their names written close to the numbers, a Pimlico practice which began about the same time Bill Veeck started it with the White Sox.

The field was led onto the main track and not until the public address announcer went through a rundown on each Preakness horse and the field had paraded by the stands did the bands strike up "My Maryland."

The break from the starting gate was just like that of the Derby; all broke evenly except Candy Spots, which was a little late and veered to the outside.

Never Bend took command immediately, as he had in the Derby, and Rural Retreat (which had finished second in the Preakness Prep) went with the leader, playing No Robbery's Derby role. Jockey Bill Shoemaker got Candy Spots straightened out and began picking up horses going by the stands the first time. Chateaugay was sixth, on the rail behind Country Squire (which turned up with a case of hives the day of the race) and Sky Wonder.

Into the first turn, Never Bend continued to set the pace with Rural Retreat close on him. The fractions were not spectacular—:24$\frac{1}{5}$, :47$\frac{2}{5}$—for the first two quarters. Candy Spots moved up to third on the first bend while Chateaugay remained in sixth place, with Lemon Twist and On My Honor trailing.

Straightening out for the run down the backstretch, Never Bend was still being pushed for the lead by Rural Retreat. R. L. Baird on Rural Retreat said later, "I don't really know Never Bend, but he didn't look like he was running right to me. Here I am, a 99-1 shot, and I'm going easy, almost head and head with him."

Manuel Ycaza said Never Bend "did not run his race. He was like swimming. The pace was not fast like in the Derby."

Candy Spots was coasting along in third place, three lengths off the leader, while Chateaugay still lingered in sixth place, nine lengths behind Never Bend.

Approaching the half-mile pole, Candy Spots began his move to the lead, disposing of Rural Retreat without the slightest difficulty and catching Never Bend on the turn. Chateaugay also made a big move on the turn.

Never Bend had run the first six furlongs in 1:11$\frac{3}{5}$, the mile in 1:37, and he was through. Candy Spots went by without his offering the suggestion of a counteroffensive.

Shoemaker let Candy Spots go to the lead on his own entering the stretch. "He's inclined to loaf on you when he makes the lead and I was worried about Chateaugay coming up behind me," Shoemaker said.

81

Chateaugay made the same valiant run, and at the same part of the race, that he had in the Derby. It was to carry him past Never Bend again, but he was to draw no closer than 1½ lengths to the spotted horse.

Chateaugay had not lost a race since he propped, or shied, in the stretch run of the Pimlico Futurity last fall. It was at about the eighth pole in the Preakness that he gave up his determined drive to catch Candy Spots.

"I kept after my horse," Shoemaker said, "hit him four or five times right-handed, then switched and hit left-handed and he leveled off." He pulled away from Chateaugay easily, winning by 3½ lengths but with the authority of 10.

Never Bend finished another 4½ lengths behind Chateaugay. Lemon Twist, winner of the Illinois Derby the week before, came from seventh place to nose out Sky Wonder for fourth money. Rural Retreat finished far ahead of On My Honor, the Derby fourth, which never hit a lick in the Preakness, and Country Squire.

Candy Spots' time of 1:56⅕ was the third fastest for the Preakness since 1925, when it was first run at 1³⁄₁₆ miles.

The winner's share of the purse was $127,500, which put Ellsworth's horse and cattle operation out of the red for the month.

Ellsworth was quoted as saying, "My stable led the nation in money last year with more than a million dollars, but over all we came close to missing the break-even point."

It was the fourth Preakness try for Shoemaker, who had finished second with Correlation in 1954 and Sword Dancer in 1959, and nowhere with Silky Sullivan in 1958.

"He ran like I thought he could today. I've always thought he was a great horse and now I'm certain he could be," Shoemaker said of Candy Spots.

Groom Josen Kascandi led the winner back to the barn and halted him in front of a water hydrant. While other Preakness runners were being sponged clean from buckets of warm water, Kascandi sprayed Candy Spots with cold water from the hydrant. Candy Spots stood placidly. While hosing a horse after a race is common in South America, it came as a surprise to some casual observers, who quickly cleared the area as water splattered off the Preakness winner in all directions.

Harry Guggenheim and trainer Woody Stephens studied Never Bend closely. "We have absolutely no excuses," Capt. Guggenheim said. "It was a well-run race and nobody had any trouble. There were three good horses and we finished third."

Cold water bandages were put on the front ankles of the world's greatest 2-year-old money-earner. Capt. Guggenheim and Stephens were joined by

82

Ycaza and they went into a huddle. For some time they had been thinking about taking a shot at the May 29 English Derby if Never Bend came out of the Preakness in good order.

Monday morning, Never Bend's front left ankle felt cool to the touch of Stephens. In the afternoon, it was warm. Capt. Guggenheim then announced: "It is time now to call a halt. We will stop on him until he is completely well. No good horse should be asked to run unless he is at the top of his form."

On Tuesday, Stephens said there was still a possibility Never Bend would go in the Belmont Stakes on June 8. "We had the ankle X-rayed extensively and there are no indications of any fractures. Thus we must assume that the trouble (evidenced by heat since April at Keeneland) has been in a sprain or strain.

"You may say we are not out of the Belmont Stakes at this moment. If Never Bend shows us he is sound and if we are able to make the necessary training progress, he will start. Otherwise, he will remain on the sidelines."

Meanwhile, Candy Spots is being pointed for the May 30 Jersey Derby, then the Belmont, then the Chicagoan. If he continues to run as he did in the Preakness, Ellsworth should have no trouble meeting the bills.

## Gotcha!

A comment of sorts on women drivers showed up in the winner's circle at Monmouth Park recently—a 2-year-old filly by Turn Right, out of All Action, named Next Left.

## At The Podium

DURING the Thoroughbred Club Dinner Purse festivities at Keeneland, new Thoroughbred Club President Dr. William R. McGee (1) presented winning rider Bobby Gallimore with a neo-classic purse of 500 coins, the neo being the copper showing through silver; (2) called upon Dinner Purse winner Caribbean Line's owner, T. Alie Grissom: "You're waiting for me to stand up here and tell you how smart I am to win this race, but I'm gonna sit down before you find out how dumb I am;" (3) introduced the owner-breeder of the season's leading money earner, whose sire and material grandsire top the current general and broodmare sire lists, America's current leading owner and leading breeder—Mrs. Cloyce Tippett.

## So Why Answer?

DETROIT'S big race, the Michigan Mile and One-Eighth, which was called the Michigan Mile and One-Sixteenth for a few years, has reverted to its maiden name, Michigan Mile. It still will be run at a Michigan mile and one-eighth this week, which is all right because the Mile Trial Handicap was run at a Michigan mile and one-sixteenth.

Identifying alliteration could have been preserved with Detroit Distance Dilemma. This would fall more or less naturally into conversations, "He wasn't quite ready for the Dilemma," or, "In the Dilemma the boy couldn't decide whether to stay on the rail or go around." Then, too, the fixture's history would include the 1964 dead heat of Going Abroad and Tibaldo. The Trial could be called the Perplexing Prep.

But us, nobody asked.

## Get It In Writing

WE have arrived at the conclusion that one cannot learn to win from a book. Vince Lombardi wrote a book on football, Adolph Rupp one on basketball, Preston Burch one on training horses. Inasmuch as no one has taken these books in hand and managed to put down the authors at their own game, there is a suspicion that some vital points were omitted from the manuscripts, or that a winning formula cannot be reduced to writing.

Ben Jones never bothered to write a book on training, but then his exploits will be passed on as long as race-trackers study overnights. At Santa Anita, the subject came up about when a trainer should give a horse his final blowout before a race.

84

Eddie Neloy gives Buckpasser a little more than three furlongs on Thursday, then gallops him on Friday and the morning of the race. Other trainers like to "blow out the hay" on Friday or the morning of the race.

Venerable Bill Finnegan was talking to *Daily Racing Form*'s Oscar Otis: "Who's to say what a successful pattern for a horse is? We've been asking ourselves that question on the backstretch ever since Ben Jones—right here at Santa Anita—wanted to get a horse out of a race on Saturday afternoon. It was not a stakes and he did not have the right to scratch at will, so Jones worked the horse Saturday morning a mile in 1:42."

The stewards made him run anyway. The horse won.

## In Old San Juan

THINGS can get turned around pretty easily in Puerto Rico, where the National Association of State Racing Commissioners held its 37th annual convention March 22-26.

Christopher Columbus on his second triumphant tour of the Caribbean landed on the island in 1493 and named it after the Spanish prince, San Juan. He thought the bay on the north side provided a rich port, hence Puerto Rico. Somehow in the ensuing four centuries, these names got turned around; the island became Puerto Rico and the rich port became San Juan.

The gold business went sour early and the first governor, Ponce de Leon, re-invested in coffee and sugar cane before taking—like any tired executive today—a vacation cruise to Florida looking for the fountain of youth or something. Over the years the coffee and sugar cane played out and now the best business on the island apparently is cab driving.

One day was set aside on the NASRC convention progam for a trip to Luquillo. We visualized this as a visit to Belmont winner High Echelon's dam, but it turned out to be a great beach party with barbecued pigs, cock fights, ragged-brimmed straw hats, coconut milk and rum, hosted by the Puerto Rican racing commission.

A hundred or so racing commissioners were lined upon the hotel steps awaiting buses for Luquillo Beach when a pack of cab drivers arrived with the announcement that the first bus driven up to the hotel would be flipped on its back. The sincerity and simplicity of this statement went unquestioned by the bus drivers. A few labor-relations attorneys among the commissioners thought of obtaining an injunction and calling the sheriff, but this seemed turned around somehow, inasmuch as the host was a governmental agency, in essence the governor. So the 28-mile trip to Luquillo was made by cab.

The next day's program called for lunch at the El Comandante track as guests of concessionnaire Max Jacobs, a resourceful man who decided to alter busing arrangements in favor of cabs. Normal cab fare to the track is $2. Jacobs was informed by the union leader the job would amount to $4 a cab. An hour before lunch, in the absence of buses or cabs, Jacobs put in a call and learned that the price had risen to $7.50 a pop, whether the cab was loaded, half-filled, or empty—and cash on the barrel head. Jacobs abruptly defined a location where the cabs could be parked.

Obviously the union leaders had not been listening to Arizona Congressman Sam Steiger, who, for more than a year now, has been charging, in the House of Representatives and before sundry racing commissions, that the Jacobs family's $50,000,000 Emprise and Sportservice corporations are tied into the Mafia. The Jacobses have spent a good deal in legal fees and time refuting these successive charges and have reached a point where they can smile a little.

Max Jacobs said he had a suit altered last year in Toronto, then flew to California, where Sportservice has the concessions at Bay Meadows. His brother, operating the concessions at Woodbine, called and said the tailor had finished, had sent the suit to Buffalo, where Jacobs lives, and wanted to be paid. Jacobs said he did not want to pay until he tried on the suit, that he would return from California in 10 days. His brother called again, said the tailor was pushing him about the bill. Two days later the same report. Three days later the same report—the tailor wanted his money. Then a story appeared in a Toronto paper quoting Congressman Steiger and his charges that the Jacobses were associated with the Mafia.

"I got another call," Jacobs said, "from the tailor. He said not to worry about the bill, any time; if the suit wasn't right, forget the whole thing."

At any rate, we did get to El Comandante. It is a nice track, built 14 years ago to accommodate 18,000 fans, but the stands will be razed soon and the track's 500 acres developed with high-rise apartments and offices. The San Juan Racing Association, which only last week was cleared for listing on the New York Stock Exchange, has been granted a 10-year license to conduct racing at a new track to be constructed six miles east of El Comandante at a cost of $25,000,000. The license grants the association exclusive right to conduct racing in Puerto Rico, 156 days or nights, and on-course and off-course

86

betting thereon. There are 470 off-course betting shops and, apparently, no bookmaking. Most of the betting is on the "5-6 pool" on which a player once bet 25 cents and won $79,000 for picking six consecutive winners; bookmakers historically avoid handling such action.

## Whip Control

RACING Hall of Fame rider Ted Atkinson, known as The Slasher, may never have made it in Australia. Man down under by the name of Walter John Hoysted does not like jockeys to use whips, and you better believe it. He delayed the start of the Flemington races last month to discuss the matter, calmly, "I would not have hurt anyone." Netted him fines, however, $30 for being armed with a shotgun, $20 for firing the weapon "without authority," and $30 for assaulting a policeman.

## Not Quite The Same

BEFORE Joe Widener became involved in it, Florida racing was nothing more than a series of tent meetings—impromptu affairs arranged by bookmakers looking for action in such odd racing places as Jacksonville and St. John's, where the betting ring operated under a tent.

In 1923, Widener gave a million dollars to Jimmy Bright to build a race track at Hialeah, a town Bright and flier Glenn Curtiss were reclaiming from the Everglades. Widener went off to Europe and, when he returned, he found Bright had built a concrete and steel grandstand in front of a mustard-yellow oval surrounding a brown infield—no Belmont Park (of which Widener was to become president), but lengths better than a tent. Widener also found Bright had spent $200,000 more than the stake, part of this going for rows of royal palms and 20 pink flamingos. Widener went for the birds, bought 100 more at $50 a pop, and a pink tone was set when Hialeah opened for the first time on Jan. 15, 1925.

Nothing of consequence really happened there until legalization of pari-mutuels in 1931. Then Widener came in with a rebuilding program and

Hialeah emerged in structural splendor unmatched by any track in the United States. He incorporated architectural features he liked at Longchamp, Saratoga, Chantilly, Belmont, Ascot, and Deauville. From France came the saddling stalls, the iron-fenced walking ring, and carriage entrance; from England came a turf course; from Australia came the automatic totalisator. Class and style came to winter racing.

Prior to Widener's Hialeah, the important New York stables wintered in New York (Sunny Jim Fitzsimmons stayed at Aqueduct and broke yearlings) or at the old Bennings track in Washington, D. C., or in Aiken, Columbia, and Camden, S. C.

In 1938, Ben Jones brought Lawrin off Hialeah winter racing and won the Kentucky Derby. Jones' subsequent success with Calumet horses racing up to the Kentucky Derby from Hialeah changed the concept of training up to the classics, from resting in winter quarters to racing at Hialeah; wintering a stable in the North became a rarity.

While Santa Anita provided class racing during the winter for west coast stables, most of the prominent New York stables shipped to Hialeah. Oh, there were Florida meetings at Tropical Park and Gulfstream Park before and after the Hialeah meeting, but these provided only winter racing. Hialeah was class racing, during *the season*.

In 1946, a law was enacted in Florida which gave the season—40 racing days from mid-January to early March—to Hialeah as the track which returned to the state the most pari-mutuel tax revenue. The "Hialeah law" first was challenged by Gulfstream Park in 1947 and it was upheld by a 4-3 decision of the Supreme Court.

Over the years, Gulfstream Park endeavored unsuccessfully to have the law amended by the legislature. Challenged in court again, the "Hialeah law" was ruled unconstitutional by a 6-1 decision of the Supreme Court last Feb. 22. The Florida Racing Commission, however, exercised its discretion and awarded Hialeah its traditional dates for 1972 anyway. About that time, the Florida Racing Commission was abolished, its regulatory responsibilities assigned to a Board of Business Regulation, which reviewed the old date controversy and ruled the former commission had not erred in giving Hialeah its traditional dates.

Gulfstream went back to court. On Oct. 15, the Supreme Court in a 6-1 decision ruled that Gulfstream should get the Jan. 17 through March 2 dates, that Hialeah should try a meeting running from March 3 through April 22.

With a new shift of population up the beach to Hallandale's bristling new high-rise apartments and motels, Gulfstream Park, with the choice middle dates, probably will do well as to crowds and mutuel handle. Gulfstream's purses will rise. If the money is there, the horses will run for it.

Yet money alone is not class. There lingered at Hialeah, as the fragrance of bougainvillea, a certain style and grace that Joe Widener had brought to it; this attracted owners of good horses at a special time which was called the season. Somehow, Gulfstream Park, although well run, clean and bright, modern in every way, does not have the same allure.

With the longer racing season in New York, many prominent stables may be expected to spend the winter in the North, shipping out for occasional races at Liberty Bell or Laurel. Others are applying for stalls at Santa Anita for the first time. Perhaps the "season" now for racing's fashionable will be spent commuting between Palm Springs and Arcadia, Calif.

The Florida court certainly changed racing in the East. If they only had ordered the re-opening of Bennings, it would be like old times.

## Nota Bene

PARENTS of several members of the eighth grade Latin class at Sayre School in Lexington raced horses at Keeneland. On the last day of the meeting, the class pooled its resources (amounting to $2, plus bits of information gleaned from Ceasar, Cicero, and dinner-table conversation) and put the whole on a 3-year-old filly named Prim Lady, which was bred, owned, and trained by a member of the Sayre Parents Club. Prim Lady came down smartly by six lengths, returning $VI.LX. This was to be divided into three parts, like all Gaul, for a combination ticket on the Derby.

## Well, Now

AN announcement in Miami papers stated that the Hialeah management was going to donate a three-year accumulation of nickels, dimes, and quarters from the track wishing well to a local children's hospital.

Last week a newspaper reader jumped into the wishing well and started

89

scooping up coins with a tin cup. Then he jumped out, leaving in such haste as to forget two large piles of coins.

There is a five-foot alligator in that wishing well.

## Maybe Next Year

ANOTHER Christmas has come and gone on its merry way, leaving some wondering what to do with garish ties, six cigarette lighters, and several toys immobile because Santa is bad about batteries.

It is our understanding that one Lexington breeder, whose older children have had their own riding horses for some time, finally got around to getting a pony for his youngest son. The pony was done up brightly, red and green ribbons in its mane and tail, and was led to the front door of the house on Christmas morning.

The littlest angel stared dumbly at the gift. Tears came to his eyes.

"What's the matter? Didn't you want a pony?"

The youngest slumped to the floor and wailed: "I wanted a zebra!"

## Providing Insight

REPUBLICAN GOVERNORS, in Lexington for their spring conference during Kentucky Derby Week, are going racing.

There is a distinction between going-to-the-races and going-racing. The former is hurried, to get down on the Double; the latter is leisurely and involves taking some friends to the box, arriving in time to see the filly led into the paddock for the maiden race, and leaving after the feature.

The governors are going racing at Keeneland on April 30. The spring meeting will be over by then, but a special 2-year-old race, 4½ furlongs, the inaugural running of the Republican Governors' Race, will comprise the day's program. Every governor will be an owner, two assigned temporary ownership in each of the 14 entrants in the race. Everyone will be a winner, which is the ideal way to go racing, for each owner, trainer, and rider in the Republican Governors' Race will be awarded a silver julep cup.

In addition, the governors will acquire permanent ownership in a yearling Chateaugay colt presented by the Thoroughbred Breeders of Kentucky. Each of the governors will have a corporate share in the Governors Stable which will race the colt. The Thoroughbred Breeders of Kentucky will pay the training expenses, and any profits of the Governors Stable will go to the Grayson Foundation for equine research.

This should be a good thing, an opportunity for racing to recommend itself, providing some insight into the sport for some of the governors. California Gov. Ronald Reagan, of course, needs no introduction to the game for he has been breeding and selling yearlings at Del Mar for some years now; he and Mrs. Reagan bred 1962 stakes winner One Peso. For most of the governors, however, it will provide a new point of view of racing, that of the horse owner. This can be kaleidoscopic.

For example, Keeneland programmed a similar event in 1958 for a Southern Governors Conference. It was a great show. Joe Wolken put on a spread, about 25 yards of roast beef, ham, chicken, shrimp, and incidentals. Keeneland went all out to explain racing to the governors, even to the extent of using a public-address system (ripped out before the regular fall meeting started). J. B. Faulconer explained the history of the Thoroughbred. A blacksmith, track vet, and paddock judge explained their duties. Trainer John Ward gave instructions to his jockey over the PA set. The starting gate was demonstrated. A saliva test was taken in front of the stands and Spencer Drayton was on hand to explain racing's preventive measures against stimulation.

And then a ruled-off jock won the exhibition race with a ringer. Right there at Keeneland, in front of God, 17 governors, Drayton and everybody.

This came about casually enough. Jimmy S. Jones had some horses in training at Keeneland at the time and, when asked if he had anything ready to work a half-mile, he said he had a colt named Law Man that would do for the race. Law Man was duly printed on the program. Jones, however, decided to work Law Man the day before the governors' race and substituted another colt for the exhibition (Palm Beach, a $39,000 yearling half-brother to Neptune, second-best 2-year-old in France the previous year). In assigning program owners for the race, Gov. Frank Clement of Tennessee, a former FBI lawman, drew Law Man and he liked that, loudly proclaiming willingness to bet $10,000 on his colt if somebody would start the Tote board working.

91

The program listed S. Griffin as the rider of "Law Man." Now Strother Griffin had been a prominent jockey in the 1920s, but he was reluctant to don silks for the race and the unlisted substitute rider was Andy Lo Turco. Ruled off the Turf for an accumulation of things, Lo Turco had authored an article in the *Police Gazette* entitled "I Was a Crooked Jockey." In the paddock, Gov. Clement said he would take Lo Turco's case to the racing commission if he won the race. Lo Turco won easily. He is still down, though.

Arkansas Gov. Orval Faubus, then engaged in another race problem, won a side bet by picking against the filly running in his name, Miss Narwood, by Southern Pride—Idunno.

Nonetheless, the program was pronounced a success. The upcoming Republican Governors' Race can be an even greater success—if they check the lip-tattoos of those riders.

## What Is The Question

The first six-word name accepted by The Jockey Club was submitted last week by Alfred Vanderbilt: To Be or Not To Be, a yearling out of Soul Searcher, by Turn-to.

## Democrat Eater

CHET LAUCK attended his first National Association of State Racing Commissioners convention last week in San Francisco. Some years ago, as Lum, he pondered problems with Abner in the Jot-Em-Down store over to Pine Ridge. Now 70 and in the advertising business in Hot Springs, Lauck was appointed last February to a five-year term on the Arkansas State Racing Commission.

In his report to the convention, retiring NASRC President Fred Davis of Vermont urged that his successor draw upon the rich experiences of men who had served as racing commissioners for more than 20 years. Davis specifically recognized Emmet Kelley of New Hampshire and George

Greenhalgh of Rhode Island, each of whom has been a racing commissioner for 26 years; Paul Dundas of Maine, 23 years; Ben Poxson of Colorado and Hugh Mehorter of New Jersey, 22 years; and Harry Frost of Nevada, 21 years.

Davis was thinking in terms of racing-administration experience, but if a man were to ignore racing and draw upon some of Ben Poxson's other experiences, he could put together a long-run television series. During the last 80 years, Poxson has served as a county judge and as a governor's secretary, and has been involved intimately in Colorado banking, mining, politics, and history.

Donner's Pass is the subject of a new book, which reminded Poxson, "We had a man-eater in the southern part of the state some years ago. My mining partner played poker with him, just after the blizzard let up, you know, and he had made his way to town. My partner probably won some of the victims' money, 'cause the man-eater—that's what he became known as—had these fellas' wallets and things in his room when the marshall finally got to asking him about what happened to the fellas he was with when the snow came up.

"Anyway, they tried and convicted him there in that town—small place, thinly populated in that area of the state then; not much of a place now, some Texans bought up the whole town few years ago—and when the judge sentences him, he says, 'We only had six Democrats in this county, and you ate four of them, so you're going to hang, mister.' "

Unsinkable Mollie Brown? "That's a true story, told me herself, she did hide that roll of 99 thousand-dollar bills in the stove, and her husband came home late and lit the fire; when she told him the next morning, poking around in all those ashes, he said that was all right, he'd find her another mine.

"Well, a man lucky enough to discover one big mine like that first one—he's never going to find another one. But, you know, he did, within a year. She built that big old house in Denver, but the society people never accepted her, and she went off to live in France.

"She came into the office one day in the late 1920s, asked to see the governor. He had known her from 'way back, always called her Maggie; she says to him he ought to take that big house for the governor's mansion, and Gov. Adams says, 'Why, Maggie, that's awful kind, but you know I've always lived in the hotel and they've been real nice to me, taken care of me. Being a bachelor, I don't know what I'd do in a great big house like that all by myself.' And Mollie, she says, 'Why, Bill, if that's all that's bothering you, stop worrying; I'll move in with you so's you won't be lonely.'

"Oh, she was some gal, Mollie was. When the *Titanic* went down, you

93

know, she just happened to have this pistol stuck in her belt..."

The 1960 NASRC president was interrupted by the 1969 NASRC president, Harry Farnham of Nebraska, "Only six Democrats in the county and you say he ate four—I dunno, Ben..."

Well, you get a bunch of racing men together and it is hard to find complete agreement on everything.

## Midsummer Derby

"THE 'Hell' here is very elegantly kept up and patronized by gentlemen," chronicled a somewhat petulant correspondent for the Boston *Journal* during Travers Week at Saratoga.

"Shoddy seems to be pre-eminent, and there are government officials here who are doing their best to aggravate the evil that is now cursing the land. Honest men may make money out of the government, but no man who has any respect for himself or regard for his country will revel at Saratoga when the times demand sobriety and economy.

"What the women spend in dress, the men spend in 'liquoring up,' until they can't stand, in horses and in gambling. We heard of several young men in society who 'fought the tiger' so persistently as to be (using the elegant vernacular of the place) entirely 'cleaned out,' and obliged to borrow of the bank to get home. One gentleman lost $1,000 in one evening with the greatest nonchalance... The races attracted nearly all the sporting community of the country."

Well, things have not changed too much since the above was written a century and three years ago. Then, there was an insurrection going on elsewhere called a civil war; now it is called a riot, or civil disturbance, or a situation which cannot be controlled without federal troops, but not a certified insurrection.

At any rate, Saratoga has not changed too much. Oh, the gambling casinos are closed. The Piping Rock, where Paul Whiteman played and Ted Lewis somehow made losing seem funny, burned down a few years ago; on the other hand, John Morrissey's Elegant Hell has not burned.

When Old Smoke began construction of his gambling spot in the middle of Congress Park a century ago, a town father happened by and inquired what name was to be given the completed work. Morrissey thought The Casino would catch it, but town fathers traditionally lean toward euphemism, and in 1869 when the former world champion bare-knuckle heavyweight, U. S.

94

congressman from New York, and *de facto* founder of Saratoga racing moved his gambling tables from Matilda Street to the park, it was into a brick building named The Club House.

Be that as it may, the place was generally referred to, outside of Saratoga Springs, as Morrissey's Elegant Hell, later as Dick Canfield's Casino, and more recently as the Museum. There this week the New York Turf Writers Association will hold its annual ball.

We are about to enter upon another Travers Week at Saratoga. While Morrisey invented Saratoga racing as an afternoon diversion to prep his clients for serious play in the evening, there never was a scintilla of written evidence that he owned a piece of the race track. It is inconceivable that any action in Saratoga at the time was not controlled by Old Smoke, but he remained in the background as to the race track, preferring that operation to be headed up by wealthy racing men. Before New York society was expanded to a list of 400, it consisted of William R. Travers, Leonard Jerome, John Hunter, Francis Morris, August Belmont, and a few of their friends.

Wall Street broker, clubman, connoisseur of fine wines, Travers had something of a speech impediment which he bore with good humor. He was the originator of a venerable vaudeville bit: Early one morning he was sneaking up his front stairs with his shoes in hand when his wife broke the dark silence:

"Willie! Is that you?"

"Uh, wh-wh-who were you expecting?"

Travers was up front at all New York society sporting events—yachting, driving, card playing, and such. He naturally was named president of the racing association which held its first meeting in 1863 over the Horse Haven track in Saratoga Springs.

Property was then purchased across Union Avenue and a new course was laid out, essentially where the present track is. The first race on the new course was run on Aug. 2, 1864, and it was named the Travers Sweepstakes, for 3-year-olds, 30 subscribers, value of stakes $2,500.

As chance would have it, Travers owned the best colt in America at the time, in partnership with John Hunter (first chairman of The Jockey Club) and George Osgood. The colt was out of Magnolia, a mare given to Henry Clay, who placed twice and finished out of the money in three presidential elections and who passed the mare on to his son John. Magnolia was 20 when she produced Kentucky, which ran off with the inaugural Travers, easily defeating Zeb Ward's Tipperary, Francis Morris' Throg's Neck Jr., J. S. Watson's Patti, and James A. Grinstead's Ringmaster in a matter of 3:18¾.

The entire meeting consisted of only 12 races, including a walkover, in four days, so it is hard to comprehend how a Boston writer could be perturbed about the racing program; only last Saturday, patrons at Charles Town had a shot at 19 races for a single admission price.

A total of 22 horses raced at the 1864 Saratoga meeting and five of these raced in a hurdle event. In addition to the Travers, there were two other stakes: The two-mile Sequel Stakes, value $1,750, was won by Kentucky, of course; the mile Saratoga Stakes for 2-year-olds, value $1,250, was won by Hunter's Knight of St. George filly, named, fittingly enough, Saratoga.

It may be noted that the track president and his partners won all the stakes at the meeting, but J. S. Watson, not known to have a proprietary interest in the track, won half the races: Watson's 4-year-old Capt. Moore, by Balrownie, won dash races of 1½ miles and two miles on the same day and then was given a walkover; Watson's 4-year-old Aldebaran, by Commodore, won two races at two-and three-mile heats, and his 3-year-old filly, Patti, by Eclipse, carrying 73 pounds, including a jockey named, or perhaps described, in the summary as Boney, won a 1¼-mile selling race. (Allowed 14 pounds because she was entered to be sold for $600, Patti was reported as sold after the race for $610. It is suspected here some fellow of no social standing whatever entered that $600 bid, for Patti was brought out two races later in the afternoon and finished fourth and second in a mile-heat race carrying again the colors of Watson.)

Kentucky was born of Lexington. Literal-minded historians favoring Boonesboro contest this, but Col. Sanders Bruce's *American Stud Book* is our authority. Lexington also sired unbeaten Norfolk and Asteroid in the same 1861 crop and it has been suggested that no other sire came up with such a triumvirate until Bull Lea sired Citation, Coaltown, and Bewitch 84 years later.

Norfolk beat Kentucky in the 1864 Jersey Derby, but no other horse did in Kentucky's 21 other races. Travers, Hunter, and Osgood bought Kentucky and a good filly, Arcola, from Clay for $6,000 just before the Jersey Derby. With Norfolk shipped to California, Kentucky took the Sequel Stakes, then the Travers and its Sequel, the Jersey St. Leger and its Sequel, and a match race against Aldebaran.

At four, Kentucky ran out of competition. Allowed to walk over for two purses, he won a pair of two-mile heat races and a pair of three-mile heat races before taking the inaugural Saratoga Cup. Asteroid was entered for this race, but was not shipped up from Kentucky.

At five, Kentucky won four more races and the Saratoga Cup again before the grand opening of Jerome Park. Asteroid was shipped to New York for the Inauguration Stakes, but the long-awaited meeting between the two sons of Lexington was canceled when Asteroid broke down a week before the race. Kentucky won the opener at Jerome Park easily, four-mile heats in 7:35 and 7:41¼.

While Jerome was the builder of New York's first fashionable race course, he had yet to own a horse. Travers and Hunter sold him one—Kentucky. For a record $40,000! Kentucky won only one race for Jerome, the $1,000-added Grand National Handicap.

In 1867, the Annieswood Stable was formed, partners being Travers, Hunter, Jerome, Belmont, and Sir Roderick Cameron. A comparable syndicate today would be composed of Ogden Phipps, John Galbreath, Jock Whitney, Charles Engelhard, and Alfred Vanderbilt—just to give an idea of the Annieswood strength.

Kentucky was absorbed into Annieswood, which, it quickly was discovered, had virtually all the good horses around resulting in absolutely no action at all. Consequently, Annieswood was broken up so the partners could bet against each other. At the 1868 dispersal, Belmont bought Kentucky for $15,000 and stood him at his Nursery Stud at Babylon, L. I., where he was to sire champion filly Woodbine, winner of the 1872 Alabama and Monmouth Oaks. Belmont also bought Bertram, winner of the 1876 Jersey Derby and Monmouth Sequel Stakes; Caroline, winner of the 1874 Hopeful; Silk Stocking, winner of the 1872 Kentucky Stakes; Count D'Orsay, winner of the 1873 Weatherby and second in the Belmont; Medora, winner of the 1872 July Stakes, and high-class runners Countess and Lord Byron.

Lexington, America's leading sire for 16 years, more or less left the Travers Stakes as a legacy to his progeny. The second winner of the Travers was Lexington's daughter, Maiden (later to produce America's leading money winner, Parole); the third winner of the Travers was Merrill, also by Lexington.

Champion Ruthless, by Eclipse, took the fourth Travers after winning the inaugural Belmont Stakes. Then there came The Banshee, Kingfisher, Harry Bassett, Tom Bowling, Sultana, and Duke of Magenta, all Travers winners sired by Lexington—nine of the first 15 winners of the race.

From its beginning, the Travers was a championship race. Its roll of winners include 29 horses recognized as the best of their rivals at three: Kentucky, Maiden, Ruthless, Harry Bassett, Joe Daniels, Tom Bowling, Sultana, Baden Baden, Duke of Magenta, Falsetto, Hindoo, Inspector B., Henry of Navarre—names which come whispering down to us from another century.

In the 1918 Travers, Sun Briar was first, Belmont winner Johren was second, Preakness winner War Cloud was third, and Kentucky Derby winner Exterminator was fourth.

97

In the 1926 Travers, Mars beat Pompey and Display. In the 1930 Travers, Jim Dandy brought about a new expression for feeling fine, fit, and happy by scoring at 100-1 over champion Gallant Fox and Whichone.

Then there came Travers winners Twenty Grand, Granville, Whirlaway, By Jimminy, One County, Native Dancer, Sword Dancer—champions all.

In 1962, however, the greatest Travers of all was run. Ridan and Jaipur raced head and head the entire way, and at the end the camera showed Jaipur the winner by a nose. Ridan, which was to whip Jaipur soundly in both meetings the next season, broke even with him in their two encounters at two, but Jaipur was voted the champion. He had won the Travers.

Last year, champion Buckpasser beat the Belmont winner and Suburban winner in the Travers, and it was hoped that Dr. Fager and Damascus would settle something in the 98th running of the mid-summer derby. Alas, Dr. Fager has been declared from the race.

Well, the determination of a championship, while adding significance, is not essential to a good horse race. This year's Travers winner no doubt will be a good one, which would have prompted William R. to inquire, "Yes, b-b-but what do you imagine he'll pay?"


## Quiet, Please


AT Belmont Park there is a goat in Barn 28 named after Phainting Phil Scott, a British heavyweight noted for a tendency to fall into a horizontal stage of shock at the first hint of violence.

Fainting Bill the 3-year-old goat is called. He passes out cold at the slightest show of hostility or any sudden noise. In his own quiet way, Fainting Bill has revolutionized the role of stable pets. As a usual thing, goats, dogs, cats, chickens, ducks, guineas, and such living with the horses serve as fiercely protective, self-appointed stable guards or as tranquilizing companions. It is the other way around with Fainting Bill; the horses watch out for him and the dogs are careful not to frighten him.

"This mare," said Mrs. John Cotter, "is the third to take care of Bill. First we had Perth Assembly, then Royal Audrey, and now Portico II. Each mare has adopted Bill as her very own. He seems to arouse their maternal instinct and they apparently sense he isn't quite right. Portico II won't let anyone make a threatening gesture toward the goat and she's apt to bite if you get too close to him. At night she covers him with straw, and she raises a fuss when we separate her from the goat for her workouts."

Mrs. Cotter said that boys around the stable used to show off Fainting Bill's trick by shouting at him before friends, but this was stopped. "Now, everybody is careful not to frighten him, but it can't be avoided all the time, and he still collapses. We found out long ago that he always comes to without help."

## Blind Faith

THE late Col. Phil T. Chinn once remarked that the most serious mistake he made when he took his first horses to the track was in the selection of a name. He showed up at Nashville in 1895 with a 2-year-old filly by Wagner which the young trainer was confident could run a hole in the wind, an ability of which he had personal knowledge to the exclusion of all others and consequently a source of hope for winning an adequate sum at good odds.

"But I named that filly—in those days you named when they first started—in compliment to the citizenry of Nashville after the luminary of the day, Helen Keller," Col. Chinn recalled, "and don't you know, everybody in town bet that name. My hideout horse, a legitimate 70-1 shot, wins at 7-1."

There are a couple of horses in Canada which figure to draw considerable action irrespective of form if they ever run as an entry. One has the comfortable name of Good Old Mort while the other is named after several personal acquaintances, Poor Old Sam.

## Mementos

A JOINT showed up in the dirt near the starting gate at Hialeah last week. We had the thought that all the batteries, buzzers, and more refined electrical devices had been buried with the old Kentucky Association track. In 1935, the track which since 1828 had sustained the thundering hooves of

99

mighty Lexington and Enquirer and Aristides and Ten Broeck and Himyar and Hindoo and Clifford, Chant, Halma, Agile, and Chacolet was razed to make way for a federal housing project in Lexington.

There was a slight rise around the last turn and this was called a "hill" by losers, "nothing at all" by winners. When this portion of the track finally was leveled by bulldozers, an arsenal of joints and buzzers was unearthed. These were not auctioned, as was the gate post embossed with KA which now stands at the entrance of Keeneland.

Electrical devices are not uncommon equipment in a stable training Quarter Horses, but we had not thought of them in association with Thoroughbred racing until Hialeah stewards suspended Puerto Rican jockey Francisco Rivera for 60 days. An assistant starter thought he saw something in Rivera's hand as Rivera entered the gate with Camilo II for the ninth race on Jan. 21. Starter Charles Camac was so advised. The start was delayed, Camilo II was scratched, and a battery was retrieved from the dirt. Rivera admitted to no knowledge of any joints. The stewards recommended that Rivera's license be revoked.

## Engine Trouble

DON Brumfield rode Mike Ford's Kauai King to victory in the Kentucky Derby and Preakness last year. In the Blue Grass Stakes last week he rode Solar Bomb, owned by Ford and Dr. R. T. Murphy and trained by Ford. Solar Bomb finished last, 27 lengths behind Diplomat Way.

Said Brumfield: "Had the right Ford—wrong motor."

## The Generosity Of Col. Bradley

THERE once was a race horse man who believed that every child at Christmas deserved a toy and a big Christmas dinner. A gambler by trade, he backed his convictions pretty well, and he came off a winner.

The man was Col. Edward R. Bradley.

In 1921, Col. Bradley had one of the best 3-year-old fillies of the year in Bit of White, by Sunstar. She had finished second in the Alabama Stakes to Prudery, and second in the Latonia Oaks to Flambette, and second in the Saranac Handicap in which Kentucky Derby winner Behave Yourself finished fourth.

Shipped to Churchill Downs in October, she was the best thing on the grounds and easily won the Falls City Handicap. Ten days later, she came out as an odds-on favorite for the $5,000-added Louisville Cup.

"If she wins," declared Col. Bradley, "the purse shall be donated to the orphans of Kentucky." She could not have won bigger. Giving 14 pounds to her closest rivals, she took a commanding lead soon after the start, opened up by eight lengths the first time around, and "hard held" at the end of two miles, she was a winner by 15 lengths in 3:22⅗, breaking the track record by nearly seven seconds.

The winner's share amounted to $4,720. Col. Bradley rounded it off at $10,000 and donated the whole with the stipulation that it be used only for Thanksgiving and Christmas dinners for Kentucky orphans.

Col. Bradley was a gambler, according to his sworn testimony before a United States Senate committee, and a superstitious one, not given to stoping once he had a good thing going. His first good race horse was named Bad News, and for the next 43 years Bradley-bred horses' names started with the letter B.

Thus when the Louisville Cup was discontinued in 1922 and there was little reason to expect Bit of White to win a $5,000 stakes every year, Col. Bradley had to come up with something else to keep the orphans' Thanksgiving and Christmas parties going.

He asked Bob Saxton, sports editor of the *Cincinnati Enquirer*, to solicit contributions for the orphans' fund from horsemen. Saxton collected about $2,200 and Col. Bradley supplied the balance to bring the figure up to $10,000 again.

In 1928 with the hope of going over the $10,000 mark, Col. Bradley decided to hold a one-day race meeting at his Idle Hour Farm near Lexington, immediately after the Latonia meeting and just before the fall sales.

Approximately 8,000 persons on Nov. 12, 1928, crowded around the mile training track (now covered by turf but still used for exercising King Ranch horses). Six races were carded, with Col. Bradley putting up purse money for five $1,000 races plus the $5,000-added Orphanage Stakes for 2-year-olds.

Winner by six lengths of the inaugural Orphanage Stakes was Herbert P. Gardner's Clyde Van Dusen, which six months later won the Kentucky

Derby. Winner of the supporting feature, the Armistice Day Handicap, was Sen. Johnson M. Camden's Martinique, trained by Roscoe Goose.

Profits from the sale of admission tickets, programs, box seats (literally), and the betting amounted to $24,623 for Kentucky orphans.

Only 5,000 turned out in miserable weather for the 1929 meeting, when Gov. Flem Sampson presented a silver trophy to Brownell Combs after his filly Manta won the Orphanage Stakes. It was a good card. Mrs. Payne Whitney had a filly in the stakes. Hal Price Headley ran three horses. A. B. Hancock Sr. entered game old Whiskery, but scratched the 1927 Kentucky Derby winner at the last minute.

The most successful of the meetings staged by Col. Bradley was held in 1930, when the orphans received $27,048.60. Sewell S. Combs, president of the Kentucky Association race track and member of the Kentucky State Racing Commission, trained winners of both divisions of the Orphanage Stakes that year. Plumage, by Ballot, beat Greentree's Blue Law in the first division. Oswego, by Cherokee, upset Robert W. Collins' highly favored Don Leon in the second. Both winners were owned by Combs in partnership with Allen Gallaher and both were ridden by Herb Fisher, who two years later on Head Play lost the Kentucky Derby by a nose to Col. Bradley's Brokers Tip after a stretch-long, saddle cloth-snatching and whip-slashing duel with jockey Don Meade. (Fisher gained a momentary measure of satisfaction by busting Meade in the mouth in the jocks' room, but was suspended for fighting and consequently was on the ground when Head Play won the Preakness.)

The last of the one-day meetings was held on Armistice Day of 1931. Adm. Cary T. Grayson came from Washington to serve as steward, along with Walter S. Vosburgh of New York and Charles Price of Churchill Downs.

Joseph E. Widener presented a trophy to J. W. Parrish of Midway, Ky., after Depression, by North Star III, won the Orphans' Matron Stakes by a head over Al Sabath's I Say. The Nash Brothers' Minton, by Angon, won the Orphans' Junior Stakes as some 5,000 persons huddled in the rain. In attendance were George D. Widener and his trainer, A. J. Joyner; The Jockey Club chairman, William Woodward Sr.; Mrs. Payne Whitney and her son, John Hay Whitney; Walter Jeffords, A. C. Bostwick, P. A. B. Widener, Arnold Hanger, Col. Phil T. Chinn and W. T. (Fatty) Anderson, Samuel D. Riddle, Col. Matt Winn, cartoonist H. C. (Bud) Fisher, E. J. Tranter, Maj. Louie Beard, John Hertz and many others.

Profits from the four meetings totaled $101,619.96. Thereafter, Col. Bradley found a less involved means of raising money for the orphans' Christmas—he wrote out a personal check each year until his death in 1946.

There were some who said this money was not directed through the proper channels, that it could have been better allocated for new buildings, more equipment, better salaries for supervisors.

Col. Bradley gave it for turkeys, rag dolls, toy trains, balls, peppermint canes—nothing of real significance, unless, of course, one feels, as did this race horse man, that one of the most important things in the world is a child's smile of joy at Christmas.

## Gentlemen, Please!

AS a usual thing, disputed Turf matters in 18th century England were submitted for arbitration to The Jockey Club, "A society being composed of men of high rank and fortune, conversant in the laws which usually regulated amusements of this nature, and who determine all appeals made to them on the strictest principles of honour consistent with the prosperity of the Turf."

A problem arose, however, out of the running of a sweepstakes at York on June 2, 1791, when the aggrieved party was not altogether certain he would receive a fair shake before The Jockey Club, inasmuch as all other parties to the controversy happened to be members of that body.

Thus came about "The Famous Turf Cause of BURDON Against RHODES" tried at the Guildhall, York, before Mr. Baron Thompson and a special jury on the night of Aug. 10, 1791.

An action of assumpsit was brought for 120 guineas had and received for the use of the plaintiff, Mr. Thomas Burdon, by the defendant, Mr. Rhodes, clerk of the course at York.

The circumstances were these: Mr. Burdon and 11 others subscribed 10 guineas each for a sweepstakes to be run with hunters which had never won a race, to be the property of the subscribers, to carry 12 stones (168 pounds), and to be ridden by Gentlemen. Mr. Burdon's chestnut horse, Centaur, ridden by Mr. C. Rowntree, won the race, but Mr. Palm. Chichester, who finished second on his hunter by Highflyer—Marianne, objected on the grounds that Rowntree was no Gentleman at all and the clerk consequently held up the purse, for which Mr. Burdon sued.

Testimony for the plaintiff established that Mr. Burdon was a subscriber,

Centaur was his horse, a maiden and a hunter, that Mr. Rowntree had carried the proper weight and had won the race, and that the clerk had refused to pay over the winning purse.

Sir William Foulis, Bart., testified that he did not consider Mr. Rowntree to be a Gentleman in the general acceptance of the term but that Mr. Rowntree had hunted to hounds with him and had enjoyed the sports of the field like other Gentlemen for some time. (He was over 70.) As to his general character, "I know nothing against him but on the contrary have a good opinion of him and think myself obliged to him for assisting me in preserving the game on my estate." Did Sir William ever know Mr. Rowntree to do a dirty action? "I never did."

Farmer John Preston, asked if he reckoned Mr. Rowntree to be a Gentleman, replied, "Aye, to be sure I do," and added that Mr. Rowntree had two estates, worth about 180 pounds annually.

In his opening statement for the defense, counsel acknowledged uncertainty in defining Gentleman, admitting "no positive rules by which it may be distinguished. We must consider, however, the nature of the agreement in which this term is inserted. Obviously enough, the subscribers were not under the necessity of riding their own horses but might procure another to ride for them, provided that rider should be a Gentleman.

"Could it be supposed that such a man as Rowntree would be permitted to ride? That a man like as he has been represented to you was a fit person to associate and keep company with, even in a ride, the other gentlemen who rode? Good God!

"Can you for a moment believe it was the intention of the parties that men of his description should ride? We mean not to deprecate the character of Mr. Rowntree, to arraign any part of his conduct, even on this occasion, for he seems to have been made the unwilling instrument of another's want of propriety.

"Mr. Rowntree may be, from what we have heard we doubt not he is, a useful worthy member of society, in the situation in which he is placed. We oppose not his pretentions to merit. He may possess as much as those in a superior station of life. It is only to the character of a Gentleman that we mean to resist his claims."

Robert Dension, Esq., one of the York stewards, testified that Mr. Chichester had objected to Mr. Rowntree's riding before the race and that in his opinion Mr. Rowntree's "appearance then did not bespeak the Gentleman, but I do not know him."

George Baker, Esq., a subscriber to the race, testified that Mr. Rowntree and other farmers had hunted fox with his hounds but that he did not think

Mr. Rowntree was a proper person to ride in a Gentleman's race. "I went up to him and he appeared glad to see me. I asked him how he could make such a fool of himself in his old age as to ride for a Gentleman and he said that he was sorry he came, that he did not pretend to be a Gentleman, but that he had made a promise to Burdon when he was drunk to ride his horse for him and that he would sooner go home dead than break his word." Did Mr. Baker ever know Mr. Rowntree to do a bad or dishonorable action? "I never did."

Hon. George Monson testified that he also had protested Mr. Rowntree's appearance and had stated he would not ride in the race against him.

S. Barlow, Esq., testified that Mr. Rowntree was "a very honest man but is neither considered by others or himself as a Gentleman."

John Wharton, Esq., testified that neither Mr. Rowntree nor Mr. Burdon were Gentlemen but that the former was a man of good reputation.

Sir H. Goodricke, Bart., testified that although he had never seen Mr. Rowntree until two days before the trial, he did not appear to be such a person as, when he subscribed to the race, was intended to ride. "I would not have ridden against him."

Christopher Wilson, Esq., another subscriber to the race, testified that Mr. Rowntree "certainly is not such a man as we intended should ride; he would be objected to on any race ground in England. I have rode in similar sweepstakes with the Prince of Wales and I am certain if Rowntree had attempted to ride on such occasions, he would have been kicked off the course."

With the evidence closed, counsel for the plaintiff rose and for his closing argument said:

"I have now sat almost three hours to hear a man, confessedly allowed by all parties to be a man of probity and worth, degraded and villified as the outcast of mankind, as the refuse and scum of the earth.

"Gentlemen of the jury, amidst all this obliquity, all this wanton and ungenerous abuse of a respectable character, amidst all this arrogance and pride—too often the appendages of high rank or fortune—which have been most lavishly displayed here this night, no one has favored us with a definition of the term, 'Gentleman'.

"In such absence, I take the liberty of offering my definition. I believe the strong traits, the striking features of a Gentleman to be: A good education, liberal manners, moral good conduct, and independency of station.

"In which of these characteristics have they proved Mr. Rowntree to be deficient? His education and manners have not been impeached. Every witness has borne ample testimony to his moral good conduct, and to the high estimation of his character—even those who in all the arrogance and pride of superior consequences have denied him a title to their society.

"Far be it from me to arraign the character or conduct of any other Gentlemen who have been examined this night. But surely it is not presumptuous to say that the character of Mr. Rowntree—for integrity, honor, and worth—stands as unimpeached as does theirs.

"Mr. Rowntree's dress has been severely criticized by some witnesses. Now, I never before heard that dress was the criterion by which a Gentleman might be distinguished. It would seem to be a most uncertain test.

"But let us try the title of Mr. Rowntree by three criteria which seem in the opinion of my learned friends to form the Compleat Gentleman: An hereditary estate, the enjoyments of the sports in the field, and a freedom from any business or profession.

"In none of these requisites does he fall short. If to be idle and useless are prominent features of a Gentleman, he has most fully proved his claim to that distinction.

"But to these criteria, I add another—Honor. Honor in the strict adherence to a promise, that exquisite sensibility which prepares one to meet public insult and private inconvenience rather than break a promise—even a promise made in a moment of partial inebriety and consequently nugatory.

"I think the character of Mr. Rowntree on such a view must stand high in the estimation of every man.

"Added to these qualifications is yet another virtue, which apparently has caused him to be the object of contempt and ridicule by the witnesses. I am referring to the virtue of economical, prudent conduct—not restrained to his house—but apparent in his dress, which a numerous family of 14 children claim from him.

"Shall such an amiable virtue be so distorted into a contemptible trait of character? Shall an honest, respectable man in whom every public and private virtue is united—the good husband, the provident father, the peaceful member of society—be degraded as the scum of the earth, deserving to be kicked off the floor of society for daring to lay claim to that rank in life which his conduct and situation entitle him to?

"Gentlemen of the jury, there are such rights as the rights of man. I am now standing up in support of those rights."

At this point, extended applause came from court observers, cries of "Scandalous!" from members of The Jockey Club.

"Gentlemen of the jury, in considering this case, we need not be led away by the ideas which men—in all their fancied superiority of rank and station—may annex to the character of a Gentleman. The true ground on which this matter stands is the obvious interpretation of the term as applying to the written agreement entered into by the subscribers.

"Can anything be more plain, more apparent, than that the term 'Gentlemen' is here used as opposed to 'Jockey' or 'Groom'? Can it be doubted that the intention of the subscribers was that none of the horses should be rode by men whose professional skill would give them an advantage in point of jockeyship?

"In this light I am inclined to regard the term. This is the construction it deserves. But in any construction, I trust we have removed every objection that can be made to the rider and fully proved our title to the sum in question, by our perfect compliance with the subscribed conditions. I trust you will be of the opinion the plaintiff is entitled to a verdict."

The jury was.


## Skoal!

IT is difficult to separate racing from international news, what with Damascus winning the Belmont on one day and being mentioned as a bombing target the next. Exhibition Park in Vancouver has a series of races going named Salute to the Americas, Salute to Canada, Salute to Britain, Salute to the Orient, Salute to Northwest Europe—which would seem a vague place for the addressing of a salutation—and this may not escape diplomatic notice. The first three named are handicap and allowance races while the Orient and Northwest Europe salutes are for claimers.


## A Little Fishy

EDGAR ZANTKER, who bred Quiz Show, First Minister, Miss Blue Jay, Blue Skyer, and other nice ones from a small broodmare band, stopped by the office this week and explained how difficult it was to find a good broodmare prospect: "All I see is sardines."

Sardines?

"When I am a little boy, it is during the first world war and it is very difficult to find sardines, because they must come from Portugal. But one day I find 10 cans of sardines, and I buy them, and I take them home, to show my

107

mother, so she will know how smart I am finding sardines. But we open a can, and they smell, they are no good. We open all the cans, and none of them is good.

"So I go back to the man where I bought them and I say I opened all the cans of sardines and they are no good and he says to me, 'Edgar,' he says, 'I thought you were a smart boy, but I see different now. You do not eat sardines; they are for trade.'

"Now I am looking for some fillies that I can race and maybe retire as broodmares, and all I can find is sardines."

## A Christmas Story

RACELAND was dead, to begin with. There is no doubt whatever about that. The register of its burial was signed by the racing secretary, the sheriff, the trustee in bankruptcy, and the chief mourner. Scrooge signed it. Old Raceland was as dead as a door-nail. Scrooge and it had been partners for a few years, but Scrooge had not been so dreadfully cut up by the sad event that he was not an excellent man of business and on the very day of the funeral, he had solemnized it by getting three other tracks started in the same area.

Once upon a time—of all the good days in the year, on Christmas Eve—old Scrooge sat busy in the state revenue department building, or counting-house as it was called.

"A merry Christmas, uncle!" cried a cheery voice. It was Scrooge's nephew. Fred, who had dropped by to ask if Scrooge wanted to fly South for the Christmas Handicap at his small track; it was not a big stakes, just $10,000 added for the nice older horses on the grounds, but it would be a fun trip.

"Bah!" said Scrooge, "Humbug!"

"I am sorry, with all my heart, to find you so resolute," Fred said in leaving, "But I have made the trial in homage to Christmas. Change your mind, give me a ring. Merry Christmas!" and he left.

An owner and breeder entered, asked for Raceland or Mr. Scrooge, and when informed that Raceland had died some years ago, inquired, "We have no doubt his liberality is well represented by his surviving partner?" Scrooge frowned at the world liberality.

The owner and breeder were soliciting donations for an economic survey of racing "some slight provision for the Poor and destitute who suffer greatly at the present time."

108

Scrooge dismissed these gentlemen with the promise of nothing and, since the hour was late, started to close the office. Bob Cratchit, state racing commission chairman, stopped writing his annual report in the outer office and rose to go.

"You'll want not to race tomorrow, I suppose," Scrooge said.

"If quite convenient," said Cratchit. "We've been going for 364 days, we're having trouble getting horses to fill the races, and the jocks are complaining about the condition of the track."

"It's not convenient," Scrooge growled, "and it's not fair, but I suppose you must have the whole day." They left, Cratchit returning to his three tracks and Scrooge to his lonely rooming house. That night, Scrooge was visited by an apparition, the ghost of Old Raceland.

Raceland came with a dreadful clanking of a long chain of mistakes it had forged and from which it would never be free, links of bad management, dropping attendance, bad location, poor horses, high state licensing fees. The spectre of Old Raceland said it had come to warn Scrooge that he would be visited by three spirits and that from these, Scrooge would have a chance to free himself from the chain of mistakes he was forging but would not acknowledge. Raceland then took its leave, returning to its phantom company of Havre de Grace, old Empire City, Tanforan, and Jamaica. Every one of these wore chains like Raceland's ghost; none of them was free of the misery of its mistakes.

The first of the three spirits to visit Scrooge was the Ghost of Christmas Past. The wraith took Scrooge to Salisbury Plain on Long Island where Col. Richard Nicolls was presenting a silver porringer bowl to the winner of the first two-mile Newmarket Cup race and the governor of New York was explaining that racing "was not so much for the divertisement of the breed of horses." Then Scrooge saw George Washington in the stewards' stand for the sport at Williamsburg; next they fell in with the huge crowd of merrymakers journeying to the Union Course to see the great Boston vs. Fashion Match; then Francis Morris' filly, Ruthless, winning the first Belmont Stakes at Jerome Park, and the clicker machines Col. Matt Winn was using for pari-mutuels at Churchill Downs, mounted police at Sheepshead Bay closing down the meeting, and the day Equipoise threw two shoes and still got up to beat Twenty Grand and Mate in the Pimlico Futurity, and finally the day the totalizator board was put up in the Belmont Park centerfield.

The second spirit, the Ghost of Christmas Present appearing as a horn of plenty, took Scrooge to Bob Cratchit's where the racing was meager, but still operating as well as possible under the circumstances—prices were rising, but the income was fixed and horsemen were demanding bigger purses; a half-mile track named Tiny Tim was about to go under although it was cheerfully proceeding with a crutch of night racing. Scrooge looked in on his nephew Fred's meeting, which was not a big one, but everyone seemed to be having a marvelous time.

The third spirit, the Ghost of Christmas Yet to Come, took Scrooge onto the street and he saw people that he had known before as great racing fans and one of them said he had heard that it had died, and two others talked about going to see the Packers play. The spectre took Scrooge to an abandoned race track where the centerfield was being used for a golf driving range, the stands had been stripped of seats and all hardware that could be sold, a junk dealer was using the walking ring to store wrecked cars, the barns had all burned. Scrooge asked the spirit if anyone were sorry that racing had died and the wraith took him to Cratchit, who was grieving over the loss of Tiny Tim.

And then Scrooge awakened from his troubled slumber to a bright, new Christmas Day, and he flung open the shutters of his window. He called down to a boy to run to the television network that was offering a big turkey prize of a contract and tell them to send that TV pact over to Cratchit's place. And then Scrooge hurried out onto the street, bustling about with sincere good cheer, building up his public relations; and that afternoon he flew down to Fred's track and had a thoroughly enjoyable time. The next day when Cratchit came into the office, Scrooge told the commissioner that Scrooge's take of the mutuel play thenceforth would be cut back to three per cent and might the season be merry.

And Tiny Tim did *not* die. Its operator had discarded the crutch and cried, "God bless Us. Every One!"

## Take That!

AT Hawthorne two weeks ago, Jose Martinez lost his whip while bringing a second-choice up from last place. Danny Rosier was backing up to last on a 45-1 shot at the time, and Martinez, just in passing, asked if he could borrow Rosier's whip. Inasmuch as Rosier had no apparent use for his whip in the last three furlongs, he tossed it to Martinez, who thereupon brought his horse down at $8.80 for $2. Both riders were fined $100 each, however, for such gestures happen to be against the rules.

110

Our man in Chicago, Joe Agrella, was talking about this to Hall of Fame rider Ted Atkinson, now Illinois state steward. "I remember about 30 years ago that Johnny Adams and Silvio Coucci were battling head and head with their mounts late in the stretch," Atkinson said. "Adams was just hand-riding and Coucci yelled to him, 'I'd beatya if I hadn't lost my whip!'

"So Adams just handed Coucci his whip—and then beat him to the wire."


## That's Racing


WHEN H. A. (Jimmy) Jones was with Calumet Farm, he had his hands on six Preakness winners. He assisted his father, Ben, who saddled Whirlaway in 1941 and Pensive in 1944, and he tightened the girth on Faultless in 1947, Citation in 1948, Fabius in 1956, and Tim Tam in 1958.

Now, as director of racing at Monmouth Park, Jones was among the visiting firemen as 10 3-year-olds were led into the centerfield at Pimlico to be saddled for the 93rd running of the Preakness.

Dan Barnette, who had rubbed Whirlaway, brought Forward Pass from the barn. The betting favorite, Forward Pass looked the part—big (16.2 hands tall and well proportioned), calm, his coat fairly glistening condition.

Jones eyed the Calumet horse, resting his round chin on three pudgy fingers, wiggling the little one: "Look how good Henry has him." Jones folded his arms across his chest and watched Henry Forrest saddle the big bay. "If he don't beat these horses today, you can set me down as crazy."

Eddie Arcaro, who rode six Preakness winners, liked Forward Pass: "I'd give Henry my 10 per cent just to have the mount. This race is made for him—it doesn't have the early speed the Kentucky Derby had. I don't believe Milo rode him well at Louisville. Over there Milo hit the horse to get him running, because he had that outside post position, and then he tried to rate him and it is hard to hold a horse once you've got him stirred up, and then he asked him to go. The horse didn't know what to do—he's just a horse, not a Rhodes Scholar. I don't think Milo will ride him that way again. If he ever gets a two- or three-length lead in this race, I'm just going to get in line."

Jack Price, owner-breeder-trainer of 1961 Preakness winner Carry Back, said he thought the race should be split: "Forward Pass and Dancer's Image could have a match race for 85 per cent of the purse, then let all those other horses run in another division for 15 per cent of the purse." [The Preakness

**111**

was split in 1928, War Cloud beating nine rivals and winning $12,250 in the first division, and Jack Hare beating five for $11,250 in the second.]

Peter Fuller, owner-breeder of Dancer's Image, who had been absolutely certain his horse would beat Forward Pass in the Kentucky Derby, had reservations about the Preakness: "I don't really see Forward Pass having too much pressure on him in the early part of this race; there is no Kentucky Sherry or Captain's Gig to carry him that fast first three quarters. I see him saving something, and when we come to him at the head of the stretch, I don't know, but Forward Pass just might draw away like he did in the Blue Grass Stakes.

"I'd like to say I was confident Dancer's Image could take him in this race. I notice the experts in the *Telegraph* pick Dancer's Image all the way across, but the way this race shapes up, with no real early pace, I'd have to think that Forward Pass should be the logical favorite. We would like to win this race, of course, but I really think the *real* test between these two horses will come in the Belmont Stakes at a mile and a half."

Price's second division of the Preakness did not include the kind of horses one expects to be running for a $195,200 purse.

Trainer Max Hirsch sent Robert J. Kleberg Jr.'s Out of the Way from New York after the Mamboreta colt had finished fourth in the Withers. Neither trainer nor owner showed for the Preakness and it was apparent that the stable connections did not consider Out of the Way as good as his stablemate, Call Me Prince, which had won the Withers. Last year he had finished last in Forward Pass' Flash Stakes; this year he had finished fourth, beaten almost nine lengths by Dancer's Image in the Wood Memorial, won an allowance race, and was beaten by less than four lengths in the Withers, an encouraging performance.

Gene Goff, owner-breeder of Arkansas Derby winner Nodouble, said he figured he had "more nerve than anybody in the race." He had shipped his horse out of Chicago, where he had been listed at 2-1 in the morning line for the $75,000-added Illinois Derby, to pay $12,000 in supplementary and starting fees "to see how the horse shapes up against the tops" in the Preakness.

Miss Judy Johnson became the first woman trainer to saddle a horse for the Preakness when she sent out Tri Colour Stable's Sir Beau, which had beaten Dancer's Image in the New Year's Handicap at Laurel and had finished second to him in the Governor's Gold Cup. "Don't know whether we can win it, but he's never been better."

Most of the pre-race speculation centered on Dancer's Image. Forward Pass appeared to be a solid horse with little question about him. "He's as good as we can get him and we won't have any excuses," declared a confident Henry Forrest.

On the other hand, Dancer's Image had his right front ankle tapped early in the week, had an injection of cortisone, had not been seen by his regular trainer or assistant trainer since Churchill Downs stewards announced their ruling Wednesday night suspending Lou Cavalaris Jr. and Bob Barnard as a result of finding Butazolidin in post-race urinalysis after the Kentucky Derby.

With Runnymede Farm manager Bob Casey substituting as trainer, Dancer's Image was worked three furlongs in a quick :35⅕ on Friday morning. "He went a little faster than we wanted," reported jockey Bobby Ussery, "but he went real good."

Forward Pass seemed the logical choice for the Preakness and he was installed the favorite at $1.10 to 1; Dancer's Image was the sentimental choice, going off at $1.20 to 1, for he was foaled at Alfred Vanderbilt's Sagamore Farm, not far from Pimlico, and there were many who wanted the gray colt to substantiate his first-place finish in the Kentucky Derby. Next in the betting was Out of the Way at 15-1.

At the start, Forward Pass ducked out with his first jump from the gate, brushing Dancer's Image. It was nothing. Ussery was going to take back on Dancer's Image anyway and Valenzuela immediately straightened out Forward Pass.

Nodouble sprang from the No. 1 post position and burst into the early lead while Valenzuela looked to his right and saw Martins Jig and Ringmaster hustling from their No. 8 and No. 9 gate stalls to get good positions going into the first turn.

Dancer's Image was along the rail, inside of Wood-Pro, Jig Time, and Out of the Way, four horses heads apart and trailing the first five going past the stands the first time.

Martins Jig made it to the turn first, by a slight margin over Nodouble, the latter taking the shorter route along the rail while Ringmaster tracked Martins Jig in third place. Around the turn Forward Pass was running easily in fourth place, four lengths off the pacesetter.

The early pace was nothing such as that of the Kentucky Derby, nothing to set a man waving his handkerchief to slow it down. Martins Jig, with his closest pursuer being Nodouble, raced the first three quarters in fractions of :23, :47⅕, and 1:11. Three years ago Flag Raiser set the fastest early pace in the history of the Preakness (:22⅖, :46, and 1:10⅗), a factor which assisted Tom Rolfe as he passed tiring horses in the stretch.

Meanwhile, Forward Pass coasted along in fourth place, going fairly easily

113

entering the backstretch some three lengths behind Ringmaster and four lengths in front of Yankee Lad, which was leading a pack of horses. Out off the Way stayed just ahead of Dancer's Image, which was bidding his time in seventh place well off the rail going down the backstretch.

"I didn't want him to get right on the fence," Ussery said later, "because I thought it might be a little deep in there."

Passing the half-mile pole, Valenzuela clucked to Forward Pass...nothing urgent, just a suggestion to pick it up. He did. With only casual urging Forward Pass began what appeared to be his move; actually, the leaders may have been coming back to him, for Forward Pass was taking the overland route, passing Ringmaster and then drawing up alongside Nodouble, which had regained a slight advantage over the rail horse, Martins Jig, entering the last turn.

Around the bend it seemed that Forward Pass was hanging in that he did not continue his surge to the front, and Out of the Way was moving at a faster rate on the outside behind him. Valenzuela, however, was going to the lead under wraps.

Meanwhile, Dancer's Image was beginning a little move. Ussery dropped him in on the rail to save ground going around the turn and he seemed about to run over Yankee Lad; Ussery, who rides high anyway, appeared to be standing up near the three-eighths pole and admitted later that he had to check his horse a bit on the turn because of the traffic. Ussery hit Dancer's Image once on the left side and quickly slipped between Yankee Lad and Ringmaster.

Up at the front end, Forward Pass coasted to the lead on the outside of Nodouble and Martins Jig. He was just galloping between the three-eighths pole and the quarter pole. Valenzuela had been criticized for his ride in the Kentucky Derby; it had been said that he had burned up his horse getting him to the leaders at the head of the stretch and had nothing left to withstand the closing rush of Dancer's Image. In the Preakness, Valenzuela brought his horse to the leaders with only mild urging, and at the head of the stretch he had a good deal of horse under him. Valenzuela drew his whip for the first time and Forward Pass spurted into command.

Behind the Calumet horse came Dancer's Image, rolling again after his slight check in the middle of the turn. The gray horse was full of run and he gained momentum. Yankee Lad was along the rail inside of him, Out of the Way was outside of him. Martins Jig and Nodouble were in front of him as Forward Pass began to draw away.

Rounding the elbow, Martins Jig began to tire and Nodouble began to drift out. With his horse full of run, Ussery was thinking of going outside

114

Nodouble, inside of Forward Pass, but Nodouble was going wide on the turn and a small hole opened between Martins Jig and Nodouble, a hole that for a moment approaching the three-sixteenths pole appeared that it might open wider if Nodouble continued to drift. In that split second, Ussery elected to go between Martins Jig and Nodouble.

Willie McKeever, an apprentice boy on Nodouble, at that same moment straightened his horse and the hole did not widen. Too late. Ussery already had pointed Dancer's Image for the opening and in the midst of a powerful run the gray colt's course could not be altered again.

Dancer's Image ploughed into the hindquarters of Martins Jig, bouncing him sideways; Martins Jig's head thus closed the hole even tighter. Joe Culmone started to turn Martins Jig's head toward the rail, but saw Yankee Lad trying to come up through there and was left with no choice but to try to keep Martins Jig straight.

Consequently, the hole just was not there. Dancer's Image created his own trouble when he hit Martins Jig, and Dancer's Image had to make the most of it. The most-of-it consisted of shoving a couple of 1,000-pound horses down the track for 70 yards. To Baltimoreans, it was like watching Alan (The Horse) Ameche crashing through the scrimmage line.

When Ussery made his decision as to a hole, Dancer's Image was running faster than any horse in the race. When Dancer's Image got caught in the switch at the three-sixteenths pole, he was only two lengths behind a fleeing Forward Pass. Had Dancer's Image got through...

"We had just started to get rolling and then I get knocked around for 100 yards," Ussery said after the race. "Oh, I think I'm gonna win it, if I get through."

When Dancer's Image finally bulled his way through, shoving Nodouble out in the track while Martins Jig dropped back, there was an eighth of a mile to go. He was three lengths behind Out of the Way and eight lengths behind Forward Pass. Dancer's Image dug in again and began his third run of the race. Driving hard, he closed the gap, but it was too much. He caught Out of the Way a jump after the wire, losing second place by a head, with Forward Pass coasting home six lengths ahead of this pair. Time for the 1$\frac{3}{16}$ miles was an ordinary 1:56$\frac{4}{5}$, more than two seconds slower than Nashua's track record set in the 1955 Preakness.

The stewards flashed the inquiry sign immediately after the race. Bill Phillips, Triangle Publications chartman, thought he had seen a jockey stand up in his irons at the sixteenth pole; he asked the stewards to check it when they reviewed the films.

Probably the only person, other than Phillips, in the crowd of some

40,000 who noticed what McKeever was doing while Dancer's Image was making his desperate late charge was Nodouble's owner, Gene Goff: "The boy stood up on my horse at the sixteenth pole. Maybe he was trying to pull a Shoemaker."

Immediately after the race, the apprentice rider did not seem to know precisely what happened. "He ran real good, but perhaps I shouldn't have rushed him so early," McKeever was quoted. "I don't think I was involved in any trouble at the top of the stretch." McKeever then suggested Nodouble "was trying to throw a shoe. He bobbled and I started to pull him up."

Close study of the patrol films did not confirm this in the minds of the stewards, who fined McKeever $100 for misjudging the finish line. The race was confusing to other riders.

Culmone was quoted after the race: "My horse tried to duck in at the eighth pole. (Steward Fred Colwill said Martins Jig had a run-out bit, which may have caused the horse's head to be turned in toward the rail.) I couldn't get past Dancer's Image when he went for the hole."

Of course, Culmone already was ahead of Dancer's Image, being one side of the hole.

Ussery was vague. "Some horse crossed in front of me and made me alter my course. I don't know who he was. Then this other horse started knocking me around. I don't know who he was. I really can't say what happened until I see the pictures."

At first viewing, the stewards disqualified Dancer's Image from third, placing him behind Martins Jig, which had finished eighth. They told Ussery to wait until after the ninth race to see the films again when it would be determined whether Ussery would get a suspension for foul riding.

For Dancer's Image's owner-breeder, this was a second, staggering, chest blow. First money in the Kentucky Derby had been withheld when a Churchill Downs stewards' ruling confirmed the chemist's report of the presence of Butazolidin in a post-race urinalysis of a sample from Dancer's Image. Now Dancer's Image had failed to beat Forward Pass in the Preakness, and additionally had been disqualified.

Dancer's Image's loss in the Preakness was bound to ratify in the minds of many that he had been helped in the Kentucky Derby. Fully aware of the vindictiveness of a crowd which had bet at $1.20 to $1 on a loser, Fuller elected to follow his colt back to the barn, walking the eighth of a mile in front of the stands to the gap into the barn area.

As Fuller followed his horse, there were no jeers. People jammed the rail and offered consolation.

"We're with you, Mr. Fuller."

116

"Tough break, fella. Bad racing luck."

"You're the best, Mr. Fuller."

"Hang in there. You'll get 'em in the next town."

"They ganged up on you, Pete. Three or four of them got together and stopped us cold."

Fuller grinned. "Thank you. I really don't know what happened." Fuller checked his horse at the barn, found a slight burn in the area of a stifle, dismissed it as not serious, and inquired if the patrol films of the race might be seen.

Colwill, after reviewing the films with Ussery, invited Fuller into the showing room in the jockey quarters. The head-on shot of the race between the three-sixteenths pole and the eighth pole was rerun several times—in slow motion, backward, forward.

Colwill said he did not believe Ussery should be penalized. When Ussery made his decision, in that split second, the decision was not a bad one—it turned out to be a bad one. Dancer's Image definitely interfered with Martins Jig and justly warranted being placed behind Martins Jig in the order of finish. It was an infraction of the rules of racing.

An infraction of the rules, however, does not always result from bad judgment, or fraudulent intent, or deliberate wrongdoing, or wanton carelessness. The stewards found that Ussery made a split-second decision that was reasonable at the moment he made it, that Dancer's Image was so full of run his course could not be altered again once he was directed to a hole that closed, that Ussery was blameless and would not be suspended.

Did Fuller have anything to say?

"Oh, we have no complaints. This is racing. This is the chance you must take with a come-from-behind horse. We have gotten through the hole before. In other races it has opened up for us; this time it did not. That's just racing."

## Taken

DR. ROBERT. W. COPELAN spends his weekend removing bone chips from horses' knees, watching Ohio State football games, collecting horse paintings by Henry Stull, and trading knives. He picked up a single-bladed Russell Barlow from trainer Dewey Smith; it was rusty and dull, but Smith,

117

still selling after he had sold, advised that sharpening would reduce the knife's value. At Keeneland, Dr. Copelan proudly drew out his new-old Russell Barlow and proceeded through the ritual of cutting off a chew of tobacco. A parking attendant observed this closely. "See ya got one of them Rusty Barlows. Best dollar knife I ever had. Heard some crazy man paid $75 for one just the other day." Dr. Copelan hardly had time to spit.

## Nijinsky And The St. Leger

IN 1851, Queen Victoria was aboard the Royal yacht attending the first of what has become known as the America's Cup races. These challenge affairs, renewed this week off Newport, were begun by Turfman John Cox Stevens, owner-breeder of the celebrated four-mile mare, Black Maria, and president of the old Union Race Course on Long Island. Stevens also was the first commodore of the New York Yacht Club and owner of the schooner *America*, with which he challenged English seamanship to a 53-mile race around the Isle of Wight.

Queen Victoria was said to have dispatched a steamship to get a report on this first race as it was nearing its conclusion. Upon the steamship's return, Queen Victoria reportedly asked the signalmaster, "Are the yachts in sight?"

"Only the *America*, may it please Your Majesty."

"Which is second?"

"Ah, Your Majesty, there is no second."

This apocryphal line has survived the century because it is handy in reporting other sporting events, such as the oldest English Turf classic, the St. Leger, run Sept. 12, at Doncaster for the 194th time.

Had Queen Elizabeth II, represented in the race by her homebred Charlton (Charlottesville—Ibrox, by Big Game), inquired of the Earl of Halifax or any other of the stewards as to the second horse in the St. Leger, the historic response would have been more appropriate.

Although eight horses were asked to race against him, there really was no second to Nijinsky, the Canadian-bred son of Northern Dancer—Flaming Page, by Bull Page, owned by American Charles W. Engelhard. He was the whole of the affair.

Actually, David Robinson's Meadowville (Charlottesville—Meadow Pipit, by Worden) finished second, a length back, with Mrs. Ogden Phipps' Ameri-

118

can-owned Politico (Right Royal V—Tendentious, by Tenerani) another half-length back in third. But these margins were by sufferance.

Along the one mile, six furlongs, and 127 yards of the race, champion jockey Lester Piggott permitted Nijinsky to run only about a furlong, then brought him home with confidence under a hard pull.

The outcome of the race, as we were repeatedly advised prior to its running, "really is just a formality; nothing here can touch him."

Getting to these formalities was an informal adventure for a green man from Scott County, Ky., putting on shoes for his first trip abroad. Duly qualified by birth and attitude as an Out-of-Towner, we encountered difficulty with the plane situation in New York. It was suggested that the jumbo jet would depart at 8 p.m., but the matter of frisking some 200 potential hijackers for hand grenades, and such, delayed boarding for an hour and a half, resulting in congestion on the taxiways that required another two hours before the 17-plane queue inched onto the runway. Once away, dinner was served, a movie was shown (appallingly mis-classified as for mature audiences), and suddenly it was dawn—five hours having been dumped somewhere in the Atlantic.

Arriving at London's Heathrow Airport, we naively hired a car with the intention of driving directly to Doncaster for the day's races. Now for the dullest Englishman, this would be simple indeed.

We encountered trouble at the onset, however, from the moment we realized that 25 years of reflex actions—adequate enough when the steering wheel is on the left and everyone drives to the right—were a serious handicap on the lanes and highways of Britain.

Driving proved to be a matter of stiffling constant terror, occasioned by the sight of apparently driverless cars whizzing by carrying one intent passenger and by negotiating the succession of traffic circles which Christopher Robin calls round-abouts. Then there was the fruitless attempt at reconciling the road map to road signs designating villages and routes omitted from the map.

We circled the airport, making adjustments all the while, visited such places as Slough, Staines, and Heston, several times, and then, with the kind assistance of most courteous petrol station attendants, made our way through Uxbridge, Richmansworth, Watford, and finally happened upon the main, northbound motorway. Briefly, this was not the most direct route and is not recommended.

Once on the motorway for the 180-mile journey north, a degree of confidence returned, for this was comparable to our interstates, with three lanes on both sides of a median. For future American travelers, it is well to know

119

that passing on the left is counted unseemly and will occasion a certain amount of headlight blinking, the polite English equivalent to our own whatthehellareyoudoing, trying to kill somebody?

The motorway cuts through the middle of Britain past Luton, Northampton, Leicester, Nottingham, Rotherham, and Doncaster, on to Hadrian's Wall and Scotland. It slahses through rolling farmland which for hundreds of years had been sectioned only by hedgerows and infrequent plant fencing.

For years we had though that Sir Alfred Munnings overdid it a bit in painting the skies above his racing subjects, but all we saw in England were Munnings' skies. It rained four times within an hour, each shower interspersed with what a weatherman had predicted would be "some bright spots early on."

E. Barry Ryan, wise in the ways of the English Turf, had arranged through the British Bloodstock Agency for our lodging at Wentbridge House, only 11 miles north of Doncaster—if one knows the way. Wentbridge, of course, did not appear on our map and, after a series of inquiries at Doncaster, we headed off on some lanes so narrow that the question of driving on the left became moot—until meeting another car. The preponderance of mini-cars in England is readily accounted for; two Pontiacs could not pass.

Eventually we came upon a two-lane road and abruptly entered Wentbridge, a village of perhaps 15 stone cottages set immediatley upon the roadway, with cattle grazing in neatly clipped pastures just beyond. The Went River is half as wide as Elkhorn Creek; its bridge has been watched from Wentbridge House for two centuries. Wentbridge House is a two-story structure with ivy climbing its stone walls and shingle roof. Smoke from its chimneys promised warmth and hospitality as evening settled in with misty rain and the temperature dropping to 40.

Dick Ratcliff, a big, handsome, jolly man who has been observing English racing for *The Blood-Horse* for the last 21 years, was there with a warm welcome. "Oh, ho—first time, is it? Imagine you'll find things a big different. We'll have a look about tomorrow, but you will join us for dinner now, won't you? Vincent O'Brien, brilliant man, most knowledgeable, and Lester Piggott, our champion rider, and his wife, Susan, daughter of Sam Armstrong, who trains for many Americans..."

Dinner was a feast of melon, veal, potatoes, green beans, eggplant, wine, strong coffee, and the best of racing talk. O'Brien, perennially Ireland's leading trainer, has a quick mind and sure grasp of racing and breeding in both Europe and America, and nimbly jumps from one to the other.

O'Brien said he had been going to Saratoga for some years and had never found it so hot and tiring as last August. "We were hard at it there, looking at yearlings, putting together the Nijinsky syndicate for two nights, then up to Canada to see the Buckpasser colt we got last week for $180,000, then back here to race; finally got away after eight straight days of that sort of thing and took a two-day vacation."

Piggott, Europe's Bill Shoemaker, is reticent to speak, but quick to smile. In a matter of minutes, O'Brien obtained brief but definite appraisals of important horses Piggot had ridden or ridden against: "Nothing special...he's all right...no...bad ride...she may be...he's a nice horse...nothing..."

Piggott had six mounts scheduled for the next day at Doncaster, then was to ride Sunday in France, the next day at Goodwood in England, the next at Atlantic City (aboard Cheval in the United Nations), and on Thursday would be back for the Ayr Gold Cup in Scotland. He asked about Fort Marcy, Mr. Leader, and Red Reality. (At midweek, Piggott canceled his United Nations engagement.)

"Minsky will do," O'Brien said of Nijinsky's 2-year-old half-brother. "He must be rated the tops in Ireland." Nothing was said of Nijinsky, nor the morrow's St. Leger, which Piggott was to win for the fifth time (St. Paddy in 1960, Aurelius 1961, Ribocco 1967, Ribero 1968) and O'Brien was to win again for an American owner, having saddled John McShain's Ballymoss to win in 1957.

A deep and delicious sleep under three blankets was interrupted early Saturday morning by a knock on the door and the appearance of four English papers, hot coffee, and milk equally hot. Ratcliff was cheery and ready to get on to the race course, "traffic you know," and as he whipped his sporty MG onto the road, we began a breath-taking chase to Doncaster.

The St. Leger has been run on the Town Moor (except for shifting about during World War II from Thirsk, to Newmarket, to York) since 1776. The course is 60 feet wide and measures a mile and seven furlongs around, in a pointed-egg shape; the St. Leger field begins on one side near the pointed end, races a flat half-mile and then up a hill.

"I'd say the top of the hill is the best part of 60 feet above the flat; it wouldn't be 80 feet, but it's a good 60 feet," Ratcliff said. "They start the climb up there, and then down they come; it's much steeper coming down than it looks, quite steep, and then from there in it's all on the flat, nearly a half-mile around until they reach the straight, and then 4½ furlongs down to the finish. It's a very fair course. No horse has any excuse for being beaten here, there are no bad-luck stories. If they are good enough, they will win.

"It really isn't one of England's most beautiful race courses. Goodwood is; it is magnificent; you can't see a house, just rolling, lovely country—just

121

beautiful. But this is a good course for the horse. Did you ever see better turf? Right now it is good going; if it were to rain heavily for two hours now, it would not become heavy here, or even soft, might become good-to-soft."

Grazing on the golf course in the vast centerfield were some ponies belonging to the gypsies whose tents and trailers surrounded the carnival equipment, merry-go-rounds and Tiltawhirls and such, which already was in full swing for early arrivals on St. Leger day.

For more than a century, viewing of the last half of the runs for the St. Leger has been obtained from a series of steps under steel-pier-supported roofs, literal grandstands, located well back from the course and parallel to it for the last two furlongs. Last year a modern Members' Club replaced one of the old grandstands at the finish line. It has some seats, two tiers, and a private box section on the cantilevered, pre-stressed concrete roof. It overlooks the new parade ring.

Accommodations for bookmaker stalls were provided on the ground floor in the Members' Club, but the bookies refused to use them, the Tattersalls ring moving out on the lawn, between the Members' Club and weighing room where some 40 brightly painted slates posted varying odds.

Starting odds are fixed by four racing journalists, the chief of whom since 1957 has been Geoffry Hamlyn of *Sporting Life*: "This form of betting has been in existence here for over a hundred years. I don't think anybody else has it; it is a unique system which apparently works only in England.

"We set the starting prices and the prices by which all the off-course bets are settled throughout the country. We starting-price reporters take a composite return; we know all these bookmakers intimately—there are only about a half-dozen that really are worth returning at all—we know these chaps and we take the prices off the good ones, not the bad ones, and we four agree among outselves what we think is a fair return for each individual horse. This is transmitted and accepted by all bookmakers throughout the country and they pay out on what we say.

"By and large, the starting price beats the Tote, because it takes 23 per cent off the top, you see, and it is easy to compete with that sort of deduction, isn't it?"

Bookmakers handle 10 times more than the amount of money wagered through the Tote machines, which apparently appeal only to women bettors. Hill's and other big bookmakers occupy the front line in front of the Members' Club. Tick-tack men, stationed on boxes near the Tattersalls ring, relay the fluctuation of odds as posted by the major bookmakers to other bookmakers in the Silver ring, and these in turn are relayed to other bookmakers

122

operating in front of the grandstands farther up the track and in the infield. David Hedges of *Sporting Life* estimated there were about 140 bookmakers operating that day in various betting rings. The tick-tack men, wearing white gloves, relay odds or layoff money between bookmakers with quick, intricate, precise hand signals; waving off a gnat could cost somebody £1,000.

A goodly portion of the "conjectured" crowd of 30,000 was on hand well before the 2 o'clock post for the first race. It was not as large as those which came to the St. Leger immediately after the war, for the St. Leger has diminished greatly in popularity in recent years. Five football teams were playing at home in Yorkshire on Saturday, commanding most sporting attention. Nijinsky's appearance drew those who came to Doncaster, rather than the race itself.

Phil Bull has gone so far as to suggest that the St. Leger be run at weight for age, open to older horses, to put more appeal into the classic. With first money of $88,977, the St. Leger ranks second only to the Derby among England's richest prizes, but in recent years has not always drawn the best of the 3-year-olds.

O'Brien elected to send Nijinsky in it because it fit well in a training schedule leading toward the Prix de l'Arc de Triomphe, and only incidentally because Nijinsky would become the first English Triple Crown winner since unbeaten Bahram in 1935. If rain had softened the course too much, O'Brien had said he would just as soon ship Nijinsky over to France for the Prix Royal Oak run the next day.

(Old Charlie Smirke, who rode Bahram to victories in the Two Thousand Guineas, Derby, and St. Leger 35 years ago, did not count it significant that Bahram's feat was duplicated: "He was just a good horse in a bad year. Nijinsky is better than Bahram, has more speed and is a bigger horse altogether, but he has not got much class against him either. I know a horse that could have beaten either of them with two legs tied together—Windsor Lad.")

Admittedly, there was not much in the way of credentials among Nijinsky's eight rivals for the St. Leger and he was installed favorite at 2-7. None of the others had won stakes at two and only four had won stakes this season: Meadowville (20-1) had won the Great Voltigeur and Derby Trial at Lingfield, finished second to Nijinsky in the Irish Sweeps Derby, and third when Politico (20-1) had won the Chester Vase, his only stakes victory for Mrs. Phipps. F. R. Hue-Williams' Rock Roi (Mourne—Secret Session, by Court Martial) had won the Warren and Gordon Stakes, finished second to Meadowville in the Great Voltigeur, and his price was set at 33-1. American

123

Lawrence Gelb's Rarity (Hethersett—Who Can Tell, by Worden) had won the Athboy and Desmond Stakes in Ireland, and he was installed at 8-1. The Queen's Charlton, third in the King Edward VII Stakes, was the only other to place in a stakes and he went off at 10-1. Outclassed were Miss P. Wallis' Melody Rock (Sayajirao—Deirdre, by Vimy). H. G. Copsey's Whindamus (Mandamus—Whinberry, by Wilwyn), and Hue-Williams' King of the Castle (Relko—La Montespan, by Tantieme), the last three to get home.

It started out to be a trying day for Piggott. In the first race, he finished second by a nose on the favorite. In the second race, the $2,009 September Stakes, he had the mount on Engelhard's favored Leander, trained by Jeremy Tree; Leander came away from the gate like a bronco, bucking four times before dumping Piggott, who rides extremely high. The St. Leger, third race on the program, was delayed until Leander finally was caught. Piggott took a hard fall, but he is all man and shrugged it off. He appeared in the parade ring for the St. Leger with a large green grass stain on the left side of his riding breeches.

Engelhard shook Piggott's hand. "I commiserated with him," the precious-metals tycoon said, "apologized for the rudeness of Leander. Jeremy says he has been bucking like that at home; we're going to have to teach him to do differently. I don't believe Lester will want to get on him again."

Nijinsky had been led across the four-lane highway, separating the barns from the race course, between two mounted Bobbies and he looked something special, with or without escort. He is a big, handsome bay, with no sign of the much-publicized skin disease which was thought for a while to prevent his running in the St. Leger. He was quiet and composed.

Mrs. Phipps, wife of the chairman of The Jockey Club, was on hand to see her Politico run. E. P. Taylor of Canada, who bred Nijinsky and sold him to Engelhard as a yearling for $84,000, also was in the parade ring. Jimmy Stewart of Hollywood Park flew up from Switzerland; he said he had been president of the Thoroughbred Racing Associations when the last American Triple Crown winner was honored and had presented the trophy to Mrs. Gene Markey for Citation. Champagne Larry Boyce of Maryland, who had said before his Hark the Lark had run last in the Preakness and Belmont that he was prepping the horse for the St. Leger, said Hark the Lark just was not enough horse; he said he had a Citation colt, though, that was a sensation and that he was pointing him for the next year's St. Leger.

Dark clouds had threatened rain for an hour, but as the St. Leger field left the parade ring, walked down in front of the stands, and then "cruised" back across the finish line, the sun cut through to brighten the stage for the 194th running of the St. Leger.

124

In American races, every step of the running is vital, many races being decided right at the break, or by positions reached within the first furlong; pace means nearly everything in American races, a fast one or a slow one being determinative.

In most English races, the St. Leger in particular, what happens during the first 10 or 12 furlongs seems to have no bearing on the outcome. At least there is no interest in the first part of a race. The horses just gallop along, their riders waiting for the important running, which is at the end.

Thus Whindamus and King of the Castle bounded off to the lead and no one much cared. Politico settled into third, followed by Rarity, Charlton, and Melody Rock. Piggott sent Nijinsky away leisurely; he had only Rock Roi and Meadowville behind him for the first mile.

As the field began to climb up the hill in the distance, Whindamus had the lead by three-quarters of a length over King of the Castle, followed by Politico, Rarity, Charlton, Melody Rock, Nijinsky, Rock Roi, and Meadowville. Over the top they went, and then down, out of sight to spectators and to the film patrol.

Looming into view again with a mile of flat to go, Whindamus had drawn out to a 10-length lead over King of the Castle, which was beginning to tire. Politico was still third, followed by Melody Rock, Charlton, Rock Roi, and Rarity. At this point, Nijinsky was 20 lengths back and had only Meadowville beaten.

On the long sweeping turn toward the junction with the straight-mile course, Whindamus began to weaken and Politico closed the wide gap. Melody Rock, Charlton, and Nijinsky began to move up, preparing for the race that would begin when they hit the straight and contest the last half-mile.

Politico took the lead entering the stretch as Whindamus suddenly dropped out of it. Charlton took aim on Politico and Nijinsky was right behind him as Meadowville suddenly came to life. Three furlongs out, Politico had the rail and the lead with Charlton at his flank. Piggott then eased into a comfortable position on the outside of Charlton and bided his time, keeping Nijinsky under wraps until approaching the final furlong pole.

Then, suddenly, Nijinsky spurted forward. In a matter of a half-dozen strides, he passed Charlton and flew past Politico into a commanding lead.

Piggott looked back on his right to size up Meadowville's run, thought it nothing, and wrapped up on his horse, coasting home with a safe length advantage over Meadowville, with Politico third.

Four lengths later came Charlton, four in front of Rock Roi, which finished 2½ lengths ahead of Rarity and Melody Rock, these two separated by a head margin. Whindamus and King of the Castle trailed far behind.

125

As Nijinsky came cantering toward the finish, a polite patter of applause rose from the Members' Club, accompanied by such remarks as "Brilliant," "Yes, indeed," "Awfully nice colt, you know," and this while Nijinsky still was a sixteenth of a mile out with Meadowville close up on the outside of him.

For our money, Piggott was drawing it pretty fine; to the knowing British, Piggott had the thing in his pocket all along, "Ah, much the best. Easiest sort of thing."

Nijinsky's time for the mile, six furlongs, and 127 yards was 3:06$\frac{2}{5}$, a full two seconds slower than the course record set when the race was run five yards farther, but 5$\frac{2}{5}$ seconds faster than Intermezzo's time when he won the classic last year. Time for English races, however, is counted as nothing, mere trivia to be discarded or ignored—like the order of the early running.

We had thought we might get a photograph of Engelhard's champion, perhaps with Engelhard or O'Brien leading him in. Guy Wilmot, director of W. W. Rouch & Co. Ltd., horse photographers, warned that this would require cheek. We had the cheek; it was the muscle we lacked. Long after Nijinsky had been led into the winner's enclosure, we managed to squeeze through the tight throng rimming the fenced semi-circle in front of the stone-pillared weighing room; this was done by closely following a tall, broad-shouldered man, dapper in blue pin-stripe and bowler, obviously a mainstay of the champion Leeds football team. Alas, Nijinsky already was being led away.

Engelhard had been there before, of course, having won the St. Leger with Indiana in 1964, and the American-bred brothers Ribocco in 1967 and Ribero in 1969.

Accepting a silver bowl, Engelhard said, "The horse ought to be here; he did the work. It was an exciting race and indeed a thrill to have such a horse. Once in a lifetime. This is the one. But I'm glad to have this, I'll tell you that, and I certainly am proud to be here. Thank you." Engelhard, accompanied by Mrs. Phipps, Taylor, and Stewart, then was invited into the weighing room to view films of the race.

O'Brien said Nijinsky never looked better, was quite calm, won without difficulty. He said he was headed for the Prix de l'Arc de Triomphe to be run at Longchamp near Paris on Oct. 4, "then we'll take another look at it in regard to racing in America."

Engelhard thought the Man o' War Stakes at weight for age, 1½ miles on the turf at Belmont Park two weeks after the Arc, would be a likely spot. Consideration also is being given the 1¼-mile Champion Stakes to be run the same day at Newmarket; O'Brien had used the Champion two years ago with Sir Ivor as a stepping stone between the Arc and the Washington, D. C., International at Laurel. This year the International will be run on Nov. 11, 3½ weeks after the Man o' War and Champion.

Nijinsky now has won 11 straight races: The Dewhurst, Beresford, Anglesey, Railway Stakes, and an overnighter at two, the English Derby, Irish Sweeps Derby, St. Leger, King George VI and Queen Elizabeth against good older horses, Two Thousand Guineas, and Gladness Stakes this season. In earning $572,919, he has passed Sir Ivor and now ranks second only to Sea-Bird ($645,645) as the greatest money-earner in the history of European racing. He has been syndicated for a record $5,440,000 and is scheduled to stand next spring at A. B. Hancock Jr.'s Claiborne Farm near Paris, Ky.

Is Nijinsky a good horse? The best there is today.

## The Late Show

RARER than a day in June, if, J. R. Lowell is still asking, is a good movie on the Late Show. Thus it was an unexpected pleasure when, because we were slow in shutting off the TV after the news, Will Rogers galloped into the yard, casually slid out of his saddle before his mount stopped, and this was explained as the title came on, "In Old Kentucky."

It is an old, incredible, enthralling story reworked several times in Hollywood, most sumptuously about 30 years ago with Walter Brennan and Loretta Young. It is the story of an attractive young girl left with naught but a farm whose fences have not been painted since the Civil War and a young colt with the Look Of Eagles In His Eyes; next door the fences are white, must have 60 horses in training, trainer wears breeches as if he were a jump-up man; the whole thing comes down to the big race at Churchill Downs and the surly rich guy next door has the favorite, but the old homestead, marital bliss and everything else is riding on the colt with the L.O.E.I.H.E., and you know who has to win this race.

We look forward to the day when Truman Capote and John Huston attack this story, but until then, we will ride with Will Rogers, Bill (Bojangles) Robinson, and Dorothy Wilson. Robinson taps through the kitchen, preparing eggs, biscuits and such: "That's nothing," observes Rogers, "you should see his routine for dinner."

The movie had a historical note: Years before Penny Ann Early was born,

127

Churchill Downs jockeys did *not* refuse to ride against Miss Wilson; at the last minute, Gray Boy's regular jockey took himself off—obviously part of the skulduggery to permit the favorite to win—and Rogers with little trouble gained the stewards' permission to let Miss Wilson ride her own horse.

Then, too, there was the problem of Gray Boy's bad right forefoot; Rogers said he needed rain for a muddy track. A water tower exploded and flooded the track as the field raced into the far turn. Gray Boy, alone, was unperturbed by this catastrophe and Miss Wilson brought him down by a half-length. The sheriff handcuffed Rogers to the fence at the scales, it finally began to rain, Robinson danced away, and that was the end.

Moviemen are now working on "The Reivers," a grand racing story that won William Faulkner's last Pulitzer prize, but they are going to have to come from far out of it to beat "In Old Kentucky."

## A Visit To France

TAKING into consideration the setting in the Boulogne woods of Paris—the distance, shape, elevation, and descent of the course; the size and quality of the field; the anticipation leading up to the race; the number of people who bet and the amount wagered on it; the size of the purse; and the high-fashion style of the assemblage attracted to its runing:

Upon these considerations, the Prix de l'Arc de Triomphe must be counted the greatest race in the world.

To the 49th Arc de Triomphe on Oct. 4, American Charles W. Engelhard sent mighty Nijinsky, unbeaten in 11 starts, the most valuable horse the world has ever known (syndicated two months ago for $5,440,000). Fresh from his triumph in the 1¾-mile St. Leger, in which he became England's first Triple Crown winner in 35 years, the Canadian-bred 3-year-old had trained to the complete satisfaction of Ireland's leading trainer, Vincent O'Brien, and was to be ridden again by England's champion jockey, Lester Piggott.

Professional horsemen and some 5,000,000 Frenchmen who bet the race fully expected Nijinsky to spread-eagle his field. With some $15,000,000 wagered (compared to the American record of $2,625,524 on the Kentucky Derby), Nijinsky was a heavy favorite at 2-5.

In the 15-horse field, Nijinsky's only serious rival was thought to be

128

American Winston Guest's long-striding Gyr, a Kentucky-foaled son of 1965 Arc winner Sea-Bird which had finished second to Nijinsky in the English Derby. Considered the best 3-year-old in France after defeating older horses in the Grand Prix de Saint-Cloud, Gyr was installed second choice at 7½-1. To bet the Tierce in France, one must name the first three in order of finish, and Italy's best 3-year-old, Ortis, winner of the Italian Derby and St. Leger, was installed third choice at 9-1. The rest of the field drew little support, French Derby-St. Leger winner Sassafras being next in the betting at 19-1.

Nijinsky is by Northern Dancer, a stocky, sprint-type horse whose trainer, Horatio Luro, insists was best at 1⅛ miles, but which won a particularly searching Kentucky Derby at 1¼ miles. Nijinsky's distance capacity was suspect until he won the 1½-mile English Derby, 1½-mile Irish Sweeps Derby, and then the English St. Leger at 1¾ miles and 127 yards.

In these three races, Nijinsky merely cantered along the first mile or so, well off the pace, then came with a flashing burst of speed for two furlongs that put away all his adversaries, permitting him to coast home the last furlong.

For the Arc, Piggott was confident (as was everyone with whom we talked—before the race) that this two-furlong burst would suffice; it invariably had theretofore. It was of little concern that Nijinsky trailed early (12th, seven lengths back ascending the hill), or that he was three horses wide going downhill around the turn.

Nijinsky lost the Arc three furlongs from home. He already had begun his two-furlong sprint. With momentum started, he rounded the final elbow and found no room between Blakeney and Beaugency. Piggott had to check his mount—ever so slightly—but check that run he did. As A Chara and Grandier faded, Nijinsky was afforded room to go around Blakeney and commence his run again. Quickly, he moved up from eighth place and took aim on Sassafras, four lengths in front of him. Nijinsky's second run carried him to the front, perhaps by as much as a head a sixteenth of a mile out, but then he hung. Piggott drew his whip and hit Nijinsky twice. Nijinsky drifted left.

In his earlier races, Nijinsky's uninterrupted spurts had carried him to the front by clear margins and his rivals folded; in the Arc, Nijinsky did not gain clear command. Sassafras, incapable of any sudden turn of speed, merely continued on his even pace. France's eight-time leading rider, Yves Saint-Martin, joyously saluted with his whip after crossing the finish with Sassafras a head in front. He had brought down the unbeaten champion.

The full import of the Prix de l'Arc de Triomphe cannot be comprehended by popping over to France for one day and witnessing the race. Just a race it

129

is not. The Arc is the focal point of all European racing, its climax for the season. Further, the Arc serves as one of Paris' major social functions and, consequently, produces an important, elegant fashion showing. Since Charles V moved the royal residence from the Isle of City to the right bank, it has been generally known that Paris cannot be done in a day; we tried to do it in four, and considerable was left unaccomplished.

In the sixth grade Miss Topham introduced us to *Totor et Tristan, le Soldat de Bois*, and this faint reference material surprisingly carried us pretty far. Root words often can be inferred from variant spellings—albeit not always correctly: The countless number of brasserie shops mystified us, for quite obviously very few French women were buying the garment we had in mind; on our second day we learned brasseries sold beer and sandwiches.

The singlemost important traffic law in France is loaded toward the right, that is, drivers to one's right have the right-of-way. This law is strictly observed by nonchalant cabbies to one's right, routinely ignored by daring stunt men on the left, making traffic circles very gamy propositions indeed. There is no discernible flow, or thread, of traffic in the roundabouts or public squares such as the Place de la Concorde. Cars leap forward and screech to a halt eight feet later—at acute, right, and obtuse angles. Meanwhile, an imperturbable policeman with a quick flash of a white glove will stop all cars and beckon an elderly pedestrian off the curb. When the old man has shuffled halfway across, the policeman will flick his wrist, signaling the game to begin: As cars hurtle down upon him, the old man will quicken his step and unleash a rapid succession of expletives addressed to the policeman personally and drivers generally. We were to witness essentially this same scene on three different occasions and, miraculously, each time all parties survived.

We arrived at the Hotel de Crillon in the center of Paris, one of two stone-pillared buildings dominating the Place de la Concorde in which the Treaty of 1778 had been signed and the 13 United States recognized by France. After traveling some 4,500 miles, we walked into the Crillon lobby and found we had never left home. There was New York steward Cal Rainey talking to Jockey Club member Gerard Smith and Hollywood Park's Jimmy Stewart. Louisville insuranceman Ed McGrath and trainer Bowes Bond were struggling over an evening's itinerary with Monmouth's David (Sonny) Werblin, who has all the speed of Silent Screen and more stamina—which is handy in Paris. Whitney Tower of *Sports Illustrated* invited us to go racing at Masions-Laffitte before we could unpack.

In a suburb of Paris, Maisons-Laffitte is a French Keeneland—plus a couple of centuries. It has a 1¼-mile straight grass course beginning out of sight to the right of the old stands and runs parallel to the Seine for a while. The old wooden stands with stucco walls and Burgundy-painted support timbers showing through in Norman style, will accommodate about 2,000 persons.

Behind the stands is a forest of chestnut trees shading what must have been a private chapel. Its Romanesque stained-glass windows and 30-foot-high vaulted ceiling enclose the weighing room; an elaborately decorated fireplace attracts owners and trainers. The tiny walking ring in front of the old weighing room has been abandoned for a larger and treeless new one circled by concrete tiers.

Not more than 2,500 people were on the grounds, perhaps 500 milling about the seatless grandstand; the front lawn immediately emptied after each race. Attendance and on-track handle bear no relation to the healthy purse distribution (averaging $6,456 for each of the seven overnight races on Thursday), this money coming from off-course betting which closes at 1 p.m. each day in tobacco shops all over France.

On Thursday night, the Societe d'Encouragement pour l'Amelioration des Races de Chevaux en France, which directs racing and controls off-course betting in all of France, held a press party at Longchamp. This began with a prepared address by a tall, dignified track official whom Hollywood would have cast as a general in Napoleon's army or a New York head waiter; laudatory in nature, the speech commended the responsibility and perspicacity of the assembled Turf journalists. By custom, a French journalist responded by reading off a series of compliments directed specifically to racing officials who revived Longchamp after World War I and caused the rise of the Arc to its present pre-eminence. Then everybody went for the champagne. Churchill Downs was never like this.

We made a date to visit the training grounds at Chantilly early the next morning with Pierre Franckel, the most prominent racing man in Sweden before World War II when he won the Swedish Derby and who has been reporting French racing for *The Blood-Horse* for many years. Franckel stopped his car a few steps from the front door of our hotel, on the spot where a guillotine ended Louis XVI's way of going in 1793. We drove north for about 45 minutes, into the City of the Horse.

Last year in France, 6,881 horses started. About 5,000 of these raced at the courses around Paris with 3,000 trained at Maisons-Laffitte and the remaining 2,000 at Chantilly.

We stopped in the center of town and walked into Les Aigles, 547 acres devoted to training the Thoroughbred. If a horse cannot show something here, he should be put down as useless.

"This is called the Eagle's Ground," Franckel said of the vastness of unob-

131

structed turf, "where Napoleon trained and paraded his imperial guard." The whole comprises a number of grass courses and dirt tracks, each open on different days, varying in length and shape from a two-mile dirt oval and 1¾-mile grass oval, to 1¼-mile straight on turf and 2½-mile straight on dirt, to a 6½-furlong hurdle course.

Dense hedges and saplings provide verdant, 40-foot walls separating the training paths. Lords of this domain are the trainers whose stable yards and homes ring the training grounds or are located a few blocks away in the city. Sets of 20 horses under the direction of Francois Mathet, who would not speak to a Cabot, Lodge, or Adams—in French, and 83-year-old Willie Head, a most genial man, jogged across the Eagle's Ground to a training path. It was dark, cool, drizzly, and the horses loved it.

The race course at Chantilly is magnificent. From its small, white stands, one can look toward the head of the stretch at one's right where the old chateau (now a state-owned museum), and the huge stables begun by Prince Conde in 1719 and completed in 1735 (now operated as a riding stable and training center for dressage horses), provide the world's most dramatic background from which race horses can emerge. We could not help but stand in awe, accustomed as we were to views afforded at Aqueduct, Miles Park, and Hawthorne.

We crossed a horse bridge, over a train carrying passengers at a 100-mile-an-hour clip, into another forest, in the center of which was a small sandy circle from which an official directed the traffic of horses coming and going along the spokes of race paths extending from the hub.

We met Miguel Clement, who trains Prime Action, a 3-year-old Porterhouse colt, for Reginald N. Webster. Jack Cunnington Sr., who has more than 100 horses in training for American owners, came by with a set of 25 horses. Trainer Albert Klimscha, who has enjoyed considerable recent success with the horses of Countess Batthyany of Germany, said that Sword Dancer, which sired champions Damascus and Lady Pitt while standing at Darby Dan Farm in Kentucky, had arrived at the countess' stud for duty next spring.

We returned to Paris in time to attend class at the Ecole de Tower, offered for bewildered people from Scott County, Ky., a tutoring service by Whitney Tower, who knows racing like Walter Vosburgh and Paris like De Gaulle. Evidence of this knowledge is Tower's reservation of a car and driver for the trip to Saint-Cloud and Friday's races. Paris racing shifts daily from track to track and races are run over different courses at a single track, to preserve the turf. Purses are relatively uniform, and high, at each of the tracks, independent of attendance and handle at each track. (Purses at Saint-Cloud for

132

seven overnight races averaged $6,217.)

Weekday attendance is small, perhaps averaging 2,000; attendance is not published. These are, on the whole, persons genuinely interested in seeing horses race; the type of player who folds the outer pages of the *Racing Form* over the arm of a seat in front of a television monitor in the bowels of Aqueduct does not have to go to the races in Paris, for he can get his action in the tobacco shops in the morning. This effect of off-course betting, dramatically decreasing track attendance, is most enjoyable for a man accustomed to fighting for a parking place, dodging scurrying players, arguing with ushers and waiters, and struggling for survival in the crush of average crowds at American tracks.

Saint-Cloud is the only track in France at which the races consistently are run counter-clockwise as in America. This is one of the reasons the rich Grand Prix de Saint-Cloud, 1¼ miles at weight-for-age in July, was selected for foreign showings of American champions Buckpasser, Arts and Letters, and Assagai (only the latter made the trip; he finished fourth).

Saint-Cloud was built in 1901 and recently was remodeled along lines similar to new Belmont Park, with its brick back and concrete cantilevered roof, but about one-tenth in size. It has only 20 boxes. The track is owned by the Societe Sportive d'Encouragement, as is Maisons-Laffitte, whereas Longchamp, Chantilly, and Deauville are owned by the Societe d'Encouragement. For all the French progressiveness in the mechanical complexities of handling off-course betting, there is no electronic Tote board at the track. Serious players concerned about current odds check small slips of paper, three inches wide, six or eight inches long, on which are scribbled next to the saddlecloth number the odds to win and odds for "place" (comparable to American show betting); these slips of paper are posted from time to time on trees behind the stands and taped to columns and bulletin boards under the stands.

A large number of Americans race horses in France. Training costs were raised 12 per cent last month, up to about $9 a day (some New York trainers are now charging $24); there are no vanning bills, the tracks handling shipping from the training centers to the various race courses. (Saturday's races at Longchamp averaged purses of $11,239; Sunday's six stakes including the Arc involved $570,132, averaging $95,022 a pot, which gives some indication of what off-course betting can do for racing when properly organized and administered by racing men.)

The fourth race Friday at Saint-Cloud was won by New Yorker Murray McDonnell's Mister Snob (two days earlier, McDonnell's Burd Alane had won the Discovery Handicap at Belmont Park) from Texan Bunker Hunt's

133

Clems Match, by Clem. The last race was won by The Yankee Dancer, a son of Native Dancer, owned by Peter Fuller of Boston, from a field which included horses owned by Robin Scully of Lexington, Abram S. Hewitt of New York and other places, and Daniel Wildenstein, France's leading owner who resides in New York.

That night, photographer Jerry Cooke, who has covered sporting events in nearly every major city in the world and can get lost in any of them, volunteered to direct us to Ami Louis, which when finally located proved to be a restaurant 20 feet wide, 100 feet long, inadequately lighted, with mustard-painted walls of early railroad-station-men's-room decor, lightning-quick waiters, and the most delicious food in the world. At the next table was Robert Lytle of California, who raced Correlation a few years ago.

Saturday's races were held at Longchamp. Although we have always been partial to the patterned-stone architecture of Keeneland, the glistening new whiteness of the Longchamp stand which can accommodate 30,000 persons with perfect ease is about the best looking new plant we have seen. It was completed in 1966, a section at a time off on a corner of the track property and then scooted by rail into place without interrupting the race progams.

The feature of Longchamp, unique at present, but certain to be copied by every American track owner concerned about racegoers who want to see the horses, is the oval amphitheatre which can accommodate 18 rows of persons with a close view of horses in the walking ring. Some 7,000 persons ringed the paddock when the field for the Arc was paraded.

On Saturday, the final, straight three furlongs of the Arc course was fenced off with a temporary rail. The 1½ miles of the Arc is begun at the far left with the gate stationed in front of a windmill that survived several centuries of storms but was damaged by World War II bombings. The field races a straight six furlongs, the first two furlongs of which are flat; French racing rules prohibit horses from crossing over during this initial first quarter. The Eiffel Tower, rising about the Bois de Boulogne, provides a sight-line from the stands where the half-mile climb begins; the ascent, much of which is hidden from spectators by a solid clump of trees (the public address announcer calls the order "approaching the woods" and, after a pause, the order "emerging from the woods"), amounts to a 33-foot elevation above the level of the homestretch. At the peak of the rise, the horses begin a right-hand turn for a quarter-mile, all downhill, then hit the flat for a run of one furlong that is virtually straight, to the last small turn into the three-furlong straight to the finish line. This course has tested the best horses in the world since the Arc first was run in 1920.

By Sunday, the number of arrivals from America gave rise to concern as to who was minding the store. Hollywood Park president Mervyn LeRoy worked the Arc into a trip on which he was to accept movie awards in France and England. Atlantic City president Bob Levy arrived with results of the Matchmaker Stakes, New York Handicapper Tommy Trotter with news of the Woodward. Charles Engelhard's American trainer, Mack Miller, and Rokeby Stable trainer Elliott Burch flew in, as did trainers Angel Penna, Jack Weipert, and Horatio Luro (who trained Nijinsky's sire and dam). Also present: Laurel's John Schapiro, who issued invitations to the Washington, D. C., International (declined for Sassafras; no decision yet for Nijinsky; yes for Park Top, England's Horse of the Year last season); Raymond Guest and E. P. Taylor who spoke at Marcel Boussac's traditional black-tie dinner at Maxim's on the eve of the Arc; Leslie Combs II and A. B. Hancock Jr. of Kentucky, Reginald N. Webster, Mrs. Richard C. du Pont, and the John Butlers of Maryland; W. R. (Fritz) Hawn, on hand to see his horses race and accompanied by Eddie Read of Del Mar; Col. and Mrs. Cloyce Tippett, Maj. C. C. Moseley, Mrs. F. E. (Jimmy) Kilroe of California ("I told Jimmy for heaven's sake—don't keep those home fires burning"); Eugene Constantin of Dallas, whose colors in France are the white and green hoops of Col. E. R. Bradley's Idle Hour Farm; Wendell P. Rosso of Virginia, whose Bold Fascinator, a $120,000 Bold Lad filly purchased at last year's Keeneland summer sale, finished third in the important Criterium for fillies; Peter Fuller, who raced a half-sister to Dancer's Image the day before the Arc, and Dr. Joe O'Dea, president of the American Association of Equine Practitioners who flew over for the Arc from a veterinary symposium in England with a crowd of vets.

In sharp contrast to the sparse weekday crowds, an estimated 65,000 persons came to Longchamp on Arc day. And they came dressed to the teeth. Now, confessedly there are horsemen with a keener, more practiced eye for a horse, but we bow to no man as a critical judge and admirer of stunningly attired attractive women. The thought came that cost of the dresses and outfits, including some originals, in and around the paddock quite possibly exceeded the value of the horses—Nijinsky's syndication not excepted. Fashion photographers were all over the place, pausing only briefly for some candid shots of Omar Shariff and his long-curled companion, popular singer Antoine, but primarily concerned with the midi outfits, big-brimmed hats, boots and tucked-in gaucho pants, which have pushed mini skirts into total eclipse in Paris.

An increasing number of American owners have looked at our tax legislation, training cost-purse earnings ratio, strife between racing organizations, stall allotments, and racing facilities, and compared these with the French tax-free gambling winnings and purse earnings, lower training costs, marvelous training and racing facilities, and have decided the French style of racing is more enjoyable than ours.

The French style of racing, of course, is essentially set by Marcel Boussac (textiles, Christian Dior), president of the Societe d'Encouragement, and this organization runs a taut ship under the directorship of Jean Romanet, an amalgam of Marshall Cassidy, Jimmy Kilroe, Everett Clay, and George Smathers.

At any rate, among the Americans who completely enjoyed French racing on Arc day was Lou Doherty, owner of The Stallion Station near Lexington, where Sir Ribot stands. The $50,220 Criterium des Pouliches drew a dozen of France's best 2-year-old fillies for one of their most important tests at a mile. Doherty watched as his Two to Paris (Sir Ribot—Running Account, by Tuleg) was saddled by Jack Cunnington Sr. in the race preceding the Arc. It was her second start and she went off at 27-1; Rosso's Bold Fascinator was 8½-1, and Howell Jackson's Take a Chance (Baldric—Never Too Late, by Never Say Die) closed at 12-1. Two to Paris came back a winner by a half-length, a performance which may place her tops among the fillies on the year-end Handicap Optional. Doherty rented a Paris apartment. Tension mounted after the Criterium des Pouliches as the horses for the Arc were saddled out of sight in the receiving-barn area and a full house stared almost in silence for 30 minutes at a horseless walking ring.

Then they came. Gyr (Sea-Bird—Feria, by Toulouse Lautrec) pranced into the ring, nervous, already broken out, giving his handler fits; he is 17 hands tall with a disproportionately small head. The Italian champion, Ortis (Tissot—Orientale, by Nagami), seemed almost as tall, with a thick neck and much heavier than Gyr; he is a liver chestnut with dark spots, like Arts and Letters, and Elliott Burch noted that he had the right coat. Nijinsky, four inches taller than his sire at 16.2 and rangier in build ("like his dam," said Horatio Luro), seemed calm and composed, but his rider, Piggott, said later that he was a trifle excited by the crowd surrounding the walking ring. At the time, there seemed no real reason to study the others. After the parade in front of the stands, Gyr was galloped off and displayed a stride that challenges comparison; that big chestnut surely must go in 30-foot bounds. But his long stride was to no avail in the Arc; his rider was to say that Gyr ran his race before entering the starting gate.

Both Gyr and Ortis had entrymates calculated to set an honest pace. Guest leased Prix Ardan winner Golden Eagle (Right Royal V—Aquilla, by Nasrullah or Princequillo) from his sister, Mrs. Allan Manning, to run with Gyr. Lar, which had won five consecutive overnighters in Italy and had been

136

coupled with Ortis in the Italian Derby and St. Leger, took the early lead from Golden Eagle soon after the start of the Arc. Saint-Martin got Sassafras away third, then came Ortis, Blakeney, Miss Dan, Beaugency, Soyeux, A Chara, Gyr, La Bijute, and then Nijinsky 12th, beating only Quinqueut, Grandier, and Stintino, which was left at the post (his owner is Irishman Gerald Oldham, who spent 1950 rubbing horses at Claiborne Farm in Kentucky: "When Nasrullah arrived at Claiborne, I took care of him; very difficult horse to handle, bad tempered, did not care for anybody to clean out his feet.")

Lar and Golden Eagle led the way up the hill with Sassafras running easily in third. Miss Dan followed in Sassafras' tracks, two lengths further back; Gyr was to drop in behind her, while Nijinsky dropped into the same file, 12th, seven lengths off the pace.

At the top of the hill, the field swung right and Piggott took Nijinsky three horses wide while Saint-Martin had Sassafras on the rail during the quarter-mile downhill run around the turn. Leveling off for a straight furlong run, Lar began to fold and Miss Dan challenged Golden Eagle for the lead with Ortis to her right, forming a three-horse wall which prompted Saint-Martin to take Sassafras off the rail and to the outside of Ortis. Gyr had good position and was no more than three lengths off the leaders. Nijinsky was blocked behind the fading Lar, Beaugency, and Blakeney—ninth, five lengths back, and beginning his run.

At the final turn into the homestretch, with three furlongs to go, Piggott checked Nijinsky slightly as no hole appeared between Beaugency and Blakeney (Piggott said later this momentary check had no bearing on the race). Then as A Chara and Grandier swung wide, Nijinsky finally was freed to move up and around the outside of Blakeney; he spurted forward.

Miss Dan had taken the lead along the rail, Gyr had not a straw in his path, and Sassafras was inching to the front when Nijinsky ranged up alongside of him with 1½ furlongs to go. Nijinsky got his head in front. O'Brien, Hancock, and Taylor, all watching from a point a sixteenth of a mile from the finish, saw Nijinsky get the lead; it occurred to no one in that section of the stands that he could lose it. But he did. Piggott hit him twice and Nijinsky drifted off into defeat.

In time of 2:29.7, only a fraction slower than the course record 2:29 flat set in last year's Arc by Levmoss, Sassafras won first money of $248,364 by a head margin over Nijinsky, whose second money of $86,400 raised his total earnings to $659,319, surpassing Sea-Bird's previous European record of $645,645.

The game filly Miss Dan, which had relinquished the stretch lead only af-

137

ter an extended duel, finished two lengths back in third for a $43,200 prize, and 1½ lengths in front of Gyr, which picked up $21,600 fourth money.

Others in order of finish were: 5th Blakeney, by a short head; 6th Beaugency, by two; 7th Soyeux, by three-quarters; 8th Quinquet, by four; 9th Grandier, by a neck; 10th A Chara, by three-quarters; 11th Ortis, by 1½; 12th Stintino, by 10; 13th Golden Eagle, by eight lengths over the early leader, Lar, with La Bijute eased.

Thus, Nijinsky suffered his first defeat, to an even-running 3-year-old not previously considered the best in France. The thought persists that Nijinsky would beat Sassafras the next nine times they met, but there is only one renewal each year of the Prix de l'Arc de Triomphe. Voila.

## In Good Order

A month ago we flew to Paris to see Nijinsky II. This week we drove, for Paris, Ky., is only 25 miles down the pike and Nijinsky II had arrived at A. B. Hancock Jr.'s Claiborne Farm Tuesday night.

Kentucky on a fall afternoon is better than color TV. October rains have kept paddocks green and these are framed by white plank fences and rows of maples and chestnuts waving pompons of bright yellow, red, and orange against gray skies.

On the Paris Pike we drove by what once had been the Old Hickory Farm of Col. Phil T. Chinn ("Never sell a Zacaweista mare, never buy one by Crusader") and the Longridge Plantation of Col. W. V. Thraves, winner of the Madden Cup (presented by John E. Madden, along with co-sponsors Chinn and A. B. Hancock Sr., in tribute to the horse seller "who has out-hornswoggled each of us at least once.")

Then the glistening white, new Kentucky Training Center with its tall Corinthian columns, then a field of John R. Gaines' weanlings behind the old stone fence that continues along the frontage of Mrs. Charles Payson's and John Hay Whitney's Greentree Stud, with Maxwell Gluck's Elmendorf Farm and E. Barry Ryan's Normandy Farm on the other side.

The Paris Pike then runs between T. Alie Grissom's red and white Duntreath Farm and the black plank fences of Dr. Charley Hagyard's farm, where stands America's new leading sire, Hail to Reason. Bold Ruler, leader for the last seven consecutive years and again this season through September racing, dropped back to second place when Hail to Reason's Personality won the Woodward and his Limit to Reason picked up rich prizes in the Champagne Stakes and Pimlico-Laurel Futurity.

Claiborne Farm begins at the Paris city limits. We stopped at the office and asked to see Bold Ruler. We walked by the stallion barn that houses champions Buckpasser and Tom Rolfe; Herbager has Princequillo's stall, Hawaii has Nasrullah's, and Pretense has the one in which we last saw Blenheim II.

In a paddock lined by an eight-plank fence and honeysuckle, 16-year-old Bold Ruler raised his head to inspect an intruder leaning on his gate. He snorted. Bold Ruler still has a trachea tube in place, but Dr. Walter Kaufman, resident Claiborne veterinarian, estimates he uses his nostrils for 85 per cent of his breathing. Since his return last month from Auburn and cobalt treatments for cancer, Bold Ruler has regained some weight. He stared for a moment, then wheeled and cantered off, as if to demonstrate his fitness.

In Bold Ruler's barn, brass plates indicate stalls for Round Table, Bold Lad, Sir Ivor, Sir Gaylord; there is a door without a name plate. One is being made for Nijinsky II.

At present, Nijinsky II is stabled at the Xalapa Training Center of Claiborne, 10 miles farther into Bourbon County, in the magnificent stone barn the late Ed Simms designed by drawing the plan in sand with his cane.

Luther Jones led out Nijinsky II for inspection. We can add nothing by way of description to Richard Stone Reeves' painting. "We put him out in the paddock for three hours this morning," Jones said. "Had 31 men out there, you know, so he wouldn't run any place. I led him around couple of times on a shank, let him put his head down and pull on some grass; then I let him go. He just kept on eating."

The world's most costly Thoroughbred (syndicated for $5,440,000 last August), this week voted England's Horse of the Year, had arrived in Kentucky in good order.

## Affair To Remember

IT is an easy thing to have an affair with Saratoga. One knows at the onset that it will last only a week, the month of August at the most, before return to the cares and responsibilities of everydayness. But for a fleeting time, problems of a troubled world seemingly are arrested while the racing man

139

directs his attention to such things as the way the Hail to Reason—Affectionately filly goes behind, the quality of Hand melon, the size of the Travers field, getting a seat for the sales, the proper time to leave the Hollywood Park cocktail party on the Reading Room lawn to get to the steeplechase affair under a pink-striped tent in Mrs. A. C. Randolph's yard, the William Woodward collection of Herrings and Stubbses exhibited at the National Museum, the dearth of handicap horses, the schedule for the Saratoga Performing Arts Center, the space problem in a box caused by wide-armed wicker chairs substituted for bentwood numbers—a fleeting, delicious time when one can enjoy the luxury of trivia swelled into importance.

An affair with Saratoga can begin at an unlikely hour, 6:30 on Saturday morning at Oklahoma, the training track across East Avenue from the sale yards. In adjacent barns are horses of Wheatley Stable and Ogden Phipps trained by Eddie Neloy, the horses of Charles W. Engelhard trained by Mackenzie Miller, the horses of Paul Mellon trained by Elliott Burch. The next barn houses the Hobeau Stable, so named because Jack Dreyfus thought it had the casual lilt of a man of the road. Pigeons swirled over the barn; trainer Allen Jerkens hates them, certain they have kept his horses from winning; it would seem that the head of the NYRA, who with a wave of his hand converted the blacktop of Aqueduct into a park, could keep pigeons away from his barn.

Activity on the walking ring at the Rokeby barn began at 5:30. Burch checks the ankles of a chestnut filly that has a white umbrella between her eyes; she is by Exbury and cost a record sum as a weanling in England two years ago; named Canterbury Tale, she made her first start early in the meeting, finished nowhere, promises to improve. She is followed by another 2-year-old filly, a bay by Ribot—All Beautiful, and thus a full sister to champion Arts and Letters; she is named Fairs Fair, and won her only start impressively.

Breakfast on the clubhouse terrace is crowded, busy, and the melon disappointing. Gov. Nelson Rockefeller, in town for Eugene Ormandy's birthday celebration at the Saratoga Performing Arts Center, did not show for breakfast. Breeders from Virginia, Kentucky, Florida did, and there were families from Troy and Albany. Racing secretary Tommy Trotter says the astounding increase in attendance and handle at Saratoga must be due in part to population explosions in Albany and other nearby towns. Another factor might be that many upstate families are skipping vacation trips this summer, taking in events near home; ballet at the Performing Arts Center also had a record attendance.

State steward Francis Dunne, fight referee, happened by. In the first race

140

of the previous day, Eddie Belmonte, Puerto Rico's Tod Sloan (dandy rider, dandy dresser), thought he had a 9-1 field horse home until Jacinto Vasquez pressured him a little at the head of the stretch with a first-time starter, then went on to win, Belmonte finishing third. At Saratoga, the jockeys weigh in in front of the stand, walk through the clubhouse and paddock to return to the jocks room; Belmonte caught up with Vasquez in the paddock, rapped him smartly about the head and shoulders, for which the stewards gave him the meeting; Vasquez continued the thing in the jocks room, which cost him a $250 fine.

Dunne said being a steward was not like it used to be 40 years ago at Agua Caliente: "Of course, the name itself means if you're there, you're in hot water. But we had a perfect rule book—nothing printed in it. Somebody wanted to do something, all you had to say was it was against the rules. Nowadays, everybody has his lawyer with him to be sure it's all right to say good morning, and they all want you to show them where it says something in the rule book. In Mexico, all we had to say was it was against the Agua Caliente rules and that was the end of it."

On Saturday morning, lookers were few in the sales yards. Yearlings still were arriving by van, nervous about new surroundings, and some consignors, talking about it, were worrying still about flooring in the tack room to keep dust down for their help. Mrs. Cloyce Tippett had flower pots and a fuchsia sofa ready for lookers at her consignment.

Highlight of the racing program was the 43rd running of the Whitney. Favored was H. Carl Vandervoort Jr.'s 4-year-old Pleasure Seeker, winner of the Hollywood Gold Cup and second by a head in the Brooklyn to Bill Perry's syndicated Bold Ruler colt, Dewan, second choice for the Whitney. Third choice was Meadow Stable's homebred Hydrologist, which finished less than two lengths back, in third place, in the Brooklyn two weeks ago. With the exception of Nodouble, the Whitney had about the best of the East's handicappers, such as Haskell winner Gladwin, last year's Whitney winner Verbatim, Gleaming Sword, Red Reality, and such. Among these was 3-year-old Judgable, overlooked at 28-1 by nearly everybody except Saul Nadler, who claimed him for $15,000 last December, and his son Herbert Nadler, who trained him.

Bobby Woodhouse got Judgable away from his No. 10 post position in a hurry and crossed over to the lead before the field got to the first turn. No one thought much about this, because Judgable often goes to the front, then dies when something looks him in the eye; when Silent Screen caught him in the mile Saranac, Judgable faded to fifth. So no one really cared much when Judgable drew out to an easy three-length lead going down the backstretch. Mike Phipps' Argentine-bred Dorileo, a field horse, ran at the leader around the last turn and was turned back easily. Nothing else tried until it was too late.

Judgable had been permitted to run by himself on the front end four weeks ago and had come home an easy winner in the Dwyer Handicap. The same thing happened in the Whitney. Hydrologist came up with a big run from last place, but it concerned only second place, which he got by a nose over Dewan, another nose in front of Verbatim, all three older horses finishing three lengths behind Judgable.

Victory at nine furlongs added a new dimension to Judgable, a son of speedy Delta Judge, for although he was getting seven pounds, he was carrying equal weight by scale against leading older horses.

In old Saratoga, Saturday racing was followed by dinner at Edgar Wooley's Grand Union Hotel, presided over by Victor Herbert, who was engaged for the season at a storied salary (usually lost at the races) to conduct evening concerts in the Grand Union's garden on Broadway. This week, Saturday racing was followed by dinner at Siro's, just outside the clubhouse gate, with the evening's music provided by the Saratoga-Potsdam chorus and Philadelphia Orchestra conducted by Eugene Ormandy. Seated on the lawn of the Performing Arts amphitheater, listening to Vladimir Ashkenazy handle Chopin and Ravel on the piano, one is struck by the thought that the only thing missed with the passing of the Old Grand Union evening is the proprietor's son, Monty.

Sunday morning, misty and early, Mrs. Ethel Jacobs, her son Tommy, and daughter Patrice, were in the trainers stand near the six-furlong pole when son John brought out the winner of the Preakness, Wood Memorial, and Jersey Derby. Personality worked seven furlongs in 1:25: "Impressive," noted the clocker. "Pretty good for him," said John Jacobs.

Trainer Mike Freeman, who breezed Whitney Stone's Shuvee five furlongs in 1:01⅕, talked with Alfred Vanderbilt. "Looks like a three-horse Travers—Personality, Judgable, and Jimmy Conway's horse."

About that time, Conway arrived, parking his Volkswagen next to some Rolls and Cadillacs. He had spent a pleasant Saturday afternoon at Monmouth Park, saddling Saddle Rock Farm's Twice Worthy to win the $100,000 Monmouth Invitational and close the meeting.

A son of Ambiopoise, Twice Worthy was started only once by Conway last year at two, and was beaten 22 lengths when Silent Screen broke his maiden at Saratoga. Thus there was little form on the colt when the late Robert Lehman's racing stock was dispersed last winter and Conway got him for Saddle Rock on an $18,000 bid.

142

This season, Twice Worthy has started four times: He won a maiden race by seven lengths in June, next broke a 1 1/16-mile turf record at Aqueduct in winning an allowance by five lengths, next equaled Delaware Park's 1 1/16-mile dirt record in winning the Rosemont Stakes by nearly four lengths, and then clipped two-fifths of a second off Monmouth's 1 1/8-mile record winning the Invitational by four lengths.

Smiling as congratulations were thrown to him by trainers and exercise boys, Conway said, "Kinda caught some lightning in a bottle." The implication was that it did not happen often, which was a modest and happy lie for Conway, who has been developing important horses for more than 30 years.

Down an oiled path on which cars are not permitted until after training hours, sets of horses are walked to and from the main track. At Donald Ross' barn, trainer Buddy Raines had a big roan colt grazing at the end of a shank. "This is my pink horse," Raines explained. He is from the last crop sired by gray Native Dancer and is the first foal out of gray champion handicap mare Open Fire, she by gray Cochise.

"Had Cochise out in Chicago, win the Arlington Handicap with him," Raines began as though 20 years ago were only last week, "and I'm 6-5 to win the Washington Park Handicap with him when Mr. Ross calls me to ship up here for the Saratoga Cup because he thought it was good to support the meeting here. Well, the Saratoga Cup was 1 3/4 miles, and the race was only $11,000 or something, so we skipped that $100,000 in Chicago and come up here and the gray horse won the Saratoga Cup and I guess it was the most satisfying thing we ever won." Which covered such territory as Greek Song beating Bed o' Roses in the Arlington Classic, and Greek Song's son, Greek Money, beating Ridan in the Preakness, and Cochise's daughter, Open Fire, beating Summer Scandal and Old Hat in the Spinster. What about this 2-year-old colt?

"Well, I don't know, Haven't breezed him yet. He gallops faster than the average horse can run. Thought we'd wait on him; he's 16.2, must weigh close to eleven hundred pounds, have to keep a club handy to keep him off or he'll walk all over you. But if you try to do anything with a colt growing this fast, you come up with knees, or splints, or something that will get you nothing. He'll be along. He's pink, isn't he?"

Activity picked up at the sales yards. Lookers were everywhere, some with an intent to buy, some to talk: "Do you really think they will get off-track betting started? Maybe we can get the casinos going again here."

"Old-time racing is a thing of the past. You know what's wrong with the NYRA? The people who own it are all nice people, all successful in their own businesses, but they don't have any money in the NYRA. They have

$50 worth of stock they can't sell. That's why they won't fight anything—they don't have any money in it. When they went non-profit, they hung up their gloves."

"Now my daddy raised a real race horse." This is Ben Ferguson of Kentucky talking. "Billy Barton won the Cuban Derby on the flat, then he killed a man and they ruled him off. But he came back as a jumper.

"And I mean a jumper. In the English Grand National, he cleared not only Becher's Brook, but Jolly Roger who was hung there; old Billy was squeezed between horses on both sides of him, so he just cleared the fence, and Jolly Roger. Had the lead at the last jump, but the boy wouldn't let him have his head when he came down, and he stumbled, boy came off; he got back up, though, finished second by a half-length. Now old Billy was a great horse, I'll tell you."

Stories spun in the Spuyten Duyvil garden next to the sales yards at Saratoga in August have the soothing affect of a log fire in December, lulling a listener into a comfortable state easily misconstrued by a casual passerby.

These stories seldom are encumbered by fact. Thus, old-time champions run faster, steeplechasers jump higher, and trainers appear craftier than those of today.

Billy Barton did not clear Mrs. Payne Whitney's Jolly Roger hung on the fence at Becher's Brook: It was Easter Hero which had landed on the fence, and at the Canal Turn; Billy Barton jumped over rail, ditch, fence, and Easter Hero, but more than half of the field of 42 did not.

Easter Hero had been purchased two weeks before the race by Alfred Loewenstein, Belgian millionaire and gentleman rider, and was installed fourth betting choice at 11-1. Howard Bruce of Baltimore owned American-bred Billy Barton, 10th choice at 33-1. Harold Kenyon's Tipperary Tim, at 100-1, was the longest shot in the biggest field ever assembled for the Grand National up to that time. (There were 66 in the field the next year when Easter Hero finished second for John Hay Whitney.)

Approaching the eighth jump—which consisted of a rail, ditch, and fence, immediately followed by an absolute right-angle turn to the left, if one wished to avoid the canal which parallels the course for the next four jumps—Easter

Hero had the lead, closely followed by Billy Barton, Grakle, Darracq, and Maguelonne.

Easter Hero either took off too soon, or slipped on the rain-soaked turf, but he landed on top of the fence and slowly slithered back into the ditch. With a prodigious leap, Billy Barton cleared him, but two or three horses behind him were pulled up sharply. Easter Hero scrambled out of the ditch and proceeded to wander back and forth for a while, thoroughly discouraging all others from making an attempt at the obstacle.

As a result, the field suddenly was reduced to 11, with Billy Barton leading the survivors. Only two were left with riders to rise to the 30th and final jump and when Billy Barton stumbled as he landed, Tipperary Tim remained to amble home alone. T. Cullinan remounted Billy Barton and completed the course 30 seconds later, the winning margin being declared a "distance."

After the yearling showing under the awning of the walking ring, about a thousand people moved over to the Saratoga Golf Club for the Fasig-Tipton cocktail party that annually gets the sale week into full swing. The talk continued.

"What do you imagine the Bold Ruler—Luquillo filly will bring? Hirsch Jacobs turned down $200,000 for her as a weanling, I heard."

"I was never stroking the ball so well, one over par after 14 holes, and these doctors I'm playing begin to get these messages, you know, urgent calls, see, from the clubhouse. I said now fellas, just hold those emergencies till we finish the eighteen. Kept them right there, came in with a 73. Won four operations."

Sunday night the C. V. Whitneys shifted the Gideon Putnam Hotel Terrace Room back into another era with a dinner taken from a United States Hotel menu dated August 1895. The ladies wore boas and bows; James P. Mills came in a yellow checkered suit complete with false mustache, while George Poole showed in tails, snappy vest, and sundry items he estimated as amounting to forty pounds overweight. There was considerable picture taking, society editing, and dancing to Burt Bacharach tunes until two in the morning.

A very few hours later, many of the same people were on hand for Hall of Fame installation ceremonies at the National Museum of Racing. Among those elected this year were unbeaten American Eclipse, foaled in 1814; Sam Purdy, who rode him in his famous match race against Sir Henry; Gilpatrick, who rode champion Boston in the 1840s, Lexington in the 1850s, Kentucky to win the first Travers in 1864, and Ruthless to win the first Belmont in 1867. None of these had the patience to wait around for a century to attend the ceremonies, so John A. Morris was on hand to accept their plaques; his great-grandfather bred and owned Ruthless, and Gilpatrick wore the all-scarlet silks that Pete Anderson wore when he booted home Morris' Missile Belle in this year's CCA Oaks.

Marion Van Berg, America's leading owner for the last 10 years, flew in from Omaha to hear himself described as representing the mainstream of racing and to be inducted into the Hall of Fame as a trainer. Frank (Dooly) Adams, eight-time leading steeplechase rider, was up from South Carolina to accept his plaque, owner-breeder Ogden Phipps and trainer Eddie Neloy representing Buckpasser. Neloy said: "Every sport has its stars. Buckpasser was a star that never missed a curfew, never had a contract dispute, and always showed up for training."

Among the new pictures on display in the museum are those of the William Woodward collection borrowed from the Baltimore Museum. These included such sporting masterpieces as John Sartorious' Darley Arabian, John Wooton's Godolphin Arabian, George Stubbs' Eclipse with Mr. Wildman and sons, and Stubbs' Diomed, and sundry Herrings. As Capt. O'Kelly bet him two centuries ago, "Eclipse first—the rest nowhere." But then, there are racing men who would take John Herring's pictures first.

Favored for Monday's Saratoga Special across Union Avenue from the museum was Charles Engelhard's $60,000 Raise a Native colt, Raise Your Glass, which had dead-heated with Gedney Farm's Tamtent in the Tremont in June. Second-choice was Edward Sawyer's tough little Three Martinis, winner of the Great American. Raise Your Glass bounded away at the start as though he had beaten the gate, breezing the first quarter in :22, the half in :45⅕. Three Martinis caught the chestnut colt at the head of the stretch and would not let go, the two drawing away from Tamtent by nine lengths. At the wire, Three Martinis got the money by a head, with six furlongs in 1:10⅘.

"At this time of year, 2-year-olds should be running six furlongs in eleven and change," E. Barry Ryan said. "The track is about three-fifths of a second too fast." Ryan was ready with answers for steeplechasing's problems: "First off, make the brush championship, the Temple Gwathmey, and the hurdle championship, the New York Turf Writers Cup, weight-for-age races rather than handicaps. Next I would divide the jumping season three ways—from

146

March 12 to May 1, then move them all out of New York, give those 200 stalls to the flat runners. Let the jumpers race here at Saratoga, and come into New York again from Oct. 16 to Dec. 12. See, there always is trouble filling flat races early and late in New York, so a jumping race on the card could help there; the stall situation becomes very critical in the summer and moving the jumpers out—to Monmouth or Delaware or the farm—would be a big help. You might hear some talk that they couldn't get their horses ready by March or the ground might not be good in December, but the steeplechase season in Europe starts in the fall and ends in the spring."

At the Hollywood Park cocktail party after Monday's eighth race, the Godolphin Darley, French newspaperman, breeder, and bloodstock agent, was talking about the success of off-track betting in France: "It can only go with gimmick betting. It will never become widely popular with straight betting, winning four dollars for two. In France we have the Tierce, on which a man can bet 60 cents and win maybe ten thousand if he picks them one-two-three. The most important aspect of the French system is that the off-course betting is operated by the tracks, and an adequate portion of the handle goes to the tracks to provide good purses. The greatest danger in having big betting payoffs is the inducement to fix races. That really is the big problem with off-course betting, keeping the races honest."

The crowd at the Hollywood Park party shifted almost en masse to Mrs. A. C. Randolph's party, a mile away on Caroline Street, when the rains came. They watched from under a tent as steeplechase champions Neji and Bon Nouvel, flown into Saratoga just for this party, were paraded while Humphrey Finney announced their accomplishments.

## Filling The Void

ABOUT eight centuries ago, King Richard and some friends were crusading through the Gaza Strip on big horses which could trot and sometimes canter with 450 pounds of armored knight up. By and by some Bedouins showed up wearing sheets and ran rings around the Europeans, night and day, with little dish-faced horses weighing no more than 900 pounds and standing 14½ hands tall. Well, in no time at all, two or three centuries, the English caught on about these desert horses and began to import them to England, identifying them by their point of departure, Arabs from Arabia,

147

Turks being Arabian-descent from Turkey, Barbs being Arabian-descent from the Barbary Coast and Moorish Spain. Infusion of the Eastern strains began to produce a blooded horse in England which had speed and stamina; trials as to this speed became more numerous and more interesting, and by 1727 John Cheny began to make a record of such races run for prizes worth 10 pounds or more. In 1743 Cheny began to include some pedigrees and these were a primary source for James Weatherby Jr. when, in 1791, he published *An Introduction to a General Stud Book*. While all registered Thoroughbreds today trace in tail-male line to the Byerly Turk (1680-96), Darley Arabian (1700-33), or Godolphin Arabian (1724-53), the purebred Arabian has more or less been distanced by the Thoroughbred. H. Keene Richards imported some Arabians before the Civil War, bred them to top Thoroughbred stallions and mares and got nothing that could warm up a son of Lexington or Glencoe. Beginning with Vol. 20 of the *American Stud Book*, The Jockey Club decided not to list Arabian horses, much to the disgust of Robert Sterling Clark, who took all his horses (including American-foaled Never Say Die) to race in England.

At any rate, the Arabian Horse Racing Association of America now has been formed; Arabian races at 1 9/16 miles were held at Evangeline Downs in Louisiana for the first time with pari-mutuel wagering on Sept. 2, 4, 7, and 9. This week, the Arizona Racing Commission, impressed by the mutuel handle's reaching $23,300 on one Evangeline Downs Arabian race, has granted permission for pari-mutuel wagering on Arabian races at Turf Paradise.

Says the AHRAA: "The advent of the Arabian as a distance racer in the United States adds a third dimension to the world of horse racing. Quarter Horses will always be the short-distance horses, the Thoroughbred will continue to be the intermediate distance horse, and now the Arabian will fill the void of long-distance races."

## Good Choice

ABOUT noon on Nov. 12, Wells Fargo man Thomas Raftery left Aqueduct headed for the Morgan Guaranty Trust Company and stopped in Brooklyn for a sandwich. It cost $1,377,000. Just think of the tab if he had ordered pie.

The money represented a portion of two days' receipts at Aqueduct. Three gunmen followed Raftery back to his armored car after lunch, suggested that the two other guards not do anything foolish, drove the armored car two blocks down the streeet, and transferred 10 of 12 bags containing unmarked paper currency to a getaway car. Then they whisked away, the biggest winners since John Bet-a-Million Gates.

About an hour later at Aqueduct, a horse named Call a Cop was late, missing by 2½ lengths in the third race.

This was the day the New York Racing Association happened to announce that Jack J. Dreyfus Jr. has been unanimously elected to succeed James Cox Brady as NYRA board chairman. Now there have been new sergeants terrified by their first inspection of the books after recently being placed in charge of an NCO Club, but we doubt there ever was a man before Dreyfus who walked into his new office and as to his first day of business received news that he was $1,377,000 short.

People who keep such statistics as the time-trial record for the second quarter-mile on a half-mile track by a 4-year-old filly pacer with a Dan Patch windshield, report that this robbery was bigger than the Brinks job in Boston and second in America only to the $1,551,277 heist from a mail truck near Plymouth Rock in 1962.

Fortunately for the NYRA, the Aqueduct receipts were fully insured, but the robbery reflects the immediacy and magnitude of problems confronting the new head of racing's biggest show.

Again fortunately for the NYRA, Dreyfus is a big man. He succeeds a big man and it is seldom today that a replacement can be found equal to his predecessor. Weeb Eubank and others have awakened screaming from nightmares conjuring next year's replacement quarterback for the Jets.

Brady is a thoughtful man of keen intellect and forceful determination unsuspected before his election as NYRA head eight years ago. A Yale man, head of Brady Security & Realty Corporation, board chairman of Purolator Products, and a director of Chrysler, Brady lent extraordinary, big-business organizational talents to the NYRA. Lent, because if the NYRA board chairman's salary were doubled, it still could not entice a man to undertake the problems intrinsic to the position, for the salary is zero dollars.

Brady, as his father before him and his son after him, is fascinated by the prospect of breeding and racing the good horse. He loves the game. So he assumed the burden of this position and by his leadership effected the blend, with just the right touch of vermouth, of old and new architecture and modern economic considerations that is the new Belmont Park; rendered structurally sound while retaining the dignity of racing's Dowager Queen at Sara-

149

toga; sponsored more filly racing and nurtured distance racing; and, most importantly, got the money—by negotiating with the state to permit retention of a greater portion of the mutuel handle and by re-financing the long-term mortgage—needed to rebuild the plants and raise purses. Last summer, Brady decided it was time for someone else to take a turn at the position.

By virtue of being a gentleman, Brady was necessarily inhibited in shout-to-shout combat with horse trainers and owners who declare racing is a business in which every participant has a vested right to receive some money, from somebody.

This is one of the basic philosophies, along with hypotheses that all NYRA trustees are dishonest, cheating bad horses out of money by putting up big purses and alloting stall space for good horses they own, which prompted Howard (Buddy) Jacobson and the HBPA to file an anti-trust suit against the NYRA and others considered part of The Establishment.

In sharp conflict with the HBPA position are tradition, statute, and case law. By tradition, racing is a sport, a game involving winners and losers. By statute, racing is a privilege rather than an inalienable right. By case law, the licensed privilege to engage in racing and the opportunity to win or lose on the track may be revoked. Still further, a West Virginia case taken this month to the Supreme Court of the United States held that three licensed jockeys—Robert Wilkerson, Russell Applebee, and Milton J. Dalgo—could be denied admittance to Waterford Park by track management, the lower court ruling that the track had "the absolute common-law right to exclude, whether it be patron, rider or anyone else."

At any rate, the new head of the NYRA can more than handle the job. No less a gentleman than his predecessor, Dreyfus is a quiet, self-effacing man with a lightning-quick mind and a marvelous sense of humor. An outward appearance of soft calm belies an insatiable appetite for competition—be it in Wall Street, tennis, bridge, golf, or horse racing—and an appreciation of the bizarre: He introduced the lion and ping-pong table to investment-firm advertising and painted his Hobeau Farm plank fences blue. A graduate of Lehigh, he worked for Merrill, Lynch, Fenner, & Beane between bridge hands, in 1945 started his own investment firm, Dreyfus & Co., and in 1965 became chairman of the Dreyfus Fund. In 1967, when his Hobeau Stable led the owners list, he was the single man who effected a compromise between the state, NYRA, and HBPA that resulted in horses returning to race for higher purses in New York; that same year he was honored with a testimonial dinner by the Thoroughbred Club of America and was elected to the NYRA board of trustees. Last August he was elected to The Jockey Club.

We first encountered him walking around the backstretch of Churchill

150

Downs in his shirt sleeves, looking for his horse, Beau Purple, which had just won the 1960 Derby Trial to become the first stakes winner Dreyfus ever bred. Why had the colt not raced at two?

"Well, he had some ankle trouble and we wanted to give him some time. I'd like to say he was so fast we couldn't catch him, but I'm afraid that's too old a gag," and he smiled almost in apology.

"This breeding thing really fascinates me. I've been reading *The Blood-Horse* for some time now and, as I understand it, everybody agrees that the formula for success is simply matching the best with the best. Well, now, there is a trick there: What is the best, and how do you get to it?"

In selecting a new chairman, the NYRA trustees would seem to have managed it.


# Wonder Horse

WITH his Kentucky Derby style of running (an unhurried 18th on the first turn and down the backstretch) firmly fixed in our mind, we were totally unprepared to believe it was Canonero II rushing up on the outside to challenge Eastern Fleet on the first turn of the Preakness.

Well, we thought, Canonero II has run off with his boy. Eastern Fleet will knock the wind out of him going down the backstretch. Then, as they battled head and head, five lengths in front of the rest of the field, down the backstretch and around the last turn—we began to realize, again, how wrong we can be.

Two observations brought this to our attention:

(a) The time—the first three quarters were being run by this pair steadily faster than any early running in the long history of the Preakness, :23²/5, :23³/5, :23²/5. The first six furlongs were run in a Preakness-record 1:10²/5, the mile in a Preakness-record 1:35 flat.

(b) Gustavo Avila was riding high, just galloping Canonero II outside of Eastern Fleet. Avila had his seat in the air as high as Lester Piggott until he reached the three-eighths pole; then he sat down like Manuel Ycaza and went to work.

More than five million Venezuelans, half the population of the entire country, watched Canonero II win the Preakness via satellite telecast. It seemed the other half of the country was on hand at Pimlico, shouting, jumping, kissing the track, singing, hugging friends and strangers, as trainer Juan Arias, wiping tears of joy from his eyes, proclaimed it was "no race" at all.

There can be no doubt now about Canonero II: He is a real good race horse. He can come from behind, he can go to the lead; he can sprint and he can stay; he can look a good horse in the eye for a half-mile and put him away.

Canonero II is a wonder horse. We wondered who he was two weeks ago; now we are wondering who can prevent him from becoming America's first Triple Crown winner since Citation.

## In The Cassidy Style

THE adventurous life of Marshall Cassidy ended Oct. 23 after 76 years. Last August near Glen Cove, Long Island, a truck lost its rear wheels and axle, careened across a road divider and crashed into a Mercedes driven by Cassidy in the opposite direction; hurtled, somersaulting through the air, the automobile was ripped in two. Cassidy suffered multiple injuries from which he never recovered.

A man of honesty, strong will, and vision, he looked for the right of things and was unwilling to compromise for what he thought was less than right. He was racing's Man For All Seasons.

Racing was a member of the Cassidy family. In a day gone by, the quality of the man starting the races more or less determined the quality of the meeting; the starter was a man held in awe, the most important and highest-paid official on the track. Tallest of these giants was Mars Cassidy, for a quarter-century the starter in New York. Upon his death in 1929, a son, George, succeeded him as starter in New York. Another son, Wendell, became presiding steward and director of racing at Hollywood Park. Another son, Marshall, tended to the upbringing of the other member of the family, racing, from a small, roughneck, unruly sport to the conglomerate, smooth, gray flannel business of today.

Marshall Cassidy improved race starts by designing starting gates. In his seven years as an assistant starter under his father working with the old Maxwell barrier, he developed a conviction that there had to be a better way. As starter at Tijuana, young Cassidy tried a moving start, with an old

152

McGinnis barrier mounted on Ford trucks (the truck driving was tricky, and this idea was abandoned). Then he built permanent starting chutes, 21 feet long, that kept horses separated and straight, at Tijuana, at four tracks in Canada, and at Bowie. At Agua Caliente he put doors on the permanent chutes. Then he designed the overhead structure with suspended partitions, the whole mounted on wheels for moving the structure from one starting point to another. This essentially is the gate used today in America, and only recently adopted in Europe, largely through Cassidy's influence in international racing.

Marshall Cassidy improved the accuracy of determining the order of finish in a race. For centuries the placing judges and stewards were located in stands on the finish at ground level. Cassidy moved the judges atop the grandstand roof at Hialeah so they could see something. He developed a camera to photograph what the naked eye might miss. At Tijuana he came up with three high-speed cameras whose shutters were tripped manually when Cassidy thought the horses were about at the finish. Later at Hialeah he set up on the roof a camera whose shutter was tripped by the first horse past the finish line, breaking a thread. Then came the photo-electric eye. To dispel the thought that the camera favored the outside horse, Cassidy placed another camera on the inside rail, and suspended another over the middle of the track at Belmont Park. Later, he settled on one finish camera, with a mirror on the inside rail to photograph both sides.

Marshall Cassidy improved the running of a race by developing the film patrol. Before an all-seeing eye recorded every step of a race, riders had a tendency to do things which seroiusly affected the outcome of a race and which patrol judges failed to note. Foul riding, and just plain bad riding, can be scrutinized by jockeys and stewards upon review of patrol films and corrective measures taken. Jockey Eddie Arcaro frequently has stated that the film patrol has proved to be the greatest safety device for riders, horses, and the public ever introduced to racing. Cassidy caught Arcaro in a foul the first time he mounted a camera on his binoculars in the Empire City stewards stand in 1941. As special consultant at Hollywood Park, Cassidy worked with Jack Mackenzie to get cameras placed in patrol towers to record entire races. Faster developing processes after World War II permitted viewing of films immediately after a race.

Marshall Cassidy devised an improved method of horse identification which virtually has removed the problem of "ringers" in New York. Marshall Cassidy instituted the Jockey Club School for Officials which has provided a much-needed opportunity for new officials to become acquainted with their duties and older officials to review efficient procedures. As New York state

153

steward in 1934, Marshall Cassidy increased track security, introduced the saliva test, hired a third placing judge to provide a majority opinion, required jockeys to ride out their mounts regardless of how far beaten, maintained for the first time a record of equipment used on each horse and posted changes. As executive secretary of The Jockey Club, Marshall Cassidy developed a blood-type indentification system which helps eliminate double-parentage in pedigrees, devised a card-index file which can handle registration of racing colors for all stables in America, and inspired better communication between leaders of all segments of racing and breeding at The Jockey Club Round Table Conference at Saratoga. As director of racing in New York and chairman of the planning and building committee, he supervised the construction of Aqueduct.

On the side, Marshall Cassidy was actively engaged. As a youth he exercised flat runners, schooled steeplechasers, and rode in amateur races in New York, Maryland, and Mexico. In school he played football, basketball, and baseball, boxed, and studied mining engineering. At the age of 19 he picked up a little practical application working in a mine in Gallego, Mex. The mine was overrun by a band of insurrectors, followers of Francisco Madero, and Cassidy joined them in a brief campaign to overthrow the government of Porfirio Diaz; as a demolition expert, he blew up train tracks before joining the siege of Juarez. He operated a motor stage line between Glove and Phoenix, Ariz., for a while, clerked and served as bouncer in a hotel, participated in some prize fights, performed as a motorcyclist in a side show, punched cows and rode broncs in rodeos. This palled, and he returned to work for his father as assistant starter for Donerail's 1914 Kentucky Derby.

One day in 1915, Cassidy struck up a conversation with a pilot who was in the business of flying thrill-seekers around the Statue of Liberty. In need of an attention getter, the pilot suggested that Cassidy do some wing-walking, in exchange for flying lessons. It was agreed. Cassidy in 1929 became one of only two men at the time to obtain a commercial license in Canada and a transport license in the United States, with hours logged in various types of planes from the two-cylinder English Gadfly to the tri-motored American transport. While a starter at Caliente, he was given an expert deep-sea diver certificate for his underwater efforts in locating a torpedo off San Diego.

Marshall Cassidy rose to life's adventures with style.

In his recollections, Marshall Cassidy wrote: "Because certain innovations in racing are credited to me, I rather welcome the opportunity of explaining why I do not deserve special acclaim.

"Evert effort of mine that was successful has been rewarded a thousand times over in my satisfaction that I was contributing to the welfare or improvement of the sport I love. Perhaps, now that life is nearly over, I can be excused for being extremely happy in boasting that I never accepted a cent for any project I introduced. My life has been letter perfect for me and I would not change a single thing if I had it to do over again."

## As It Was Meant To Be

WITH no racing at Keeneland on Monday, Colonel Elsworth dropped by the office to set things straight, starting with a slight adjustment of a prized pencil sketch of Himyar hanging on our wall.

"I suppose you know how he got his name," Colonel Elsworth remarked. Would you believe a Negro groom, in response to Maj. Barak Thomas' inquiry as to the best colt among the Dixiana 2-year-olds of 1877, pointed to him and stated, "Him yar?"

"I had supposed the late Mr. Joe Palmer had scotched that story long ago. Himyar's third dam was Flight. His second dam was Hegira, an Arabian word meaning flight, as particularly applied to Mohammed's flight from Mecca to Medina in 622. The first dam was Hira, which formerly was the capital city of Arabia. Himyar was the name of a ruler of the Himyarites, a Semitic people who inhabited a part of Arabia. So, some meaning for his name might be found in his first three dams, quite independent of anyone's dialect," the colonel said.

"Himyar was 1-4 for the Kentucky Derby, shortest price in the history of the race. Graustark could be an even heavier favorite if he continues as he has at Keeneland and nothing new turns up in the way of a challenger.

"Graustark, though, has not yet shown himself at a distance as Himyar did. He had won the 1½-mile Belle Meade Stakes in the mud in Nashville with the greatest ease, and had won the 1¾-mile Phoenix Hotel Stakes in Lexington 'pulled double' in his two starts before the Derby.

"He got off badly in the Derby, however, and I understand when he began picking up his horses the jockeys yelled up the line, 'Here he comes! Don't let him through!' Finished second by two lengths and caused a panic in every city that had betting shops, for the Derby was just catching on then as a big race."

Having submitted his historical footnote for the day, Colonel Elsworth

155

deftly jumped 88 years to Keeneland. "Greatest place to go racing in America today. You know, you can go to the races and watch closed-circuit TV in winterized stands at many tracks, but this is not going racing in my mind—has little to do with the horse. Keeneland and Saratoga are about the only places left one really can go racing, where he can walk out on grass, under trees, and actually see a horse being saddled. This is a quite enjoyable part of racing which has been omitted at nearly all of our modern plants today."

Yes, but that grass turns to mud holes in rainy spring weather, and while you may see the horses being saddled there are seats in the new grandstand section at Keeneland from which it is impossible to see the race from the five-sixteenths pole to the eighth pole, and no public-address system is available to inform players what has happened to horses which seemed to be making a move on the last turn.

"True, there has not been as great concern for the betting public at Keeneland as at Lincoln Downs, Aqueduct, Hazel Park, or nearly any other track. Personally, I think the want of commercial get-up-and-go to attract the kind of players who will wager an average of $90 or more, as in Florida, New York, or New Jersey, is the very aspect which makes me like Keeneland. I care nothing about big crowds or $5,000,000 mutuel handles, I just like to watch good horses in the company of well-dressed persons who designate horses by name rather than number. School teacher friend of mine drove down from Madison, Wis., 10 hours, to see Graustark and Moccasin run. He's not a player. Just wanted to see them run at Keeneland."

Keeneland does advertise, though, asking the public to come to its races, and for its first two Saturdays this spring Keeneland outdrew Gulfstream Park by more than a thousand (for these days, betting per capita at Keeneland was $46.66, at Gulfstream $94.35). In the Ashland Stakes, with nine betting interests, show betting was prohibited and no prior announcement of no show betting was made. The concession stands are undermanned; it is possible to wait 20 minutes to buy a hot dog.

"I believe Keeneland's attitude toward the public is much like Herman Hickman's toward the Yale alumni when he was football coach—do just enough to keep them sullen, but not mutinous. There was considerable criticism of Hialeah and Gene Mori when no betting was allowed on the Flamingo, it being suggested that the track ought to gamble a little, too, on a minus pool—the track's gamble being less chancy than players' because the track will show a profit on all other races for the day even with a minus pool.

"Yet I would side more with Keeneland than Hialeah on prohibiting a

156

form of wagering to avoid the chance of a minus pool being subtracted from the track's share of the mutuel handle. Nearly all of Keeneland's take goes into purses—72 per cent over the last 30 years—while only 43 per cent of Hialeah's take goes into purses. All tracks should be forced to gamble a little on a minus pool, but I would hate to have a number of minus pools cut into Keeneland's take to such an extent that purses would be reduced.

"I have no sympathy for a man who goes to Keeneland to buy a hot dog. He should go to Keeneland to see horses. It is the only track I know primarily concerned with horses and horse breeders. I think it is a great thing for racing for a track to give a party honoring breeders of good sales yearlings, as Keeneland did last week.

"The Thoroughbred Club Dinner Purse this week is a delightful part of Keeneland. The fare is considerably more than hot dogs and the very essence of a social dinner tied in to the winning of an otherwise insignificant 2-year-old race makes racing at Keeneland more personable, more fun than other places which have bigger purses and bigger crowds.

"Keeneland is for horses. Graustark and Abe's Hope are here, as were eight of the last nine Derby winners, and local breeders ship in good stables for the short meetings. I believe this is partly because there is more satisfaction to winning at Keeneland than is derived from the purse money alone.

"Yes, Keeneland could do a great deal more for the general public—it's not perfect—but in my view it is the track putting on the most enjoyable racing around today.

"By the way, I do think Graustark will make it around those two turns in the Blue Grass."

Colonel Elsworth adjusted Himyar again and sauntered on.

## All Smiles

BILL VEECK has a sense of humor. This in itself is something of an innovation among track presidents. The new head of Suffolk Downs has a barnful of innovations, some of them pending and unannounced, which adds to his confessed flare for rocking The Establishment.

Racing has a show of inherent excitement and color, intensified by the monetary involvement of its spectators. Yet while the nation's discretionary dollars multiply and leisure hours lengthen, daily average attendance at race tracks declines. Track presidents worry over this apparent anomaly constantly and at the annual TRA conventions, diverse plans and methods for attracting new racing fans are discussed in seminars.

Into this solemn group of track executives comes brash Bill Veeck, smiling and confident, leaving a trail of sports triumphs in rollicking Chollie Grimm's Brewers, a midget pinch hitter for the Browns, and an exploding scoreboard in Comiskey Park.

Racing braced itself for something that might be deemed bad taste. What bizzare gimmick would Veeck foist upon Boston? Alligator wrestling? A Pilgrims Progress Handicap for 5-year-old maidens? A free gate for everybody named Prescott on Bunker Hill Day, when nothing but white-eyed horses are entered?

Veeck's first moves drew approving nods from track managers. He called for some paint, and he remodeled the rest rooms. Then he knocked out the clubhouse admission price, and some track people frowned.

Later he said he had $200,000 for horses capable of going two miles on grass on June 14. Well, this was a first: There are no other $200,000-added races in America, and no two-mile turf races in memory, although they may have been quite common before the Union Course opened in 1821 with a skinned track. No one had thought of the Yankee since Never Bend beat Chateaugay in it six years ago, but the $200,000-added Yankee Gold Cup is instantly topical.

This week, Veeck announced the actual scheduling for April 19 of the $10,000 Lady Godiva Handicap, a spectacle he had been jawing about for some time. Veeck said he had five jockettes committed for the race with three more girl riders on the line. They are to ride fillies. The Lady Godiva is to be followed on April 21 by the $5,000 Guys and Dolls Purse in which four jockettes are to ride against four male jockeys.

At Suffolk Downs, the tide is about to come in.


## A Kind And Gentle Man


FOR more than 30 years, Joseph Alvie Estes was *The Blood-Horse*. He stood for honesty and integrity; it marked all he said or wrote.

He was a scholar. He also was a gag writer. He was a statistician, and a poet. He was a handicapper, and a geneticist. He was a historian, and a computer programmer. He was a master of whimsy, and a deft literary infighter. Past president of Rotary and the Thoroughbred Club of America, he was a frail little man of towering intellectual strength, a kind and gentle man—a light, that was extinguished by cancer Sept. 9 in a Lexington hospital.

Joe Estes was born in Graves County, Ky., 68 years ago. He worked his way through the University of Kentucky writing for the Lexington *Leader*, of which he became sports editor, and then the Lexington *Herald*, of which he became sports editor, and then city editor. He also edited the campus weekly, and following graduation studied at Columbia; while in New York, he became turf editor of the *Morning Telegraph* and something of a tout in verse known as Pete the Poet. In 1930, he returned to Lexington and joined *The Blood-Horse*.

Painfully honest in thought and deed, he poked at hypocrisy in racing for more than three decades. Writing with objectivity, he often was found opposed to popular opinion. When the Butazolidin controversy first arose some 10 years ago, Estes did not advocate use of the medication, but opposed its being banned on untenable grounds. He criticized a report on the toxic effect of Butazolidin presented at an NASRC convention:

"There is nothing wrong with the report except that the Racing Chemistry Research Fund directors had it presented out of context, in an apparent attempt to provide commissioners with justification for maintaining that it was dangerous, deadly, and detestable."

J. Samuel Perlman, then publisher of Triangle Publications, retorted: "As the editor of *The Blood-Horse* attended the convention in Toronto, he should have known that his statement was completely inaccurate."

Under personal attack by racing's most powerful press, Estes promptly replied: "As to the statement which Mr. Perlman says we should have known to be 'completely inaccurate,' we are now ready to make one amendment in it. Strike out that word apparent."

In 1962, the Thoroughbred Club got around to recognizing one of its own, honoring The Estes for his many contributions to racing with a testimonial dinner. The testimonials were long: W. T. Bishop read from the prospectus Estes had written for the original founding of Keeneland; Humphrey Finney explained how Estes had revised the presentation of pedigree information in the sale catalogues; Haden Kirkpatrick extolled Estes' constructive commentary on racing; Dr. Dewey Steele set out the significance of Estes' many studies in genetics and the value of the Average-Earnings Index Estes devised for evaluating racing and breeding success; Alfred Vanderbilt spoke of the man, and Brownie Leach said he could not find the words for the respect, admiration, and love he had for Joe Estes. Testimonials came by

159

letter and telegram, from past honor guests, E. P. Taylor, Marshall Cassidy, Max Hirsch, and from Dr. Jack Robbins, Preston Burch, Harry Guggenheim and Rex Ellsworth, who said it was Estes who had selected Khaled for him.

And it was at this testimonial dinner that Estes proposed the information center of automated data:

"Racing in the United States is now so big an operation that it may be endangered by its own size. As it sprawls and grows bigger, there is no possibility of intelligent centralized control of its growth or its lesser problems. The challenge now is to make possible, through access to information, intelligent decisions at state and local levels. The folklore of yesterday is not a sound basis for the racing of tomorrow. This is the age of automation, and the time has come for automation in racing," Estes said eight years ago.

"If such a center of automation comes into being, it can deliver us from the evil of ignorance. And in these days, ignorance has become a luxury we can no longer afford."

As a result of this talk, The Jockey Club undertook to finance the enormous task of reducing racing and breeding's mountainous statistics to computerized data. Because no one in the world was better equipped to direct such a task, Joe Estes resigned as editor of *The Blood-Horse* in the spring of 1963 to do the job. He did it.

Joe Estes was physically weak from a series of operations when he attended the Keeneland yearling sale last July. We sat down on a bench and talked of his doing another book. Well, he was still in the process of revising the chapter on Thoroughbreds for the *Encyclopedia Britannica*. Yes, but a new generation of horsemen needs those studies, needs that information which you spelled out over the last 40 years, needs the light only you can throw on the dark myths of horse breeding, needs the textbook that only you and the computer can put together.

He said he was tired, but that he would take a run at it as soon as he was off the vet's list. And then he grinned. He always did.


## Gang Wars

A barn burned at Washington Park last week, killing groom Michael Sprieker, 22 Thoroughbreds, and a lead pony. Wagering dropped almost four per cent and attendance fell six per cent last year in Illinois. Night racing was tried at Arlington Park. The richest race in America, the Arlington-Washington Futurity, was discontinued as the result of a dramatic alteration of Chicago racing dates by the new racing board. Marje Everett was relieved of her duties as executive director of Arlington Park by new owner P. J. Levin, who is interested in real estate and only incidentally in racing—if it shows a profit; Mrs. Everett has filed suit over her severance from the race track operation.

While class racing has been a sometime thing, there seldom has been a want of excitement in Chicago racing. It was not too long ago that Ed Corrigan at Hawthorne was fighting George Hankins at Garfield Park for survival; Hawthorne had to close and then the mayor, not aligned with Hankins politically, tried to shut down Garfield. Police moved in the barn area and, unfortunately, happened upon little Sheriff Jim Brown, who was known to other horsemen as a sagebrush killer best not to arouse. Unaware of Brown's temperament, two policemen fired at his feet as a suggestion for him to move on; he promptly killed them both and winged a few others before a dozen policemen brought him down, riddled with holes, beside a manure pile.

That was a yesterday. The gunplay has subsided in Chicago racing. But not the squabbles.

## Recalling Raceland

PRELIMINARY notification has been served on the Kentucky State Racing Commission by Don Stafford, president of Pyramid Company, that his firm has obtained options on property near Ashland, Ky., with the thought of building a race track.

So here we go again.

Col. Phil T. Chinn, reminiscing several years before his death in 1962, confessed that he once was the man of the hour in such a proposition. That was in the 1920s during a period when he was selling yearlings in quantity at prices that would command the respect of Leslie Combs II.

He had picked out Sarazen, which proved to be the best horse in his crop, raced him at two... "Made a sucker play on that horse—sold him to Mrs. Graham Fair Vanderbilt for $30,000 and he was worth $100,000."

He had bred Black Maria, best 3-year-old filly of 1926..."Sold her and her

161

dam, Bird Loose, to W. R. Coe for $10,000 and thought I was cleaning him out; of course, she and Imp were the best two mares that ever lived."

He had imported Carlaris and sold him to W. H. (Fatty) Anderson, for whom Carlaris won seven of his first eight races early in 1926, including the Tijuana Derby by seven lengths, reducing the track record by two seconds, and the Coffroth Handicap by eight lengths, reducing the track standard by 1⅕ seconds.

According to the colonel: "Tom Cromwell, Jack Keene, and I were having dinner one night at the Lafayette Hotel in Lexington and in a casual way I introduced a suggestion that we build a race track to go in opposition to Polk Laffoon. At the time, Laffoon about owned Covington; he had the power company, the transit company, the gas company, the bridge, some banks, was president of Latonia track and vice chairman of the racing commission.

"They asked where we would set up this operation. I said I didn't much care—Bowling Green, Paduach, Ashland. Well, one day we went over to Ashland and after I looked over the layout I weakened. So did Cromwell. But Keene was a great builder.

"Cromwell and I laid back, let Keene have his head and sort of walk over the ground. Cromwell said he wasn't too game about going into the thing and I said I wasn't an enthusiastic man about losing money. This man we had, J. O. Keene, while one of the finest men in the world—there was no more chance of limiting him to $250,000 than of holding John D. Rockefeller to a dime's worth of gasoline.

"We had some intimate discussions with Jack on the matter and he finally convinced us $250,000 would be enough, so we said go ahead. It was called the Tri-State Fair and Racing Association and Charley Berryman was president, a local man named Williamson was vice president, Keene was general manager, Cromwell secretary, handicapper, steward, and other things, and John S. Barbee was treasurer.

"Well, it wasn't long before Keene had spent $300,000 for the finest stables in the land, but he had no grandstand or track. We needed more money. Berryman had exhausted his people. There was only one man who could raise any more money—P. T. Chinn. So I went to New York and got $100,000 from Elmer Smathers. That was spent before I returned, necessitating a trip to Chicago. Charles B. Shaffer sprang for another $200,000 . . . finest sportsman in the world...he said at the time the track would never go. 'You have one of the finest plants I have ever seen. Only one thing wrong with it, it's in the wrong place. Should be in New York.'

"You know, the day before the track was to open, it was not completed.

162

Keene had the stretch in the wrong place, 'way over to the left instead of down in front of the stands. So I said to Jack, 'Where are your blueprints? Let me see the blueprints of this track.'

"He didn't even look at me, said, 'I don't use blueprints; I build by eye.'

"Actually, the track never really got started. They held a couple of meetings, but from the onset there was financial stress, and then one day—I believe it was Black Maria's year—Charley Berryman came to me and suggested it would be a great personal favor if I would be kind enough to ship my stable to Raceland.

"Seeing no way out of the situation, I agreed that I would. The purses there were not in keeping with my needs, but I figured I might be able to make the mutuels pay the freight inasmuch as I had a considerable number of maidens only one man knew anything about—namely, P. T. Chinn.

"I conned Fatty Anderson to go with me. He had the best horse in the country at the time, unbeatable in the West, but he was not too keen about going to Ashland. I told him it was the greatest place in the world to summer his horses, and in addition there were places to dine unrivaled this side of the Atlantic. I described the mountainous servings of fried chicken, accompanied by diverse delicacies—I knew nothing about the place, really— and Anderson finally agreed to ship in.

"Well, we went over there for opening day, the entries came out, and he said what about it? I replied that it appeared I would win three races out of my stable and he decided there was only one thing to do.

"He took a night train to Cincinnati, arranged with (bookmaker) Louis Katz to obtain the best possible price on all three horses with all the money he could get on, and returned at 9 o'clock the following morning.

"I saw him early in the day and he appeared haggard—quite possibly the railroad from Ironton was the roughest railroad in the world—but he said he was going to bet all the money he had on him through the machines on other horses in the races to build up the odds on my horses, and that I was in for half on the Cincinnati deal."

On July 5, opening day of the 1926 meeting at Raceland, Col. Chinn ran three horses.

The second race was won by P. T. Chinn's 2-year-old maiden filly, Muriel H., by Rock View, trained by C. E. Patterson and ridden by Graceton Philpot, paying $3.60 for $2.

The fifth race, the $2,000-added Ashland Handicap, was won by W. C. Baxter's Malcolm B. Jr., by Torchbearer, bred by Col. Chinn, trained by Patterson, and ridden by Philpot, paying $3. He won by two lengths, setting a track record for seven furlongs.

"I had sold that horse to Baxter, but kept him in my stable because I more or less managed all his racing interests. After Malcolm B. Jr. won, Anderson came up to me and said, 'You know how much money we've won so far?' I had no idea, but I figured it would not be much because nobody would handle a good sum on opening day at a small track. 'Fifty thousand? I'm not talking about pocket change,' Anderson says, 'We've got an unlimited bet on and the clocker tells me he can't find a work on this third horse you're running. Not one! And we've got everything going back on him!'

"I said, 'Anderson, I'm deeply sorry about that, but it is too late to work him. The horse is going on the track at this moment.' "

The sixth race was won by P. T. Chinn's Hot Time, by High Time, which Philpot eased home by six lengths. He paid $8.80 for $2.

"So I saw Fatty and suggested that we take in one of those chicken places about eight miles down the road, and he said, 'That's the idea, let's get some of that chicken, corn-on-the-cob, radishes—eat this big day off.'

"It just so happened a flash flood came up just as we arrived. No chicken. We got back to Ashland about 11 o'clock and, of course, all the eateries were closed. We went back to the hotel and had some beer.

"It was terribly hot, and virtually impossible to sleep, but we finally settled down. We were staying in Ironton, you know, and about 3 o'clock in the morning Henry Ford's coal train came out of one of those mountains with must have been 200 cars going a mile a minute right under our window.

"Wake a man in the horse business and you'll never get him back to sleep. Anderson decided it was time for him to depart. He dressed, went downstairs, ordered his car, and was then informed by the attendant that the fellow who had borrowed the car for the evening had not returned. About that time, the night clerk handed Anderson a wire.

"Anderson turns to me and he says, 'Phil, this certainly is a delightful place and I have enjoyed myself. That was a lovely dinner last night; the train, I can assure you, has left town; my car has been stolen, and now I learn that the three races we won were to no avail inasmuch we did not get five cents down on them. I imagine about the only way you could attract me to Raceland again would be with a log chain.'

"As you can understand, I felt somewhat derelict as host in this situation, but I believed our friendship would not be altered appreciably if Carlaris brought off the Raceland Derby—and I was as sure of that as Citation in a $1,500 claiming race.

"I had Malcolm B. Jr. in the Derby and Strother Griffin was to ride him. The morning of the race I went out on the track with a pony and I said:

'Strother, I know you'd like to win the Derby, but you haven't got a 1-1,000 chance of beating Carlaris, so don't punish our horse, just get him off good and let him run; there isn't a horse in the country can beat Carlaris right now.'

"Anderson called me later that day, said he had $50,000 on Carlaris and was declaring me in for $5,000, which was stretching me pretty well. Anderson thought no more of betting $100,000 than I would about smoking a Corona-Corona.

"They had a band follow the horses to the post, cymbals clanging and all that. Carlaris was a nervous horse under normal conditions, but he was finished that day before the race was run. He broke on top by 15 lengths after a quarter-mile was run, was 10 lengths on top going into the backstretch, then collapsed over at the three-eighths pole.

"Strother rode a perfect race on Malcolm B. Jr. Won by a length going away. Well, I never felt so bad in my life. Here I had just dropped $5,000 and lovely people were all around me, congratulating me, patting me on the back, and somebody put a wreath of roses around my neck. I thought I was going to choke to death."

## Fair Call

FOR the last eighth of a mile, our eyes were fixed on the top pair, Iron Liege and Gallant Man. We had an absolutely unobstructed view, along with several hundred other writers lined along a furlong of Churchill Downs roof, and nothing diverted our attention from the exciting duel to the finish of the 1957 Kentucky Derby.

Yet we missed the most important aspect of that drive. We somehow never noticed that Bill Shoemaker stood up on Gallant Man at the sixteenth pole. Don Fair did.

We did not learn about it until five minutes after the race when reading Fair's chart footnotes: "Gallant Man moved up determinedly in the early stretch, reached the lead between calls and was going stoutly when his rider misjudged the finish and he could not overtake Iron Liege when back on stride." Films confirmed Fair's report.

Fair had been calling race charts for the *Daily Racing Form* and *Morning Telegraph* for more than a quarter-century at the time, in Detroit, Kentucky,

Hot Springs, and New Orleans, but he moved to New York after the 1957 Kentucky Derby. Five years ago he was named director of the Triangle Publications field correspondents.

On Futurity Day, at the age of 73, Don Fair, the best of them all, said he had called his last race. The New York pressbox will never be the same to us without his usual greeting: "Hey, Dogpatch! Didn't Col. Chinn ever teach you anything about racing?"

## One Better

CLIFFORD MOOERS was an adventurous little man who ran a small stake into something considerable gambling in gold, oil, and things. He thoroughly enjoyed betting on his horses.

One day when he had Cyclotron and Traffic Judge in adjacent stalls, he beckoned a man down the shedrow, out of the grooms' hearing, thumbed toward a stall, whispered: "That's the fastest colt in the world!"

When this revelation elicited an appropriate response of awe, Mooers drew his visitor closer, hissed: "And that one there can beat him!"

## Prologue

AT 6:30 in the morning it still was dark in the Hialeah barn area, naked light bulbs illuminating the shedrows as grooms readied horses for the first set. A few walkers were on the ring. A suggestion of dawn silhouetted uppermost needles in the tall pines Joe Widener had set along the horse path between the barns and the track.

Through this colonnade of pines supporting a brightening sky came a set from the Harbor View barn led by a slight man sitting tall in a western saddle and wearing a cowboy hat. This was trainer Ivan Parke, America's leading rider in 1923-24 and a top steeplechase jockey in 1931.

"Been up to the farm at Ocala, clearing fields, building fences. Nice to be back at the track and take it easy."

Trainer George Poole limped by. "Aw, I broke a toe," he explained. "Pony

166

fell with me—I had time to drink a cup of coffee while he was going down—thought he'd get right back up, you know."

Daylight still was faint and V. J. (Lefty) Nickerson clicked on a light in the stall of Elmendorf Farm's High Tribute, winner of last year's Jerome at 78-1 over In Reality and Tumiga. A plastic tube, a sixteenth of an inch in diameter and about three inches long, poked out of High Tribute's head, about two inches below his left eye.

"Sinus," Nickerson said. "I ran him at Aqueduct a month ago and he wasn't right. He began draining from one nostril, and the day before Christmas, Dr. Bill Reed poked a hole in there so he could get some medicine right into the infection. I can begin galloping him again today.

"About 20 years ago I was working for Cecil Howard and we had a filly named Ocean Brief, owned by Carr Hatch of Canada. She was a nice filly. We beat Double Jay, War Allies, and Mafosta in a handicap at Santa Anita, then when we took her to New York she came down with this same thing. She smelled real bad around her head and she drained from one nostril. The vet knocked a hole in her forehead, big as a silver dollar, let all the infection drain. Had to turn her out for a year. Of course, we didn't have the medicines then we have today.

"King Ranch bought her for a broodmare, but Max Hirsch brought her back the next year as a 5-year-old and she won six races, including the Correction, Colonial, and set a track record in the Camden Handicap.

"Mr. Right had this same kind of treatment for sinus and came right back to win the Trenton and Queens County Handicaps in November," Nickerson said.

Injection of medicine directly into the infection, about 1½ inches deep in the forehead, by means of a plastic tube is relatively new. Dr. Reed said the treatment had been used for about two years.

At the Phippses' barn, trainer Eddie Neloy crossed his arms and studied Vitriolic on the walking ring. Champion at two and winterbook favorite for the Kentucky Derby, Vitriolic is the big horse, figuratively and literally. Well over 16 hands, the son of Bold Ruler—Sarcastic, by Ambiorix, has not grown taller in recent months, but wider. He towered over a lead pony accompanying him to the track for a gallop.

While Vitriolic looked the part he is expected to play this season, Queen of the Stage, voted champion 2-year-old filly last year, was still bothered by the ankle to which her sole defeat, in the Selima, was attributed. Neloy had the daughter of Bold Ruler—Broadway, by Hasty Road, standing in a tub of cold water.

Walking down the shedrow of the Phipps barn, glancing at the pedigree

167

cards on each door, one finds reason to suspect the dominance of the Phippses' stable will continue for some time. Of the 26 horses, 18 are by five-time leading sire Bold Ruler.

What in the way of 2-year-olds?

"Well, the babies are getting ready to go to the track now," Neloy observed. "First one there is a half-sister to Buckpasser, a Tatan filly named Navsup. Next one is a full sister to Vitriolic, named Cutting; that's a full sister to Bold Monarch named Big Advance; that chestnut there is a full brother to Bold Lad and Successor named The Heir; then comes a full brother to Queen Empress named King Emperor; that's Noble Leaf, by Bold Ruler out of Cicada's dam; have one more here, oh, full brother to Queen of the Stage—he's coughing."

At the track kitchen, trainer Kenny Noe Sr. shouted in a casual way: "Called Mrs. Joe Goodwin in Kentucky last night. She said they had seven inches of snow. I turned down my air-conditioning a little. Better to be here broke than anywhere else rich."

Trainer Woody Stephens got some coffee and sat down. "Had a little filly for H. B. Delman, the shoe man, a few years back. Believe she foundered a little and I had Bill Reed heel-nerve her, got her back to training and right up to the point she is going to win a race on Saturday. But Delman dies on Wednesday and the lawyer says I can't run; got to sell the filly. So I told Humphrey Finney to announce loud and long that the filly was heel-nerved, and she didn't bring much; I bought her for $1,300. So I bring her down here and she win, paying $38, with Pete Anderson riding her.

"Next morning, Pete's bringing a horse back from the track and goes by Luro's barn there and the good senor calls to him: 'Ah, Pete,' says Horatio, 'I see now that the man is in the box, Woody, he let the filly run!' "

Sammy Smith and Moody Jolley were there and the discussion veered rapidly from bets won and lost to Boo Gentry's firing a man ("for habitual drunkenness, which was as sound a reason as ever was as he has been drunk all his life") to the case of a trainer who happened to hit a starter (being heard by a steward who holds the track record for slugging assistant starters) to the owner who was hesitant to bet "unless you give him a story" ("he has to have a story, like, I like this horse pretty good because he had bad luck last time out; and then he'll ask did he have *real* bad luck, and you say the worst you ever saw, and then he'll bet you good; he's gotta have a story").

Stephens said he had to drive up to St. Lucie to meet James Cox Brady and inspect the young horses. Brady was flying over with Ogden Phipps in a helicopter.

"You better get you a bird, too," Jolley advised. "Nobody drives up there anymore. Have a flat on that road and crocodiles eat you before another car comes by."

And this was prologue, almost two weeks before beginning the other part of the game, horse racing at Hialeah.

## Evolution

ALL things change, of course, even Saratoga. Hugh Bradley said Saratoga was "the town that used to be, in a land that never was." Actually, Saratoga was never so much a town as a setting.

Saratoga today, however, is not the rich, laughing, naughty resort it was known to be for nearly a century and a half after Gideon Putnam built his tavern on Broadway in 1802. It no longer is John Morrissey's Saratoga of 1861-78, or Dick Canfield's Saratoga of 1893-1907, or Richard T. Wilson Jr's Saratoga of the 1920s. It is not even the Saratoga of 20 years ago.

In 1946 the majestic old United States Hotel with its 2,750 feet of piazza— Millionaires Piazza—was razed, and in 1953 the magnificent old Grand Union Hotel was leveled to make way for a shopping center.

In a way, the elegance and grandeur of Saratoga was the Grand Union. This was Putnam's Tavern which Alexander T. Stewart, the merchant prince purchased in 1871 for $500,000 and spent double that amount in remodeling.

The Grand Union was the largest and most lavish hotel in America, The Hotel for the nation's old and new rich, Presidents and petty politicians, southern breeders and New York gamblers. It covered seven acres and was surrounded by a mile of porch, 48 feet high.

Its dining room measured 306 by 70 feet and 250 waiters thought it a usual thing to serve some 1,600 at one sitting a dinner of: Oysters on Half Shell, Sauterne, Green Turtle Soup, Olives, Boiled Salmon, Lobster Sauce, Potato Balls, Sauterne, Sweetbread Cutlets, Peas, Claret, Fillet of Beef, Mushroom Sauce, Champagne, Roman Punch, Supreme of Chicken, Truffle Sauce, Terrapin, Saratoga Chips, Partridges on Toast, Salted Almonds...and on, and on, to the Cigars and Benedictine.

At the Grand Union, White Hat McCarthy bet James R. Keene $50,000 one of his unnamed 2-year-olds could work three-eighths in less than 35 seconds while Victor Herbert played soft music in the courtyard. And there

169

was a time Herbert turned over his baton to the young son of the Grand Union's proprietor, a boy who was to grow into "The Man Who Came to Dinner"—Monte Woolley.

Whispers of the past are the low murmurs of Lillian Russell, Diamond Jim Brady, John Bet-A-Million Gates, John Drake, Reggie Vanderbilt, Jim Fisk, and Jay Gould.

The passing of the old hotels was not mourned by all, for the elegance of 1890, while becoming when viewed from the piazza, did not hold one's fancy when represented by a small wash basin on the bedroom wall and a tub down the hall. We remember the fire escape—a large rope coiled in a corner of the room, stiff, brittle, untouched since Stewart installed it. The place was musty and smelled of Ulysses S. Grant's cigars when it sighed its last.

If the old hotels gave Saratoga class, John C. (Old Smoke) Morrissey gave it spice. He was a tough raised in the gutters of Troy who bullied his way into ward politics in New York City and once was elected to Congress. His most notable contribution to parliamentary procedure was his open challenge to several members of the House of Representatives to settle a dispute with bare knuckles on the floor of the House.

Old Smoke once claimed the American heavyweight title after whpping some mining-camp bruisers in California and winning from George Thompson by a foul on Aug. 31, 1852. The following year he fought Yankee Sullivan and was losing after 36 rounds, but during the rest period Sullivan jumped out of the ring to thrash Old Smoke's second and, thus occupied, failed to hear the call for the 37th round.

Old Smoke quickly brought this point of rules to the attention of the referee and acquired the champion's belt. He defended his title in 1858 against John C. (Benecia Boy) Heenan, whom he had fought frequently in the streets of Troy as a boy. Benecia Boy broke his right hand in the first round, but managed to hang on and did not quit until the 11th. Old Smoke refused a return bout and retired undefeated.

Morrissey operated a gambling establishment in New York City with H. Price McGrath (who was to breed and race Aristides, first winner of the Kentucky Derby) and, with the outbreak of the Civil War, decided to extend his operations to Saratoga. His game was heavily patronzied by wartime profiteers and, as a further service to occuy his patrons' afternoons, Old Smoke organized a race meeting. William R. Travers, Wall Street broker and society wit, was installed president.

Morrissey started building a gambling casino in Congress Park in 1867, completed it two years later and was said to have netted a half-million dollars in his first season of operation. New Yorkers called it "Morrissey's Elegant Hell" and Saratogians drew awesome parallels when a series of fires ravished Broadway.

Old Smoke died in 1878 and his Saratoga gambling house passed to Charles Reed, the man who had purchased St. Blaise from August Belmont on a single record bid of $100,000. Reed was said to have extended Belmont's gambling credit until the point was reached where he tore up the St. Blaise sale slip.

After Reed came Albert Spenser, and then Dick Canfield, and in our day the out-of-town help who operated tables at the Piping Rock. Arrowhead, Riley's, and less luxurious establishments, but these all were covered with white sheets during Gov. Thomas E. Dewey's administration.

Gone now are the old hotels, the gambling houses, even the tracks by which trainloads of the nation's wealthy and great, beauty and sport were brought for a hundred Augusts to the platform in the Grand Union court-yard with their Saratoga Trunks.

All things change, Saratoga perhaps more slowly than most. Old Smoke's club house still stands in Congress Park and his afternoon diversion on Union Avenue now provides the finest racing in America. The elms are taller than Gideon Putnam could have imagined. The new Performing Arts Center is something Dick Canfield would have sponsored. The new Holiday Inn on Broadway has better plumbing than the Grand Union. Paul Whiteman no longer plays for guests at the Piping Rock, but the price remains the same for a fine dinner at The Dorian. People still take the "baths" of the spa. Max Hirsch is still serving breakfast at his barn. There probably is more horse talk now than when John Madden and Tom Piatt, and H. P. Whitney and Francis Hitchcock discussed yearlings on the Grand Union piazza. The track and the grounds are in better shape than George Bull ever had them.

Unchanged, however, is the place to be in August.

## The Black Archer

MOTION has been made by the heirs of Isaac Murphy, and approved by the Fayette County Fiscal Court in Lexington, to exhume the body of the Hall of Fame jockey for reburial near the grave of Man o' War.

Born in Lexington on Jan. 1, 1861, Murphy died of pneumonia on Feb. 12, 1896. For 20 of those 35 years he was a race rider the like of which may

171

never be seen again. He was the first jockey to win three Kentucky Derbys—on Buchanan in 1884, Riley in 1890, Kingman in 1891—and he won four American Derbys and five Latonia Derbys; when Salvator beat Tenny, Isaac Murphy was the winning rider.

He rode his first race in 1875 at Crab Orchard, 50 miles south of Lexington, and is said to have won 530 races with 1,538 mounts. When Bill Shoemaker can win that many races in two years, Murphy's record does not seem impressive, but he was riding *34.5 per cent winners!* And Fred Archer, or James McLaughlin, or Arcaro, or Shoemaker never did that. He was in America the Black Archer.

Murphy was only an occasional rider in his later years (20 mounts in 1895, 30 in 1893) and was reputed to be the owner of a string of horses campaigned in 1892 by J. J. Sellers. Near the old Kentucky Association track he owned a large house whose walls were graced with oil paintings of horses he had ridden. His funeral was attended by an estimated 500 persons and he was buried in the East Seventh Street cemetery. A wooden marker over his grave disappeared in ensuing years and it was not until 1961 that the actual gravesite was identified by Eugene Webster, who said his father many times had pointed out the grave to him.

## And A Great Day For Omaha, Too

MICHAEL J. FORD is tall, blond, amiable, a youthful 41 with a grin as open as the Nebraskan plains. A Marine corporal on Saipan, he returned to Omaha after the war, skipped college, and with his father invented and began manufacturing a grain door for railroad box cars. It is corrugated paper reinforced with metal strapping and, costing about $7, it quickly replaced the $30 barricade that had been used for bulk loads of grain or salt. In 1959 he sold out to International-Stanley Corp. for enough money to "retire" at the age of 34. He turned to racing and in six years had a Kentucky Derby winner.

Whereupon he met the press, jointly and severally.

What was the first thing he thought about when Kauai King went across the finish line?

"Well," Ford grinned, "thought I was going into orbit.

"My wife's name is Veronica—she's over there, I think—but everybody

172

calls her Ronnie. Yes, I have three children and they're here. No, that was not my boy, that was Henry's—Henry Forrest is my trainer—little boy named after Bear Bryant; think he is 3½. Last year at this time? Well, I guess...well, I was home watching the race on television. Yes, this was a great thrill."

The quesitons and answers were interrupted from time to time when matronly women in extraordinary hats rushed up to buzz congratulations. Let me get that kiss again, ordered a photographer.

"But, she isn't my wife. Suppose that will be all right?"

What instructions did he give jockey Don Brumfield? "Well, we told him just to get a good position on the first turn and then ride it as the race came up, because he knows the horse. I thought it was a beautifully judged ride. You can't give enough credit to the rider. He's one of the best in the business.

"Yes, you have to give credit to Maryland; he was foaled in Maryland at Mr. Alfred Vanderbilt's farm. Yes, you have to give credit to Virginia, because Dr. Frank O'Keefe is the breeder and he raised the horse at his farm in Virginia. Say, fellas, it was a great day for Omaha, too, you know."

There was champagne, plus crushing congratulations, and flash bulbs, and more questions Ford tried to answer as best he could. It was hot in the dining room after the 92nd Kentucky Derby and Ford repeatedly wiped perspiration from his forehead.

"You know, the nerves set in only this morning," he confided. "I began to get a little washy in the paddock, but believe me, this is no bother. You just can't inconvenience a winner. How did I get into racing?

"Always liked horses, and most people don't know this but Omaha is a great racing town, probably stronger per capita than Chicago. You look at the daily handle at Ak-Sar-Ben, only a little bit off Chicago's and we have only about a tenth of the population to draw from that Chicago has."

Louisville Mayor Kenneth Schmied introduced himself to the winning owner and gave him the key to the city. "Certainly glad you brought your fine horse to Louisville and hope you come back again," the mayor said as photographers recorded the key business. "I was on Abe's Hope," he added.

In response to further inquiries, Ford said it was the second Kentucky Derby he had seen in person, that he had seen Tim Tam's Derby in 1958, and yes, he enjoyed this one more. He asked if he could have some of that champagne and sat down again.

"In June of 1960 my father and I both liked racing and we bought a horse for $5,000, privately, named Mortgageman, a 2-year-old gelding by Money Broker. Then we started claiming some and losing some. Best one we had was Tonco (by Two Ton Tony), won eight races in 10 starts from February to

May in 1961. But he got hurt and then I went on my own, trying to buy better horses at the yearling sales.

"I had been associated in business with Reno Renfrew, who had a horse farm near Lexington, and I think he recommended Tommy Gentry to me. Can't give enough credit to Tommy.

"Yes, thank you, yes it certainly was a great race.

"Tommy acted as my agent in picking out and buying the yearlings. Bought Royal Gunner (earner of $274,255) and Umbrella Fella (earner of $239,926). We got together on this Native Dancer yearling after the Virginia yearling tour and settled on a price range of $25-$35,000.

"I was with my family at Del Mar and Tommy went to the Saratoga sale. He called me, told me he had to go to $42,000 to get him, which was all right," Ford grinned, "but you kinda like to shake up your agent a little bit and I said, 'that's $7,000 over our limit, how do you think we're going to pay for him?'

"Well, less than two weeks later Royal Gunner and Umbrella Fella ran 1-3 in the Futurity Trial in Chicago [netting $41,700; two weeks after that they finished second and third in the Arlington-Washington Futurity, netting $125,000], so it worked out all right."

How did he happen upon the most variously pronounced name of a Kentucky Derby winner since Leonatus? "Well, we vacationed in the Hawaiian Islands, and we had this colt by a Polynesian horse, and the king of the island of Kauai was never supposed to have been conquered. I believe it is pronounced koo-ow-ee out there, but I don't believe it much matters."

How did he feel about the Preakness? "I feel pretty good right now. He has a pretty good opening lick. We'll ship Monday or Tuesday, have to talk with my trainer about that. Can't give enough credit to Henry Forrest—he trained the horse to perfection. No, we are not entered for the Belmont, but we can supplement to it if things come out right in the Preakness. Boy, it's hot in here; wonder if I could have some of that champagne."

It had been a hot, exciting Kentucky Derby and the biggest estimated crowd of 100,000 in memory had installed Kauai King as the betting favorite over Abe's Hope, Stupendous, and Amberoid, the only candidates in the field of 15 thought better than 10-1.

An auxiliary gate was required to provide a 15th post position for Williamston Kid. The break was good for all except Amberoid in No. 1 and Rehabilitate in No. 4, neither of which was ready and both stumbled coming away. Quinta brushed Abe's Hope immediately after the start, but it was of no consequence.

Kauai King broke in stride, taking the lead at once and became the first

174

Kentucky Derby winner to lead every step of the way since Jet Pilot 20 years ago (Swaps and Dark Star assumed command shortly after the break).

It was thought that Quinta and Dominar would set the early pace and that Kauai King would go into the first turn probably in third place, but Brumfield sent the son of Native Dancer a first quarter in :22⅘ and had a length to spare on Quinta, almost two lengths on Dominar, when he went to the rail easily at the turn, quickly opening up a three-length lead.

Meanwhile, Advocator broke alertly and went past the stands the first time in fifth place, Stupendous ninth, Blue Skyer 10th and Abe's Hope 11th. Around the upper turn Kauai King set a relatively fast early pace for a 10-furlong race, going the first half-mile in :46⅕. He was three lengths in front of Quinta, which was another three lengths in front of the pack, into which Dominar was quickly receding, his serious running concluded for the day.

Down the backstretch Kauai King maintained his margin of three lengths, as did Quinta approaching the five-eighths pole. Advocator moved into third place and Stupendous was two lengths behind him on the rail. Blue Skyer was seventh, a neck in front of Rehabilitate, with Abe's Hope another two lengths farther back in ninth place.

On the last turn Johnny Sellers took Advocator up on the outside of the pacesetter while Braulio Baeza sent Stupendous up on the rail and both horses got within a length of Kauai King.

"He seemed to give himself a breather between the three-eighths pole and the quarter pole," Brumfield said later. "When Advocator came up on the outside I hit my horse once on the left and took a hold of him. He likes you to hold his head up and that's when he goes to running."

Rounding the elbow, Kauai King pulled away from Advocator, which was taking the longer route, while Stupendous, on the inside, took over second place. Blue Skyer moved up to fourth on the outside of Advocator, Rehabilitate stayed on the rail in fifth place, while Abe's Hope swept wide and started his final run down the stretch from sixth place.

At the three-sixteenths pole, Stupendous drove to within a half-length of the lead, his high-water mark.

"I don't know how many times I hit him in the stretch [eight]," Brumfield said. "About the eighth pole the only thing I was thinking was 'help me now, Lord, I need it.' "

Kauai King pulled away with good daylight between him and Advocator, which was only a head in front of Blue Skyer. Abe's Hope had made his run, getting to within two lengths of the leader ony a sixteenth of a mile away from home.

175

"We had a good shot at it," Bill Shoemaker said. "I thought those horses in front were getting weary and we could go right on, but my horse didn't have it."

Kauai King was tiring, but not as badly as were Abe's Hope and Stupendous. Advocator and Blue Skyer finished fastest of all, save perhaps Rehabilitate. Right at the end both Advocator and Blue Skyer closed the gap, picking up a length on the winner in the last 20 yards.

"I don't know how much he had left," Brumfield said. "I was getting all I could out of him."

It was enough, by a half-length. Brumfield had set a pace of progressively slower quarters—:22⅘, :23⅖, :24⅖, :25, and :26⅖ for the final time of 2:02—matching the time Dark Star needed to beat Kauai King's sire by a head in the 1953 Derby.

Kauai King's time for the last quarter was the slowest of any winner in the last 18 runnings of the Kentucky Derby. None has needed more than 26 seconds to close it out since Citation coasted home with a :27⅕ stretch run over a sloppy track. Make what you will of that.

Last year Lucky Debonair ran the final quarter in :24⅕ and just made it, by a neck, when Dapper Dan turned in a phenomenal final quarter of :23⅕. The year before that, Northern Dancer finished out the final two furlongs in :24 flat while Hill Rise ran it in :23⅗.

There was nothing around this year with a 24-second lick at the end, but then horses race against horses, not against time, and there was nothing in this year's Derby that could head Kauai King during any part of it.


## Fast Footing

JOE DANIELS (Australian—Dolly Carter, by Glencoe) was the best 2-year-old of 1871. He confirmed this with a smashing triumph in the $2,100 Central Stakes at Pimlico in the fall when, ridden by James G. Rowe Sr., he soundly defeated Sir Roderick Cameron's Inversnaid and Gov. Oden Bowie's Rebba with a mile in 1:54¼.

My, how times, literally, change. Last fall at Churchill Downs, Charles

176

Engelhard's 2-year-old Evasive Action defeated Miss Mary Fisher's Hard Work in the Kentucky Jockey Club Stakes with a mile in 1:33⅘.

Joe Daniels was the best of his crop whereas Evasive Action was weighted 20th high on the Experimental Free Handicap. It is suspected here that a nice 2-year-old of today is not 100 lengths or so better than a champion 2-year-old of yesterday.

Horses, generally, may be faster than they were a century ago—but not much faster. Track surfaces are. Construction of dirt tracks has become so sophisticated, 2-year-old fillies now can run 4½ furlongs in :50⅖ (Kathryn's Doll at Turf Paradise, Dear Ethel at Miles Park, both in 1967).

Having peaked out on dirt, our scientists went back into the lab to get something faster in the way of track surfaces. The artificial Tartan surface at Tropical Park last month produced a new clocking for 4½ furlongs when Bushers Rule, a 4-year-old gelding by Apollo, was timed in 50 seconds flat. We can look forward to even faster times when they perfect the racing plates with those little tiny wheels.

Or, we can turn them out on grass and let them run.


## Something Special


ONE of the many pleasures of racing at Keeneland in the spring is the Thoroughbred Club Dinner Purse.

Now, this is not a big deal in a money way, such as the Champagne or Garden State Stakes, but it is long on special interest and good fun. The event is raced over 4½ furlongs for a $6,000 purse and a set of julep cups, and is restricted to 2-year-olds owned by Thoroughbred Club members who like to talk about the thing over drinks and dinner after the race.

It was started more than 30 years ago at a Saturday luncheon meeting in Lexington of the Thoroughbred Club of America, more than likely arising out of a discussion of sensational works by maiden 2-year-olds owned by the discussants.

Inasmuch as the conditions require that the 2-year-olds be maidens at the time of subscribing for the dinner, it is surprising how many winners of the Thoroughbred Club Dinner Purse have proved to be good horses.

In the very first running of the race in 1940, Alsab beat Some Chance. Alsab, of course, was champion of his crop at two and three, while Some

Chance won the Futurity and nine other stakes. In 1947, Bewitch beat colts, which she was to do many times before her retirement as America's greatest money-earning mare with $462,605. Romanita won it in 1956, the year she was voted champion 2-year-old filly. Other winners of the Thoroughbred Club Dinner Purse which went on to win stakes were Bagdad, which earned $353,422 and became a prominent sire; Spotted Line, Red Curtice, Judy Rullah, Provocative, Matisse, Mr. Prosecutor, Delnita, Mays Relic, Roman Bow, Mlle. Lorette, Volt, Golly, Feudin Fightin, Quick Swoon, and Miss Bally.

In some years, the number of entries for the race required its being run in two or three divisions. In 1963, subscribers toasted two winners presenting, at once, different types of racing men and the essence of the racing game:

Winner of the first division was Ouzo, owned and bred by Cornelius Vanderbilt Whitney, whose riches include the enjoyment of having bred more stakes winners than any man alive; winner of the second division was Mays Relic, owned, bred, and trained by Strother Griffin, a former rider who had only one horse in his stable.

This spring, only six 2-year-olds were entered for the Thoroughbred Club Dinner Purse. Tinkham Veale II's Corporation sprinted to a clear lead and held it almost to the end. Millard Waldheim's Busted trailed Corporation into the stretch, then started to lug in; favored Busted was outside Corporation at the eighth pole, suddenly ducked inside, almost clipping the leader's heels, then dug in and won by a nose.

In the Keeneland dining room three hours later, trainer Tony Basile was asked how he felt about his colt running such a race:

"It scares me to death. He's been spooky like that since we started racing him. Does it in the morning, too. Down at Aiken, he must have run five-eighths of a mile in a quarter-mile race. His mother was the same way, did the same thing right here at Keeneland four years ago."

Basile also had trained Waldheim's homebred T. V. Commercial, earner of $404,034. "I would have to say this colt Busted might be just a little bit better than T. V. Commerical was at this time. We'll run him in the Lafayette Stakes and then we'll know more.

Mickey Solomone, who rode Busted, was presented with a silken purse of coins, in keeping with an old race-track custom discarded many years ago; the purse was hung on the finish post, sometimes on the wire stretching across the track, requiring the jockey to stand on his saddle to pull down the purse. The Thoroughbred Club Dinner Purse award for the winning jockey is in the green and white colors of Col. E. R. Bradley, first honor guest of the Thoroughbred Club.

Bill O'Neill, manager of Bwamazon Farm and Waldheim's racing and breeding interests, represented the winning owner and breeder in accepting the six silver julep cups.

"Solomone says he might put the blame on Tony for this colt's running crooked and Tony has been asking me what to do with him. None of us know, but as long as he keeps winning, we don't particularly care. His sire, Creme dela Creme, was like that. The first time he started, he threw Don Brumfield three times going to the post, but he still won. He went on to win the Rancocas and Jersey Derby before he got hurt. Busted's dam, Bwamazon Lady, was in front in her first start here at Keeneland four years ago, and the rider folded up on her and a filly trained by Ralph Kercheval (current Thoroughbred Club president) beat us a nose. Next time she ran out on the turn and a filly trained by Mack Miller beat us.

"You know Judy Rullah won the Dinner Purse for us in 1955. She went on to win the Arlington Lassie and Pollyanna, then produced Creme dela Creme, sire of this colt. This is a kinda 'round-the-mountain thing, keep going around and wind up back at this Dinner Purse."

Did Bwamazon have something else this year?

"Well, we have got one or two that we haven't started yet. Everyone has a better one back in the barn and we are no exception. Right now, though, I'll stick along with Busted for a while."

It is not a big race, an important event in the over-all view of the Turf, but it is one of the nice things that makes racing in the spring at Keeneland something special.


## Keep the Change


AT SARATOGA, the days are long, eventful, and at times befuddling. A man rises at dawn to see his horse work, rushes through Hand melon and eggs, attends two or three meetings (for example, the National Steeplechase and Hunt Association had simultaneous meetings at two sites, the Holiday Inn and the Reading Room, presumably one for gray horses and one for bays), drinks lunch, goes to the races, leaves early for a cocktail party, and, before attending the yearling sales has dinner either in a home or at one of Saratoga's superb restaurants.

At any rate, toward the end of a day it can become difficult to ascertain

179

precisely where one is, or about. One prominent yearling buyer showed up at a dinner party, had some more martinis, and decided it was time to go to the sales. He put down $300 next to his plate and asked for his bill. The butler, immune to all behavioral maladies of Saratoga house guests, coolly ignored the situation and returned to the table with the salad. Presuming this was his change, the horseman grabbed the bibb lettuce, dressing and all, stuffed it in his coat pocket, and departed for the sales.

## We Don't Buy It

WHITNEY TOWER in *Sports Illustrated* quotes an anonymous trainer, apparently one who does not have any of Bold Ruler's 10 stakes winners this season in his barn: "Bold Ruler won't make it. His get are better at two and at three. The threes are better than the fours, and at four what is there of his that has been a valuable addition to the handicap division? Only one of the first crop, Lamb Chop, proved that Bold Ruler could sire a distance runner. And one Lamb Chop doesn't make a sire." And when Bob Cousy started with the Celtics it was suggested that he was too small, had too much razzle-dazzle, the pros would eat him up.

## For Art's Sake

THE DAY after Fort Marcy won the International, his owner-breeder was talking about George Stubbs (1724-1806), one of the first great English artists to paint what, to the casual eye of today's racegoer, is a recognizable horse.

When Paul Mellon talks of Stubbs, he knows whereof he speaks. Much of the vast Mellon art collection is on exhibit in the National Gallery of Art in Washington, which was built and filled originally by Mellon's father, former Secretary of the Treasury; Mellon is president of the National Gallery and privately has added considerably to it in the way of wings and pictures.

Many of his sporting pictures, after exhibition at the Virginia Museum of Fine Arts in 1964, have been returned to his Rokeby Farm, some gracing

the walls of his residence (the Degas painting of horses at the start, reproduced on posters and distributed about Paris to advertise this year's running
of the Prix de l'Arc de Triomphe, hangs in the dining room; Benjamin
Marshall's famous "Studies of Horsemen" is in the living room).

Most of the Stubbs paintings hang in what is called the "brick house" at
Rokeby, where there is excellent lighting and ample wall space for one of the
largest collections likely to be encountered under one roof. There also are
animal and sporting pictures by Jacques Laurent Agasse, Henry Alken,
Edgar Degas, John Ferneley, John F. Herring, James Pollard, Francis and
John N. Sartorius, James Seymour, James Ward, and John Wooton.

Mellon said Stubbs had become quite popular in the last four or five years.
"Some of his better and bigger paintings have been coming up, you know.
There was a portrait of an Indian holding a cheetah which was supposed to
be about to chase a deer—a wonderful picture—that was sold last year. I
didn't bid for it because I thought it ought to stay in England. It is a real museum picture. The Manchester Museum has it now. It sold for a very big
price, £125,000 or something like that."

Just inside the brick house front door is a 12 x 16-inch Stubbs painting of
the rubbing-down house at Newmarket, which Stubbs often used as a background for paintings of Eclipse, Gimcrack, and other famous race horses of
the 18th century. Mellon adjusted a light over a 33 x 39-inch Stubbs painting
of John Pratt's Pumpkin, by Match'em—Old Squirt Mare.

"This is my favorite of all," Mellon said. "I got it sometime in the early
1930s, one of my first. I like the horse and I like the boy in his cherry-col-
ored jacket. I just think it's a beautiful picture."

In a corner was Stubbs' "The Farmer's Wife & The Raven" depicting an
episode taken from the *Fables* of John Gay, published in 1727. The volume
rests on a table below the painting with a marker in it indicating the subject
fable.

On another wall was "Reapers," which Stubbs painted on a 30 x 40-inch
oval Wedgewood plaque in 1795. He painted on porcelain, copper, wood, "always experimenting with different things."

Next to a small self-portrait in oil, there hung the initial drawing Stubbs
had made on squared paper and from which larger or smaller paintings
could be executed in proper proportion.

Under these was "the only photograph I have here." It was Marshall
Hawkins' famous picture of the First Lady negotiating a fence her horse
would not, one arm outstretched to break the headlong fall.

"It happened in one of our fields here and about a month later we were out
hunting again and I said that if I could get a copy of the picture, which had

appeared on the cover of *Life*, I would like her to autograph it for me. A week later I got this one from the White House."

Hand written on the mat was: To MFH—I will get off to pick up your cigarettes anytime. Jackie."

No attempt will be made here to describe the treasury of sporting art in the Mellon collection, for words hardly can re-create the pleasure of viewing the horse as painted by Stubbs, or Ward, or Wooton, or Sartorius, or Herring, or Degas—and these in every direction.


## Traveling Salesman

ON the clubhouse terrace at Saratoga one morning this week, a man drew up to a table, looked in vain for an empty spot for his *Daily Racing Form* and sale catalogue, finally stashed them under his chair, and opened the conversation: "Well, what can I sell you gentlemen a part of?"

He was from Kentucky.


## Down Mexico Way

SPECULATION began shortly after noon on Tuesday, May 7, 1968, when a bomb exploded on racing in the form of an announcement that Dancer's Image had carried prohibited Butazolidin in his system when he finished first in the Kentucky Derby.

Speculation has simmered ever since about how "somebody" somehow "musta made a bundle" betting on the race. "A lotta smart money" was reported bet in Miami. Topical at cocktail parties has been the "million cleaned up in the Caliente future book."

Speculation continues because it has never been determined who administered the Butazolidin which the state chemist, the stewards at Churchill Downs, and the Kentucky State Racing Commission have found as fact was administered to Dancer's Image.

Talk of Who, goes toward Why, and stops at the Big Bet. If a single individual bet a great deal of money on Dancer's Image at Churchill Downs, he

182

will forever remain unknown. For one thing, a player has all day Friday and most of Saturday to bet in small denominations on the Kentucky Derby, unlike other races on which track wagers must be placed within 20 or 30 minutes. For another thing, the Kentucky Derby wagering pool is so big (a record $2,350,470 in 1968), heavy play on a recognized contender is undetectable. Dancer's Image figured to be second choice off his past performances; before any money was bet at the track, the track handicapper set his line on Dancer's Image at 3.50 to 1; when all the large and small bets were put through the mutuels, Dancer's Image paid 3.60 to 1. Thus, no unexpected money on Dancer's Image appeared at the track.

Well, then, how about the action in Mexico? How much money was bet in the Caliente future book?

In Los Angeles last month for the NASRC convention, we decided to visit Caliente. We called its San Diego office. "Come on down, take you only 20 minutes to fly," invited Caliente publicist Ken Rojens. It would take 55 minutes to get to the Los Angeles airport, a 30-minute wait before takeoff, the flight down there, and then the trip from the San Diego airport...it was decided to rent a car.

Problems arose immediately. Hertz does not care for customers driving in Mexico because, in the event of an accident, fault often is determined by nationality and cars can be impounded for six months or more. Then, too, nobody takes the San Diego Freeway to San Diego because it goes to Long Beach. The Santa Ana Freeway is better, if rush hours are avoided. Once past Disneyland, the traffic and swearing subsides.

It is easy to confirm a proper direction for, driving south, one runs out of road signs bearing Santa Anita stakes names like San Gabriel, San Juan Capistrano, and San Marcos and comes upon Del Mar fixtures such as Oceanside, Escondido, and La Jolla. The interstate streams by the Gulf of Santa Catalina surf and where it mets the turf at Del Mar. In San Diego, a high curving bridge to Coronado nears completion despite indignant and persistent protests from those who prefer the ferry. Passing ship after ship docked in the San Diego Naval Station, one quickly reaches the border.

There, the United States and many things that one takes for granted— paved roads, traffic signs, street curbs, cleanly painted signs, new cars, the hurry—stop. The Hertz was U-parked and we walked across into Tijuana, abruptly another place entirely.

Hot dust swirled up from the lot where drivers of 10 yellow cabs hustled fares to Caliente for 75 cents. Owner-drivers of two blue-and-white cabs waited in the rear of the lot for fares to Caliente for 50 cents. It seems that many of the cars in Tijuana are rebuilt, after extensive stock-car racing;

183

every driver in Tijuana has the right-of-way, which makes intersections exciting. There is an extensive muffler-repair business, about a mile of hand-painted signs advertising muffler maintenance on the premises, grassless yards in front of shop-residents. A truck was stopped in the middle of the main road and, as workmen patiently filled chuckholes with dirt, drivers skidded around the truck, raising more dust.

The most substantial structures in northern Mexico are churches, and Caliente. The race track was built 40 years ago with little thought of cost, Marshall Cassidy doing much of the design and supervising construction, Jack Campbell and Francis Dunne serving as officials. It was part of an elaborate resort complex, golf course, gambling casino, and grand hotel. A wisp of splendor still remains in the casino portion of the Caliente stands, the terrazzo dining terraces, the heavy doors, high vaulted ceilings, elegant chandeliers, and dark paneling.

The day's business, the foreign book, is conducted in a newer yet more-worn section of the stands. While many track operators lie awake at night trying to figure ways of utilizing a 10- or 20-million dollar property when their race meeting ends, the Alessio brothers have no such problem.

Caliente is in use all day and most of the night, year around. Players wander in to play the first races in Florida and Maryland about 10 a.m., and there is a shuffling of patrons of the foreign book as the day wears on with results being posted from Fair Grounds, Oaklawn Park, and Santa Anita. At dusk, an elevated dog track is rolled in front of the stands and a new, entirely different crowd of bettors arrives for dog racing, five nights a week. On Saturdays and Sundays, Thoroughbred racing is conducted. Last month, old-time handbook slates went up on the grandstand apron for Saturday and Sunday players who prefer Walter Mary's line to the crowd's odds as established through pari-mutuel pools. If there is a lag in the action, players can take a flyer on the Kentucky Derby future book.

"We don't like to be immodest," said John Alessio, "but we have the reputation of providing all kinds of betting down here. We have the quinella, the Perfecta, the Daily Double, the 5-10, the 1-2-3, and now the old-style books which are very popular in England and Australia and which I think will put a little more life into this thing."

John Alessio is the head of a large family which moved to San Diego from West Virginia. He is small, neat, has the manner of a banker, which he is, and the acumen of a corporate executive, which he is. His assistant is brother Tony, a short, round, rumpled man who runs the foreign and future books. John sat behind a large desk and thumbed through a stack of correspondence as we talked. Tony crossed his ankles under his chair, studying an

184

old issue of one of his lines on the 1968 Kentucky Derby future book.

"There are two or three things that we have to clear in our discussion," John began. "We are American citizens and we run this track as a corporation for Mexican people and we are necessarily limited in our discussions.

"How much money is bet here in the Kentucky Derby future book? Not that we keep that as a secret, but we have never given that out. We have not said that we won all the time or lost all the time. I can say that our business on the Kentucky Derby future book has dropped off considerably since the post office ruling prohibited bets coming through the mail. The future book—we don't handle a lot, a comfortable amount. Well, you might ask, is it a couple hundred thousand? I would say to you right now, no."

Tony laughed and said he had heard that he had laid off $400,000 on the Kentucky Derby last year. "That's asinine," John said. "If we lay a horse at 25 to 1 two months before the race, why would we lay it off on the day of the race when the horse's odds are 2 to 1? That doesn't make sense; it's not logical."

The Alessios said that the Kentucky Derby future book pool was 85 per cent less than what it had been before 1957 when mailed bets could be accepted. They said that they continue making a Kentucky Derby line for its publicity value to Caliente. In addition to advance betting on Tony's line in the future book, they also offer betting at Caliente on the day of the Kentucky Derby and those bets are paid off at track odds, that is, odds fixed by the mutuel play at Churchill Downs.

"The year Swaps won, we had a $32,000 minus pool here at the track," John said. "We paid off what Swaps paid at the track, $7.60. If we had paid off on the basis of what was bet at Caliente that day, it would have been $3.40."

Tony said he based his future-book line on the money he handled, trying to keep it as balanced as possible. "Money makes the price. My odds change every day. We send out a line every week for publicity purposes, but all future boks are subject to change without notice and I revise my line according to what kind of action I have."

Has there been occasion to refuse to take a bet? "I don't think I have ever turned anybody down. If a man comes in with a big bet, I might give him a different price."

Is a $10,000 bet usual or unusual? "Unusual," Tony said, "unless you come up with a horse like Graustark. Remember how wonderful he was? I took a $10,000 bet on him at 8 to 5, would have cost me $16,000. You have to take money on the favorites."

"Reminiscing a little," said John, "when we could take bets through the

185

mail and over the phone and all that, a man called from Palm Springs and wanted $10,000 on Citation. We took it at 8 to 5. Next week he calls up and bets another $10,000, and the next week he bet another $10,000." No mention was made of an unbalance book in 1948 when Citation won the Kentucky Derby.

What about last year? The Caliente future book listed Dancer's Image at 30 to 1 on the opening line of March 3 and through April 1. After Dancer's Image won the Governor's Gold Cup, he was dropped to 10 to 1 and then to 8 to 1, fifth favorite. After Dancer's Image won the Wood Memorial, he was dropped to 5 to 1, second favorite to Forward Pass, and his final posting was 4 to 1.

"I think $200 was the biggest bet I took on Dancer's Image," Tony said. "We got good play on Forward Pass, Iron Ruler, Proper Proof, Verbatim, Don B. ...this was a good book because they took everything early. But $200 was the biggest I had on Dancer's Image and that was early, at 30 to 1. A good pal bet me about 15 horses at $200 a shot and I stumbled on that one. Nobody collected more than that $6,000 on Dancer's Image. He was one of our regular customers; don't think he has ever been to a Kentucky Derby."

As to a big betting coup on the 1968 Kentucky Derby future book, the Alessios future sayeth not.


## Now You're Talking Real Money


LOOKING at racing's vital statistics as presented by economist David Novick, we find that $5 billion was bet on Thoroughbred horse races in North America last year, $731,649 per day, $98.82 per person each day.

This seems like a good deal of betting money. We were checking on something in an old volume of *The Blood-Horse*, however, and happened upon a story John A. Drake related to editor Tom Cromwell concerning serious wagering.

John W. (Bet-a-Million) Gates, who started with a hardware store in West Chicago, went to Texas with some barbed wire in the 1870s and returned with a fortune. This was parlayed into a magnificent sum by a series of corporate mergers, which by 1892 was the monopoly styled Consolidated Steel & Wire Co. Five years later, Gates organized a trust that was to control all the wire and steel that glistened; it was so grand that J. P. Morgan stepped in and took it over. So for $20 million, Gates left U. S. Steel to Morgan and turned his attention to railroads, oil, and the race track.

At the turn of the century, American racing men with any pretense of class raced a few horses in Britain—August Belmont, W. C. Whitney, James R. and Foxhall Keene, Pierre Lorillard, plus Richard (Boss) Croker and Ed Corrigan (both of whom had been ruled off in New York, for different reasons), and John W. Gates.

Gates' horses were in the care of American trainer Enoch Wishard and ridden by the celebrated American brothers, Johnny and Lester Reiff. Gates bought an aged horse whose name struck his fancy, Royal Flush, with which he won the Royal Hunt Cup at Ascot in June of 1900. The following month, Royal Flush was entered for the Stewards Cup at Goodwood.

Drake, friend and partner of Gates in many Turf exploits, said he left the business of getting down the bets to Gates: "I didn't see him for a couple of days and when I finally met him, I asked him how much he had placed on the horse. He said he didn't know, and took out his memorandum book, started turning pages.

"Well, every page he turned represented a sizeable investment with a bookmaker, and after he had been fingering pages for quite a few minutes, I took out my Waterman and drew a line across his book, telling him that was as far as I wanted to go.

" 'Hell, John,' Gates explained, jumping to his feet, 'you don't mean to tell me you've heard there's something the matter with our horse!' "

Royal Flush, with Johnny Reiff up, won the Stewards Cup by six lengths at 11-2 starting odds. Second was Croker's Americus, also trained by Wishard, and ridden by Lester Reiff. Drake said he and Gates won nearly $2 million on their bets.

"I met him the next day in the hotel," Drake related, "and he tells me, 'John, if you hadn't dumped cold water on me, we could have taken some real money from these people.' "

## Racing Men Never Retire

Checking yearlings at the sale, as has been his wont for more than 70 years, was George H. Strate. Since he broke Imp and galloped her at two and three in Ohio for Uncle Dan Brossman, Strate has seen the promise of a thousand young horses.

He was born in Louisville; his mother died when he was six, his father

187

when he was nine. "I ran away from the orphanage when I was 14½ years old, joined Sam Bryant's stable at Churchill Downs, but they found me about six weeks later and took me back. Then I ran away again, caught on with Col. Robert L. Baker at old Oakley Park. That was my first regular job, working around the barns and getting on a few horses. Rode a little at Ohio and Indiana fairs.

"You know, Uncle Dan didn't care much about Thoroughbreds, only to cross mares with Standardbred stallions to get trotters. He didn't think much of Imp either when she was racing around in Ohio, but when she went to New York she win the Suburban (1899) and beat all the good colts around then."

In 1904, Strate was foreman for C. E. (Boots) Durnell. "You know, I saddled the first Kentucky Derby winner ever bred and owned by a lady. Mrs. Durnell owned this colt by Free Knight bred by a lady out in Missouri (Mrs. J. B. Prather). Mrs. Durnell came around one day—we were racing out at old Ascot Park in California—and she was wanting to know how to get eligible for the Kentucky Derby, so we nominated Elwood and Boots didn't know anything about it.

"We shipped over to Churchill Downs and Boots went on to Chicago, and then he come down to see Elwood's final workout, which wasn't much, and he says, 'He ain't gonna do anything; he's too fat,' and went on back to Chicago.

"Well, only five horses run in the Derby that year and we were the longest shot in the field at 15-1, but we win by half a length. You never saw anybody as pleased as Mrs. Durnell. We won the Latonia Derby with Elwood, too, that year."

Strate saddled two other horses for the Kentucky Derby. Mrs. Frank Heller's Agrarian finished third to Cavalcade in 1934 and H. S. Nesbitt's Staretor finished second to Whirlaway in 1941. "I win the Hollywood Derby with him."

The best horse Strate ever had?

"Inchcape. Never beaten. Would have been a great sire but he got burned up. Bought him as a weanling for $2,000 from John E. Madden. Sold him for $150,000 as a 2-year-old to Harry Sinclair.

"After I left Nevada Stock Farm, I went to work for John H. Rosseter, vice president of Grace Steamship. I built that farm out there (Wikiup Rancho near Santa Rosa, Calif.) for him, 1,100 acres, and he sent me to Kentucky to buy some stallions. Got Disguise out of the Wickliffe Stud dispersal, then went out to Madden's to see Friar Rock.

"I had letters of credit in my pocket amounting to $250,000. Madden and

188

me got to dickering around there and I finally bought Friar Rock for $60,000. Madden kept after me, though, trying to find out who I was buying for. I wouldn't tell him. But he found out. Met Mr. Rosseter in New York later and they worked out another deal where Madden kept a half-interest in the horse and would stand him a couple of seasons at Hamburg Place and then he would stand two seasons at Wikiup.

"Well, that was when I got Inchcape (1918); he was in Friar Rock's first crop. I had bought Passing Shower from Madden for Mr. Rosseter the year before for $7,000. Win the Spinaway with her. Fred Burlew was training for us and Inchcape win his first start at Aqueduct and 10 days later come right back and win the Tremont by seven lengths."

Sam Hildreth, then assembling the powerful Rancocas Stable for Harry Sinclair, and George D. Widener each reportedly made offers of $100,000 for Inchcape which were refused. The record price for a 2-year-old at that time was the $75,000 Louis Winans had paid Madden for Sir Martin in 1908. Within a week after the Tremont, Inchcape was in the Rancocas Stable, the transfer being made for a reported $150,000.

Inchcape did not meet Tryster or Prudery, generally regarded as the best 2-year-olds of 1920. He raced only one more time, as a 3-year-old, in Sinclair's colors, winning an allowance race by 10 lengths at Saratoga before he suffered a training injury. Rosseter refunded the sale price and took Inchcape to California.

"I rented a place here to keep Mr. Rosseter's mares when we bred to Kentucky stallions. Rented from Price Headley for $700 a year, what he called the whisky farm—used to make whisky there in a building next to the creek—that's where the Campbell House is now. Had a half-mile training track out there in the middle of the golf course. I never used it. Only kept broodmares there.

"I used to race a lot out west. Before I went with Mr. Rosseter, I trained for George Wingfield (1915), who had the Nevada Stock Farm. I saddled the first winner ever sired by Sweep, a filly named Washoe Belle; won a little stake with her at Denver. Win the Nevada Derby with Star Shooter at Reno that year and Wingfield gave me a $650 stopwatch. Another good mare I trained for him was Celesta, by Sempronius.

"Before that (1905) I win the California Derby at Tanforan with Dr. Leggo, by Puryear D., for Charlie McCafferty."

Since he saddled his first winner, Nettie Regent, on April 20, 1899, at Newport, Ky., for Mrs. Kate P. Shipp, Strate has trained a large number of good horses for many owners, including Willis Sharpe Kilmer ("One year; had the second string, won a lotta races"), the Tedluc Stable, for which he

189

won the 1930 Prince of Wales Plate in Canada with Spearhead; Royce Martin, for whom he won a divison of the 1944 Kent Stakes with Kaytee; Brae Burn Farm, for which he won the 1951 Astoria and Colleen Stakes with Star-Enfin; Ogden Phipps, for whom he won the San Marcos Handicap with Great Captain; Carleton Burke, Walter Dupee, and Greentree Stable.

"I was with the Lester Manor Stable for 33 years. Owned by Frank Heller, carpet man from New York, and Benjamin O'Shea of Union Carbide. Compliance won the Alabama and Monmouth Oaks for us in 1948. Open Show won the Benjamin Franklin Handicap. Bevy of Roses was the last good filly I trained; won the Miss America Turf Handicap in California in 1959. They had a farm in Virginia but we kept all the Lester Manor horses with Leslie Combs. First foal out of Bevy of Roses, a yearling filly, sold here two years ago for $52,000."

Strate says he retired four years ago, but racing men never retire, really, as long as there is a crop of yearlings coming on. He now lives in Little Rock, Ark., and serves as an advisor for Gene Goff's Verna Lea Farms in Fayetteville, Ark.

"We're selling that good filly, Nilene Wonder, at Ocala next month. She beat Tosmah and Miss Cavandish last year, you know; would have been best but went wrong.

"Say, I better do some studying here on this catalogue. Some of these yearlings'll get by me. If you're going to write anything, sorta soft-pedal it. Never cared much for publicity."

George Strate, with more than 70 years of racing, looks forward to the next sale.


## Any Takers?


RAYMOND GUEST was sitting in the Hotel de Crillon bar, adding some sauce to the speech he had prepared in French for Marcel Boussac's traditional black-tie dinner at Maxim's on the eve of the Prix de l'Arc de Triomphe.

Guest's Irish-bred L'Escargot last year as a 6-year-old was voted champion American steeplechaser after jumping the Atlantic several times and winning the Meadow Brook Steeplechase on this side. This year, L'Escargot won the important Cheltenham Gold Cup and was a subject of rumor that he was

190

to be run on the flat in final preparation for the $100,000 Colonial Cup at Camden, S. C., on Nov. 14.

"Listen pal," confided the former eight-goal polo player who a few years ago became the first United States Ambassador to Ireland to pick up a blue ribbon in an Irish hunter class, "a horse can get hurt pretty easily going over jumps.

"That old guy knows all there is to know about fences, so all he needs for the Colonial Cup is a little zip and some shipping money. See, he's used to carrying 170 pounds over jumps; he gets into the Irish Cesarewitch Handicap [Oct. 17] with only 122 pounds. He's going to think he has No Boy up for two miles on the flat and I figure he's worth a five-oh bet he finishes in the top four."

## With Eddie Neloy

### WEDNESDAY

6:30 a.m.—An orange full moon rested just above the San Gabriel mountain range. In the Phipps barn at Santa Anita, seven rays from electric bulbs in each stall slanted through the doorways and hit the shedrow floor like Indian lances. Steam rose from the dirty straw Ofelia Tiziani pitched out on a muck sack. It was 36 degrees. Assistant trainer John Campo's white ducks noisily enjoyed mud and puddles left on the walking ring by Tuesday's four-inch downpour. Disciplinarian (3-year-old son of Bold Ruler—Lady Be Good, by Better Self), winner of the San Miguel Stakes by seven lengths in the rain, snuffled.

Eddie Neloy, who last year saddled the Phippses' horses for 281 races and won 93, including a record 41 stakes for unprecedented year-earnings of $2,456,250, left his car in the track parking lot and picked his way through mud to Barn No. 37. On Saturday night he had been in New York accepting a Bill Corum Memorial Award at the B'nai B'rith sports dinner; on Sunday morning he had been at Santa Anita to see Buckpasser work and made the decision to have 28-year-old Joe Grasso, Standardbred trainer and blacksmith, fly out from New York and apply a plastic patch on Buckpasser's right forefoot; on Monday he was at Hialeah, where he has the main division of the Phipps horses (25, plus the same number of 2-year-olds at Gulfstream Park with Al Robertson); on Tuesday afternoon he had flown back to California to spend the last four days with Buckpasser before the $100,000-added Charles H. Strub Stakes.

"Good morning, Father John," Neloy said to his 28-year-old assistant as he walked under the shed. "See you picked up another duck."

"That mallard? Wandered over from Charlie Whittingham's barn. Her mate died over there so she come over here where it's more interesting. Whittingham says we beat him in the stake yesterday (Whittingham trained Tumble Wind, which had finished second to Disciplinarian) and now we're stealing his ducks."

Neloy walked directly to Buckpasser's stall and felt both front ankles. The champion did not care for Neloy's applying any pressure on his right forefoot and moved his leg back and forth quickly, trying to wrest it from Neloy's grasp.

"You just don't like me, do you," Neloy stated more than asked. Buckpasser finally ceased his efforts and Neloy studied the patch on the inside quarter and small swelling just above the patch on the coronary band.

"Hot. Has a little pressure place there, John, just above the patch."

"Not as hot as it was yesterday, boss."

"Well, we'll see if it goes down when we take him out on the track this morning. Main track's closed because of that rain, I suppose. Let's gallop him on the training track with a pony."

7:05 a.m.—Ogden Mills (Dinny) Phipps, owner-breeder of Time Tested (5-year-old son of Better Self—Past Eight, by Eight Thirty, two stalls away from Buckpasser) and who was in California with the Ford team for the Riverside-Motor Trend 500-mile race for stock cars, came under the shed-row.

Neloy went into the tackroom and drew a picture of the inside of Buckpasser's right forefoot. "Couple of weeks ago, these two small cracks showed up here. They didn't mean anything, no heat, but last week it got a bigger crack here, little farther back on the quarter and higher toward the coronary band.

"After he worked Sunday, this one opened a little, so we called Joe out here from New York to put the patch on and stop the crack before it got up into the coronary band, where we would be in trouble. There was no heat in there Sunday night. Monday, after Joe put the patch on, we did get a little heat there while the left ankle was cold. Of course, any time you do any cutting, you're going to get some inflammation. Left a little hole above the patch to let it out. This morning we find a little pressure built up in a spot there above the patch. We have to see about that."

Poker (4-year-old son of Round Table—Glamour, by Nasrullah), which

192

was to run in the San Pasqual Handicap on Thursday, was taken to the track with Helpful (3-year-old daughter of Bold Ruler—Lending Hand, by Turn-to), a maiden. Neloy zipped up his windbreaker against the cold. He was wearing a white shirt, blue sweater, gray flannels, and black shoes that were quickly losing their shine en route to the training track.

"Man could make a lot of money selling overshoes this morning. Hi, George. Oh, doing all right, I suppose, but probably shouldn't have won by so far yesterday." Approaching the trainers' stand, Neloy reached for a condition book in his back pocket. There was none.

"Dinny, that's a great tailor you recommended. No back pocket." Young Phipps casually inquired if Neloy had bothered to suggest to the tailor that a back pocket was desired. "No, never had to ask a man for a back pocket before." The horses galloped twice around the muddy six-furlong training track and headed for the barn; Neloy and Phipps headed for the kitchen and coffee.

7:25 a.m.—"Well, how about it? Shall we make an announcement about the foot? May be nothing, then again may amount to something and they would come up with a $100,000 race and nobody in it?"

A jockey's agent drew up to the table, inquired about a mount. Neloy got a condition book. It had no calendar in the back, so he ruled off one, meticulously writing in the dates and noting on appropriate squares when stakes were to be run and horses he might have ready for each. Phipps said one of his cars at Riverside had a flat, that when the race had been stopped on Sunday because of rain all cars had been locked up and no one was allowed to touch them, so when the race was resumed, seven days later, the car would have to go the first lap with a flat tire.

Ricardo Diaz, writer and co-producer of a television show on racing, a half-hour segment on an all-sports, 12-part series entitled "The Professionals," drew up a chair. "Mr. Neloy, here is the script. We're scheduled to shoot this morning that scene from the exercise boy, camera mounted on his helmet, and we'd like to have him ride a bay if you don't mind. We can do the thing about a leg bandage on the pony. Have you gone over the script I sent you?" No, he had not, but if all he had to do now was see that Warren Fourre wore the special helmet and rode a bay, he could get that done with the next set. Diaz left to make final arrangements for the shooting.

"Well, shall we tell them? The press?" Phipps said he thought it would be best to make a full disclosure, and to do so as early as possible. "We've never held anything back before." Neloy nodded, and on the back of the TV script he began writing out a statement:

"Inasmuch as it has been our policy to keep the press and public informed

193

of Buckpasser's status for all races, we wish to say Buckpasser suffered a—how many r's in recurrence?—recurrence of the crack on the inside quarter of his right forefoot. It is in the same area in which the crack occurred that kept him out of the Triple Crown races last spring.

"It does not run into the coronary band, and if it did there would be no possibility of his running in the Strub Stakes on Saturday. In an effort to keep the crack from running into the coronary band, we called in Joe Grasso, whose patch was used last spring. He applied a patch to the area on Monday. There is a small buildup of—don't want to say infection; what's another word?—inflammation—that's the word; thanks, Dinny, where would we be without you?—in the area of the coronary band at present.

"It will be touch and go as to whether this inflammation can be cleared up before Saturday, and his starting on Saturday will depend on whether the inflammation subsides by that time. Eddie Neloy."

Whittingham sat down with a cup of coffee. Neloy silently passed him the statement. Whittingham read it slowly. He had two horses nominated for the Strub. Pretense and Drin.

Whittingham: "Gonna go?"

Neloy: "If I can get the inflammation down. Don't want to tub him because the water will loosen the patch."

Whittingham: "What you need is Butazolidin. Best thing in the world."

Neloy: "Too close to the race."

Whittingham: "Might try a light. I've had good luck drawing with a light."

Neloy: "Well, we'll know more after he gallops today."

7:55 a.m.—Joe Grasso greets Neloy at the barn. "Joe, will the water on the training track bother that patch?" "Not enough to worry about." "OK, we'll take him along in the middle of the track then." Neloy then hurried to the racing secretary's office to see Jimmy Kilroe.

"Thought we better tell you, Jimmy, it's touch and go whether we can run Saturday, and if we get a statement out now you might draw a better field."

Kilroe read the statement, said he appreciated Neloy's making it, was sorry his secretary had not yet arrived to type it. "I'll type it; an electric typewriter doesn't scare me," Neloy boasted. His secretarial work concluded, Neloy returned to the barn where the television crew had assembled, along with a small crowd of casual observers. Fourre, with camera helmet, was up on Vocalist, a 4-year-old bay gelding by Charlottesville—Arietta II, by Tudor Minstrel. In the same set was Top Bid (3-year-old son of Olympia—High Bid, by To Market), which Neloy wanted to get in an allowance race before the Santa Anita Derby.

Randy Sechrest, who at Neloy's urging had purchased Bold Bidder two

194

years ago and had won the 1966 Strub with him, was in the trainers' stand as Vocalist and Top Bid were galloped. "Got some mighty fine boots there, Randy," Neloy observed.

"Thybens givem to me for Christmas about 15 years ago."

"I been spending all kinds of money with him for a dozen years and all I ever get is a calendar." Kilroe entered the trainers' stand and Neloy handed him the typewritten statement. Kilroe said he would see that it was released to the press.

8:25 a.m.—At Barn 37, Mrs. Alice Carr de Creeft, in knee boots and blue-jeans, had set up modeling stand and roundtable and was adding bits of clay to a sculpture of Buckpasser on which she had been working for a week. The television crew was setting up a scene in which a leg bandage would be put on an absolutely sound lead pony. Diaz worked with the cotton.

"Boy," Neloy called, "you can sure tell you're a greeny." Diaz said he did not want to take up the time of one of the grooms and, since it was to be a close-up shot with only the hands showing, he thought he could do it. Neloy stooped under the shed rail and took the cotton, shook it out, rolled it, wrapped it around the pony's left foreleg. Then, with the professional pride of a man who had rolled a sufficient number of bandages in his 31 years on the track never to lose the knack, deftly did up the leg, smoothly and neat as a "pin—who's got a pin?"

"Did you zoom in on the hands?" Diaz asked the cameraman. "Now back it up and get Mr. Neloy. Right. Right. That's fine. Thank you, Mr. Neloy."

The trainer stooped back under the shed rail. "John, you go with Buckpasser. Give him once around. If he takes a bad step, or acts like he is not interested, or goes wrong in any way, bring him back to the barn. If he is going all right and seems to want to, go twice around." Neloy walked through the tunnel under the training track to take a vantage point in the center-field.

"Believe that was the pony that stumbled, not the horse," Dinny said. Buckpasser felt good in the brisk cool of the morning and galloped as though he would prefer that Campo on the pony would let him go. They galloped twice around. Neloy met them as they came off the track.

"That was the pony, wasn't it?"

"Yeah, boss, stumbled a little. The horse went good. Wanted to go." Neloy stopped by the secretary's office in the stable area and entered Top Bid in an allowance race (which did not fill), then returned to the barn where Buckpasser was being washed down. Mrs. de Creeft worked frantically on her sculpture, and a sizable crowd in addition to the television crew assembled.

Neloy took a clean rub rag and briskly dried Buckpasser's right foreleg. He

195

felt the coronary band. "Gone down. Feel a lot better about this thing now." Tiziani threw a cooler over Buckpasser and walked him away, up the ramp at the end of the barn and under the shedrow. "Hasn't taken a bad step yet. Had a chance to when he made that turn to go up under the shed."

Dr. Jock Jocoy drove by the barn. "Hey, Eddie, want to talk to you about a horse when you get time. Bid. Top Bid." Neloy was not ready to put a price on the horse. Dr. Jocoy drove on. Neloy and Grasso moved away from the crowd into the tack room and discussed the possible cause of the quarter crack. Grasso suggested it was a fundamental weakness in the area of the foot, or it might be the horse's way of going which put unusual stress on that particular quarter. Neloy thought it might be because the patch had been applied last year and may have interfered with normal growth of the hoof in that area. It was agreed that the slight inflammation was to be expected, was not serious, and since it had gone down after the slow gallop might be of no consequence.

11:10 a.m.—Neloy took a white feed sack, cut a corner from the bottom, punched some holes in the top of his small, inverted tent. Campo brought two jars of Dr. B. F. Brennan's Osmopack, a bottle of peroxide, and a small tube of cortisone ointment. Neloy sat down in the stall, dipped fingers in a jar of Osmopack and slapped a liberal portion of the turquoise material on Buckpasser's foot. A scrap of brown paper was slapped on and the horse was permitted to put the foot down. Neloy cleaned the coronary band with peroxide, covered the pressure point with cortisone ointment, then spread Osmopack over the entire hoof and pastern, and dressed the whole in the white sack, which he tied at the top by threading a piece of cloth through the holes.

"Now, we'll let nature do something for us."

## THURSDAY

6:50 a.m.—"How about it?" Neloy asked Campo as he came under the shedrow and headed for Buckpasser's stall.

"It broke, boss."

Neloy knelt in Buckpasser's stall and felt the right front coronary band, which the day before had evidenced a swelling above the quarter crack. The swelling was gone and the heat was less; Buckpasser was frisky, apparently feeling strong and ready to do something.

"Oh, I feel real good about this," Neloy said, ducking under the webbing to emerge from the stall. "Bold and Brave won the Royal Palm at Hialeah yesterday, John, by a neck. Beat Bold Tactics. When I'm in Florida, you win the stakes out here with Disciplinarian, and when I'm out here they win the

196

stakes in Florida. Wonder if Mr. Phipps thinks about those things.

"Say, John, I had dinner at Lou Rowan's last night and Mrs. Rowan wouldn't mind having a couple of your ducks. Guarantees nobody will eat them. (Naw.) Good home."

"You take care of the horses, boss," Campo said. "I'll take care of them ducks. How's Bold Monarch, boss?"

"Can't tell. He seems to hold his breath, swells up, then when Baeza hits him on the flank, whoosh, and he levels off and starts running."

7:05 a.m.—The public-address system announced to a small assemblage of early-bird racing fans that Helpful, from the Ogden Phipps barn and trained by Eddie Neloy, was coming onto the track and would work. Neloy walked toward the finish line, where he could clock the filly. Randy Sechrest asked if there were a price on Disciplinarian.

"We're not averse to selling him. You get Liz Tippett to put a price on Tumble Wind and we'll sell Disciplinarian for that figure." Sechrest thought Mrs. Tippett might price the horse at more than a million. Neloy smiled. Ricardo Diaz asked if the television crew could take a shot of Neloy clocking a horse at the gap. Neloy said he had better remain where he was, perhaps the scene could be taken after the workout.

"How'd she do?" Campo called from the track after Helpful had worked. Neloy had clocked her seven furlongs in 1:35.

A trainer asked about Successor, last year's 2-year-old champion. "Filled out good. You know what you hope will happen when you stop on a 2-year-old? That's what happened to Successor."

7:42 a.m.—Walking back from the track, Neloy pondered what to do with Buckpasser. "Think we ought to work him this morning?" he asked Dinny Phipps. "If he irritates that spot, we'll have another day with him before the race. Of course, Oscar Otis says it's OK if we work him Friday or Saturday.

"Say, Dinny, I was talking to your grandmother the other day and suggested you weren't getting much recognition about owning half of Successor. She said that was all right—you were getting half the money." Phipps said he was satisfied with the arrangement.

Neloy ducked into Buckpasser's stall and felt the colt's ankles again. "See, yesterday, the pressure had built up here; like a boil, during the night it broke. I feel very, very good about it this morning. He is 99 and 44/100th OK."

Grasso appeared at the stall door and was asked in. "Want to ask you," Neloy said, "See where this went down, the patch seems a little loose at the top."

"That's all right," Grasso said quickly. "It doesn't matter there. Down at

197

the bottom it matters. It doesn't matter toward the front or at the top."

Neloy emerged from the stall, inquired again whether John wanted to give away two ducks with guaranteed good homes, and then, quickly: "John—we'll breeze him a half. Let's put some Vaseline on that spot before we take him out there."

8:25 a.m.—An eight-man television crew recorded Buckpasser's walk with Time Tested through the barn area to the track. Neloy and Phipps walked behind the horses, followed by a suddenly large crowd of volunteer television extras who had heard The Big Horse was going to work.

Race track communications are worthy of serious study by RCA: On Wednesday, trainer Buddy Hirsch, who has horses in the same barn with Buckpasser, called Greentree Stable trainer John Gaver in Aiken, S. C.

"How's Buckpasser's foot?" Gaver asked.

"Hasn't even appeared in the papers, out here," Hirsch reported. Ah, but Neloy had called Mr. Phipps, who told Mrs. Phipps, who had seen her brother, Pete Bostwick, in Miami and he plays polo in Aiken, where Gaver rehashes tomorrow's news in the trainers' stand with horsemen who received *Daily Racing Form* two days late.

Time Tested, on the rail, and Buckpasser broke from the half-mile pole. They raced evenly to the eighth pole, where Buckpasser without apparent effort pulled away to finish a half-length in front. The track still was off from Tuesday's rain and was classified as good.

"Forty-eight," said Neloy studying his watch. "Very good, very good. Time doesn't mean much; the main thing was that he wanted to do it. This horse will tell you if he's not feeling right. At Rockingham Park last summer he just did not want to do it. Something was wrong. Forty-eight. Didn't want him to go that fast."

Neloy hurried to the track and walked toward the clubhouse turn as Fourre brought the champion back on the outside rail, then turned under the stands and into the paddock, where Neloy stopped them. Blood showed from Buckpasser's right forefoot above the inside quarter. Dinny Phipps handed the trainer a clean handkerchief. Neloy dabbed the bloody spot. He grinned.

"No pus. The blood is good and clear. Looks like we've got it all out. Now we have two days for the surface to heal and we're in good shape."

Harry Silbert, Bill Shoemaker's agent, joined the parade back to the barn. "Eddie, I'd appreciate it if you'd take a page in the dinner program. Horse worked good, eh? Just sign at the bottom here." Neloy said he had been tapped in Florida.

8:45 a.m.—Neloy asked Campo to get some peroxide and cotton. After

198

Buckpasser was washed off, Neloy dabbed the small opening at the coronary band with cotton and peroxide, then poured on the remainder of the contents of the bottle. "What do you think?" he was asked.

"I think he's going to run."

Neloy hurried to the racing secretary's office, entered Buckpasser in the Strub and Top Bid in an allowance race, then went out to the track to film a scene at the rail. En route, a member of the Santa Anita publicity staff advised Neloy that at 2 p.m. he was to have his picture taken for *Sport* magazine, accepting a plaque on behalf of Buckpasser.

9:35 a.m.—Buckpasser walked off with two careful steps, possibly a recurrence of something in his hind quarters which showed up a month earlier. Neloy frowned. A photographer wondered if Buckpasser could be led out again because the light was right.

"How about catching that tomorrow? He's had an awful lot today," Neloy said. A local TV sports announcer introduced himself, asked if he could have a moment, the camera moved in, and Neloy was asked again what a quarter crack was, about Buckpasser's condition, and the probability of his racing in the Strub. "Very satisfied with his workout this morning; if nothing else comes up, I believe he will race Saturday."

Neloy walked back to the tack room, passing Mrs. de Creeft. "I'm not an artist, of course, so my opinion doesn't mean anything, but I think you might want to build up his shoulder a little here and bring him up in the back there because he really is much straighter than you have him right now." Mrs. de Creeft thanked him.

"Joe, I want to talk to you later about that foot, after I get a chance to think about it." Neloy went to the track with Vocalist, which was to be breezed a half-mile with Fourre wearing the camera-helmet. At the rail, Neloy did another scene for the television show, explaining breeding and Thoroughbred racing in general. Walter Blum came by on a horse and Neloy asked him if he could stop by the barn Friday morning and put a good three-quarters in Top Bid (whose race did not fill again).

10:25 a.m.—Grasso showed Neloy a drawing on a large envelope, suggesting a steel bar shoe be tacked on Buckpasser's right forefoot on Monday, the same thing on the left to balance it. Grasso and Neloy then entered Buckpasser's stall, Neloy holding up the foot while Grasso cut out a portion of the pad between the shoe and the foot. Buckpasser had two layers of a pliable plastic compound which served as a cushion between the plate and foot; one layer was cut out immediately under the cracked area of the hoof to relieve any possible pressure. The pad when first applied had been yellow, but had turned green from the application of Osmopack. The pad under Buckpasser's

199

left front shoe was red rubber.

"We've got stop-and-go shoes on this horse," Neloy noted. "At least we've got the green one on the right foot." Campo and Neloy then applied a brace to Buckpasser's hind quarters.

"Walked off a little funny behind about a month ago after Braulio had worked him here—had to go around a couple of horses. We did the same thing with him then, and he walked off fine ever since. Try the same thing again." Neloy then repeated the procedure he had employed on Wednesday, cleaning the coronary band with peroxide, then applying a cortisone ointment, the Osmopack, and the sack.

11:25 a.m.—"OK, let's do him one more favor. Let's leave him alone." There was a television scene to shoot on the walking ring, another which required several walks through the barn area.

"I'm sorry this foot business came up, Ricardo; my mind's on other things and I'm not as co-operative as I should be."

Dr. Jocoy drove by. "Hey, Eddie, can I see ya a minute?" There was a brief discussion involving the possible sale of a horse, then Neloy returned to camera. At 12:20, Neloy wondered if the shooting could be stopped for the day inasmuch as he had lost his bookkeeper and had to write out the checks for 44 employes in Florida and get them in the mail before the races. He was to saddle Poker in the San Pasqual Stakes; Mr. and Mrs. Ogden Phipps were scheduled to arrive.

# FRIDAY

6:50 a.m.—Neloy walked into Buckpasser's stall and removed the sack on the colt's right forefoot. "Wash it off, Tiz, but don't put too much water on it. I want to see if there is a scab." There was none. Neloy took a clean rag and rubbed the leg dry. Campo led Buckpasser out of the stall as Neloy watched closely. The horse walked carefully at first, then normally. Neloy told Campo to walk him "a good 45 minutes."

7:15 a.m.—Neloy, by appointment, entered a radio shack behind the barn area entry booth for a five-minute interview. He said he felt very good about Buckpasser; the inflammation evidenced on Wednesday had abscessed, broken, and appeared to have drained completely. He was pleased with the workout Thursday and was confident of Buckpasser's chances of going in the Strub.

8:00 a.m.—Walter Blum dropped by the barn as Campo was getting out Top Bid. Disciplinarian was in the same set; he would be galloped. Ogden Phipps and Mrs. Phipps arrived.

"See you got the car past the gateman," Neloy smiled.

"Oh? Not supposed to drive in here?" The chairman of The Jockey Club hurried down the shedrow and told his chauffeur to move the limousine. Neloy and the Phippses then walked behind Top Bid and Disciplinarian to the track. As Neloy was clocking Blum and Top Bid breaking from the three-quarters pole, sports telecaster Gil Stratton approached and asked him to step down to the rail for a short interview:

"Sure, Gil. Can you step aside there just a bit, I want to catch this colt at the pole here." Five furlongs in :59$^2$/5, six in 1:12$^4$/5. Then Neloy and Sratton were on camera as Blum walked Top Bid back along the outside rail.

The interview completed, cameraman Joe Burnham, who does the TRA color film of the season's champions and has teamed with Stratton on many television racing shows, asked Neloy if he wanted to see a tape of the interview in the truck next to the stands.

"I know you're a ham, just want to see how big a ham," Burnham said. "I can always tell—if they smile the first time they see themselves on television." Burnham watched Neloy closely as the trainer viewed the tape rerun. Neloy did not smile. "So," said Burnham with feigned disappointment, "I knew he had class. Just kidding him."

8:40 a.m.—"Eddie," said the owner of the best horse in America, "she's come all the way out to California. You're going to have to show her the foot." Neloy and Mrs. Phipps went to Buckpasser's stall. Neloy explained the position of the cracks now covered by Grasso's patch (Nu-Hoof), the treatment with poultices to draw out inflammation, the place where the inflammation had erupted, plus the etiology ("weakening of the wall due to excessive drying or excessively thin walls") signs ("an exudate under the cracks or simple inflammation of the laminae may result, depending upon the size of the opening into the sensitive tissues; infection of cracks may cause foot abscesses which break and drain at the coronary band in a fashion similar to 'gravel' "), and of quarter cracks in general. The latter portion of his explanation was phrased in technical terms consistent with Dr. O. R. Adams' *Lameness in Horses*, 1966 edition, a copy of which Neloy had in his traveling bag.

9:55 a.m.—Waiting between scenes of television shooting, Neloy leaned on the stall webbing and stared at Buckpasser, which was sleeping on his side in the straw. "He's not what you would call a good doer. He eats all his feed up, but he takes his time doing it. We'll let him sleep and pack his foot later. I've got plenty of time."

The television crew wanted a scene with the ducks. They were not readily amenable to direction. Someone wondered what the mallard was doing among seven large white ducks.

"Well, a man came by here yesterday and said John had to integrate his

201

flock or there was going to be picketing of the entire stable area. We call him Stokely Carmichael. Here Stokely," Neloy called.

4:00 p.m.—Neloy returned to the barn, where Whitney Tower and two photographers from New York were waiting to take his picture with Buckpasser for a *Sports Illustrated* cover. One of the photographers asked that the horse be led out into the sun of the walking ring. Neloy was hesitant, for Buckpasser was wearing a sackful of Forshner's Hoof Packing with a dash of turquoise Osmopack around the top. Just a few head shots. Campo led out Buckpasser. He limped perceptibly, favoring his poulticed leg. Buckpasser posed like Barrymore.

4:15 p.m.—Neloy did not like the way Buckpasser walked. Perhaps the opening above the quarter crack was irritating him, perhaps stinging, the way a scratch on the back of a person's hand might feel when healing. Neloy walked over to the track first-aid room and asked the physician what he would recommend for Sandy Koufax if a scratch on the arm were bothering him the morning of a game.

"No. Anything with procaine in it won't help me," Neloy said. "I don't want to soak it, either. Thanks, doctor." Neloy returned to the barn, took off Buckpasser's poultice, put epsom salts packs around the leg, bandaged him. Tiziani smelled something burning. No he didn't. Neloy smelled something. No he didn't. Yes he did. Down the shedrow, might be something on fire in Buddy Hirsch's tack room! Quick! Knock that lock off the door! Nothing in here boss.

Fire alarms sounded. Engines raced to Barn 37. Santa Anita President Robert Strub, closely followed by a Santa Anita vice president, Fred Ryan, hurried from Peter McBean's party for the Phippses in the directors' rooms.

An old rag in a culvert near the barn smoldered and was quickly extinguished. A rumor which came out of the fire—that all was not well with Buckpasser—swept through the party in the directors' room. The rumor was not extinguished.

# Saturday

6:05 a.m.—Depressing headlines in a Los Angeles *Times* extra: The first Apollo astronauts, Virgil Grissom, Edward White, and Roger Chaffee, had perished in a flash fire.

6:15 a.m.—Neloy waited for his usual telephone call from Florida. "Got bad news, boss. Great Ruler shattered a leg pulling up from a gallop; had to destroy him." A large price had been turned down recently for the 2-year-old full brother to Bold Monarch.

Neloy skipped his usual coffee eye-opener and drove across the Santa

Anita parking lot to the barns. "I don't know yet. If the horse is not 100 per cent right, we should not run him. If he is just 99 and 44/100ths and runs, and something happens to the other leg, you never forget it the rest of your life. Well, take a good look this morning, go over all the thinking again with Mr. Phipps, then make a definite decision. Yesterday morning, I was positive he was going to be able to run; this morning, we have a borderline decision."

A gateman signaled for Neloy to stop. He had a message for Neloy to call Dr. Peter Chamberlain, the track physician. Neloy, thinking one of the men had been hurt, hurried to the barn. "Everybody all right, John?"

"Groom in Jim Nazworthy's barn was kicked...died last night."

"Oh, that's awful. All your men OK?"

"Dunno; Warren's not here yet. Boss, did you take that pack off?" No. Neloy quick-stepped toward Buckpasser's stall.

Buckpasser stood with hindquarters in a corner and pawed the ground with the right front foot. He had been doing so for some time, the straw being swept back in the corner, and he was digging into the dirt floor.

6:55 a.m.—Neloy took Buckpasser by the halter, "Come up a step." Buckpassesr did not want to, but he did, without putting down the right forefoot.

"Well, he made the decision for us," Neloy stated flatly.

Neloy knelt in the straw. An abscess had developed on the outside at the coronary band. There was no swelling on the inside above the quarter cracks.

"He's sore. He won't run. Tub him, Father John. I'm going to get some coffee."

7:05 a.m.—Jimmy Kilroe and Dinny Phipps sat down in the kitchen with Neloy. "Can't do it, Jimmy. Sore this morning. Thought you better know so an announcement could be made as soon as possible. Don't want to be getting any boos from the public." Kilroe thanked him and left to inform press, radio, and television. Neloy told Phipps about Great Ruler's suffering a broken leg.

"What a day! And I even get a bad time from the gateman; said he had checked on me and I didn't have anything to do with the Phipps barn. I almost couldn't get in here this morning."

Neloy called Dr. Chamberlain. He had been thinking during the night about that cut on Koufax' arm and had a suggestion. Neloy thanked him, said it was too late.

7:15 a.m.—Neloy stopped at trainer Bob Wheeler's barn. "Looking at the race in the paper last night, Bob, and the way the speed in the race shapes up, I think your horse (Rehabilitate) has a good shot at it. He's good right now. Baeza is due in here to ride my horse and he can't go. You can have

203

Braulio if you want him."

Wheeler said he already had named Esteban Medina as his rider and would not be permitted to switch this late, but "Sure nice of you to think of us, Eddie; sure appreciate it." Neloy returned to Barn 37. Campo had Buckpasser's two front legs in a rubber tub of hot water. Neloy went to the track with a set. Trainer Jim Maloney passed and inquired quietly, "Is it true what I hear?" Neloy nodded. Maloney shook his head.

A player watching the workouts talked to himself: "Just my luck. I bet the 12 horse yesterday and that's just where he finished. And Buckpasser, a horse I can really even up with, probably won't even run." Neloy said he had heard that Buckpasser had been scratched. The player stared in disbelief. "That's right, man down there at the gap told me himself." The player thought about that verification for a while, "Yeah, but I bet they never tell the public 'til they all get out here this afternoon." Moments later, the announcement came over the track public-address system. Local radio and television stations also broadcast the word early in the day.

8:02 a.m.—As Neloy returned to the barn with the first set, Ogden Phipps walked down the shedrow. He had seen Buckpasser. "He made the decision easy, didn't he, Eddie?" Neloy then reported the bad news from Florida. Phipps thought a moment. There are owners who at this point might inquire about the condition of the track or question whether a trainer exercised proper judgment in galloping or working, or sending the horse out on the track at that particular time.

Phipps said: "You know, something must be the matter with that mare. She's had Progressing, Conquering, and now Great Ruler—three of her foals have broken their legs."

A man with two small girls bearing stable-area passes appeared. "My daughter here wrote a letter to Mr. Campo and he said she could come out and see Buckpasser."

Neloy nodded. "Well, he is hurt this morning and will not race today. He can't even come out of the stall for you because he is standing in a tub of hot water," and Neloy explained the whole problem in minute detail to three wide-eyed listeners.

9 a.m.—Grasso removed the patch from Buckpasser's foot and cut the shoe back to a three-quarter plate, removing all pressure from the cracked quarter. The swelling was down perceptibly. Dr. William Schmitt administered Butazolidin to help reduce inflammation. Neloy applied a flaxseed meal poultice mixed in hot water and bandaged the right foreleg.

"Well, Eddie, how long will it be?" Phipps inquired. "Will he be able to make the Widener?"

"Maybe we better wait awhile before deciding, Mr. Phipps. You know, if we set up a schedule and point for a particular race, we have a tendency to take short cuts to make the race, trying to shape this thing to fit the schedule rather than trying to fit the schedule to the injury. Maybe we better wait awhile, take another look, see how he is coming along, and then we can tell better." Phipps nodded and left.

Lou Rowan came by to offer condolences and Neloy went through the history of the injury again. Rowan shook his head at the ill fortune.

At 45, Neloy has more hair than Whittingham, but considerably less than Robert Kennedy, and is grayer. He bowed for Rowan to see, "See what training horses can do to a 31-year old man?"

## Jest The Thing

CHICK MIFFLIN, whose pickings have produced, among other things, as fine a collection of engraved announcements of 19th Century funerals as anyone would want to see, has presented us with a crisp and sere race program from Cuba's Oriental Park for Feb. 9, 1921.

President of the Cuba-American Jockey and Auto Club, which ran the show at Oriental Park a half-century ago, was C. A. Stoneham Sr., while the second vice president was John J. McGraw. This was in the winter. In the summer, they worked up north in the baseball business, as president and field manager of the New York Giants, winning the National League pennant whenever they chose.

According to the late Col. Phil T. Chinn, Stoneham and McGraw were great betting men. Especially McGraw. Again according to Col. Chinn, who had no need for outside sources on what happened in racing from about 1885 through 1961, McGraw was "an easy mark. The smallest kind of story would get him very excited, and he would come up with the money to finance a betting coup in a matter of minutes. We are talking now about a sizable investment, well up in five figures, for an arrangement with Phil T. Chinn in those days involved more than pocket change. I do not mean to convey the impression that McGraw was a betting man in the class of Harry Sinclair or Ed Simms, but he was enthusiastic. Could be set up with a story you might be embarrassed to give another man."

Col. Chinn had nothing going at Oriental Park on Feb. 9, 1921, at least under his own name. W. R. Coe (for whom, about this time, Chinn was buying, selling, and managing a breeding operation which produced such champions as Cleopatra, Pompey, and Black Maria) had a horse named Shy Ann, which finished second in the second race at 3-5 odds. Bill Finnegan, who died last year, owned and trained Mister Jiggs, which finished out of the money on the same race. Mose Goldblatt, who had trained Iron Mask before taking over a division of the H. P. Whitney stable, was listed as owner and trainer of a stakes-winning daughter of Peter Pan—Frillery, named Furbelow, which finished third in the $1,000 feature race won by Mrs. C. H. Gilroy's Mayor House.

We are as uncertain what to do with this thing as was Mifflin. If anyone is short on 50-year-old race programs, we have one here.

## Just Between Us

SOME of these terse announcements by stewards are fascinating, such as the following from Park Jefferson in South Dakota: "Groom Pat Rother is fined the sum of $50 for conduct detrimental to racing (instructions to a jockey)."

What on earth could the man have said?

The late Hal Price Headley reported his father said that Col. James E. Pepper told him—all of which comes perilously close to the hearsay rule and make what you will of that—"That rider didn't follow a single one of my instructions!" Col. Pepper's horse had not raced up to expectation, getting off last, and failing to improve his position. "I told that boy to get out in front and stay there!"

## I. D. Please

AT Belmont Park, Fred Capossela entered a back gate and that usually means only one thing: Post time was a few hours away, however, and Triangle Publications columnist Herb Goldstein reported that a new Pinkerton stopped Capossella and asked for identification.

206

Now, Capossela might be known in some quarters as a stamp collector, or ham radio operator, or as a former amateur jai-alai champion of Florida, and he once was known for his column in the New York *Post* on billiards. In 1934, however, he began calling the races at Tropical Park, in 1940 at Hialeah, and for the last 28 years generally has been known as the "Voice of New York Racing."

Capossela stared at the Pink. "I'm Freddy Capossela, the announcer," he said lamely. Goldstein reported the skeptical Pinkerton walked around the car returned to scrutinize the driver, finally said, "Okay, let me hear it."

Capossela got out of the car, took a deep breath, and announced: "It is now...Post Time!" The Pink nodded, "Okay, you're him."

Security is tight at New York tracks and the Pinkertons do a marvelous job keeping out unlicensed persons from the stable area and undesirables from the stands, particularly touts, self-styled "turf consultants."

Before Belmont Park was rebuilt, all the New York races were run at Aqueduct and the grass courses became worn. The NYRA hired a grass specialist, a Ph.D. from Cornell, to keep the jumping and turf courses green.

The first day the professor from Ithaca encountered a Pinkerton at the Aqueduct entrance, he identified himself as "a turf consultant from upstate." Never got by the gate.


## Now He Likes It


SUN leaked through a roof of morning mist supported by tall columns of elms in front of a long row of stalls known as Barn 62 in Horse Haven. A chicken named Barbara clucked along the shedrow, looking for a spot to lay an egg. Steam rose slowly from a barrel of water as hotwalkers casually led three horses around a path formed for that purpose a century ago.

One of the hotwalkers was Victor (Lefty) Nickerson, a tall, balding, 37-year-old trainer who enjoys—not necessarily in order—walking his horses, Van Cliburn and Eugene Ormandy at the Saratoga Performing Arts Center, Italian cigars, and having a Bold Ruler in his public stable.

He put his horse away and walked with another set to the near-by Oklahoma training track. "You know," he said quietly, "I've been coming here for 19 years and never really enjoyed Saratoga before last Saturday afternoon."

The place had taken on charm when Nickerson saddled J. J. Brunetti's

207

Staunchness, by Bold Ruler, to win the $50,000-added Whitney Handicap at 18-1 odds. Did Staunchness' victory, his first since beating Hail to All in the Dwyer nearly 13 months ago, surprise him?

"I'm surprised to win a $3,500 claiming race," he said softly and suggested a smile. He bears his frequent surprises with equanimity. Last fall he was one of the leading trainers at Aqueduct after taking over the Gedney Farm horses and saddled 33 per cent winners from starters at one stage of the meeting. He also had trained stakes winners Notch and Lord Date and stakes-placed Reely Beeg for Alfred Wohl.

Nickerson came around the race track when he was 14. "My mother wanted me to run away from home and didn't care whether I went to the race track or with the circus. Don't write that; I was just kidding."

He was rubbing horses for Stanley Lipiec at the old Fairgrounds in Detroit in 1945, the year Lipiec led the nation's trainers in number of wins with Mrs. Lottie Wolfe's horses. "John Stanley, who bred Double Jay, was there with some horses called Leystan and Freddie's Pal, and he said to me, 'Boy, what are you going to do when you grow up?'

"I told him I wanted to be a trainer. 'Get yourself some broodmares, go down to Kentucky, and be a breeder.' I think I should have taken that advice."

Instead, he rubbed horses until he went into the Army during the Korean War. He wound up in Germany, where he bought an 11-year-old race horse for $500. "We raced this horse six months, picked up $20 for finishing fourth once, then gave the horse back to the Germans for free. We were promoting good will."

Following his discharge, Nickerson started training for himself in the United States. In 1956 he claimed a Rustom Sirdar filly from Lou Doherty for $6,000. He ran her back and she won by seven lengths, so he upped her to $7,000 and she won by 11 lengths.

"So about this time I'm thinking maybe I had something more on my hands than I had figured. Her name was Scampering, out of a Pilate mare. Ninety days after I claimed her she won the Gazelle Handicap, beating Cosmah and Dotted Line. Never was any good after that, developed osselets, and I sold her privately. I believe Tom Satterwhite has her now as a broodmare in Kentucky."

After he sold Scampering, Nickerson went to France, visited museums, theaters, and other points a man touches in Paris, returned broke and decided he had better train for other people.

What has Staunchness been doing since he won the Dwyer? "I don't really know. I didn't get him until April of this year. He had been fired in his front ankles and was turned out last winter. I have him and two other horses for Mr. Brunetti." Nickerson brought Staunchness back to the races in June, finished second, then sixth and fourth in overnight races. He had worked once at Saratoga, going six furlongs in a leisurely 1:15⁴/₅ on Tuesday before the Whitney.

This was not terribly impressive and Staunchness was made sixth choice in the field of seven for the 39th running of the nine-furlong fixture. Canal, Pluck, and Malicious disputed the early lead, going three abreast into the first turn as Staunchness settled into fourth position.

Malicious gained a slight advantage going down the backstretch with Pluck at his throatlatch most of the way. As Canal began to retire for the afternoon, Porlijo challenged. Staunchness remaining in fourth position about two lengths behind the leaders.

Malicious finally disposed of Pluck and entered the upper stretch with a short lead, but Staunchness came sweeping up on the outside and Prolijo slipped through on the rail, Staunchness taking command and holding Prolijo safe by a length. Odds-on Malicious finished third, another 1¼ lengths back, while second-choice Bold Bidder, never in serious contention, finished fourth.

Where would Staunchness race next? "I don't really know. I don't think there is anything more for him at Saratoga and we don't have him staked for anything."

Wohl, who came out to see some of his horses in Nickerson's care, said he had some tickets for the Performing Arts Center. Would Lefty care to go?

"I would be delighted." He lit up another cigar and observed that Saratoga was getting to be an enjoyable place.

## Improving With Age

AL HIRT'S first job was as a bugler at the Fair Grounds in New Orleans. He said he got $6 a day, union scale in 1941, "and it wasn't bad in those days." Well, they were running only seven races then. On Preakness Day at Pimlico they ran nine and Hirt got $25,000, so you can see how expenses go up when you add a couple of extra races to the card.

Hirt, recovering from the brick-in-the lip he drew during the Mardi Gras, said he was only about 90 per cent when he played the national anthem at the Kentucky Derby, but that he had gained 10 points for the Preakness. With his New Orleans combo, Hirt spent most of the afternoon captivating the picnic set in the Pimlico centerfield.

Sedate, generally older, whole families with young children, many coats and ties, with only a token showing of hippies, the Preakness infield crowd appeared much different from the boisterous, college-age, T-shirted throng that fills the infield on Kentucky Derby Day. When Al Hirt's trombone man slid into Tommy Dorsey's old theme song, an immediate response of enjoyment came from the Pimlico crowd, which gave some indication of the age group.

## He Spoke Too Soon

DIXIANA Farm trainer C. R. (Chuck) Werstler was talking about Stan, champion grass horse of 1954: "The only way he could be stopped was for them to build a brick wall at the eighth pole." The following day in the Blue Grass Stakes, Dixiana Farm's Hard Work thought he saw some construction work beginning at the eighth pole, and he faded right out of the Kentucky Derby picture, to be reserved for sprinting events later in the season.

## Buying Time

JOHN F. CLARK JR., who in 1933 bought Clang as a yearling for $300 and earned $25,565 with him while he was running six and seven furlongs in world-record time, is in the stewards stand at the Fair Grounds, a spot he has occupied most of the last quarter-century. He helped write the Louisiana racing law and knows as much about New Orleans racing as anybody.

"See that old house there just beyond Mrs. Brown's barn—used to call that Col. Bradley's barn. That house was built by a cotton planter in 1854. When they started racing here in 1873, that house was the clubhouse. They used to watch the races from that third-floor cupola. It's not even on the grounds now, and is used as an apartment house.

"You know the old Metairic Course, where Lexington and Lecompte raced more than a hundred years ago? It's a cemetery now. The track is still there, though. I've driven around it in my car many times—measures exactly a mile. I've got a plot there, where the stands used to be, near the three-eighths pole."

Old horsemen never leave the race track.


## Tradition

TRADITION is a great thing. Everyone should have one. Most race tracks do, because tradition gives the program status, and some are more recondite than others.

At traditional Old Hilltop this week, a Maryland Jockey Club is advertising the 92nd Preakness. Old Hilltop was a name given the track by sports writers weary of trying to explain the tradition about how the site was known as Pemlicoe in 1669 because early settlers had come from a section of London noted for Olde Ben Pimlico's Tavern, or something.

At any rate, the meaning—if a small rise in the centerfield reasonably can be identified as a hill top—of Pimlico's handle was cut away 30 years ago when bulldozers leveled the centerfield to permit better viewing of the horses at the half-mile pole. So Pimlico's hill became topless, which is something of a tradition in itself in a California-tavern sort of way.

Now the Maryland Jockey Club really has tradition. It has been suggested that a club so named was founded in Annapolis in 1743, nine years before printed mention appeared of the existence of the English Jockey Club, which, outside of Maryland, is considered the forerunner of similarly named racing clubs in America.

Historian John Hervey believed there was racing at Annapolis during colonial times because he found evidence of 12 silver spoons created as racing trophies in 1721, and the Annapolis Subscription Plate trophy of 1743 presently is displayed in the Baltimore Museum.

George Washington, by his own account, dropped £1 6s at the Annapolis races in 1762 (Mark Twain always considered Washington's reputation for veracity something less than his, for whereas George could not tell a lie, Twain admitted that he could, but would not).

While substantiation of a Maryland Jockey Club's existence in early colonial days is hard to come by for want of a record of its activities, there must have been one, for it was reorganized in 1783 with Gov. William Paca and Richard Spriggs as stewards.

This club waned with the commercial ebb of Annapolis. It was merged with a similar club founded in 1823, was incorporated as the Maryland Jockey Club on June 3, 1830, moved to Baltimore and set up shop on 200 acres on the Frederick Road with a track called the Central Course. This died, as did many things, during the Civil War.

The Maryland Jockey Club was born anew in 1870 when Gov. Oden Bowie, who had promised to provide a race track on which to run the proposed Dinner Party Stakes, was elected president and arranged a 10-year lease on the 70-acre Pimlico site where a fair had been staged the previous year.

Thoroughbred racing under the auspices of the Maryland Jockey Club began at Pimlico in the fall of 1870 and Milton Sanford's Preakness won the Dinner Party Stakes. In 1873, a $2,050 race was named in honor of the first winner of the Dinner Party Stakes and was won by Survivor, but renewals of the early Preakness Stakes were forgotten when Pimlico was closed in 1889.

William P. Riggs was the driving force in reviving the Maryland Jockey Club and racing at Pimlico; in 1905, the track was bought out of receivership, a meeting was held, and racing has been held there continuously ever since under auspices of the Maryland Jockey Club, whose stewardship has changed dramatically in persons and policies over the years, leaving only the name and track the same sine 1870.

The traditional number of runnings of the Preakness are hard to account for. In its fourth season after reopening, Pimlico staged a $2,000-added Preakness Stakes in 1909 under allowance conditions.

The next seven runnings were handicaps, but a continuity developed and by 1918 the Preakness was said to be having its 10th running; it happened to be raced in two divisions that year, so the following year the race was styled the 12th Preakness (picking up its first addition). The 1923 race was labeled the 16th Preakness, but then someone remembered the 1879-89 runnings of a race called the Preakness at early Pimlico, so the 1924 renewal was tagged the 28th Preakness (picking up 11 runnings).

By 1927, when H. P. Whitney's Bostonian won the 31st Preakness, the race had considerable stature, and money ($53,100); the following year it had even more: H. P. Whitney's Victorian won a $60,000 race said to be renewed then for the 38th time, it having been found that it predated the Kentucky Derby with initial runnings from 1873-78 (picking up six more runnings).

Well, while it could be said that the Preakness was run earlier than the

Kentucky Derby, it was still short on renewals. In 1948, it was discovered that a minor race at Gravesend Course in Brooklyn was named the Preakness. Never mind that it was named in honor of James Galway and his Preakness Stable, and was for non-winners of a $1,000 race in one year, non-winners of a $2,500 race in other years. Here was a race similar in name and 15 runnings of it, 1894-1908, suddenly became part of the history and tradition of the Pimlico fixture, Citation winning the newly styled 72nd running of the Preakness.

There remained, however, a tradition gap of two runnings between the Preakness and Kentucky Derby. This was partly closed two years ago when yet another Preakness was found, not a 3-year-old affair at Pimlico, not even at Gravesend, but a $1,665 handicap for 3-year-olds and up run in 1890 at old Morris Park in New York! The only 5-year-old to win the Preakness was Montague, owned by the Preakness Stable.

So this week at Old Hilltopless, the traditional wreath of daisies painted like Black-Eyed Susans will be placed on the 92nd winner of the Preakness in front of a small replica of the Old Members' Clubhouse cupola which burned last year.

These sort of traditions are made, not born. They are unnecessary embellishment of one of America's great races.

There really is only one tradition, good and true, attaching to the Preakness: This is a race, for years beyond memory, won by exceptional Thoroughbreds.

## Personal Favor

BOB STILZ, newly-appointed Kentucky racing commissioner, was talking about Col. Phil T. Chinn: "Back in the depression when nobody had any money—you know, 25 cents meant something—my father was with the bank in Lexington and came upon a $100 bill. He stashed it away in his wallet so he could prove he was a man of parts, if the occasion ever presented itself.

"He took me up to Cincinnati one Saturday afternoon to see the Reds play. We stopped by the Netherlands Plaza, which had just opened, so we could gawk at all the splendor, the way country people will do. We were standing there in the lobby taking it all in when Col. Chinn came out of the dining

213

room there. He saw my father, whom he knew only casually, and came over to us, which pleased my father, knowing somebody important right there in the Netherlands Plaza.

"Very quickly, the Colonel inquired if my father were in a position to handle a financial matter. Well, we only had change between us after the ball game, but then my father remembered that $100 bill he had stashed. He took it out of his wallet—I had never seen a $100 bill before—and handed it right over to the Colonel.

"Col. Chinn never batted an eye. He crumpled that bill, pressed it into the hand of the head waiter, said, 'I have some important business matters to attend to young man. I would consider it a great personal favor if you would take care of Mrs. Chinn's dinner bill and retain the balance for yourself.'

"Well, father almost collapsed, because he knew he would never see that money again. The Colonel had a lot of style."

## A Helluva Way To Win A Race

ON Tuesday morning, three days after Dancer's Image finished first in the 94th Kentucky Derby, Churchill Downs stewards Lewis Finley, Jack Goode, and Leo O'Donnell announced they had received from the state chemist a report that a urine sample taken from Dancer's Image contained phenylbutazone or a derivative thereof.

Kentucky racing rule 14.04 states: "Should the chemical analysis of saliva, urine, or other sample taken from a horse indicate the presence of...a medication which is a derivative of phenylbutazone, it shall be considered prima facie evidence that such has been administered to the horse. The trainer...(and any others in attendance of the horse) shall be immediately stopped from participating in racing...pending the outcome of a hearing on same... The horse alleged to have been administered any... (such) medications shall not run during the investigation and hearing..."

Kentucky racing rule 14.05 states: "When such positive report is received from the state chemist by the stewards, the persons held responsible shall be notified, and a thorough investigation shall be conducted by or on behalf of the stewards. Then the time shall be set by the stewards for a hearing to dispose of the matter..."

Kentucky racing rule 14.06 states: "The trainer shall be responsible for the condition of the horses he enters. Should the chemical analysis of any sample

214

indicate the presence of any...medication which is a derivative of phenylbu-tazone, the trainer of the horse, together with the assistant trainer, stable foreman, groom, or any other person shown to have had care and attendance of the horse shall be subject to the penalties prescribed (in rule 23.01) and such horse shall not participate in the purse distribution."

Kentucky racing rule 23.01 states: "Whenever...the stewards acting under authority of the commission find any...licensee...to have violated any rule of this commission...the license of such...licensee...shall be subject to suspen-sion or revocation...or the licensee may be ruled off or fined in an amount commensurate with the offense. Provided, however...the decision or ruling of the stewards as to the extent of the disqualification of any horse in any race shall be final and no right of appeal shall exist to the commission or to the courts."

The stewards then announced that a hearing on the matter would be held on May 13 and that an official ruling would be issued after the hearing. The stewards further stated that betting on the race would not be altered what-ever proved to be the final placement of the horses.

Thus, at midweek, it appeared that under the Kentucky rules of racing Dancer's Image would be disqualified from first place in the 94th Kentucky Derby, that the disqualification of the horse was unappealable, that the purse money would be redistributed, that Forward Pass would be declared the official winner, and that penalties, if any were to be assessed, would not be announced by the stewards until after the scheduled hearing next week.

Among the losers of this Kentucky Derby was racing. Early reports on ra-dio and television and in newspapers blared that the winner of the Kentucky had been "drugged" with a "pain killer and stimulant." To many in the greatest audience racing probably ever had, the early bulletins meant that the horse which had finished first in America's most famous race had been doped.

Dancer's Image lost not only the purse money, but the prizes of the Ken-tucky Derby. The prize to a Kentucky Derby winner is glory, adulation, re-spect; the prize to an owner-breeder of a Kentucky Derby winner is the won-derful fulfillment of a dream and the unabashed pride in saying: "I bred that colt to win the Kentucky Derby, and he won it for me." These prizes are lost.

While Forward Pass may go into the record books as the winner, an esti-mated 100,000 persons at Churchill Downs and an estimated 10,000,000 tel-evision viewers at home saw him lose.

His rider, Milo Valenzuela, said after the race that Forward Pass had "spit out the bit at the half-mile pole," that he "did not get hold of the track," that "when he went to the front, I thought he would go on and pull away, but

215

then I saw that gray horse coming up on the inside...there was nothing I could do."

Forward Pass spent himself pushing the fastest pace in Kentucky Derby history (Kentucky Sherry raced the first six furlongs in 1:09⅘, and when the searching test came at the head of the stretch, Forward Pass needed 26⅖ seconds to finish the final quarter-mile.

Roaring down on the inside, Dancer's Image turned in a final quarter in 24⅖ seconds; he caught Forward Pass at the three-sixteenths pole and drew away. The favorite, with the best record, Forward Pass lost the Kentucky Derby on the race track last Saturday.

How could a Kentucky Derby victory produce such losers?

### The Medication Rule

This horrendous Kentucky Derby did show the public that racing officials enforce the rules of racing regardless of resulting turmoil. The same unflinching adherence to the rules of golf in the recent Masters tournament brought a mixed reaction—some praised the tournament officials' enforcement of a rule, others questioned the wisdom of the rule.

(Everybody in the gallery and watching on television knew Roberto de Vicenzo had shot a birdie three on the 17th hole; yet when Tommy Aaron inadvertently put down a four, and de Vicenzo verified the wrong score by signing the scorecard, the rule required that the wrong score stand. De Vincenzo lost the tournament by one stroke.)

The wisdom of racing's medication rules, as to the prohibition of Butazolidin (brand name of phenylbutazone) has been challenged heatedly and repeatedly for the last 10 years. For one thing, medication rules vary considerably in wording and enforcement from state to state.

Colorado's rule permits use of Butazolidin. Other states' rules do not specifically prohibit Butazolidin. It is suspected that in some states no tests are made for it.

According to reports submitted to the National Association of State Racing Commissioners for 1966, there were 89,786 post-race tests made of urine and saliva in the United States; of these, 66 revealed prohibited drugs or medications which resulted in disqualifications; 13 involved Butazolidin (five in Michigan, four in Ohio, three in New Mexico, and one in Washington). Reports in for last year show 80,666 tests, 51 positives, eight involving Butazolidin (two in Massachusetts, one each in Arizona, Florida, Idaho, Maine, Ohio, and Vermont).

Why is Butazolidin prohibited in some states?

216

About 35 years ago, federal narcotic agents wandered under a shedrow and picked up some heroin. Theretofore, the use of hop in various forms was a common, widespread practice in getting a horse up to a race. After a few trainers were shipped out to Leavenworth and Atlanta, neither of which places had racing dates, the use of heroin was sharply curtailed. Introduction of the saliva test at Hialeah revealed an astonishing number of other items being used to stimulate a horse. The fast pill and then the slow pill were declared illegal, and as the racing scene drifted from the bad, old days into the good, clean nowadays, the list of outlawed stimulants and depressants grew to cumbersome length. Rather than particularize each outlawed drug by trade name, which could be changed faster than Tote board odds, racing commissions wrote general rules which seemed to cover the situation.

Kentucky had a general rule which prohibited use of any narcotic, stimulant, depressant, or local anaesthetic. Then along came Butazolidin. It began showing up in post-race analyses in many states and the general thought among racing commissioners and chemists is that detectability is ground for prohibiting a medication regardless of its therapeutic properties.

What is Butazolidin? It is a brand name for phenylbutazone, an anti-inflammatory agent approved by the United States Food and Drug Administration for use by people and by animals.

It is not exactly an aspirin, it is not strictly an analgesic, it is not a stimulant, it is not a narcotic. Butazolidin reduces inflammation and consequently reduces throbbing pain which results from a swelled, inflamed joint. Use of Butazolidin, thereby reducing inflammation in a horse's joint or ankle, permits a horse to race to its normal ability. Prohibition of such medication to a horse which needed it requires that the horse remain in the barn longer to recuperate.

The effect of Butazolidin may be realized within eight hours. Traces of Butazolidin may be found in the urine of a horse 72 or 85 hours after administration; the period of elimination varies with the individual horse and the maximum duration for all horses has not yet been determined. (Crimson Satan was administered Butazolidin five days before the 1962 Leonard Richards Stakes; a trace was found and he was disqualified from first place.)

At the 1961 NASRC convention, a scientific paper was presented showing that if you gave enough Butazolidin to a horse, it could kill him. Of course, too much aspirin also has a toxic effect, and it has been said that a sizeable roll of bills can choke a horse. Nothing in the scientific paper indicated that Butazolidin had toxic effects when used at recommended levels of therapeutic dosage. Nonetheless, Butazolidin had been shown to be capable of killing a horse; further it was troublesome in that it had been showing up in

217

tests, so a majority of state racing commissions voted in 1961 to prohibit its use.

Kentucky did not. Illinois did not. At Arlington Park, names of horses racing with Butazolidin were posted in the paddock and further made known to the betting public in *Daily Racing Form*. The first few days this system was adopted, there was a general rush of players to get on the "Bute" horses in each race.

It was soon discovered that horses administered Butazolidin did not win an unexpected number of races, that they were running pretty much as their past racing records indicated they might. Butazolidin handicappers went back to studying early morning workout times and Illinois eventually abandoned the practice of posting the names of horses administered Butazolidin.

At the 1962 NASRC convention, however, considerable pressure was brought to bear on William S. Miller, chairman of the Illinois Racing Board, and William H. May, chairman of the Kentucky State Racing Commission, to prohibit use of Butazolidin in the interest of uniformity of racing rules throughout the United States. They yielded.

May in bowing to the majority opinion told the NASRC executive committee: "We think you're wrong and we're right... In Kentucky, where we do not test for Butazolidin, we have the most formful racing in America—up to 39 per cent winning favorites... We are reluctant to abandon our position, because our decision (to prohibit Butazolidin) represents the feeling of less than two per cent of our people in Kentucky. But we're going to be on the team."

May returned to Lexington and reported at a Thoroughbred Club of America meeting that an agreement had been reached for a comprehensive study to be made and that if the NASRC study failed to prove that Butazolidin was a narcotic, stimulant, depressant, or local anaesthetic, its prohibition in Kentucky would be rescinded.

That was six years ago. A report of the study, if conducted, never was made public and the Kentucky rule specifically prohibiting a "medication which is a derivative of phenylbutazone" still stands. Its wisdom still is questioned. Yet it is there, and every trainer who has brought a horse into Kentucky in the last six years has raced under the responsibility imposed by that rule.

By midweek, the 94th Kentucky Derby ws not officially finished. The race which began at 4:40 p.m. on Saturday and was run in 2:02⅕ would not be concluded for at least nine days, the earliest time stewards could issue a final ruling on the order of finish—and even then it might not be ended. The racing rule declaring the stewards' decision final could be contested, appealed to the Kentucky State Racing Commission (within 20 days), and a commission's decision could be appealed to Franklin Circuit Court.

Peter Fuller, owner and breeder of Dancer's Image, is a fighter. He is fiercely independent, unmindful of the opinions of others as to his choice of a proper course, proud of his horse, and unshakeably confident in the ability and integrity of his trainer, Lou Cavalaris. He is wealthy. He has retained legal counsel.

Upon learning of the chemist's report, Fuller was stunned—"tremendously shocked and grieved. It's a dream turned into a nightmare," Fuller was quoted. "This touches everything—your heart, your name, your honor."

Fuller returned to his home in Boston on Tuesday night and told reporters there that he was going to offer a large financial reward for information on individuals who "tampered with my horse." He suggested possibilities that someone could have tampered with the urine sample, or switched samples, or tampered with Dancer's Image during a security lapse. He said he planned to race Dancer's Image in the Preakness and Belmont Stakes, but only if Cavalaris could saddle him.

A strong man, with jutting jaw and deep-set earnest eyes, Fuller is a competitor, by inheritance and inclination. His father, Alvan Tufts Fuller, was a champion bicyclist who sold his trophies to set up a bicycle shop in Boston. He prospered. He was elected to Congress as an independent before World War I, then served two terms as lieutenant governor of Massachusetts, was elected governor in 1924, and retired from politics in 1928 to devote his time to a Cadillac-Olds Agency in Boston. (With son Peter as president, it is the largest Cadillac-Olds agency in the country today; last year it sold 1,800 new Cadillacs, 1,000 new Oldsmobiles, and 4,400 foreign and used cars.)

Peter was born with celiac disease, which hampered his digestion; he survived his first eight years on a tenuous, special diet, a frail little boy with an enlarged stomach. Thereafter he concentrated on his physical development and became captain of an undefeated wrestling team at Milton Academy. He took up boxing and in 1948 won the New England region heavyweight title in the Olympic Trials, at the same time taking the regional wrestling title in the 191-pound class. The next year he won the New England Golden Gloves and AAU heavyweight boxing titles; he was defeated in the national Golden Gloves semi-finals by Coley Wallace (who later was to defeat Rocky Marciano). He won 50 of 55 amateur fights. At Harvard he captained the wrestling team and was named the school's outstanding athlete. He gave up AAU boxing in 1953, but has continued wrestling, working out in the gym he has given Milton Academy and competing for a place on the Olympic team every fourth year until this year, when he found that the Trials were to be held on

219

the same day that Dancer's Image was to run in the Wood Memorial.

"I'm 46 and I figured my success in the Trials would be short, Dancer's Image success in the Wood would be long, and I made a decision to go to Aqueduct," he said.

For a Harvard-educated millionaire, Fuller is a non-conformist. He is a rugged ex-Marine who loves his horses, admires his trainer, and is absolutely unafraid to fight and buck the odds. Prior to Tuesday he had considered himself extraordinarily lucky in racing and breeding. He had been breeding Palominos at his Runnymede Farm near the New Hampshire seashore: "We would put about $1,000 into a Palomino and then someone would come along and want to buy it for $200 or $300. There didn't seem to be too much sense in that. Basically, I think along business lines. Always been interested in breeding animals; we have a purebred Guernsey herd at the farm, and we have bred French Alpine goats, and we kind of drifted into breeding Thoroughbreds. I had an idea Man o' War was a great horse—now that was a real bright idea, wasn't it—so I thought I ought to buy a Man o' War mare.

"This was in the fall of 1953 and Hal Price Headley was dispersing his mares at Keeneland. I'll tell you how green I was: I sent my farm manager, Bob Casey, to Lexington to buy Salaminia, which was by Man o' War, and I told him he could spend $3,500 to $4,500 to buy the mare. Well, she went for $62,000, of course.

"We revised our thinking there rather quickly, and drastically. I bought three mares at that Keeneland sale: I paid $1,900 for Our Louise, by Neddie, in foal to Piet; $1,000 for Fountainstown, by Rodosto, in foal to Challedon; $1,500 for Teco Tack, by Hard Tack, in foal to Equifox."

In recalling his entry into Thoroughbred breeding, Fuller recounted that he sent his first three purchases to Carter Thornton's Threave Main Stud near Paris, Ky. He asked Thornton what he thought of the broodmare band.

"He hemmed and hawed around and finally asked, 'You really want the truth?' Yeah, I wanted him to level with me. 'You've wasted your money,' Carter said. 'It costs just as much to feed a bad mare as it does a good one. Why don't you start with something good?'

"Well, let me show how lucky a green man can get:

"The Equifox—Teco Tack colt was named Equitack and won four races and earned $10,184; the Challedon—Fountainstown colt was named Challefont and he won nine races, placed in a stakes for me, set two track records, and earned $40,219; the Piet—Our Louise colt was named Discard (he had a foot turn out so bad they scratched him when we tried to start him for the first time at Rockingham), and he placed in three stakes in New York, won 39 races, and earned $155,336.

220

"So there's Carter's three bums! Cost me $4,400 and the foals they were carrying earned more than $200,000." Fuller laughed. "Carter's never forgotten it. Well, I've never let him."

Fuller said there was more to the story of his first mares: "I took Fountainstown back to Keeneland the next fall and she was sold for $200, but Our Louise didn't even draw a bid. You know, if a mare doesn't bring $100 or $200, a bid of some kind, they take up her papers and she goes to the stockyards. Well, I didn't know anything about that rule and I told them I certainly would have put in a bid on her if I'd known, so they let me have Our Louise back. En route home, we stopped off in Maryland and bred her to River War. To that cover, Our Louise produced Arpey—that was our oldest child's first intelligent word—and Arpey became the first stakes winner we ever bred when she won the New England Futurity. I've bred four foals out of Our Louise and they have earned almost $190,000."

Fuller now owns 45 broodmares and they are pretty well scattered in Maryland, Kentucky, Florida, California, Michigan, Washington, and Canada, while only five are now at his farm in New Hampshire. He owns four stallions—Pan Dancer standing in Canada, Lucky Uncle in Michigan, Multnomah in Washington, and Ross Sea at Runnymede.

"I've always had a great deal of respect for Calumet Farm. I breed to their stallions a good deal. In 1961 I bought Hillsborough and another horse named Ledlie from them for $60,000; Hillsborough won the Display and Bowie Handicaps for me, finished second in the Jockey Club Gold Cup, Gallant Fox, and some other stakes, earned about $135,000 after I got him. He sired only three crops before he died; Miracle Hill is by Hillsborough."

Fuller has raced a dozen stakes winners and has bred six. "The best horse I've ever had, of course, is Dancer's Image. He was a good horse last year, undefeated in Canada, where he was voted champion 2-year-old, but he was running under a handicap. Since March 30, when we took the blinkers off and put Bobby Ussery on, he has been a different horse.

"I told everybody I bet that he was going to win the Kentucky Derby. I brought 65 people to Louisville to see him win the race. I could see it...he was going to be last, and Forward Pass would be leading at the head of the stretch, and then Dancer's Image would come on...and he would run him down.

"And when he did it...that was the greatest thrill I have ever experienced or ever expect to experience," Fuller said the day after the Kentucky Derby.

Two days later he was to say: "Winning the Kentucky Derby was the most fantastic thrill I've ever had. This experience today is by far the biggest disappointment."

In 93 runnings of the Kentucky Derby, there never had been a disqualification. Then no one ever had bred or owned seven Kentucky Derby winners before Calumet Farm did, and the first disqualification in the fixture would give Mrs. Gene Markey's Thoroughbred farm an unprecedented eighth winner.

Forward Pass is a good horse, a solid horse, a far better horse than many which finished first in previous Kentucky Derbys. He is the first good son of On-and-On, a Brooklyn Handicap winner by a great stallion and out of a champion mare and extraordinary producer; Forward Pass is out of an exceptional race mare which, in turn, is by a leading sire and out of one of the grandest broodmares in the American Stud Book. Forward Pass thus has a pedigree from which a Kentucky Derby winner is not unlikely to emerge.

He is big (16.2 hands), and good looking. His record is that of the most consistent high-class 3-year-old of the season. He quite probably will be the betting favorite for the Preakness. He possibly is the best 3-year-old of the season, but his leadership was not established by his performance on May 4.

"I'm sorry it happened," Calumet trainer Henry Forrest was quoted on Tuesday. "I hate to win a Derby this way. This is a hell of a blow to lots of people."

# A Season Of Plenty

ABOUT 73 per cent of all racing in North America is a bore, that is, claiming events and races at less than a mile. This is fortuitous, as Candide pointed out just the other day, for it sets off in relief and permits special enjoyment of infrequent good racing.

If Keeneland ran 240 days, or if Saratoga started in July and dragged on through September, these meetings probably would become tiresome, too. As they are, however, Keeneland and Saratoga provide brief, bright, fun interludes, 15 days in April and 24 days in August, that break the monotony of the 6,867 other race days in North America.

Keeneland in the spring presents the sport at its best—good horses, well-kept grounds, colored by dogwoods and pervaded by the fragrance of honey locust blossoms, displaying the promise of new 2-year-olds, building hopes and anticipation as the Kentucky Derby candidates are sorted.

Additionally, there has developed in recent years a social adjunct to the

Keeneland spring meeting. Private parties are interspersed among the public affairs, such as the Keeneland cocktail party honoring consignors of yearlings that proved their value on the track, the Thoroughbred Club Dinner Purse, the Lexington Ball after the Blue Grass Stakes, these in prologue to Princess Margaret's visit with the Whitneys for the Kentucky Derby.

Then, too, there are April hunt meetings, the Iroquois, Oxmoor, and High Hope steeplechases on Sundays. The High Hope was moved from Doug Davis Jr.'s High Hope Farm this year to the state horse park on the old Walnut Hall Stud; Raymond Guest vanned Sir Tristram's stablemate over from Churchill Downs the day after the Stepping Stone, and Bill Hartack brought Lochris II over the rolling mile course in a $500 flat race to get second money.

While hunt racing and social whirl may not be integral to the Keeneland race program, such activity attendant to Keeneland in the spring makes it a special, most enjoyable time and place for racing people.


## A Barn Well Filled

THERE is a considerable amount of dialogue under shedrows and in track kitchens which goes largely unrecorded, partly because of a want of probity and partly because it cannot be incorporated into a race chart. It is an integral part of the fun of racing, however, and should not be ignored in chronicling the history of the Turf.

One who can hold his own, going short or long, with the best conversationalists on the backstretch is Eddie Neloy, at heart a monologuist but one who can use a straight man to advantage. Years before he became America's leading trainer, Neloy was a dishwasher.

Two weeks ago in the Pimlico track kitchen, he inspected the tableware with a professional eye, wiped a non-existent spot from a coffee spoon, and sat down with trainer Alex J. (Duck) Zolman.

"Hey, Duck, remember when you and I were rubbing horses together? For Hurst Philpot. Narragansett in 1942."

Zolman nodded and observed that New England was tough in those days.

"Remember that Italian next to us trying to sell that horse? Brought one of his friends out to the barn and says, 'Now, listen to me, before you see thisa horse, I wanta tell ya, he don't looka so good.' And the other fella says, 'Atsa all right, he looka pretty good to me, I buy him offin ya.'"

223

"Then a couple of days later he comes back, complaining about buying a blind horse. 'Ah, but I tell ya before you buy him, he don't looka so good!' "

Later that day Neloy saddled a filly for the Black-Eyed Susan that looked good, saw well, and was not for sale—Ogden Phipps' My Boss Lady. After the race, Neloy returned to the barn and asked rhetorically, "How's that for training?

"My instructions were to get in a good position on the first turn, then go to the front but stay a little off the rail where the going is good, take a breather down the backside and let the others catch up, then draw off to win easy."

My Boss Lady ran just as Neloy announced he had trained her, finishing 1¼ lengths in front of Holly-O with Chalina and Justakiss another half-length back. Unfortunately, Neloy neglected to give the filly detailed gate instructions, for My Boss Lady stumbled and unseated her rider at the break.

Moody Jolley, never at a loss for pre-race or post-race comment, was cooling out Chalina, which had been closest to My Boss Lady in the upper stretch and got second money.

"We've got Justakiss beat, but my rider doesn't know which way Eddie's loose horse is going and, while he's worrying about going inside or outside the loose horse, the winner slips by us on the outside—88 ways to lose a race, only one way to win."

Neloy observed this was wisdom of the ages. Jolley hotly protested an insinuation that he was getting on in years.

"Aw, come on, Moody, I remember you when I was a kid!" Neloy called as Jolley walked his filly down the shedrow. On his next round, Jolley still was muttering, "When he was a kid..."

"Sure, you remember that little ragged kid hustlin' you a dime for the movies," Neloy prodded. Trainer Stanley Rieser appeared under the shedrow with silks in hand, said he was shipping out for New York since Justakiss was nominated for three or four stakes there.

"Aw, you don't wanta do that, Stanley," Jolley counseled. "Eddie here is loaded up there. You'd be walking into Death Row."

In the Phipps family arsenal at Belmont Park, Neloy has several Bold Ruler 2-year-olds in the ready rack and has yet to decide which is best. In the 3-year-old colt division, Neloy has stakes winners Stupendous, Impressive, Bold and Brave, and another one coming along nicely, Buckpasser.

Last Saturday, Neloy sallied forth with a trio of Phipps 3-year-old fillies for the Acorn Stakes. Two of them had won stakes, My Boss Lady and Destro, while the other, Marking Time, had finished second in an allowance race, her only previous start this season.

224

Bill Shoemaker flew in from California to ride Marking Time, arousing suspicion that this filly was something more than an afterthought at the entry box. Dead last, 19 lengths back after a quarter-mile, she was brought patiently along the rail, then guided out into the middle of the stretch, where, with a startling burst of speed, she spurted by Around the Roses and Moccasin to win by 2½ lengths.

As regards the handicap divisions, Neloy has Queen Empress to go against the fillies and mares, and on Monday he showed what he had in the way of 4-year-old colts. Wheatley Stable's Bold Lad and Phipps' Dapper Dan going in the Metropolitan.

Bold Lad was a convincing winner with 132 pounds (since 1891 only two Met winners carried more—Grey Lag in 1923 had 133 pounds and Devil Diver in 1944 had 134), while Dapper Dan closed with his usual late run and missed third by a nose.

Second in the Metropolitan was Hedevar, Mrs. Edith Bancroft's homebred which carried the old Belair silks of her father, William Woodward Sr. The procession of colors in a big stakes was a parade of old.


# Keene Designs

IN the fall of 1961, John R. Gaines and E. V. Benjamin III purchased 252-acre Sherwood Farm for $1,200 an acre. It was a well-appointed horse farm with plank fencing, being the section of historic Elmendorf Farm on which Joseph E. Widener had built one of the finest training barns in central Kentucky, a five-furlong training track, and a rambling dormitory.

The two horsemen who barely totaled 60 years in age had found precisely the kind of farm they needed for their operation, but were able to hold it only six months before reselling the place for $2,000 an acre—in essence a forced sale. Few persons, regardless of age or circumstances, can go around shrugging off offers of a $200,000 profit.

Consequently, Gaines was left in the middle of an auspicious broodmare-buying program with no place for his purchases. He thereupon negotiated a 20-year lease with option to buy on the 88-acre Old Keen Place, subsequently added an adjacent 4½ acres, and renamed it Gainesway Farm, a name his father had used for his successful Standardbred breeding establishment.

225

For a century and a half, this was part of a large grant owned by the Keen family. In the March 14, 1789, *Kentucke Gazette*, Francis Keen ran the following notice:

"DON CARELESS, a Beautiful bay, full five feet three inches high, stands this season at the subscriber's stable and will cover mares at five dollars the season payable in cows and calves, meat, cattle, sheep, pork, wheat, corn, rye or oats at their cash price when delivered at the subscriber's house, provided that any of the above mentioned articles shall be delivered by the fifth day of December next, otherwise nothing but cash will be received in payment; good pasturage gratis, but will not be answerable for escapes or accidents.

"Don Careless was got by old Don Careless imported by Col. Taylor from England, his dam by the noted Tom Jones; his pedigree is equal to any in the district, but there need not be an enumeration of words, as the horse will show for himself. It is hoped no person will bring a distempered mare by which the horse can receive any injury."

In relatively recent times, the farm was owned by the late J. O. Keene, who in 1935 sold a portion of it containing a 1¹⁄₁₆-mile track and elaborate beginnings of a stone clubhouse and stable to a group headed by Hal Price Headley and Maj. Louie Beard. This portion is now Keeneland Race Course.

Keene was fond of building in stone. He designed and built the Raceland track near Ashland, Ky., and the stonework in the stands was much admired. A few days before the track's grand opening, however, one of the track's investors noticed that the finish line was located a considerable distance south of the beautiful stonework and asked to see Keene's blueprints.

"Blueprints? Why, son, I build by eye."

The 16-stall stone barn at Gainesway was built by Keene's fine eye. Gaines has added at the rear and center a breeding shed which is equipped with a wash rack and a small veterinary laboratory. Gaines plans to install in the center a section of the Tartan 3-M surface of the type now being used as a racing surface at Del Miller's Washington harness track. The Tartan surface will be surrounded by chipped rock, half as big as a fingernail. Gaines said he preferred the rock surface to clay, tanbark, or tobacco stems, usually found in breeding sheds, for reasons of cleanliness, drainage, ability to raise or lower for different-sized mares, and its non-slip qualities.

When Gaines started buying mares, he did not contemplate standing a stallion. However, at last year's Washington-Arlington Futurity, he met with Fred W. Hooper and agreed to syndicate Crozier (My Babu—Miss Olympia, by Olympia) for $25,000 a share and stand him at Gainesway. Hooper retained 12 shares, 15 were sold, and Gaines kept five shares. Gaines reports

226

that Crozier's 1964 book includes 28 stakes winners or stakes producers.

Gaines took possession of the farm late in 1962 and immediately turned over all sod, reseeding with 25 per cent clover, 75 per cent bluegrass. He also built new fences, four-plank black fences lining the main entrance driveway while diamond-mesh wire fencing was used on the paddocks. For the wire fence, Gaines used six-inch locust posts set eight feet apart and notched at the top to recess a 16-foot oak plank. Every 12th post was set in concrete. Gaines said the wire fencing cost $4.78 for eight running feet.

Water was piped into all paddocks, in most of which were installed concrete tanks which slant inward at the base as a precaution against a horse's scuffing a knee. The tanks were manufactured in Lexington at a cost of about $50 each.

Gaines rebuilt a 20-stall barn whose exterior is part stone but mostly board and batten. Features in this barn include a lower shelf to catch loosened leaves from the hay racks and pull catch-releases on stall doors which avoid the possibility of a horse suffering an injury from a door latch being left in a protruding position.

In reclaiming a wooded lot which had not been used for horses in many years, Gaines left some of the tallest trees, but marked them and had lightning rods installed at a cost of $5,800. Forty years ago, J. E. Widener at Elmendorf and E. F. Simms at Xalapa Farm had lightning rods placed in tall trees to guard against loss of valuable mares.

"It might be too costly today for a large farm," Gaines said, "but on a small place like this, where mares and yearlings are pretty close, the saving on one mare or yearling which might otherwise be struct by lightning more than offsets the cost of installation.

Gainesway farm manager is 40-year-old Joe Taylor, a native of Lawrenceburg, Ky., who 15 years ago started with Standardbreds at Gaines' father's breeding farm. Taylor said that in a 10-year period with a Standardbred band of 40 mares, he had averaged about 72 per cent mares in foal, a percentage, he said, which might have been helped by use of artificial insemination permitted with Standardbreds. Taylor said that last year, when the practice of palpating mares was used, 93 per cent of the mares got in foal. He is enthusiastic about palpation and follicle examination.

Taylor said he had experienced some success getting maiden mares in foal soon after they were brought back from the race track. Many horsemen have found that mares can get in foal if bred immediately after being taken out of training, but if not then, they must wait 60 to 90 days to allow the mares to recover from what is known as the "turnout syndrome" and readjust to their new environment.

227

Taylor believes that mares at the race track are kept in good condition and have normal estral cycles. He and Gaines are experimenting this year with some barren mares. The mares were taken up in December, ponied an hour daily, then kept in their stalls. They are groomed daily just as though on the race track. While in their stalls, they wear a heavy Baker blanket and may stand, if they wish, under a 250-watt heat lamp which is suspended on a drop cord to within three inches of their backs. Although the bulb is low, it is free swinging, and Taylor says none of the mares has broken a bulb.

Taylor and Gaines are not certain the heat, disciplined exercise, and grooming will help the mares get in foal. Taylor pointed out, however, that the seven mares (owned by Gaines and his clients) which had received such treatment appeared in the middle of February to be in the type of condition he ordinarily would have expected by May. He said three of the mares already were believed to be in foal. Gaines said next year they planned to augment the program with controlled illumination, that is, turning on stall lights before sunrise and after sunset during the winter months to correspond with daylight hours later in the spring.

Gaines apparently has found an answer to the problem of metal feed tubs tearing and possibly causing injury to horses which have a penchant for banging them against stall walls. GI kitchen serving kettles of 24-guage iron were purchased 15 years ago at a cost of about $5 each and not one has been dented yet.

## Straw Fever

V. W. (BUDDY) RAINES, who was a young old-timer when he was galloping Brookmeade's Cavalcade for Whistlin' Bob Smith 30 years ago, watched as Brandywine Stable's Greek Money and For the Road were being walked. He began to discuss such old-time stewards as George Brown Jr., and Tom Healey who went into the stand after he quit training.

"When you talked to them, you took your hat off. They knew all about what you were doing. I had a little gray filly going in a claiming race and Walter comes over to me and says, 'The boss put in an order for your filly. I'm gonna have to take her today.'

"Geezt, I didn't want to lose that little filly, so I rushed over the office and told Judge Healey I was gonna have to scratch her 'cause she had the worst case of colic I ever saw.

228

"He looked at me for a minute and says, 'Well, Buddy, I'm very sorry to hear that, because I know how you prize that filly. I'll have the vet go over and look at her.'

"I run back to the barn—beat the vet a nose—got in the stall and rubbed straw over her best I could so's she'd look like she'd been rolling all over the place with a bellyache. Vet looked at her, went back and talked to Judge Healey, and I come to find out they won't let me scratch out of that eight-horse race.

"Judge Healey call me in, says 'Buddy, I don't believe we can let you out of the race. Seems your filly had the colic only on one side. I don't believe she was as sick as you are. I suspect you may be running a little temperature with claimitis.'

"You couldn't fool those judges. They knew what was going on. You had to respect them. Cost me a filly, though."

## Fond Memory

EARLY on the day before the 1964 Preakness, the late Bill Finnegan sent George Pope's Hill Rise three furlongs in 40 seconds. Finnegan threw a cooler over the 4-5 Preakness favorite and turned him over to a hot walker. He said he had done all he could, the rest was up to the horse.

Finnegan already had been on the race track a couple of years when Artful beat Sysonby in the 1904 Futurity. As Hill Rise was being cooled out, Finnegan began talking about training.

"Back when I came around," Finnegan said, "James Rowe was the best trainer there was.

"He did everything by a whistle; everything about his stable was organized, systemized. They put the tubs in, did up, got their horses out—all by the whistle.

"He only got out two sets in a morning, have maybe 20 or 25 horses in a set. Had a man and a boy for every horse. All the horses would be lined up in the shedrow and he'd go down and look over each one, feel their knees and ankles, you know, look at their feet.

"Then they'd all go out to the track, line up and stand next to the outside rail. They'd all be galloped maybe a mile and a quarter, then come back and stand.

229

"He'd have Marshall Lilly and maybe a jockey and those two—well sometimes he might have three boys—would work all the horses he wanted worked.

"While Lilly and the jockey were working two horses, the others would be washed down and cooled out, right there on the track. The men would bring their buckets and rub rags with them to the track and it was all done right there on the outside rail.

"Today, of course, you couldn't do that—get run over and killed standing there on the rail trying to wash down and cool out 20 horses.

"Now Sam Hildreth was an entirely different kind of trainer, have maybe one man for three horses. Hildreth was awful strong on feed, and bedding—his horses would stand in bedding this high. They were both good men with horses but I always thought Rowe was the better."


## Court Day

COLONEL ELSWORTH eased into the office last week, sagged into a chair, and revealed: "Survived the Saturday crowd at Keeneland and the next day, because I had a single-bladed Russell Barlow I was thinking about trading, went to Court Day over in Mt. Sterling," he said wearily. "I have yet to regain my strength."

Now Court Day may not mean much to the under-70 set in other parts of the country, but for a century or so Court Day in Mt. Sterling, Ky., has been a very important event for gubernatorial candidates and a large segment of Kentuckians who like to swap knives, guns, hounds, wagons, preserves, watches, milk cows, books, pump handles, curtains, and such things.

Mt. Sterling's streets can accommodate the comings and goings of its 5,083 residents with reasonable efficiency. On Court Day, however, some 25,000 people move slowly about the courthouse square—a few steps and then stand a while, the way one must when looking for a good trade and boot—so vehicular traffic stops outside town.

"You know Albert Clay, breeds horses on his place outside Mt. Sterling; he's in the tobacco business, has a bank over there—I believe he's board chairman of the 4th District Federal Reserve Bank in Cleveland, too—a trustee of the University, and the man who got the American Horse Council started." The colonel has a tendency to annotate his name-dropping.

"Anyway, Albert invited Sonny Whitney over for Court Day. It is real easy to spot them as they work their way up to the square. Whitney's dressed about as casual as Abercrombie & Fitch will let you and Clay's scrubbed up nice.

"They're moving along slow when a man wearing two pistols, might have been from Morgan County, shoves a rifle against Whitney's stomach and asks him, 'Wanna buy a gun?'

"As you know, in the last 40 years Sonny Whitney has bred and raced more stakes winners than any man alive and I imagine during that time he has done some horse trading. He looks at the rifle, has some rust on it, 'How much do you want for it?' The man says $80.

"Whitney is comfortable in a financial way, as was his father, and his father before him, and now I know why. 'I haven't got $80,' he says.

" 'Well, how mucha got?'

" 'Forty dollars.'

" 'Ya bought chersef a rifle, mister.'

"Whitney just slung that rifle over his shoulder and smiled at Clay. He knew he had one of the first .22 caliber rifles ever made. Had his gunsmith clean it up and today he wouldn't take a thousand dollars for that rifle.

"Clay was trying to get to the railroad track where the beagles were tied to some freight cars; they ducked under a man who had just traded for some mounted steer horns that spanned six feet, and got by the sorghum dealers, but Whitney stopped at a table covered with dime-store jewelry.

"You remember a few years ago at Saratoga when a burglar hiked $781,800 worth of Mrs. Whitney's jewelry? Well, Whitney just sort of mussed through the stuff on that table, picked up something that looked like glass; they asked $4 for it and he gave $3. Mexican diamond set by a designer Whitney knew, had his name in the ring.

"So you see, what you lose at Saratoga, you can make up in Mt. Sterling on Court Day, if you know what you're about."

## The Commission

WATHEN KNEBELKAMP for the last quarter-century has presented the Broodmare-of-the-Year award at the Kentucky Thoroughbred Breeders' Derby trainer party four days before the Kentucky Derby. This week he was

231

at his usual stand at the Brown Hotel in Louisville prepared to present a plaque to Paul Mellon in honor of All Beautiful, dam of Arts and Letters.

"This award goes to a wonderful gentleman tonight," Knebelkamp said. "He not only is a wonderful gentleman and great for racing, but he also is a pretty good businessman. He paid $175 for this mare, I mean $175,000."

Mellon was quick to respond: "The first thing I would like to say, gentlemen, is that I hope the difference between $175 and $175,000 was not the commission.

"On behalf of Elliott Burch, who is responsible for everything that Arts and Letters has done, and his father, Preston Burch, who advised me to buy this mare, and the late Mr. William du Pont Jr., who really should be honored here, for he bred this mare, and myself, I thank you very much for this prestigious and honorable award.

"I am sure the mare herself would have liked to be here, but she realized this was a stag dinner, and she is very pregnant to a very good horse which stands in Upperville—Quadrangle; this, frankly, is an advertisement. But I want to thank you all for this award and being here tonight to honor this mare. It has been a great day for me and I am very glad to accept this award for All Beautiful."


## Veteran Ride


"HOW about that little hole Eric Guerin came through!" exclaimed trainer George Poole after the 46-year-old Arcadian had slipped through on the rail to win the Blue Grass Stakes with Impetuosity. "You don't see *apprentice* boys do that!" a jubilant Poole declared.

Guerin won his first race 30 years ago, before seven other riders in the Blue Grass were born. He had won with his first Kentucky Derby mount, Jet Pilot, in 1947. Over the years he had won stakes with 18 different champions—Native Dancer, High Gun, One Count, Summer Tan, Battlefield, Blue Peter, Crafty Admiral, Berlo, But Why Not, Bed o' Roses, Next Move, Parlo, Grecian Queen, Conniver, Romanita, Rose Jet, Beaugay, and Idun.

Guerin was one of America's big-name riders, from 1944 (when he rode Brownie in the Carter Handicap's famous triple dead heat) through 1963 (when he won the Kent, Leonard Richards, and Travers with Crewman). Then for five years he did not win a stakes. On the afternoon of the 1968

232

Spinster Stakes, he was chosen as a substitute rider and won Keeneland's richest event with Sale Day. The following spring at Keeneland, he won the Ben Ali with Court Recess, his 173rd stakes victory. He was two years getting his next with Impetuosity.

Guerin's Blue Grass ride was a George Blanda performance. A young quarterback for the University of Kentucky when Guerin won the Kentucky Derby, old Raider Blanda was in Lexington to be honored as Male Athlete of the Year by UK lettermen the day another old athlete showed boys some tricks in the Blue Grass Stakes.

Naked to the waist in the jocks room, Guerin looked at Poole and grinned, "Yeah, it was kinda tight in there."

## Edward Troye, Best Of Them All

EDWARD TROYE was America's foremost sporting artist of the 19th Century, more or less by default.

While portraiture of the early race horse in England was in the fine hands of John Wooton, James Seymour, and George Stubbs, these to be succeeded in the 19th Century by such as Ben Marshall, John Ferneley, and John Frederick Herring, pictorial record of early Thoroughbreds in America was not graced by such elegance.

We must rely on the primitive work of Alvan Fisher for a suggestion of the appearance of American Eclipse, Duroc, Sir Archy, Sir Charles, Timoleon, Virginian, and other foundation sires. Henri de Lattre visited from France in 1839 and left a likeness of Boston. Later in the century, Thomas J. Scott, Henry Stull, and Louis Maurer painted a number of horses, but none of these artists possessed the skill or style of Troye.

Troye was the first painter in America to evidence some regard for the individual conformation of his subjects—not with the particularity of Stubbs or Marshall—but sufficient to gain wide patronage from the most knowledgeable horsemen of his day.

A prolific painter, Troye set on canvas virtually all of America's good race horses and sires from 1832 to 1874, many of them several times, and it is from these, executed before wide use of daguerreotypes and photography, that we are left with some impression of the sturdy, distinctly American, four-mile horse from which descend our speed horses of today.

233

He was born Edouard de Troye on July 12, 1808, at Lausanne, Switzerland. His parents were French, his grandfather an exiled nobleman, his father an eminent painter whose "The Plague of Marseilles" hangs in the Louvre in Paris. In 1822, the Troye family moved to England, where the children were trained in the arts.

Troye's brother, Charles, became a noted painter in Antwerp; a sister, Marie Thirion, became a celebrated sculptress in Verona; another sister, Esperance Paligi, became the first woman admitted to the Paris Conservatory of Music.

At the age of 20, Troye sailed for Jamaica, where he worked briefly on a sugar plantation, and in 1830 he landed in Philadelphia, where he secured a position in the art department of *Sartain's Magazine*, drawing animals. None of the illustrations in this publication can be attributed to Troye, so it may be assumed he soon was fired for moonlighting or that he just failed to report one Monday morning after a trip south into the horse country.

At any rate, Troye was setting about acquiring a reputation as an animal painter. The number of people in America desiring oil paintings of animals was greater in the days before color photography and most of these were wealthy landowners in Virginia, the Carolinas, Alabama, Mississippi, Louisiana, Tennessee, and Kentucky. This was Troye's marketing district.

He had done pictures of some merit while in his teens in England, he had sketched scenes in Jamaica, and he set out through the South painting farm animals. He did not keep an inventory of his paintings nor did he keep a diary.

He painted prominent race horses, a patron's favorite mare not always distinguished for her accomplishments, cattle, family portraits, children's ponies—anything to keep the pot boiling—and many of these paintings were unsigned, undated, and today unidentifiable.

Harry Worcester Smith reported in 1938 he had located some 240 Troye paintings. There probably are many more extant.

Troye painted some subjects more than once—at different ages and in different poses, in the same pose with different backgrounds, and the same poses and backgrounds reproduced hundreds of times by lithographs and by a "secret method known only to Mr. Troye."

By 1832, Troye was well enough established as an equine artist to paint Trifle, with jockey up, for Col. William R. Johnson, who operated something of a Wheatley Stable of that day. That was the year the little (14.3 hands) filly raced 20 miles against John Cox Stevens' Black Maria at Union Course on Long Island (Trifle won the second four-mile heat and dead-heated with Black Maria in the third, but faltered in the 19th mile, being "distanced" in the fifth heat). This 1832 painting of Trifle is relatively crude as Troye paintings go, but he repainted her 10 years later, as a broodmare at Belle Meade Stud in Tennessee, by which time Troye had developed the style and technique that gave his later work lasting merit.

He painted Lexington, America's leading sire for 16 years, many times in different poses from 1864 to 1872, perhaps the pose he liked best being completed in 1868 for he copied this figure of Lexington frequently, slightly altering the background in successive pictures.

He painted Glencoe, eight-time leading American sire, as a relatively young stallion, again at the age of 21 in 1852, and then again just before Glencoe died in 1857. The latter picture was commissioned by A. Keene Richards, who had just bought Glencoe and who said it was "one of Troye's best efforts in anatomy and coloring...those who look upon it will see a truthful portrait of the old horse—with all the marks of age—as he appeared at the close of the season in his 26th year." The Jockey Club owns a replica of this painting dated 1959.

Troye frequently turned out almost precise replicas of the same horse with a different background. When champion Kentucky was sold by W. R. Travers, John Hunter, and George Osgood to Leonard Jerome in 1866, the three former owners all wanted a painting. Troye executed three paintings of Kentucky in front of the Jerome Park grandstand, the pictures differing only in the face of the coach driver in the background, the likeness of each owner appearing in the driver's box in the picture he received.

Painting his way through the Carolinas in the 1830s, Troye happened upon Col. John R. Spann, who wanted a painting, but who had sold his good horse, Bertrand, to Kentucky as a stallion. Spann commissioned Troye to go to Kentucky and paint Bertrand, which he did, twice, same pose, once with a Kentucky setting and another with a South Carolina setting. In both of these pictures Bertrand is held by skinny, short grooms, accenting Bertrand's height, which was 16 hands, considered extraordinary in that day.

On the other hand, Troye refined Leviathan to some extent. He was raced as Mezereon at two in England, but grew at an astonishing rate during the winter and came out at three, a full 16 hands, renamed Leviathan, to go unbeaten in nine starts against moderate company that year. When James Jackson of Gallatin, Tenn., imported Leviathan in 1830, the horse was not well received initially by American breeders, the thought being that he was entirely too big and coarse.

This impression did not last long because Leviathan's first foals placed him second on the sire list and he topped the list the next three years, 1837-39. In

1838 his progeny won an unprecedented 92 races and earned a theretofore unfathomable $103,437. He led the sire lists again in 1843 and 1848.

At any rate, Troye did not accent Leviathan's size by having a groom in the picture and little indication of the stallion's reputed coarseness is revealed; indeed, Leviathan appears to be inadequately supported by spindly legs.

By 1837, Edward Troye was sufficiently known to be described by William T. Porter in the New York sporting weekly, *Spirit of the Times*, in mentioning the pending publication of a new Stud Book which "would include nearly one hundred prints of well-known horses, all to be furnished by the noted animal painter, Edward Troye. We have Mr. Troye busily at work and are very fortunate in securing the services of Campbell, an artist of rare abilities, who does the drawings on fine-grained stone from Troye's paintings."

This Stud Book never got out of the pre-publication stage. Some of Troye's pictures for it, however, were reproduced from time to time in the *Spirit*. Some of these were of horses Troye quite probably never saw—Sir Archy, American Eclipse, and Sir Henry.

The only known portrait of Sir Archy painted from life was done by Alvan Fisher; Sir Archy died in 1833, shortly after Troye came to America, and if Troye did see "the Godolphin Arabian of America" it was when the stallion was 26 years old or older, when his coat had become "shaggy, some hairs two inches long." Troye's watercolor of Sir Archy, reproduced hundreds of times, probably was taken from Fisher's painting.

Troye also probably copied Fisher's earlier works of American Eclipse (generally thought the first American race horse to be subject of an oil portrait) and Sir Henry, which was defeated by American Eclipse in the first, great, North-vs.-South match at Union Course in 1829. Troye's portraits of these two were done in 1834, when American Eclipse was 20 and Sir Henry 11, and neither suggests such age. Then, too, American Eclipse often was described in the press as having straw-colored mane and tail, coloring which Troye did not accent in his several paintings of American Eclipse.

On Troye's first trip to Kentucky to paint Bertrand, he met A. Keene Richards, master of Blue Grass Park at Georgetown, and R. A. Alexander, who at Woodburn Stud was to build America's greatest Thoroughbred breeding farm. These men proved to be Troye's staunchest supporters, his principal patrons and sponsors for the next 40 years. He also met Miss Cornelia Ann Van de Graaf of Payne's Depot near Georgetown and they were married on July 16, 1839.

The Troyes had four children, all born in the de Graaf home between 1840 and 1846. Three died in infancy; their third child, Anna, died in 1924

236

in Alabama. Mrs. Troye and Anna remained at the de Graaf home, located about 10 miles from Woodburn and about seven miles from Blue Grass Park, while Troye painted cattle and family portraits for Alexander, Thoroughbreds for Richards and many other breeders in Kentucky. During the 1840s Troye also made several trips into Tennessee, Mississippi, and Louisiana painting Thoroughbreds.

For a while he tried to operate a farm near Paducah, Ky., but he was a better painter than farmer and in November of 1847 the *Spirit* noted: "Edward Troye, the eminent animal painter, has disposed of his farm near Paducah, Ky., and is about visiting Havana, via New Orleans. While there, we understand it is his intention to devote himself to portrait painting."

In the fall of 1849, Troye accepted a professorship at Spring Hill College near Mobile, and there taught French and art for six years, devoting many of his non-classroom hours to painting portraits, landscapes, and some of his finest horse pictures.

Among these was Revenue, which Troye's old friend, Col. W. R. Johnson, had been campaigning in New Orleans and Mobile when the noted horseman died. Troye painted Revenue as a 7-year-old training in Mobile.

In 1851, Troye executed what frequently is described as his best painting, that of Gen. T. J. Wells' gray Reel, dam of three exceptional race horses—Lecomte, Prioress, and Starke—and a good sire in War Dance. Troye painted Reel several times, both outside her barn and inside her stall. The latter scene, in which her coat is almost white at the age of 13 and in startling contrast to the blue-almost-black interior of the stall, is the most popular of the Troye prints today.

Among the portraits painted by Troye while at Spring Hill College was one of Phraudieus Posea Browne, to whom he gave the "Portrait of the Artist." This painting, dated 1852, is now owned by Yale University and on exhibit in the National Museum of Racing in Saratoga.

Keene Richards, with a reported annual income of $250,000, was regarded as one of the wealthiest men in the South and his enthusiasm for Arabian horses generally was received politely, but not shared. When Richards asked Troye if he wanted to join him in a search for some good Arabians to import to Kentucky and bolster his Thoroughbred breeding operation, Troye quickly terminated his six-year stay at Spring Hill College; in July of 1855, Richards and Troye embarked on a 19-month tour of Constantinople, Damascus, the Holy Land, and Arabia—with paints. Troye there completed several massive canvases, "Dead Sea," "Syrian Plowman," "Sea of Galilee," "River Jordan at Bethabara," and "Bazaar of Damascus," the last-named now hanging in the Louvre in Paris. The large paintings were taken to his

237

brother's studio in Antwerp, where Troye copied them; they subsequently were exhibited in Canada, New York, and New Orleans, and later were purchased by Richards for $6,000 and presented to Bethany College in West Virginia, where Richards had studied theology.

Troye and his patron returned from abroad with several Arabian horses in January of 1857. These horses were bred to the best broodmares at Blue Grass Park—with absolutely no success whatever in producing race horses. Probably the best thing that came out of Richards' Arabian importations were Troye's painting of Mokhladi, Massoud, and Sacklowie, described at length in an eight-page illustrated pamphlet published by Richards in 1857.

Troye remained with Richards in Georgetown for two years, painting numerous pictures of prominent horses and people, including a giant equestrian painting of Gen. Winfield Scott. "The General was very kind to me," Troye said, "and every opportunity was afforded me to obtain a correct likeness. He bore the long sittings with patience, and only murmured when we placed him on his horse and lifted him off again. His limbs were stiff from wounds and the operation of posing made him wince with pain."

This portrait, a copy of which covers an entire wall in the National Museum of Racing, originally was commissioned by Virginia Military Institute, but the Civil War came up and Virginia Military Institute became disinterested in the commander-in-chief of the Union forces. Troye unexpectedly found he had a 7-by-9½-foot painting on his hands. He tried to sell it to the government, then loaned it, and for a number of years it hung on a staircase wall in the House of Representatives in Washington. By an act approved in 1891, Mrs. Troye was paid $3,000 for the painting, which then was boxed and stored in the capitol basement until 1939, when it was shipped out on permanent loan to VMI.

With the outbreak of the war, Richards outfitted a regiment of Confederates and joined Gen. John C. Breckinridge's staff. Troye went to Europe for two years, returned with his family in 1862 and took up residence at Blue Grass Park, ostensibly serving as manager of the 2,400-acre showplace in Richards' absence. Troye spent a good deal of his time, however, at Alexander's Woodburn Stud, where he painted Lexington numerous times, also Asteroid, cattle, sheep, and trotting horses such as Abdallah and Bay Chief.

In 1866, Troye began another publishing venture, "The Race Horses of America," a series of volumes hoped to "transmit to posterity the circumstances and characteristics which gave to them their fame," text by Troye, illustrations by Troye.

"These portraits," reported *Turf, Field and Farm*, "will be from the works of the artist, reduced and colored by a process known only to himself and

238

every one possessing a copy of this work will have a series of portraits in oil from the brush of Troye." The first volume in the series described Boston and Lexington. Subscribers paid $15 for the book and also received two 11-by-13-inch paintings of the subjects.

Troye's "secret process" involved the taking of photographs of his earlier paintings and having them lightly printed on canvas or sepia paper. These were then colored by Troye, signed, and dated. Kentucky and Sir Henry, with similar small portraits, were scheduled next in the series, but the series never made it to the second volume.

While in New York in 1867, Troye reproduced on canvas, by his secret process, a large number of his earlier paintings of Boston, Lexington, American Eclipse, Sir Henry, and Kentucky; these replicas in oil, 22 by 17 inches, were sold for $30 each or $50 a pair and many are extant today.

Richards gave Troye a 750-acre cotton farm in Alabama after the Civil War and the artist took another run at farming. This paled, however, the *Turf, Field and Farm* reporting in June of 1870 that Troye had been "rusticating at his rural home in Alabama...has broken the spell that has kept him silent for so many months, and contemplates visiting New York and Saratoga this summer...a large number of gentlemen here are anxious to commission him to paint their horses. A portrait from the easel of Mr. Troye is made valuable by the fact that it is the production of our most famous animal painter."

Troye left the Alabama farm to the management of his wife and daughter and returned to Georgetown. Blue Grass Park was his headquarters for the last four years of his life while he made brief forays to New York, Memphis, Vicksburg, Nashville, and parts of Kentucky to paint the best horses of the day. He died on July 25, 1874, and was buried in the Georgetown cemetery.

Troye was an artist, a good artist, the best equine artist in America in the 19th Century. He did not reproduce on canvas an exact replica of a horse, a photograph in oil, but he painted a sufficient likeness of a horse to please solid horsemen of his day.

He thought it made a better picture to have a sprung tail and nearly all of his horse paintings show horses' tails in an unnatural position. It became a characteristic of his paintings, as familiar as his trademark "Troye tree," an old tree, or branch with dead foliage, or bushes, which provided a touch of red on one side or both sides of his pictures painted after 1835.

In 1872, Schreibers and Sons sent a man from Philadelphia to photograph horses in Woodford County. From these pictures it is possible to compare Troye's paintings with photographs of three subjects.

Frank Harper's Longfellow was painted by Troye and photographed by

239

Schreibers in the same year, when the champion was five. Troye painted a longer horse, a straighter shoulder (he always did), and in no way approached approximation of a leg, pastern, or foot on which a horse might be expected to stand.

Troye painted Asteroid when he was a 4-year-old in training; the Schreibers photograph was taken when Asteroid was 11, had served four seasons at stud, and had developed a stallion crest. Again, in Troye's rendition, the tail is sprung, the shoulder straight, the legs too spindly.

The painting and photograph of Australian probably were made within a year of each other and quite possibly—save for the rabbit ears—Troye produced a better likeness of the horse than did the photographer, who may have been at a slight angle and apparently focusing on Australian's hip.

Studying Troye's paintings, juxtaposed to photographs of the same subjects, one can see that Troye did not paint a horse precisely as the hrose was formed. Troye painted a picture—a good picture, with style and verve. Troye produced a likeness of the individual which was readily identifiable, yet he added a vitality and spirit that film could not capture.

Those who would prefer the Schreibers photograph to Troye's painting of Australian would choose a steel I-beam over a Palladian arch.

Sir Theodore Cook was talking about sporting art: "In America you had your artists, too. There are the works of Troye, Audubon, and other Americans, but Troye was best of them all."


## Legacy


OFF pedigree and performance, Bill Winfrey was 3-5 to make racing's Hall of Fame. Son of Hall of Fame trainer Cary Winfrey and trainer of Hall of Fame horses Native Dancer and Buckpasser, Winfrey was formally inducted on Aug. 9 in Saratoga.

NYRA president Alfred G. Vanderbilt, owner-breeder of Native Dancer, made the presentation: "They say about trainers that all personality problems disappear in the winner's circle, but with Bill, it never mattered whether we were in the circle. I don't have to tell you people anything about his abilities as a trainer—both Mr. Phipps and I can attest to that. I think you should know, however, that not only is he one hell of a trainer, but he is a hell of a man, and I am proud to have been associated with him."

Winfrey confirmed this by his brief acceptance speech: "When I look at the list of people who have preceded me in selections for racing's Hall of Fame, I feel I am being run here a little bit over my head, because there are a number of my contemporaries whom I feel should have come before me. I have been thinking about this, and I believe I have figured it out—in honoring me, museum trustees are honoring my father, whom we all know was a big man."

## Getting Education

Talking about times gone by and the trainers who went with them: Today's trainers, of course, are something else entirely, a new breed which has evolved under new rules, restrictions at which an old-timer would snort: "They're trying to make honest men out of thieves."

Fifty years ago it was not uncommon for a trainer to back his judgment of his horse man to man, shortcutting the circuitous route of the mutuel machines which were relatively new. The late W. L. (Duke) McCue had a tendency to announce his convictions with the volume turned up, and not infrequently he had a bankroll to support his convictions.

He trained Double Jay for the Ridgewood Stable of James Tigani and James Boines. At two, Double Jay had won the Newport and James H. Connors Memorial Stakes in New England, then the Garden State Stakes, and was shipped to Churchill Downs for the Kentucky Jockey Club Stakes.

There he was to meet his most formidable opposition of the year, Mrs. Fred Hooper's Education, the best 2-year-old in Chicago and the leading money earner of the division with victories in the Hialeah Juvenile, Elementary, Washington Park Futurity, Prairie State, Hawthorne Juvenile, and Breeders' Futurity. The speedy son of Ariel was a 4-5 favorite although a mile was a little beyond his best distance, while Double Jay was 5-2 in the morning line for the Kentucky Jockey Club Stakes.

On the morning of the race, McCue ambled into the racing secretary's office, where a suggestion was made by one of the assembled horsemen that Double Jay was overmatched.

"Duke, think your horse will ever be able to catch Education?"

McCue responded quickly, with $400 slapped on the counter. "This says my horse is in front at the quarter!" There was considerable scurrying and

241

scrambling to get this sum covered because Education was not in the habit of being beaten away from the gate. Some of the heavier trainers in the room were shut out at the counter.

McCue produced another $400. "And this says he is in front at the half!" Real activity now began and McCue, thundering above the din, continued peeling it off the arm. "And here's $400 that says he is still in front at the three-quarters! And this $400 says he is in front at the end!"

There was a clamor still for action, but McCue, with more fire than dignity, shouted: "I'd bet some real money and ruin all you guys, but I don't have any more and that's the only thing saving you!"

That afternoon Johnny Gilbert got Double Jay away from the gate fifth, but hustled to the front quickly along the rail and after a quarter in :22⅘ had the lead by a half-length over Education. The half-mile was run in :46⅖ and Double Jay still had the lead by a half-length. The three-quarters was run in 1:11⅖ and Double Jay continued to lead Education by the same margin with the rest of the field four lengths and more behind.

Then, as Gilbert gave Double Jay a breather, Nick Jemas made his move with Education and the two horses drew almost even at the three-sixteenth pole. At that point Gilbert roused his horse and Double Jay drew away with authority to win by three lengths in 1:37, fastest time for the race since Twenty Grand beat Equipoise.

McCue's was not a good bet; his $1,600 could have won $4,320 through the machines, but it was Duke's kind of bet, an old racing man's kind of action—even money, man to man, peeling it off the arm for every pole.

Today's restrictions take away the salt.


## In Praise Of English Racing


PAUL MELLON, owner-breeder of horses voted the best in America the last two years (Arts and Letters, Fort Marcy), was represented this season by Mill Reef, generally regarded as second only to My Swallow among the 2-year-olds in Europe. Bred at Mellon's Rokeby Farm near Upperville, Va., Mill Reef won the Gimcrack Stakes at York last August, thus entitling his owner to give the principal address at the 200th annual York Gimcrack Club dinner on Dec. 11.

Mellon said that he came to praise English racing, rather than bury it in a

242

heap of critical rubble. Past Gimcrack speakers have taken the occasion to emphasize undesirable conditions on the Turf. Mellon instead related the enjoyment he had received from English racing, literature, and art since the day he saw his first horse race, the 1929 Cambridgeshire.

"To me, the enjoyment of British sporting art and literature has always been inseparable from the enjoyment of racing, 'chasing, and hunting. How often we see characters and caricatures from Alken, Rowlandson, or Surtees in the hunting field. When we go racing, there in the paddock and on the course are Seymours, Stubbs, and Ben Marshalls."

An English Turf writer, bored to death with past Gimcrack talks, had suggested that this year's might come off better in rhymed couplets. Mellon obliged with an acrostic, a short poem with a significant arrangement of letters at the beginning of each line.

> Grey was I, well-proportioned, but so small
> In stature that I scarce could shade a child.
> Many a master had I, from the mild
> Callow young lad who rubbed me in my stall
> Right on through Count Lauraguais, who asked all
> And more of me, for which he was reviled.
> Courage restrained me from becoming wild:
> Kindness and English grass soothed my deep gall.
>
> Swift as a bird I flew down many a course,
> Princes, Lords, Commoners all sang my praise.
> In victory or defeat I played my part.
> Remember me, all men who love the Horse,
> If hearts and spirits flag in after days;
> Though small, I gave my all, I gave my heart.

## Right On

JAMES P. Ross Jr. was foaled just after the running of the sixth race at the old Kentucky Association track on Sept. 14, 1907. His father, J. P. Ross Sr., was superintendent of the track at the time. Here was a lad born to racing, Kentucky racing, and—when his father moved on to Havre de Grace in

1919—more generally American racing. But what he knows about European racing is a caution.

Through the years, Ross has gained a reputation as one of the best racing secretaries and handicappers in the business. At Atlantic City, he annually issues appraisals of the world's best horses in the form of weights assigned for the United Nations Handicap.

Ross' ranking of American horses this year is not disputed here: Gun Bow three pounds over Mongo, four over Kelso, and eight over Colorado King; Quadrangle best of the 3-year-old colts (although two under scale), three pounds better than Knightly Manner and Roman Brother, four over Hill Rise, and five over Lt. Stevens; Tosmah best of the 3-year-old fillies, probably because she beat colts and older fillies and mares, whereas Miss Cavandish has not raced against colts and finished second in her only assay against older fillies and mares.

## No Monkey Business

THE New York racing season is on again.

"Yessir," outrider Lucas Dupps confirmed. He has been an outrider in New York and Florida for more than 20 years and is scheduled to be a patrol judge later this season at Aqueduct and Saratoga, but he says "Yessir" more often than a bellhop.

"Yessir, I was hoppin' bells in the Brown Hotel in Louisville, but I wanted to get around the race track, so one day I asked Col. E. R. Bradley, there in the hotel, about it. He said I looked like the right size all right, and if I got my mother's permission I could come down to the farm and help break yearlings in the fall."

Hugh L. Fontaine, a flying ace in World War I and a good polo player in the years thereafter, has trained 16 stakes winners from Ladysman in 1934 to Ponanza in 1962, including 1956 Kentucky Derby winner Needles. He is a man of flash and charm who has won a thousand friends in racing. He presently has a bloodstock agency in Ocala, Fla., but was manager of W. R. Coe's Shoshone Stud near Lexington when he first met Dupps.

"Well, sir, then I saw Mr. Fontaine and when I told him I was going to work for Col. Bradley in the fall breaking yearlings, he said, 'That so? Col. Bradley, eh?' and I said, 'Yessir, I'm gonna be a jockey.'

" 'What's your name son?' and I said, 'Lucas Dupps, sir, rhymes with cups,' and Mr. Fontaine says, 'Well, Dupes, we just might find a spot for you at Shoshone, see whether you'll make a rider.'

"So I hustled down to Lexington, worked all summer, and it began to look like I could stay on a horse anyway. That fall Elmo Shropshire was taking Ladysman and a bunch of horses out to Santa Anita that was just opening that year, and Mr. Fontaine gave me a contract and told me to go home and get my mother to sign it.

"She didn't care much for my going on the race track, wanted me to keep on in school, but my brother convinced her I ought to have this chance, then if I couldn't make it I could come on home. Otherwise, I'd be crying around the rest of my life about how I was going to be the greatest rider in the world but never had a chance. So she signed it.

"We went to California, the stable won a lot of races, came back, and Mr. Coe sold the farm. Mr. Fontaine then took the job with Brookmeade, so Elmo and I and the rest of us went with him to the farm in Virginia. But I kept wanting to ride, see, and finally Mr. Fontaine said all right, he'd send me out to learn something.

"He says to me, 'Now, Dupes, here's your train fare to Charles Town. You report to One-Eyed Joe and he'll fix you up.' So I said yessir and went up to Charles Town and found One-Eyed Joe and he was glad to see me because he wouldn't have to pay me anything since I was under contract to Mr. Fontaine.

"I didn't have any tack or anything, so he took me over to the shop and I really got an outfit—the heavy, medium, and light saddles, everything. Sande would have been proud. Bill came to $450.

"Well, anyway, I had to break from the gate before the stewards would give me a license, so One-Eyed Joe had these two colored exercise boys and he got out his knife and he told them, 'If he don't outbreak you from the gate tomorrow morning—don't come back here.'

"So the next morning, One-Eyed Joe put me on his best filly, and the other boys were loaded in the gate on either side of me, and I must have broke 10 on top. The stewards agreed if I could break like that I was gonna win a lot of races.

"But I didn't get to ride too many races because as soon as Mr. Fontaine got that bill for all my tack, he called me home. So then we all shipped up to Saratoga. That was 1937.

"One night Mr. Fontaine was out at the Piping Rock trying to beat the roulette wheel and it wasn't long before he was broke, so he looked around, saw Buddy Hirsch, and tried to touch him for $1,000."

Hirsch was not interested in making any loans, but suggested to Fontaine he would buy Dupps' contract for $1,500. The deal was made on the spot and Fontaine, with renewed strength, turned his attention to the matter at hand.

"Next morning he called me into the office and says, 'Dupes, I've sold your contract for $1,500 to Buddy Hirsch,' and I say, 'Gee, that's fine, Mr. Fontaine, because under our contract I get a third of that, sir—$500.'

" 'That so?' Mr. Fontaine paused a minute. 'Well, Lucas, I'll tell you about that $500. I was out at the Piping Rock and I put your $500 in this pocket here and my $1,000 in this other pocket and I went to the gambling tables and I really had a lucky streak. I was winning so much money, I began to stuff it in both pockets.

" 'Well, I got to doing so good I run out of pockets to hold money in and I got to thinking about you, since I'd got your and my money all mixed up, I just decided to take you in as a partner since I was doing so good.

" 'Lucas, I want to tell you we really had them going. We really were going good. Then, before you knew it, our luck changed and they cleaned us out.

" 'Now get your tack and hustle over to Buddy Hirsch's barn. Save your money and behave yourself because I don't want him sending you back here.' "

Dupps rode his first winner in the first race at Tropical Park on Jan. 1, 1938, and rode another 125 winners that year with 735 mounts. The best horse he rode that season was Thanksgiving.

"Yessir, I was riding for Mr. Max Hirsch then. See when Buddy would get mad at me he would send me to Mr. Hirsch, then when I'd do something wrong he'd send me to Miss Mary Hirsch, and then I'd go back to Buddy. I rode that circuit for four years. Anyway, I had been riding Thanksgiving regularly and he looked like he had a good chance in the Travers, but the day before that I won a race for Mr. Hirsch by 10 lengths. He took me off Thanksgiving, said I had used poor judgment, and gave the mount to Eddie Arcaro, who wins the race."

Dupps acknowledged that race riding had changed considerably since he had his last spill in 1942, crushed five vertebrae, and retired with a total of 258 winners.

"Yessir, I was riding in Maryland once when my horse tired on the lead. I saw this kid coming up on one of Mr. Alfred Vanderbilt's horses and I knew he was going to run right by me, so I just happened to hook my leg in front of his and we went the rest of the way together.

"I figured he might claim a foul, so as soon as we crossed the finish line, I hollered, 'Gosh, kid, you beat me a dirty nose! I sure thought I was going to win that one, but you beat me good.' I convinced him he won, so I knew he wasn't going to claim any foul, but as we come back to weigh in I saw Mr. Vanderbilt hustling through the crowd, trying to get to the scales.

"I hopped off my horse and weighed out fast, and rushed up to Mr. Vanderbilt, stopping him, see, before he could talk to his boy and find out for sure I had leg-locked the kid. I talked real fast, telling him how disappointed I was I lost, and how good a horse he had. Then the official was flashed on the board with my number on top, and I acted surprised and said, 'Excuse me, Mr. Vanderbilt,' and hustled off to the jocks' room before he could say anything.

"But you don't fool Mr. Vanderbilt much. He knew what was going on. He was president of the track then. He told the stewards about how I kept him from telling his jockey to claim a foul and they called me up next morning.

"They said they didn't want any more monkey business and I said 'Yessir' and they let me go."

The film patrol has added greatly to the game of racing. It also has taken something out of the game. Yessir.


## The Outsider

JAMES COX BRADY, as honor guest at the Thoroughbred Club of America, referred to HBPA charges that the NYRA trustees conspired to conduct New York racing for their own profit and reported one trustee's comment: "My God, if there is a conspiracy, let me in on it. I haven't won a race in a year."


## That Counts For Something

FEW experiences are more satisfying than studying the pedigree, conformation, and way of going of a racing prospect, making a judgment thereon, duly noting same in cryptic scrawl on a catalogue page, and then buying the

247

prospect on the open market for less than expected. Ratification of the judgment by subsequent racing excellence is an intellectual pleasure unsurpassed.

On the other hand, positive opinion proved wrong can occasion intricate rationale. Which reminds pin-hooker Raleigh Burroughs, long-time editor of the *Turf & Sport Digest*, of "an astute (part-time) dealer in horseflesh. This fellow bought two weanlings for $1,600 in 1967 and sold them as yearlings for $1,600 in 1968. This might not sound like too good a deal, but I had the use of them for a year."

## Saratoga Musings

THE sun, waiting for a more sensible hour, had not risen. Cold mist enveloped the Saratoga sale yard when the day's work began at 3:30 a.m. Metal doors clanged on the sleeping shacks and lights shone from the stall tack rooms as men emerged to begin the long day of yearling showing.

One man took a yearling on the walking ring while another mucked out the temporarily empty stall. By 4:30 almost all the consignors had their first sets of yearlings on the ring. Each yearling was walked 30 to 40 minutes. By 6 o'clock a peeping sun had worked its way through the mist, the yearlings had been returned to their stalls and morning ration of grain, the men had drifted to the concession stand behind the sale pavilion, singly and in groups, for breakfast.

Sales company employes mechanically lifted the piles of dirty straw outside each stall into a truck. Another company man was checking yearling markings. If they differed from those shown on the individual's registration certificate, photographs were taken to confirm the alteration of the certificate.

By 6:30 the men had returned from breakfast to remove feed tubs from the stalls and begin the brush and rub-rag work of cleaning off each yearling.

K. C. Wilson, foreman of the Jonabell Farm crew, first came to Saratoga in 1930 with the late John Carr's yearling consignment.

"The routine hasn't changed much," Wilson said as he tucked a brush under an arm, slipped a chain through an eyelet on the stall's back wall, and snapped it on the halter of a filly by Bold Ruler—Blue Norther.

"Always been getting up at 3:30 or 4 to get the yearlings ready and the

248

place cleaned up. In the old days didn't have electric lights here, hung a lantern on the door latch.

"Change a little. Used to bring the yearlings up by train two weeks ahead of the sale. Stabled them out at the trotting track; when they'd sell the first bunch out of here, we'd move in with our bunch. Come up two weeks ahead, so if anything happen to any of them we'd have more time with them before the sale showings.

"Nearly always had trouble with shipping fever then, lot of them come up with the cough and snots. Don't have hardly any of that now, you know; oil them good and give them shots now and don't have that kind of trouble with them anymore.

"I come up here first with Mr. Carr, Mr. Tom Piatt's brother-in-law. Then I went to work for Mr. Silas Mason, he had big Duntreath Farm on the Versailles Pike, but I worked for Mr. Burnett Robinson out at what we called Little Duntreath on the Paris Pike. Had a Xalapa Clown filly that wasn't any count; he told me to get rid of her, so I was leading her off and I see Col. (Phil T.) Chinn and I know Col. Chinn will buy any yearling so long it's at the colonel's price. You know, the colonel was the biggest yearling man around then, used to have that long barn across the street that Mereworth Farm uses now. So I ask the Colonel if he needs a yearling and he asks me about price, and I say I want $400 for her; he says I want a good deal of money for a $250 filly, so I sell her to him for $250."

Wilson continued to brush the Bold Ruler filly's hindquarters, then went to work on the tail as a barber stropping a straight edge. "You know, Col. Chinn was a real horse trader, best I ever heard of. One day he asks me, he says, 'K. C., how'd you like to go to Cuba?' And I say, 'Yassah, I'd like that fine,' and he tells me to come back tomorrow because that's when to ship out, and I come back the next morning, and don't you know, a man had come by and Col. Chinn sold him every horse in that barn, including the lead pony. And I never went to Cuba.

"I went to work for Mr. Pat O'Neill out to the Ernst Farm, and when he left there I come to work for Mr. Bell. Been with him ever since, about 20 years I guess."

Wilson concluded his work to his studied satisfaction, unsnapped the chain, and the filly nosed into the hay bunched loosely on the floor in a corner. The shed row was raked and another man picked up stray bits of straw which had fluttered onto the manicured lawn which served as a showing area in front of the barn.

"People'll be coming around looking after a while, after they get through training over to the race track, so we'll have to get our signs tacked up on

249

the stall doors. In the old days we just used to tack the catalogue page on the door.

"This Bold Ruler filly will be busy. We'll bring her out for a man to look at and, if he's interested, he'll come back and look at her again. Then he'll bring his trainer with him next time, and he'll try to slip in here during the races when hardly anybody's looking at yearlings, so he can look at her real good. Then, if he really is serious, he'll come back the night just before the sale, and he'll bring his family or his friends, and he'll get them to look at her and ask them that they think.

"Of course, sometimes the same man will look at a yearling four or five times, and then I'll watch him after I take the yearling to the ring, and sometimes he won't make a bid. You think you know who's going to bid on them, but you never know."

The sun was well up, the mist had cleared, and across East Avenue from the sale yard activity picked up at the Oklahoma training track. At the Phipps barn, trainer Eddie Neloy and owner Ogden Phipps watched a set of nine horses, headed by Buckpasser, walk with riders up on a ring animated by foreman John Campo's ducks.

On the previous afternoon, Wheatley Stable's Stupendous had won the $50,000-added Whitney Stakes with the fastest nine furlongs (1:48⅕) run at Saratoga since Kentucky started things here by winning the 1864 Travers. Our Hope in 1:48 flat beat Kelso, but had his number taken down, in the 1961 Whitney when it was run at Belmont Park; that was the fastest Whitney since 1955, when the race was reduced from 10 to 9 furlongs. Stupendous' time was three-fifths of a second faster than the nine-furlong Saratoga mark set last year by Open Fire in the Diana Handicap.

George Widener's favored Ring Twice, whose only victory this year came in the Widener Handicap, set the pace in the Whitney with Stupendous tracking him in second place. Mrs. Hirsch Jacobs' 5-year-old mare, Straight Deal, was dead last after the first half-mile. Under the allowance conditions of the Whitney, Buckpasser would have had to carry 134 pounds and thus was not enetered, leaving Straight Deal as the topweight with 116 pounds, two actual pounds more than any of her male rivals and seven pounds more considering her sex allowance.

At the head of the stretch, Eddie Belmonte began moving with Stupendous, closing the three-length gap Ring Twice had established. Stupendous reached the leader, then hung. At the same time, Straight Deal rushed up on the outside.

"You know, Straight Deal helped win this race for us," Belmonte was quoted after the race. "When we got to Ring Twice in the stretch, my horse

250

just didn't seem to want to go by, but when she came up on the outside, my horse got the idea he was in a race and came on again."

Stupendous, winner earlier this year of the Valley Forge and Arlington Handicaps, added the Whitney by a neck. Ring Twice finished less than a length in front of Straight Deal, whose third-money award of $5,620 boosted her bankroll above that of former stablemate Affectionately. Straight Deal now has earned a total of $551,476.

Presenting the Man o' War Memorial trophy to Phipps, who was representing his mother's Wheatley Stable, was John Hay Whitney of Greentree Stable. Whitney's grandfather, William Collins Whitney, was president of Saratoga in 1901 and re-introduced a touch of class to upstate New York racing after it more or less had fallen on its face during the 1890s.

With Phipps in the winner's circle had been Tim Vigors, wing commander and all that from England, who recently purchased Stupendous for something in the neighborhood of $600,000. Vigors retains a half-interest in Stupendous, the remainder being owned by the English National Stud at Newmarket, where Stupendous is scheduled to stand the 1968 season. He continues to race for Wheatley through Oct. 15.

Randy Sechrest, who saddled Ewing M. Kauffman's Moontrip to finish sixth in the Whitney, strolled by the Wheatley barn. "How'd you do down in Jersey yesterday, Eddie?"

"Got the lead in the stretch, then this other horse wheeled past and beat us by two," said Neloy, briefly describing What a Pleasure's second-place finish to Subpet in the $50,000-added Sapling Stakes.

"Well, you didn't do too bad. Got third money in Chicago (Funny Fellow in the Arch Ward Stakes on Friday), second in Jersey, and first prize here."

"Two wins," Neloy reminded. "Don't forget Heavenly Choir on Friday— $6,175 pot. That's $617.50 for me, and you know, there were six-month periods there when I didn't see $618," said the trainer who last year set a record as the Phipps horses he trained earned $2,456,250.

At G. H. (Pete) Bostwick's barn 41 in Horse Haven, foreman Scotty Riles called, "Hey, you wanna see a happy horse?"

This was one of the oldest barns in Saratoga. It had been patched and painted here and there during the last century and, nestled under tall pines, it remains one of those physical things that lend Saratoga charm and style.

The stalls were narrow and Riles had a large plastic tub at a door, filling it with hot water and Epsom salts. Riles shoved the tub underneath the webbing and MacNab, a 6-year-old Nashua gelding, quickly lifted first one and then the other forefoot into the tub. Riles then turned on a converted vacuum cleaner which set the whirlpool into action.

251

MacNab did not really laugh, or even smile, but nodded his head in obvious enjoyment.

Mrs. Richard C. du Pont drove by. Her Kelso, greatest winner of them all, was being brought out of retirement at the age of 10 for a public exhibition of jumping on Thursday in connection with the National Steeplechase and Hunt Association awards day.

Miss Allison Cram rode Kelso into the centerfield of the Oklahoma training track and sent him through some dressage drills. The gallant old gelding asked for his head; he seemed to want to gallop off.

Donald P. Ross' trainer, V. W. (Buddy) Raines, said it was great to be back at Saratoga. "I been coming to Saratoga all my life. First thing I ask the man when I change jobs, 'You race at Saratoga?' "

How often did Raines change jobs?

"Oh, ever 35 years or so, but they gotta race at Saratoga."

The week's racing began with a program which might be termed typical of Saratoga. Champion jump-up rider Joe Aitcheson Jr. won the hurdle event with a horse trained by perennial leading steeplechase conditioner, D. M. (Mike) Smithwick, and owned by the sport's leading owner last year, Mrs. Ogden Phipps.

The nominal feature on the card was the 54th running of the $25,000-added Sanford Stakes, named for a family three generations of which have been sending out 2-year-olds from near-by Amsterdam to win at Saratoga for 80 years.

The sixth race on the card, however, an overnighter with a $15,000 purse, drew Summer Scandal, voted champion older filly, and Lady Pitt, voted champion 3-year-old filly in last year's TRA balloting, plus Mrs. George D. Widener's Belle de Nuit, which was saddled by Syl Veitch in the absnece of trainer Bert Mulholland. The latter, whose name was added to the roll of Hall of Fame trainers during the day's ceremonies at the National Museum of Racing on Union Avenue, was still recuperating in a Saratoga hospital from a heart attack suffered last week.

Bursting out of the mile chute, Triple Brook, which had won four of her last five starts, including the Liberty Belle and Vagrancy Handicaps, took the lead, closely followed by Summer Scandal and Belle de Nuit. Going into the last turn, Ron Turcotte moved up Summer Scandal on the outside, while Belle de Nuit moved along the rail, three horses abreast, with Lady Pitt only two lengths behind them.

Summer Scandal took the lead, but briefly. She came wide rounding the elbow. Belle de Nuit inched in front of Triple Brook. Lady Pitt began a strong move, then from far back came Mr. and Mrs. Harry Lunger's Reluc-

252

tant Pearl, an 18-1 shot which was not to be denied. Lady Pitt finished second, Belle de Nuit third, Triple Brook fourth.

For the Sanford, Lou Wolfson entered a pair of unbeaten colts, scratched one, and his homebred Exclusive Native, from Raise a Native's first crop, was installed the choice. The chestnut Florida-bred, which had won two overnight races in June at Aqueduct and Monmouth Park, broke from the gate on top and improved his position thereafter, winning by four lengths in 1:03⅗, only a tick off the track record set 21 years ago.

Calumet Farm's Forward Pass, winner of the Flash here last week to become On-and-On's first stakes winner, was the closest pursuer for the first five furlongs, but Ogden Phipps' Vitriolic, by Bold Ruler, closed well to get second money from Forward Pass by three-quarters of a length. The others were 10 lengths and more to the rear.

The box section in the clubhouse emptied quickly after the Sanford. Mr. and Mrs. C. V. Whitney had invited friends for a tea dance, and later Mrs. Cloyce Tippett was giving a party, said to be for the purpose of meeting Cary Grant, with Jane Russell also scheduled to be on hand. Nobody intended to get shut off on a turn because of a slow start.

Seventy years ago at Saratoga they were rushing to a party to see another Russell—Lillian.

## But Now They Know It

LESLIE COMBS II was still talking about the previous day's Kentucky Oaks, which he won with his homebred Silent Beauty. "They didn't even have a name plate for her over the stall here when we were saddling," Combs said. "Nobody paid any attention to us and our little filly up from Tampa." (Silent Beauty had finished in a dead heat for first in the Miss Suwannee Stakes at Florida Downs before finishing third in the Ashland at Keeneland and second in the La Troienne on opening day at Churchill Downs.)

"She was the only filly that didn't have a name plate and Dick Fischer— he's saddling her—says 'They'll know her name after the Kentucky Oaks!' I told him to hold that braggin' until after they hang up the numbers. Never like to brag before a race—wait 'til after.

"When that Graustark filly, Grafitti, come to her at the head of the stretch and it got tight, that's when that old Spendthrift water told the story—yeah

253

man," Combs grinned. "Never get blase about winning the Kentucky Oaks. Uncle Brownell won it, you know, with Miss Dogwood in 1942. I finished second with Gold Digger in 1965.

"Fischer called me, asked whether we wanted to put up one of the New York riders on Silent Beauty. I remembered Gold Digger and I said, 'No sir, we don't want a rider out there testing the track, thinking about the Derby, and finishing second in the Oaks.' I told him to get us the leading rider at Keeneland, boy who is doing good right here in Kentucky—that's how we had Kenny Knapp.

"Silent Beauty's dam, Village Beauty, just had a beautiful colt by Majestic Prince. Half-brother to an Oaks winner, getting that Spendthrift water."

The winner of the Kentucky Derby did not have a paddock name plate, either. Sixteen saddling stalls are available in the remodeled paddock, so the four horses on the bottom half of the program (Barbizon Streak, Canonero II, Knight Counter, and Fourulla) were saddled early and walked while the 16 others in the bulky field occupied the available paddock stalls. Churchill Downs subsequently fixed up several nice name plates for Canonero II.

## When's Dessert?

Alex HARTHILL is one of the first veterinarians a man thinks of calling when his good horse comes up sore. Apart from his acknowledged technical skill, Dr. Harthill is known as a man of sentiment, not averse to a sentimental wager.

Last summer in the Arlington Park kitchen, some men from Frank Merrill Jr's barn were discussing, perhaps with embellishments, the prodigious eating habits of a man who rubbed three fillies in Merrill's barn between meals.

Harthill listened to these stores for some time and when it seemed agreed that the knife-and-fork champion of all time had been designated, Harthill sentimentally offered to cover any money which might show in the event a challenger could be found.

A good doer from Willard Proctor's barn was quickly produced. Merrill's men, smugly confident the Canadian form of their man was unknown in Illinois, backed their representative enthusiastically. The spread was put on shortly after the last set of horses had been cooled out to permit as much time as possible for the contest without interfering with Daily Double play.

254

The eaters smilingly began on six shrimp cocktails each. Then came the vegetable soup. Then bowls of mashed potatoes, peas and carrots, some corn on the cob, and eight pork chops each. Then came the two-inch sirloins. Empty dishes and coffee cups crowded each table, and by 1:30 both men were tiring perceptibly.

A stack of cobs and bones separated the contestants when Harthill's man began to falter. He sadly turned to his backer and in low tones confessed doubt he could swallow one more bite. Harthill received this news calmly, lit a cigar, and called to the cook:

"My man needs six more ears of corn and wants to know what kind of pie you got!"

On the Canadian side, a fork clattered and Merrill's foreman threw in the napkin.

## No Pampering, Please!

HAULED into court last month for permitting one of his carriage horses to tour the colonial section of Charleston, S. C., without a diaper, David Fuller challenged the city ordinance requiring horse diapers, on grounds that it inflicted unnecessary suffering and torment amounting to cruelty to horses.

In dismissing the case, Municipal Court Judge Hugo Spitz noted: "I don't think God designed the horse to wear diapers."

## Sold!

ASSAGAI'S breeder, Robin Scully, whose Clovelly Farms near Lexington include the portion of Elmendorf Farm where the late Joe Widener constructed a training track with a Belmont Park-like Widener Chute and a magnificent barn encircled by an indoor training track, was talking about his Warfare filly out of a drumstick mare.

"I was having some chicken in the Spuyten Duyvil here, you know," Scully clipped in a Brisith way which might seem odd for a scion of a family which has owned a good part of Nebraska for a century or so, but Scully has spent most of his life in England.

"Suddenly I heard over the speaker that this filly's number is coming up. I rushed out with part of this chicken, stood up at the back of the pavilion in an aisle, waved this drumstick, and bought her for $7,500."

The drumstick filly was named Palatina II, was shipped back to England, where Scully does all his racing, and proved to be one of the best filies of her year, winning six races, including the Princess Royal Stakes, Zetland Handicap, and Glasgow Paddocks Nursery Handicap, and placing in three other stakes.

Retired to Clovelly, Palatina II was bred to Warfare, the resultant chestnut filly being sold to Joe R. Straus on Thursday night for $15,000. Which just goes to show what one can do with a chicken leg.


## Going Racing

SARATOGA is the reward for suffering Aqueduct. For the month of August, horses, horsemen, and horse players are turned out upstate for freshening.

Saratoga remains, as it was in the beginning—with Travers and Jerome and Hunter and Withers, and again at the turn of the century with Whitney and Hitchcock and Wilson and Belmont—and we hope ever shall be, the place where racing is a sporting event.

The line in racing separating the sport from over-commercialism is fine and difficult to ascertain. Some commercialism, of course, is essential today to build and maintain a mutuel handle which can provide sufficient purse money to permit horse owners to survive, but too much commercialism snuffs the sport from racing.

The recognized line is somewhere between Jamaica and Saratoga Springs, for a man will say he is *going to the races* at Aqueduct, *going racing* at Saratoga.

What, really, is the difference between horse racing at Aqueduct and horse racing at Saratoga?

The management is the same. The purse structure is the same. The horses and their owners essentially are the same. The outriders are the same.

The physical plant is different. Aqueduct is new, fire-resistant, to an ex-

256

tent weatherproof, big, and accessible; Saratoga is old, has wooden posts and boxes, is cold in the morning, hot in the afternoon, smaller, and about 250 miles from the locus of big bettors. The trees in the Saratoga barn area probably are taller than those at Belmont Park.

To save a child, maybe, or even for a less urgent cause, a man could say that wooden shingles, brick sidewalks, $64 a day American Plan, and a big paddock are the distinguishing characteristics which make racing a sport at Saratoga. This, however, will not hold Vichy water.

The difference, it seems here, is in the attitude of the people who go to Saratoga in August.

This is a month, or a week, away from the business routine of the office or farm, and a man's attitude when away from the daily cares of his business is one fully prepared to be entertained.

An entire day is centered around the horse: Breakfast on the clubhouse terrace watching workouts, a trip back to the barn, a Turf organization meeting, inspection of yearlings, a round of golf or game of tennis, the third race with an entire field of well-bred maiden fillies, a stakes race, a cocktail party on the Reading Room lawn, dinner at Siro's, the yearling sales, a formal dance—and all the while the talk is horse talk.

Saratoga in August is a time of leisure and grace, Troye paintings in the museum and cold water from a hand pump, breakfast with Max Hirsch, and the Whitney, the Alabama, the Travers, and the Hopeful.

Race track presidents, breeders, and owners gather at Saratoga to enjoy America's finest racing, the whole of it, and find, year after year, there is indeed a good deal of indefinable sport in going racing at Saratoga.


## Ready But For One Thing


A half-century ago was yesterday when talking with the late Col. Phil T. Chinn. The subject was big bets won and lost.

"About the biggest proposition I ever had which fit both those categories," the colonel recalled, "came about at Jamaica. E. Phocion Howard, celebrated publisher of the New York *Press* and a fashion plate of a man, asked me to train a couple of fillies for him that he had bought out of the James R. Keene dispersal...said he thought the most expedient means of getting out on them would be to have me train them and have bookmakers pay the freight.

"Howard said he had a money man who knew nothing about racing but who would be willing to put up $5,000 as an investment if a fixture were to be found. Well, that sounded like a workable arrangement, so I took the fillies and trained them to taste. Finally I met Howard one afternoon in the Hotel Knickerbocker and advised him that the situation was pregnant, that it was time to get serious.

"Howard was a very flashy man, with many prominent friends in the theatrical world, and he again assured me that he could obtain the money. I have had a lot of these things fall through, however, and P. T. Chinn preferred to do a little talking with the money man himself.

" 'No, No,' says Howard, 'this is my good friend Charlie Schwab, president of United States Steel. This is just an investment on his part. I'll handle him.' He called him from the bar and suggested that Mr. Schwab have the five kickers in his pocket for he, E. Phocion Howard, was to proceed at that moment to his office and pick them up.

"Well, that sounded pretty solid to me, but Howard insisted he would put the money down, an arrangement not altogether satisfactory to me. The next morning I made a point of seeing Howard, and the money, before going to the track. He asked if I were sure we were going to win. I responded that the Senorita filly was absolutely ready but for one thing—the one thing she needed at the moment was $5,000 bet on her.

"I continued to the effect that if he did not immediately assure me that I was in on this deal, I would scratch the horse, or pull her inasmuch as I had control of the jockey—which was nothing but a bluff, for I did not have the boy. Howard then assured me my share would be riding on the filly."

The morning line listed Infanta, 2-year-old filly by Disguise—Senorita, at 100-1 for her first start of 1907. This apparently gave Howard some pause, for he sought counsel with various authorities on the subject of wagering and was soon brought around to the consensus that Infanta had no earthly chance and probably was over-estimated by the odds-makers at that.

While the colonel was busy saddling the filly and thinking of $5,000 going on a certain 100-1 shot ("That's a half a million dollars and I've always regarded such a sum as considerable change"), Howard remained in the Knickerbocker patting his envelope and thinking how nice it was to have it in hand.

Howard bent his elbow a couple of times, soon joined up with some actress friends and gave no more thought to Infanta until that evening. He then ordered a cabby to drive his party by the old *Herald* building, where race results were displayed.

There it was. Infanta had won the last race at closing odds of 40-1. How-

258

ard fell out of the cab, suffering a broken leg and various minor injuries.

"The next day I looked everywhere for Howard," Col. Chinn recalled. "Finally found him in a hospital. I queried him as to the events of the previous day and he apparently did not have the strength to reply, merely pointing to a table where a portion of the original $5,000 was lying.

"Well, when I realized what had transpired, I said to him, 'If you weren't lying there crippled, I'd kill ya.' I imagine Mr. Schwab held a similar sentiment. Howard was in such pain, however, I finally left him.

"This was a grave disappointment to me, as you may understand, but the previous day had not been completely wasted. I had a horse named Gen. Haley which ran in the race prior to the Senorita filly's heat. I had kept my own counsel on this matter and Phil Musgrave brought him home with a lucrative result. P. T. Chinn learned long ago it was not necessary to keep all persons fully advised as to every aspect of his business."

## Back Again

WHEN Gala Performance turned back the stretch-long challenge of Great Power to win the Jim Dandy Stakes on Friday, it marked the first New York stakes victory in seven years for Alfred G. Vanderbilt, America's leading owner in 1935 (when he had Discovery) and in 1953 (when he had Native Dancer). Previously the homebred son of Native Dancer—Red Letter Day had won the Prince George's at Bowie, the Challedon at Pimlico, and Kent Stakes at Delaware Park.

## The Pride Of Shelbyville

A man who bases his selection on pedigree for Saratoga maiden 2-year-old filly races more often than not drops a shirt. A modest $5,500 purse last week drew a full field of young non-winners, including Many Happy Returns, a daughter of Sailor—Levee which Charles W. Engelhard valued at $177,000 when she was in the Fasig-Tipton sale ring last summer; Silver Coin, by champion Never Bend out of champion Silver Spoon, by champion

259

Citation; Classicist, by leading sire Princequillo out of the dam of B. Major; Second The Motion, by Turn-to out of champion Next Move, by Bull Lea; plus daughters of Bald Eagle, First Landing, Tudor Minstrel, and some others. Something by Bold Ruler—High Voltage was on the also-eligible list.

Winner of this race was Marion Pride, by Kentucky Pride—Tea Charm, by General Don, which Sam Hinkle bred at Shelbyville, Ky. Second was Kitty Standish, she by Miles Standish, who placed at Plymouth 350 years ago.

Silver Spoon's daughter closed with a big rush, was beaten only a neck and a head, and quite probably will be heard from again.

## On Striking Gold

HENRY H. (DOC) MUNDY is a big man with gentle gray eyes, and his personality is as warm and wide open as all Texas. His face is marked by the deep lines of experience one might expect on the man who in the past 65 years has punched cows, delivered mail in Alaska, played pro football, pushed tools in Oklahoma oil fields, mined in Mexico, discovered perhaps the biggest uranium mine in America, and raced horses, and who now serves as director of a bank, a race track, and an insurance company and as president of numerous corporations of his own making in diversified fields.

In 1952, Mundy sold some 2,000 head of prize cattle, his 32,000-acre ranch near Pawhuska, Okla., and his 5,000 acres in Texas, and went to Kentucky to breed race horses.

"I figured if I was going to raise race horses, I would have to come to the Blue Grass where the best horses were raised. Just like when I started raising cattle, I went to Osage County in Oklahoma, the most fabulous all-around cattle country in the world, bar none—why the grass there is stirrup-high to a horse," said Mundy in a soft gravelly voice which could go a distance of ground with little effort.

"See, I was in Kansas City at a Shriners' convention when I met a friend I'd gone to dental school with, and he'd started practice in Pawhuska—that's Indian for white hair—and he was telling me how fabulous the place was. I had figured on taking a commission as a colonel in the British Army—this was during the first war, and they needed dentists bad—and I was on my way to the coast to catch a ship for Calcutta, India, and I said I'd stop by Pawhuska with him just to see what he was talking about.

260

"Well, I got there and the place fascinated me. It was a boom town. Oil had been discovered, and the place was a beehive, teams pulling carts of tools through town, wells spouting oil all over the place—just fascinated me. And the grass—well, I just said to myself: I can get rich here grazing cattle.

"So I borrowed my friend's car, was going down the road, no pavement then of course, when this fella was coming the other way with two mules, no bigger'n 700 pounds apiece, pulling a load of corn. I pulled over to let him by, leaned out—didn't have a roof on the car, so I really didn't have to lean out—asked him where he was taking all that corn. Said he was going to feed it to some cattle—can you imagine that?—just around the hill down there a piece.

"Well, I had to see that—cows eating corn. Back in west Texas where I was raised, there hardly was enough corn to make cornbread. We couldn't even feed it to saddle horses, let alone cattle. I'd never seen a cow eat corn. So I followed him. His name was Jim Perrier. I found out—like a lot of Indians around there, had a French name; you know those French traders coming up the Missouri mixed pretty good—and sure enough, he took a big scoop shovel and started tossing that corn to those cattle right out of the wagon.

"Those cattle were the biggest things you ever saw. I just said to myself, the grazing around here may be fabulous, but this corn trick is what's making those cattle so big. I just said to him, 'Mr. Perrier, what do you imagine those cattle will sell for?' He told me he'd had an offer just that week for $50 a round. Well, I knew cattle if I didn't know anything else, and I knew those 300 cows and 2-year-old steers and winter calves, at $50 a round, were dirt cheap. I told him right then, I just might buy the bunch."

Mundy drove back into Pawhuska, ignoring the British Army's need for dental work in India, and called the bank in his home town of Shamrock, Texas. ("Actually, I was raised in Shamrock and went to high school in Amarillo, just a little ways away—about 80 miles.") The bank directors, impressed by young Mundy's picture of opportunities in Osage County, made the loan. Mundy called his brother, told him to put his saddle in a sack and ship it to Pawhuska. He picked up a saddle horse at the livery stable and leased the back portion of Sherman Moore's ranch. ("It was the worst part of the man's spread and he didn't want it much—about 4,000 acres I guess.") The cattle were moved and one of the Southwest's most successful men was on his way.

"I later bought the 4,000 acres, added to it some, and that remained my headquarters. When I sold out seven years ago, I sold chickens, dogs, cats, machinery, everthing except a horse and the saddle I went there with. The big part of the deal was the $50 an acre for the land and the $450 a head for

261

the cattle. The other stuff was incidental, but we added it up. I'd have a barnful of hay and I'd price it at $2,500 and the man would say maybe that was worth $2,100; I'd say okay; then price some machinery at $1,000 and he would say maybe that was worth $750. We went down the line like that all afternoon, then added it all up, and it came to $1,690,000.95.

"He was writing out the check and said he might as well lop off about 95 cents, and I just said, 'Listen, we been dickering all afternoon, and I've stopped dickering. That dollar'll do me just as much good as it will you, and it won't cost any more ink. Just write that 95 cents on there.' And he did. Tell you who it was arguing with me over 95 cents: W. L. Moody, richest man in Texas, president of the American Life Insurance Company. Died two years ago with an estate of $50 million.

"All I came away with was my saddle that my brother sent me in a sack more than 30 years before and a saddle horse. I sold that saddle to Herb Stevens, and he is using it right now at Keeneland—had it recovered. Henry Forrest is using the pony."

Mundy admits to being a Good Time Charlie in his college days. He accepted an athletic scholarship to Baylor University, where he lettered in football, basketball, baseball, and track, and was graduated with an A. B. degree.

"About all I could do with that was be a teacher for $500 a year, and that was too slow for me. My mother always wanted a professional man in the family, so I scouted around and finally got a scholarship to Kansas City University, an outlaw school where they allowed me to play four more years of football while I got a degree in dentistry."

During the summers Mundy punched cows for his father for $15 a month. He spent his evenings reading Jack London and Robert Service and became "fascinated with the notion of going to Alaska." He spent his ready cash on a train ticket to Seattle, arrived broke, and visited the docks seeking means to pay the rest of his way north.

"I went up to a ship captain and asked him for a job. He asked me what I could do and I told him: anything. Actually, the biggest boat I'd ever seen before was the tub we used to take a bath in back home; but he took me on as ship's purser, and it wasn't too tough. I had a little education, and the job only amounted to checking cargo and bills of lading.

"That trip was really something. I was taken in by the spell of the Yukon I'd been reading about. The vibrations from the steamship whistle would cause those glaciers to crackle like a thousand machine guns, and down they'd come, icebergs big as a building, splashing into the water as we'd go by. The furthermost point north for the *Princess Sophia* was Sitka. I talked

262

the captain into letting me off there rather than go back to Seattle, and it wasn't long before I was sitting on the wharf with $30 pay in my pocket, wondering how I was going to get to Fairbanks and the gold fields when this Dane and I started talking.

"Come to find out his name was Koneig Johansen, and he was delivering mail with a power launch in the Aleutian group, and he could use a man who could read addresses and all. Did that for a little while, then got enough money together to go up and waller around in White Horse Pass.

"That's where one day I see this little dried-up fella come through mushing dogs and carrying the mail. No trouble to get acquainted with another man up there. That was Clifty Mooers. Didn't see him again for nearly 30 years, when I met him right here in the Lafayette Hotel, and we became the warmest of friends.

"Tell you another fella I met and didn't see again for about 30 years when I came to Kentucky, Royce Martin. I was in a little mining operation down in Mexico, and he was buying horses and mules then for Pancho Villa. What a pair of guys, two of the nicest friends I ever had."

Between Alaska and Kentucky, Mundy minded cattle, oil, banking, mining, insurance, and what not. Today he is a director of the Union National Bank of Bartlesville, Okla., director and member of the executive committee of the Mutual Founders Life Insurance Company, president of the M and H Drilling Co., president of the National Livestock Credit Corporation, president of Mundy Oil and Minerals, Inc., director of the new Latonia race track near Florence, Ky., and president of the H. H. Mundy Enterprises, a holding corporation for four manufacturing corporations.

Mundy had been racing horses, mostly Quarter Horses, and in 1946 he started breeding race horses. Since moving his horse operation to Kentucky, he has acquired 36 broodmares. They are quartered on a 400-acre section of historic Hamburg Place which he has leased from Preston Madden. There he stands Bobs Pick, 16-year-old son of Eight Thirty—Black Queen, thus a half-brother to the dams of Polynesian and Papa Redbird. Bobs Pick had 31 foals in his first five crops, including Corpick, second in the Primer Stakes; Bobbelle, second in the Coronet Stakes; and Skeno, third in the Michigan Derby.

"Not many people thought much of Bobs Pick," Mundy mused, "but I've bought a lot of high-powered yearlings the past few years and I'll tell you, it's been the Bobs Picks that have kept the Doc Mundy stable in business. I had a full book for him this year, and I sent Mah Iran and Volotime to him, so he'll do all right."

The stable carries 20 to 25 horses. One of them is Djebah, a 3-year-old colt

263

by Djeddah—Grindelia, by Bahram. He won the Graduation Stakes last year.

"I flew out to see him run in the Del Mar Futurity a year ago September. Real speed horse. He busted out there on the lead with Ole Fols and Tomy Lee, ran the quarter in :21⅗, the half in :44⅕, five-eighths in :57, and then faded back.

"I had bought that colt's full sister, Grindah, from Winn Williamson at Saratoga. She had terrific speed, but fell over a rail at Washington Park and died. I told Winn, when he and Frank Bishop put this colt up for sale as a yearling out in California, that I was going to steal it because hardly anybody knew what I did about his sister, and likely those Californians weren't familiar with Djeddah. Got him for $3,100, and the day he broke his maiden I turned down an offer of $25,000 for him."

How does a man with so many business interests have any time left for horses?

"Well, I spend only about two weeks here in the spring, come to Keeneland and tide over for the Derby. Then I'm back in Lexington for the fall sales, always looking for a good broodmare. And, of course, I have offices in most of the towns where my horses are running, so I get to see them race pretty often. I don't have to spend much time here at the breeding farm—have the best man in the world looking after things, E. M. Carr. And then I can still get around; I'm only 65.

"You know what my pet peeve is? I happened to discover and then *sold* the biggest uranium mine found up till now; sold out to the Homestake people for $28 million. But you know what my pet project is? I've got some gold property in Oregon, dredge operation, already run a pilot on it, and it's a 50-million-dollar deal, fabulous stuff. Well, what it is, is a gold mine."


## Oh! Captain


CHICK LANG, who as general manager of Pimlico hustles horses for the Preakness 50 weeks out of the year, is author of some of the funniest lines in the long run of racing's touring road show.

His father rode Reigh Count to victory in the 1928 Kentucky Derby, and the son won the 1957 Kentucky Derby by a nose with Iron Liege. He had Bill Hartack's book at the time and agents always speak in the first person singular: "I just dropped him in there on the rail, popped him twice, and then put my whip away. See, I had that other bum measured, so I just hand-rode my horse, you know; I didn't want to knock the price next time out."

At any rate, Lang is sleeping peacefully now, going to bed every night comforted by the thought that the fate of racing and Silent Screen are in the good and capable hands of trainer Bowes Bond.

Columnist Bill Phillips recorded for *Daily Racing Form* a Lang show-stopper: "Usually I take 10 lengths off of the chances for a horse to win the Kentucky Derby if the trainer has never run a Derby horse before. Not when the trianer is J. Bowes Bond, though. Not only because he's had experience saddling so many horses in other big races, but I've yet to see him lose his composure over anything. If I was caught on a sinking ship in a storm at sea, he's the kind of captain I'd like to have at the helm."

## Looking For Fillies

THE Saratoga yearling sale next week should prove exciting. The market is stronger than ever, last week's sale at Keeneland showing new records in gross ($5,910,500), average ($20,812), and individual price ($250,000 for a son of Raise a Native—Gay Hostess, by Royal Charger).

There is a strong possibility a new record will be established for a yearling filly. Next Thursday night, John A. Bell III is scheduled to sell the only Bold Ruler yearling to be offered this summer. Bold Ruler, of course, is America's leading sire now for the fifth consecutive year, and the 11 yearlings by him which have been sold at public auction have averaged $72,627. This filly is out of an exceptionally fine race filly, Fritz Hawn's Blue Norther, which beat Miss Cavandish in the Kentucky Oaks on heart alone and which Bill Shoemaker said was as good a filly as he had ever ridden.

It was at Saratoga 42 Augusts ago that the late James Cox Brady left instructions with his trainer, Howard Oots: "Buy the filly." The reference was to a daughter of Man o' War—Tuscan Red, by William Rufus, consigned by Adm. Cary T. Grayson.

Bidding on the filly was started at $12,000 by Gwyn Tompkins, representing Sam Riddle. W. R. Coe got in at $20,000. Montfort Jones of Audley Farm made the bid at $40,000. Oots jumped to $45,000, Jones went to $50,000 and Oots nudged the count to $50,500 and "bought the filly" for the highest price ever paid for a yearling at public auction in America at that time.

Oots said years later that "none out-looked her. She got sick at two and three and became a cribber. She worked well in the morning, but developed a habit of running out." Named War Feathers, she started seven times and won once at four, earning $1,350. But what a broodmare she proved to be! War Feathers produced four stakes winners—War Minstrel, War Magic, Boom Boom, and War Plumage, the latter winner of the 1939 CCA Oaks and Alabama Stakes.

As a usual thing, the average price for yearling fillies is much lower than the average for yearling colts. Fundamentally, this is because of a lamentable lack of filly racing. While more fillies are registered in each crop than colts (50.5 per cent fillies), only seven per cent of the races in North America are restricted to fillies. Consequently, fillies have relatively little opportunity to earn back their purchase price through purses.

Years ago when William Woodward Sr. was wondering how to get a nice band of broodmares together for his Belair Stud, A. B. Hancock Sr. advised him to purchase two or three well-bred yearling fillies each year, test them on the race track, and keep those which demonstrated class as runners. It would seem unnecessary to itemize the subsequent success of Belair breeding stock.

At any rate, it seems that other breeders now are looking at the yearling filly market and it, consequently, is getting stronger. It was the solid prices commanded by yearling fillies at Keeneland that accounted for the record sale average. The colt average rose only $580 above the colt average at the 1966 Keeneland sale; the filly average, however, jumped $5,020 to $20,455.

In 1961 and again last year at Saratoga, yearling fillies averaged more than the colts. The three highest prices ever realized at Saratoga were for fillies—$110,000 for China Trade and $125,000 for Belle Foulee in 1965, and the record $177,000 paid by Charles Engelhard for Many Happy Returns last summer.

## Coiffed

WHAT do people talk about in the paddock before a Kentucky Derby?

Vegas Vic's trainer Randy Sechrest introduced NYRA handicapper Tommy Trotter to Vegas Vic's co-owner, Charles Fritz of Chicago.

266

"Oh, I know Mr. Trotter," said Fritz, "he was racing secretary in Chicago when we had Sir Tribal in the 1950s." Oh, yes, Trotter remembered that gray gelding—won the Balmoral Turf Handicap twice and the Stars and Stripes. "Tell him about what happened the other night," Fritz urged Sechrest.

"Well, going to that dinner the Kentucky Thoroughbred Breeders give every year for the Derby trainers; Roscoe Goose tells me I can't bring my wife because the party's just for men. So after we win the Derby Trial, Howard Grant and I get down to the Kentucky Hotel and Roscoe says, 'Randy, you can't bring your wife.'

"I told him, 'Roscoe, I didn't bring my wife.' A few minutes later he comes around again and says, 'It's okay Randy, I finally found a seat for your wife.' Then I realize he's serious.

" 'Roscoe, you dirty old bald-headed man you—that's not my wife, that's my rider!' You know Howard, has that long hair hanging down to here."


## Kentucky Colonel


NEARLY 1,000 yearlings will be offered at public auction this week at Keeneland and, possibly, several more at private treaty at farms near by. For more than a hundred autumns, Kentuckians have mixed business and pleasure in freeing paddocks for a new crop of promising weanlings.

Save for the larger number of yearlings and the higher prices they command, the fall sales in Kentucky have not changed much over the years. Buyers are still purchasing hopes and sellers are still marketing expectancies. The discussions attendant upon the transaction, however, have diminished in subtle refinements since the passing three years ago of Col. Phil T. Chinn.

He was the real article, a Kentucky Colonel in appearance, manner, and business profession, a player and layer in the game of racing for nearly 88 years. He had a courtliness which charmed Lillian Urssell, entranced yearling customers, awed creditors, and enthralled casual acquaintances.

His father was Black Jack Chinn, noted in the legend and fact of Kentucky history as a prominent politician, race starter, owner of Kentucky Derby winner Leonatus, and chairman of the first Kentucky racing commission.

Young Chinn was at old Washington Park when Snapper Garrison delayed

267

the start for more than an hour, then won the 1893 American Derby with Modesty. He was the leading owner and trainer at the old Santa Anita meetings of 1905-06. He was at Juarez when Pancho Villa's lieutenant called a meeting of Col. Matt Winn's racing officials, jammed a knife in the conference table and announced there would be no race meeting until Col. Phil T. Chinn was re-instated—which was done forthwith. He was at Charleston when a storm blew down the betting-ring tent and one of Chicago O'Brien's biggest parlays went with the wind.

In the 1920s, Col. Chinn was America's most spectacular horse seller. After disposing of nearly 100 yearlings at Saratoga, he would return to Lexington and sell another 50 at the old Kentucky Association track. For 11 years, his Saratoga consignments sold for more than double that of the market average. He sold Hustle On for $70,000 in 1927 at Saratoga; he sold Airmans Guide for $7,500 at Keeneland in 1958. He pinhooked good-looking youngsters and breeders would seek him out in the hope of his presenting their yearlings in the Chinn consignment.

"Hiram Steele, whom I respected very much, had quit John E. Madden and returned to Dr. Marius Johnston's place," Col. Chinn recalled. "Hiram kept after me to come out and see two yearlings—said Madden, Kay Spence, B. B. and Montford Jones had been looking at them. Well I thought then they couldn't be much horses or they would have been sold, so I stalled him around.

"Finally, I came face to face with Hiram in the Phoenix Hotel and I thought, here it goes, I can't stall this man any further, I'll have to finish this deal right now. I said, 'Hiram, I've been looking for you. On my way out to your place to see those yearlings at this moment and I would be very pleased if you could accompany me.'

"Well, we rode out there in a buggy and just as we were pulling into the yard I said, 'Hiram, we've talked about everything—women, politics, who made the best whisky in Kentucky—but let us get down to the business at hand. What are these yearlings by?'

"He then said something about High Time. 'That settles it. I wouldn't want to disappoint you or Dr. Johnston for the world, so I'll look at them, but I don't imagine you could chloroform me and get me to pay more than a dollar and a half apiece for them.' "

The yearlings were in the first crop by High Time, which Col. Chinn had trained three years earlier. Intensely inbred, High Time was out of a Domino mare and was by Ultimus, he by a Domino sire out of a Domino mare. As a 2-year-old in 1918, High Time had raced six times and won once, setting a track record for five furlongs in the Hudson Stakes.

268

"He was a bleeder, though, quit faster than he commenced," said Col. Chinn. "I was not cognizant of this, however, when Mr. Sam Ross invited me to train him. Although not altogether familiar with the colt, I understood he had won a stakes and I felt that would make him eligible for the Chinn stable, so I said I would be very pleased indeed to train him. I soon found out he was a bleeder, but at that time I was confident I had an adequate remedy for such a situation.

Before long, I had him working marvelously; he was breaking all world records, the short distances he went. I thought he could fall down, jump over two barrels and crawl the last quarter to win, and I so advised Mr. Ross and his associate in this matter, Adm. Cary Grayson. I had quite some change at the time and I bet pretty fair—that was when I acquired a bad impression of this horse.

"It was at Saratoga. He went right out there on the lead, run the first half in :47 and something; but it took him about 35 to get the last quarter. He was beaten 15 lengths. Mr. Ross and Adm. Grayson came by the barn after the heat and acknowledged the horse had not run well, a point on which I agreed. I said I felt terrible about it, but I informed them I knew how they could make $1,400 on the horse: 'Gentlemen, I want you to know I have the warmest feeling for you personally, but if you can get that horse out of my barn by sundown, you may forget my $1,400 training bill.'

"So I said to Hiram, 'If I had known these two colts were by High Time, I don't believe I would have been too enthusiastic about seeing them.' But by that time we had arrived at the barn and he opened the stall door. There was Time Exposure—well, he was only five pounds back of Sarazen at two—a marvelous race horse.

"I said, 'Well, so he's by High Time. But he must have breeding on the dam's side.' Hiram said no, the colt was out of a mare that had been plowing down there in the garden. And the other colt was out of a mare Dr. Johnston gave $37.50 for, 'but he's the best horse we've ever raised here.' I asked to see the other one and Hiram was right; he was the best-looking horse I had ever seen—the perfect horse. That was Sarazen.

"Of course, there were two real horses. There was no horse better than Sarazen during his period. Of those he met, he beat them all, mud or dry, cyclone or volcano, beat them at the gate and beat them under the wire."

Col. Chinn bought the pair for $2,500. Time Exposure was to win 22 races, including the Tijuana Thanksgiving Handicap. The colonel sold him as a 2-year-old to Frank Farrell for $15,000. Sarazen was unbeaten in 10 starts as a 2-year-old.

"In his first start, I got a good, hoop-de-doo rider, an Indian named Martinez who was recommended as not one to pull a horse that was carrying a little change. You know, there was a certain kind of rider in those days who would pull a horse on you when a great deal of money was down.

"So I told Martinez, 'I'll give some consideration over and above the normal fare upon the condition you do not hit this horse, just kick him once or twice to get him away and don't win by more than a length.' Well, the boy couldn't hold him, opened up by five, won by two or three lengths.

"So I got Mack Garner to ride him next time; he's on top by four before the others leave the barrier, wins by eight lengths, pretty near tied the Hawthorne track record that day, you know; just a helluva horse. Then I took him to Saratoga, won by four, and made a sucker play—sold the horse to Mrs. Graham Fair Vanderbilt for $30,000 and he was worth $100,000."

Trained by Max Hirsch, Sarazen won the Champagne, Oakdale, National, Laurel Special, and Pimlico Serial against older horses as a 2-year-old. Champion at three, he won the Carter, Fleetwing, Saranac, Huron, Manhattan, Arverne, and Maryland Handicaps, and the International Special No. 3 defeating Epinard, Chilhowee, Princess Doreen, Chacolet, My Play, Mad Play, and Altawood. Time for Sarazen's first race at 10 furlongs was 2:00⁴/5, almost two seconds under the Latonia record and the fastest 1¼ miles up to that time, with the exception of the oft-disputed two-minute Suburban of 1913 won by Whisk Broom II.

"You know, the morning I bought those two yearlings from Dr. Johnston, I caught the first train to Washington to see Adm. Grayson. Said I was in a mind to do a little horse trading and he says with what. 'Kinda like to try that old High Time again, as a stud.' We talked around there for a while and he finally gave me half of High Time for nothing. As you know, he turned out to be a terrific stallion."

Under Col. Chinn's management, High Time led the general sire list in 1929, the same year he also was leading sire of 2-year-olds in winners and money earned. At one time Col. Chinn refused an offer of $150,000, then a record sum for a stallion.

"Adm. Grayson wrote me one day that he had received an offer to sell his half-interest in High Time and that I could match it or he would sell to the man and the horse would be moved to Virginia. I told him there would be some difficulty about removing my half of the horse to Virginia, but that to avoid any unpleasantness I would pay $50,000 for Adm. Grayson's half. I asked him when he would be desirous of payment and he said there need be no hurry—three weeks or 30 days.

"Recovering from this shock—I had no walking around money at the time—I went over to the telegraph office and addressed the following communication to my long-time friend, Fatty Anderson: "If no inconvenience to you, I would appreciate your sending $35,000 to Lexington by Monday, at which time I will have secured the remaining necessaries from my bank. Yours truly."

"Upon the appointed day I inquired of my secretary if by chance we had received any communication from California, and she informed me that $50,000 was on hand, together with a wire that said, 'Any man who can use 35 can use 50. Regards.'

"Fatty was a man of some sophistication."


## Sign Of The Times

FASIG-TIPTON COMPANY President Humphrey Finney, resplendent in dinner jacket, with black tie and matching cane, strolled up the aisle of the sale pavilion, stopping here and there for words of counsel with sellers and buyers. His eyes twinkled over spectacles as he accepted compliments on his appearance and over-all condition.

Then someone noticed he was dragging a suspender after him. He quickly retired to the company office and Miss Jeanne Barnes repaired the structural deficiency with a metal stapling machine.

"Yes, indeed," Finney reported, "staple and Scotch tape. Just goes to show you how tough things are around here."


## All Or Nothing

GEORGE STRATE, a merry 89, was busy inspecting yearlings, but had time for casual recollections. He was talking about racing at Emeryville, which enlightened the sporting element around San Francisco before the plant was closed more than a half-century ago.

"See, in those days you could help a horse pretty good. Buy it by the crate out of Mexico. Well, I had this horse that couldn't get a mile in two minutes unless you give him something. Everybody knew it though. When I brought him to the paddock, his eyes popping out and all lathered up, everybody'd

271

get on him—he'd win, but he'd only pay 6 to 5 or something like that; if he came to the paddock, head all drooping, he'd run out, of course, be about 20 to 1. Finally, the judges called me up, said 'George, we've been noticing your horse; he has long odds for a couple of races and gets nothing, then pops up at even money and wins. Do us a favor, will you? If you're not going to give that horse anything, just don't run him.' "


## Behind Closed Doors

OUTSIDE a closed—absolutely closed, locked door, armed guard, name-on-the-list to get in, and No Comment when let out—hearing held by the Churchill Downs stewards early this week, the thought persisted that it would be a long time before the official winner of the 1968 Kentucky Derby was known.

Five years ago in England, Relko won the Derby by six lengths on May 29 and he did it with such authority everybody was convinced he was the Derby winner for six weeks. On July 11, the stewards announced that they were seriously concerned that routine tests had shown positive evidence of doping in seven cases the previous April and May. Shortly after that announcement, newspapermen suggested that Relko's Derby was one of the cases involved. The stewards said nothing, however, until after a hearing on Aug. 28. Then they announced that they were satisfied that a substance other than a normal nutrient was present in Relko, but that, from the technical evidence presented, they were "not satisfied that it was administered with the intention of increasing its speed or improving its stamina, courage, or conduct in the race." The stewards thereupon continued the case for further inquiry. On Oct. 3, four months after the running of the race, it was announced: "The stewards of the Jockey Club, having considered the report of their further enquiries, are satisfied that the trainer and his employees have no case to answer under Rule 102 (ii). They found no evidence which would justify a disqualification of Relko under Rule 66 (c)."

As this was being pondered, Kentucky's attorney general, John B. Breckinridge, approached the very closed door as if to enter. He was stopped. Now there is no more illustrious name in Kentucky than John C. Breckinridge, United States senator, vice president under Buchanan, presidential nominee in 1860, commanding general of Kentucky's Orphan Brigade, secretary of war for the Confederacy, and president of the old Kentucky Association race course, by the way, but this name was unknown to the guard on the door at Churchill Downs; it was not on the list. After some delay, during which it was revealed that Kentucky law required that the racing commission be represented by the attorney general, as legal counsel, the present-day Breckinridge was admitted to the hearing, one of seven attorneys to attend.

Kentucky racing rules provide that anyone aggrieved by a stewards' ruling may appeal within 20 days to the racing commission. A racing commission decision may be appealed within 20 days to Franklin Circuit Court.

How many cases involving Butazolidin and race horses have been taken to court? Seeking learned counsel from John O. Humphreys, author of *Racing Law*, Vol. III of which is being compiled for publication by the National Association of State Racing Commissioners, we were apprised of only two Butazolidin cases. In December of 1966, a groom was charged in Michigan with violation of a criminal statute in that he was alleged to have administered Butazolidin to stimulate a horse. Wayne County Circuit Judge Joseph Sullivan, in directing a verdict of acquittal, declared: "There are drugs or stimulants that will increase a horse's speed, but testimony taken from experts proved that Butazolidin is not one of them." This case had no effect on Michigan's medication rule, which still prohibits Butazolidin, as the ruling pertained only to the criminal charge brought against the groom.

In October of 1967, an Ohio appellate court considered a case of an owner and trainer suspended 60 days because Butazolidin had been found in a post-race urinalysis—*Battles and Cheney vs. Ohio State Racing Commission*, 230 N. E. 2D 662. A lower court had declared unconstitutional Ohio Racing Rule 311 which held the trainer absolute insurer against the finding of "any narcotic, stimulant, depressant, chemical or drug of any kind or description" and left to the discretion of the stewards the penalty for both trainer and owner.

The appellate court declared the rule valid and constitutional, but unreasonable and illegal to apply in a case involving Butazolidin. Speaking for the court, Judge Guernsey said that it was in the public interest that liability be imposed when the narcotic, stimulant, depressant, chemical or drug discovered "may directly affect the racing ability of the horse," but that it was not to the public interest to impose such liability when the drug or chemical discovered "is not proved to have a direct effect on such racing ability."

"As an antibiotic medication, having qualities as a pain reliever and fever reducer, Butazolidin might, when administered in certain cases where a horse is suffering pain or fever, make that horse feel better, but there is no evidence in our record that it would, in such case, result in either an increase or decrease of its speed, and certainly nothing in our record to show that its administration to a well and sound horse would alter its capabilities for speed in any respect."

At noon, a caterer wheeled up some food to the front door of Churchill Downs' general offices. The caterer's name was not on the list, but the food was, and it got in. None of the participants in the hearing came out. Constant vigil at the office windows indicated that none of the witnesses had been called into the directors' room where attorneys apparently had spent the morning haggling over procedures.

Lou Cavalaris, trainer of Dancer's Image, finally was called into the hearing room; he was accompanied by Peter Fuller, owner-breeder of Dancer's Image. At about 6 p.m. Cavalaris and Fuller emerged from the office and immediately were set upon by two dozen writers.

"Please, we have to catch a plane to Baltimore. We're going to work the horse tomorrow morning," Cavalaris said.

"Does this mean you are going to run the horse in the Preakness?"

"We won't know until after the work tomorrow," said Fuller.

"Does this mean...?"

"No comment," advised Cavalaris' attorney.

This was skimpy, but it aroused speculation that the hearing, during which Dancer's Image was ineligible to run and Cavalaris was ineligible to saddle a horse for a race, would be terminated before Thursday's entry time for the Preakness and that Fuller and Cavalaris were confident that Cavalaris would not be suspended.

Supper was wheeled into the hearing room. Kenneth Smith, president of the Louisville Testing Laboratory, which is hired by the racing commission to test saliva and urine samples, was summoned into the hearing room Monday night. At about 9 p.m., Smith, attorneys, stewards, and others who had been locked in for some 12 hours exploded out the door, hurrying toward their cars with "no comments" tossed over the shoulders.

Attorney Millard Cox, member of the Kentucky State Racing Commission for eight years until his resignation early this year, was more dignified in his departure from the hearing room and was immediatley surrounded by a gaggle of writers. Cox represents Dr. Alex Harthill, Louisville veterinarian who treated Dancer's Image, and Douglas M. Davis Jr., owner-breeder-trainer whose horses were stabled in the barn next to that in which Dancer's Image was stabled at Churchill Downs.

"What's been going on in there?"

"Well, we have been receiving a lesson in analytical chemistry," Cox revealed and walked into the night.

When the hearing resumed again Tuesday morning, Smith apparently continued to testify before the stewards, possibly about testing procedures. Pre-race testing came to mind.

This whole controversy over the 94th Kentucky Derby could have been avoided if Dancer's Image had been given a urinalysis test on the morning of the race rather than after it. It would cost about $11 to have it taken, and it seemed it was going to cost at least $122,600 *not* to have it taken before the race.

About 30 minutes after a urine sample is drawn, initial tests signal whether the sample contains a suspicious substance. The substance cannot be specified with particularity until other tests are taken which require more time, but the initial test would afford an opportunity for a trainer to scratch his horse.

Nelson Fisher of the *San Diego Union* reported that Argentina gave horses pre-race tests as long as 11 years ago. "Horses are brought to the control barn at 8:45 on the morning they are to race; a commission man is assigned to stay with each horse and groom from the time the horse arrives at the control barn until he races. One test is taken in the morning, and the race winner, or the first five finishers, are tested again after the race."

Representing Malaysia at the 1964 NASRC convention in Chicago, Hon. Dato Sir Clough Thuraisingham, chairman of the Selango Turf Club, informed commissioners that a critical doping problem in his country had been solved by testing all horses 20 minutes before a race. Sir Clough returned to the 1965 NASRC convention and urged American commissioners to adopt the pre-race testing procedure employed with success in Malaysia. At the 1966 NASRC convention, Sir Clough said he was perplexed why the commissioners had not made a concerted effort to investigate the pre-race test.

At the 1967 NASRC convention, Dr. Phillip Murdick of Ohio State University reported on the pre-race blood test studies he had been conducting at Scioto Downs, a harness track. Dr. Murdick said the blood test, which required about 25 minutes to run, indicated the presence of some drugs, could not detect all drugs, could not specifically identify any drug, and that it would be some years before the pre-race blood test could be developed to do the job intended.

If anything constructive is to come from this unprecedented disqualification in a Kentucky Derby, it must be the obvious urgency of establishing a pre-race testing procedure for American racing—if nothing more than a pre-race warning to signal the presence of a suspicious substance—to supplement the present post-race test.

As the stewards' closed hearing dragged on Tuesday, Robert Barnard, assistant trainer of Dancer's Image, and Russell Parchens, his groom, were called into the hearing room. After a supper break, Dr. Harthill was called before the stewards, and at midnight Davis was called in, testifying until 2:06 a.m. Wednesday, at which time the stewards perhaps called it a day, although formally issuing No Comment.

The appearances of Dr. Harthill and Davis at first were assumed to indicate they were called to provide ancillary testimony as witnesses. That they were represented by counsel, however, suggested that they did not fit into a category of garden-variety observers. Absolutely no information was made public on the roles Dr. Harthill and Davis played in the matter investigated by the stewards, other than oblique reference to "certain matters brought to the attention of the stewards which warrant further investigation and action by the Kentucky State Racing Commission."

Early but not bright on Wednesday morning, the hearing was resumed. Stragglers in the press corps had reduced the door-gazers in front of the Churchill Downs general offices to about a dozen. Among those called before the stewards was Dr. Charles Jarboe, acting head of the department of pharmacology at the University of Louisville; he carried a stack of textbooks that suggested he had brought his reference library with him. It was reasonable to assume that Fuller and Cavalaris' attorneys, Arthur Grafton and E. S. (Ned) Bonnie, were inquiring rather extensively into the efficacy of Kentucky's post-race testing procedures as well as the chemical structure of various substances.

Also appearing Wednesday were Dr. L. M. Roach, veterinarian representing the racing commission; James Chinn, chemist for the Louisville Testing Laboratory who ran the initial test which first revealed an indication of the presence of a prohibited substance in the sample from Dancer's Image; and George Ralston, licensed as a trainer, who worked for Dr. Harthill.

Fuller and Cavalaris, who had returned from Pimlico at the request of the stewards to be ready to testify again if needed, emerged from the office. They went to the box of Al Schem, Churchill Downs security chief, and watched the day's racing. Fuller said he had received more than 2,500 letters, all but five of which expressed sympathy and condolences as the result of Dancer's Image's pending disqualification.

Without revealing any testimony given before the stewards, Fuller said he believed that it might be a long time before the official winner of the 94th Kentucky Derby was known. He indicated that the stewards' ruling would be appealed.

Fuller said he believed there were certain areas in racing which might need review and reassessment, areas which heretofore had been more or less

276

ignored, but which would be spotlighted as this case developed.

Fuller said he thought investigation of this case and public review of circumstances surrounding it might result in a change in medication rules and a re-examination of testing procedures which could prove to be of benefit not only to racing in Kentucky, but to racing throughout the United States.

Late Wednesday afternoon, The Door was opened and from the stewards' hearing came word that testimony would be concluded at 5:30 p.m. and that the stewards then would deliberate on the evidence and draft a ruling. At 9:23 p.m. it was revealed that a ruling had been drafted. It required more than two hours to get the wording just right and the statement typed. At 11:52 p.m., Attorney General Breckinridge on behalf of the stewards, who confessed to fatigue after about 43 hours of hearings and deliberations, appeared before television cameras and read the formal ruling of the stewards:

Official Ruling Of Stewards

On May 6, 1968, the duly appointed Chemist of the Kentucky State Racing Commission reported to the Stewards that a urine test of DANCER'S IMAGE, the winner of the 7th race at Churchill Downs on May 4, 1968, contained a medication known as phenylbutazone and/or a derivative thereof.

In accordance with the Rules of Racing of the Kentucky State Racing Commission, Lou Cavalaris and Robert Barnard, the trainer and assistant trainer respectively of the horse DANCER'S IMAGE, were duly notified, and at their request Monday, May 13, 1968, was assigned as a hearing date to consider and dispose of the matter.

A hearing was held on May 13, 14, and 15, at which times all affected parties were present in person or by counsel. After carefully considering all of the testimony and exhibits in the aforesaid hearing, the Stewards of the Kentucky State Racing Commission are of the opinion and find:

1. Phenylbutazone and/or a derivative thereof, was present in the urine of the horse DANCER'S IMAGE, winner of the 7th race at Churchill Downs on May 4, 1968, in violation of Rule 14.04 of the Kentucky Rules of Racing;

2. That the trainer and assistant trainer of the horse DANCER'S IMAGE, namely, Lou Cavalaris and Robert Barnard, respectively, were in attendance upon and had the care of the horse DANCER'S IMAGE and were responsible for the condition of the horse:

3. Pursuant to Rule 14.06 of the Rules of Racing, the purse in the 7th race at Churchill Downs on May 4, 1968, shall be redistributed as follows:

1st money    FORWARD PASS
2nd money    FRANCIE'S HAT

| 3rd money | T. V. COMMERCIAL |
| 4th money | KENTUCKY SHERRY |

The betting on the race and the payment of parimutuel tickets thereon shall in no way be affected.

4. By virtue of the investigation conducted pursuant to Rule 14.05 and the hearing held, as aforesaid, certain matters have been brought to the attention of the Stewards which, in their judgment, warrant further investigation and action by the Kentucky State Racing Commission.

IT IS THEREFORE ORDERED:

1. Lou Cavalaris and Robert Barnard, trainer and assistant trainer respectively of the horse DANCER'S IMAGE, and each of them is hereby suspended from participating in racing and denied the privilege of the grounds to and including June 13, 1968.

2. Pursuant to Rules 14.06 and 23.01 the purse in the 7th race at Churchill Downs on May 4, 1968, shall be redistributed as follows:

| 1st money | FORWARD PASS |
| 2nd money | FRANCIE'S HAT |
| 3rd money | T. V. COMMERCIAL |
| 4th money | KENTUCKY SHERRY |

The betting on the race and the payment of parimutuel tickets thereon shall not be affected.

3. Other matters which have been revealed to the Stewards by reason of the investigation conducted pursuant to Rule 14.05 of the Rules of Racing and in the hearing aforesaid are deserving of further study, investigation and action, and are hereby referred to the Kentucky State Racing Commission for such purpose.

Dated Louisville, Kentucky this 15th day of May, 1968.

/s/ Lewis Finley Jr., Steward
/s/ Leo O'Donnell, Steward
/s/ John G. Goode, Steward

At the time, Fuller and Cavalaris already had enplaned for Pimlico. The conclusion of the stewards' hearing automatically cleared Dancer's Image to enter and race in the Preakness. Last week Fuller had suggested that his horse would not race in the Preakness or Belmont Stakes if an adverse ruling as to Cavalaris prohibited his saddling Dancer's Image.

At 10 a.m. on Thursday, entry deadline for the Preakness, Dancer's Image had been entered by Fuller. Bob Casey, manager of Fuller's Runnymede Farm in New Hampshire, was listed as the trainer.

As Breckinridge read the stewards' ruling, attorneys for Fuller and Cavalaris stated that the entire matter would be appealed to the Kentucky State Racing Commission, and probably would be appealed to the courts thereafter if necessary.

Thus the absolute, buttoned-up security of the longest stewards' hearing in the history of the American Turf was for naught. All the testimony entered—apparently of a delicate nature, for transcripts of the sworn testimony were not to be made public—would be aired publicly, as required by Kentucky law, when the entire case is reheard by the racing commission. The lengthy stewards' hearing, which could have been avoided by referring the complicated matter to the commission a week ago to get it where it is now, did produce another winner of the 94th Kentucky Derby.

Dancer's Image, which came from last to finish first on May 4, now is last again. Forward Pass, which got the lead in the stretch, but lost it to Dancer's Image, now is first again. These, however, are just early calls of the race. It is not over.

The thought comes that final determination of this year's Kentucky Derby winner may slide along into 1969, at which time Forward Pass' full brother might be pointing for Calumet Farm's eighth or ninth Kentucky Derby victory.

## Saves the Farm

REMEMBER that horse with the look of eagles, that wins the big race and postpones foreclosure on the homeplace? Shows up late at night in old TV movies.

A Louisville receiver in bankruptcy was looking for him. Two years ago when the Prudential Building & Loan Association went under, the company auditor owed the firm $69,555 and agreed to turn over to the receiver 40 per cent of the earnings of his horse. This is something like a contingent remainder, not likely to satisfy most creditors, but receivers generally deal in contingencies.

At any rate, this horse happened to be a nice one, 6-year-old Knight Counter, which during the last two years won the Ben Ali Handicap twice, the Latonia Championship, Louisville Handicap, placed in five other stakes, and earned $142,662. This is very good for a horse under pressure, but the receiver petitioned circuit court last week, complaining he had trouble locating the horse and his 40 per cent, noting that he had received only $11,644. Hearing on the petition was canceled when Knight Counter promptly won again at Oaklawn Park.

The greatness of this horse, and the timing of its demonstration, would bring tears to the eyes of Walter Brennan.

## In The Bag

"I hesitate to say much too soon. I always remember Steve Judge. He and Hal Price Headley went up on the Belmont roof to see the 1940 Futurity run at them down the old Widener Chute. Judge had Our Boots in the race and Headley had Laatokka. Our Boots was on the inside and he came on steadily, picking up horses, passing Whirlaway in the last eighth, then King Cole in the last sixteenth, and Arcaro started to draw away with him. Laatokka was back in the pack, and Headley turned to see how Judge was taking it. Judge remained silent and expressionless. Then, only a few yards from the finish, when Our Boots had a clear margin of almost two lengths, Judge touched his companion's arm and remarked softly:

" 'I think I'm gonna win this one, Mr. Headley.' "

## Still Eligible

GEORGE POOLE was standing in the Keeneland paddock, waiting to saddle C. V. Whitney's You All for her victory in the Ashland Stakes, when trainer Carter Thornton passed by.

"Kinda tough on old Eddie Blind," Thornton said, referring to Poole's criticism of the Bowie starter's handling of Widener winner True North in the previous week's running of the John B. Campbell Handicap.

"Well, you don't have many chances to win a $100,000 race and I hate to have a starter blow one for me. Mr. Whitney told me I should not complain like that when we lose, but, ah, well I never really say much when we lose fair and square. That race, though...Mr. Whitney's a great sportsman; maybe he can carry me."

Poole turned his attention to a scratch sheet and marked with his thumb, as racetrackers do, the name of a horse entered Tuesday in a non-winners-of-two. A paddock wanderer expressed surprise that a horse of such quality could be eligible for a race open only to one-time winners, for among the seven entrants was Greentree Stable's Dynastic, a leading candidate for the Kentucky Derby.

"I bet I can name you six trainers just as surprised as you to find Dynastic in there," Poole said. "There are a lot of surprises in this kind of race at Keeneland in the spring. Several years ago, I brought a couple of Mrs. Elizabeth Graham's horses to Keeneland and both of them were eligible for non-winners-of-two: Gun Bow and Get Around.

"Didn't get to run Gun Bow here, but Get Around slipped into one of these and he won from here to that tree, about eight lengths. Ran him right back in the Blue Grass Stakes and he finished second by a head to Chateaugay. Mrs. Graham asked me about the Derby and I said we had better skip it. She said that was all right, but that she was going to tell the press it was my decision, not hers.

"I never had any trouble with Mrs. Graham. Of course, when I took her horses I didn't figure I'd have the job forever. But she just wanted to know everything you were doing with her horses.

"See, I figured we better duck Chateaugay and Candy Spots, so we shipped to New York and won the Withers. Then I thought the Jersey Derby would be a nice spot for Get Around, being as it was between the Preakness and Belmont and didn't figure to draw any of those horses. But Mesh Tenney won the Preakness and shipped Candy Spots right up to Garden State.

"I still had Gun Bow eligible for a non-winners-of-two. Shipped him from Keeneland to New York, then down to Delaware, and that race didn't fill either. Kenny Lennox came around looking for a horse to fill a race on the day of the Jersey Derby and I told him I'd give him one if I could get him there—Delaware Park is just a little piece down the pike from there.

"Well, Mrs. Graham comes to see Get Around in the Jersey Derby and sees Gun Bow entered in the earlier race. 'Why, you told me that horse was in

Delaware!' I explained about the race being a nice spot for him, non-winners-of-two, and Delaware being just a little ways away.

" 'Don't give me that Kentucky talk about down-the-pike-a-piece. How can
you expect a nice colt to do anything after a long van trip from Delaware?'
So, I'm already worrying about Get Around, and now I have to worry about
Gun Bow winning this little race. I got Shoemaker for him and he won by
10 lengths, but Shoe rode Candy Spots in the stakes and beat Get Around
less than two lengths.

"Those were two nice horses, though, eligible for a non-winners-of-two at
Keeneland," Poole observed.

As things turned out, Dynastic was 1-5 for the Keeneland event at 1 1/16
miles, broke through the gate, was brought back after running off a quarter-
mile, broke on top, tried to get out on both turns, and finished third; so he
still was eligible for non-winners-of-two going into the Blue Grass Stakes.

## The Middle Jewel

THe Preakness is not just a one-day affair.

It is a three-day test of speed and stamina. Fortunately, since 1931, the
Preakness has been run after the Kentucky Derby, permitting man and horse
at least a week to cool out and a few days to get set for Baltimore, bay scal-
lops, crab cakes, and a horse race.

On Thursday before the big heat, Joe and Mary Jo Pons gave a considerable party at Country Life Farm, a short expressway trip to nearby Bel Air.
Jack Price, who had Baltimore in his hand two years ago with Carry Back,
was down center again.

Carry Back's dam was bred to Saggy at Country Life before continuing a
van trip to Ocala, Fla., where the 1961 Preakness winner was foaled and
now is standing his first season at stud.

Price had a working interest in horses for years before he burst into national prominence with Carry Back. By name and nature, he had been concerned about getting another point or so and necessarily maintained a cool
objectivity in his appraisal of horses. But about the time Carry Back won the
Kentucky Derby, Price began to tumble for his horse. This is understand-
able. The hardest of hardboots have been known to get emotionally involved
with a real good horse of home breeding and become irrational on the subject.

Be that as it may, Price was still talking about his horse. "Booked him to 27 mares this spring at $6,500. The Pons here are breeding a mare to him. He really looks good. Grown tremendously. Last year in New York, we weighed him, 970 pounds, and put a stick on him, 16.1 plus. Now he's put on 150 pounds and grown taller.

"Course, he's probably the soundest horse ever retired and we're galloping him every day, you know."

Was Carry Back to be put back in training?

"Oh, I don't know about that. We were talking and C. B. says to me, 'Say, J. P., how about you and me making a tour this summer when I get through here? We can get a trailer, move around, stop at motels that have rooms with twin beds of straw, have a ball.'

"Actually, I've been thinking about taking him to Saratoga and gallop him this summer. The public will want to see him. And we can show the breeders what he looks like now."

The party was long and gay, featured by Preakness talk, an inspection of Correspondent and the rinky-tink piano of Joe Nichols of the *Times*.

Friday morning at 10:30, which seemed to be inordinately early under the circumstances, Lou Pondfield and the Cohens were ready with a spread of strawberries, eggs, sausage and much-needed coffee at the traditional Alibi Breakfast.

Preakness trainers Woody Stephens and Jimmy Conway showed in coat and tie. Mesh Tenney came straight from the barn in work clothes ("They told me to come as I was;" he cheated a little, coming up with the shiniest cowboy boots in town).

The weatherman forecast rain for Friday and early Saturday. What would be the effect of an off track?

"I don't think rain will make any difference on this track," Tenney replied. "This track is sandy and even if it rained real hard I don't think it would come up slick.

"As to Candy Spots, I honestly have no i-deea about what he would do on an off track."

Stephens said, "I never thought mud would bother Never Bend. He's a free-running horse."

Conway said, "I prefer a fast track for our horse. He ran a good race in the slop last year in New York, but as far as training is concerned, he won't even train in the mud."

Conway was asked if Chateaugay might have left his race on the track the previous Monday, when he went a mile in 1:37⅗, equalling a 40-year-old track record. Conway had been upset immediately after the drill. Part of this

283

may have been caused by Conway's suffering from a touch of virus that required an eight-hour checkup in nearby Mt. Sinai Hospital to determine he did not have pneumonia.

"I had been sick the night before that work and didn't have a chance to look at the track or anything else that morning. After looking at the track, I'd be surprised if any horse with ability could be held to much below 1:40. If he had gone as slow as I had wanted, he might not have gotten enough out of the work. No, I'm not upset about it now."

Tenney was asked again about Bill Shoemaker's ride on Candy Spots in the Kentucky Derby.

"I think Bill gave him his usual good ride," Tenney responded quickly. "There has been a good deal of second-guessing about his staying inside of No Robbery on the turn there, but that's one of the decisions a rider has to make in a race. I think anybody watching the race, at that instant, would have done the same thing.

"You're coming on No Robbery on the turn and from his reputation you know the horse bears out on the turn. But the boy held No Robbery in and Bill had no place to go right then.

"But if he had gone to the outside, and No Robbery had taken him wide, he'd probably have been ostracized from society."

On Friday afternoon, Pimlico renewed the Walden Stakes, which from 1907 to 1948 was an open race for 2-year-olds going a distance in the fall. It had been won by such as War Cloud, Mars, Mate, Chicstraw (over Discovery and Cavalcade), Firethorn, Brooklyn, Inscoelda, Whirlaway, Alsab, and Count Fleet.

The 43rd renewal of the event, named for R. Wyndham Walden who saddled seven Preakness winners, was restricted to Maryland-bred youngsters which liked five furlongs for $15,000 added money.

R and R Stable's Grey Scandal, a gray daughter of Brunetto—Nortell, by El Mono, set the pace most of the way and lasted to win by three-quarters of a length over Edgehill Farm's favored Busy Jill.

Alfred Vanderbilt, fresh out of Copenhagen on a war-veterans tour, was on hand to see his Seat of Honor finish fifth in the stakes. Vanderbilt was the brash, young president of Pimlico 25 years ago who moved the earth. Since 1870, Pimlico had been known as the Old Hilltop Course because of a 10-foot mound in the centerfield.

"Nobody in the lower boxes or on the rail could see the horses on the other side of the track," Vanderbilt recalled. So he moved in with bulldozers and cut it down, tradition be damned; a man with money on a one-run horse has one of those inalienable rights to see what's going on at the half-mile pole.

There was some talk at the time in tradition-steeped Baltimore of dropping young Vanderbilt down the old Shot Tower like a cannon ball in the making.

In response thereto, Vanderbilt stated: "Pimlico is more than a dirt track bounded by four streets. It is an accepted American institution, devoted to the best interest of a great sport, graced by time, respected for its honorable past. We are proud of this tradition, and we do not feel that the changes that have been made can alter the tradition of Pimlico any more than the shaving off of a moustache can alter the character of a man.

"The changes have been an attempt by Pimlico to adapt itself physically to the requirements of a modern race track. We don't feel that these improvements can cost us respect or tradition. On the contrary, we feel that making our track meet and stand off the challenge of younger competitors—in class of racing, in facilities, and in comfort—will add to rather than detract from its prestige.

"And so we are moving forward, guided by the will to make Pimlico the best place in America to race horses and the best place in America to see horse races."

The present management republishes these quarter-century-old remarks in the daily program. There have been many structural changes at the Old Hilltopless in the last few years. In 1956, the Members' Clubhouse, built in 1870, was remodeled. Two years later, most of the old brick and wood grandstand was replaced by a bigger one of steel and glass. In 1960, a modern clubhouse went up adjacent to the new grandstand and enclosing the saddling paddock.

Owners, trainers, jockeys, and writers got with it Friday night at Pimlico's press party. "It" was Cab Calloway's band, which shook the base of the Belvedere Hotel, which heretofore had seemed solid enough. Charles D. Morgan of New York, owner of Sky Wonder, Allied Vans and other things, amicable shouted:

"I've been in racing only four years. Tell you how it happened. My wife and I were in Florida, trying to play golf, but it was too windy—couldn't play golf, couldn't fool with the surf—so what else was there? We had to go to the races.

"I didn't care anything for the gambling, but I became fascinated with the horses themselves. So I got some, some cheap claimers.

"Well, I've since learned, the hard way, there's not much fun in that. I must have spent $40,000 and nothing came back. Had six different trainers. Wasn't their fault. They were all good trainers, but you claim a horse for $5,000, have to run him for $6,500 and he can't win, so finally you drop him

285

down to $4,500, where he can do something, and you lose him. You're right back where you started, and where've you been?

"I got out of the thing all together for about six months. Then last fall, Buddy Lepman got this horse for me for $12,000. Everything's different. We've run Sky Wonder 23 times and he's brought back 21 checks, about $90,000.

Morgan said he had two horses at present, but planned to have six by the end of the summer—"allowance and stakes horses," three with George Poole in New York and three with Lepman in New Jersey.

Raleigh Burroughs, editor-publisher of the *Turf and Sport Digest*, had an inquiry. Would it be necessary for him to send in $100 to The Jockey Club to have his name changed back again? This, it developed, was in reference to an advertisement in the last issue of *The Blood-Horse* which unaccountably referred to the author of *American Race Horses* as Raleigh "Burrows." Will the real author please stand up? Mr. Raleigh Burroughs.

This was an easy mistake, confusing two athletes. Bob Burrows was an All-American basketball player at the University of Kentucky about the same time Raleigh Burroughs was a tournament golf star. The only difference is about 18 inches in height and name spelling.

In his first game of golf, Burroughs beat Ed Furgol. "It was some pro-celebrity tournament during one of the Pimlico meetings," Burroughs recalled without specifying how he qualified.

"I never had played the game, but being a natural athlete, I got some guys to show me how to hold a club and went right out there and won. Had a little handicap, of course. Think it was 32 for nine holes. Forget now what my net score was for the nine holes they counted after throwing out my bad holes, but I got the cup.

"Thought about making a long acceptance speech, but cut it short in deference to Furgol—he's got that bad arm, you know, and I didn't want to play it too heavy."

The rain came on slowly Friday afternoon, then in earnest Friday night. Billy Robinson of Lexington, Ky., who had entered his Rural Retreat in hope of a muddy track for the Preakness, had no trouble dancing in time with Cab Calloway's beat.

This particular party broke up about 2 a.m. Joe Pons returned to Country Life Farm just in time to help a board mare foal a big filly by Correspondent. This is noteworthy here not so much as evidence of the staying power of Pons, but for the topical quality of the pedigree.

The filly's sire is by Khaled out of Heather Time. Later in the day, a spotted colt was to do something special with much the same pedigree; Candy

286

Spots' dam is by Khaled out of a daughter of Heather Time.

By 6:30 a.m. Preakness Day, the rain storm had pretty well played itself out, leaving a heavy, drizzly, wet fog. The shedrow of Barn EE, in which the leading Preakness candidates were stabled, was slick from wind-driven rain. Straw was laid over the mud.

Tenney took Candy Spots to the track first. Stephens had Never Bend and Conway sent Chateaugay out for a once-around before Candy Spots returned. The track was spotted with puddles; the dense fog limited visibility to a furlong.

The gap near the eighth pole was a slide of mud. Both Candy Spots and Chateaugay, upon leaving the sandy track, made motions as if to lie down in the mud.

"How about that?" smiled Conway. "Think my horse doesn't like mud? He wants to roll in it."

A brisk wind began to blow away the fog by 8:30, and shortly after noon the sun cut through. A track labeled good for the first four races was classified fast when 2-year-olds clipped off fractions of :22⅘, :47⅕, and :59⅘ in the fifth race.

"This morning, I wouldn't have given you 20-1 the track would come up this way for the Preakness," Conway said.

The barn party after the race as a usual thing is a turbulent affair. Pimlico officials sent 12 quarts of champagne. The victors, Rex Ellsworth and Mesh Tenney, abstain from alcohol and did not return to the barn.

Candy Spots' groom, Joseph Kascandi of Hungary, who speaks pigeon Belgian-French-German with gestures, reportedly had claimed presidency of the Mormon church in a light moment.

After Candy Spots had been cooled and put away, Kascandi addressed his attention to the champagne. Mormons do not drink, and Kascandi said then he had joined another church. He downed three glassfuls. "Ah, you come. Very nice."

Capt. Harry Guggenheim, Woody Stephens, and Manuel Ycaza, their barn conference over, toasted the winner. It was learned that Candy Spots' next objective was the Jersey Derby.

Ycaza and his agent, George O'Brien, said almost in unison, "Good race to pass up." Ycaza said Candy Spots went by him "like a bullet. Well, another day, but no 'another dollar.' "

Baltimore simmered down after the Preakness. The Monument City is in the throes of an urban renewal program. Old buildings are being dropped like and by blocks around the Lord Baltimore Hotel, which must be disconcerting to top-floor guests. Among the monuments left standing are those marking the deaths of notable clams and soft-shelled crabs, and in these eateries many of the Preakness visitors gathered. At the Chesapeake, Ellsworth and Tenney had a victory dinner to the music of a man who is a better piano player than horse player (he went for Lemon Twist).

The Preakness was rehashed for several hours, which was a feat in itself, for the running was singularly lacking in complexity. Red Smith said he thought the Preakness established that Candy Spots was the best horse in the Kentucky Derby and that Chateaugay was the best horse the way the race was run, and those who could understand it agreed.

This party inexplicably wound up at a 2:30 a.m. Printers' Mass. When the collection plate was passed, a dead one—$10 to win on Never Bend—was dropped amidst the currency. The churchman, with the casual yet careful glance of ticket-flipping professional stooper, discarded the ticket. The Preakness was over.


## Good Old Polls

THE number of polls in racing nowadays is rising. There are several Halls of Fame which require annual balloting—the one at Saratoga, another at Pimlico, and there used to be one at Miles Park. Then there are the year-end popularity polls which ostensibly bestow the title of champion on various horses in various divisions. There are polls also for the Horse Most Likely to Succeed, an informal poll taken every now and then to point up the Jockey Most Difficult for Turf Writers to Talk To, and polls on What Do You Think Belmont Park Is Going To Look Like? Without fear of disturbing anyone's fun by introducing another poll, we would like to have some voting on the horse with the most comfortable name. We vote for Good Old Mort.


## All The Champions

YEARS ago when the world was young—well, we were, and consequently not ready to accept the proposition that much of consequence had occurred

288

before we became a part of it—we accompanied our father to Mr. Hancock's place in Bourbon County to breed an old mare to Snark or Diavolo or something like that.

There at Claiborne stood leading sire Sir Gallahad III, and his son, Triple Crown winner Gallant Fox, and Gallant Fox's son, Triple Crown winner Omaha, and a new stallion Mr. Hancock was quite high on, Blenheim II, and Seabiscuit's sire, Hard Tack, and Stimulus, and...paddock after paddock occupied by horses with names that rang.

"Boy," a son said, "seems like every horse anybody ever heard about is right here on this farm."

So, a generation later, a father took his son to A. B. Hancock Jr.'s Claiborne Farm in Bourbon County to see Buckpasser. There stood leading sire Bold Ruler and his son, champion Bold Lad, and champion Round Table, and old champions Double Jay and Hill Prince, and 2-year-old champions Hurry to Market and Nadir, and Ridan, Sir Gaylord, and Decidedly, and champion Tom Rolfe, and a new stallion Bull Hancock was high on, Forli, and champion Buckpasser.

"Boy," a son said, "seems like they have all the champions here."

Perhaps the world does not grow old. Perhaps the changes are only in the generations viewing it.

It was a lazy, warm, golden morning and Buckpasser picked idly at the leaf-strewn pasture. He strolled casually over to the fence to inspect a boy's yellow hair and was patted on his nose.

"He certainly has settled down quickly."

"Come off the van from New York yestidy morning," reported Edward (Snow) Fields. "Soon as we got his leg bandages off of him, led him right up here to his paddock. Had everybody here—I counted 23 men and myself makes 24—and we're everyplace along the fence, some of the corners have two men, Mrs. Hancock and all the women down here to the gate. Led him up to that corner on the hill and turned him loose. He just jog off just a little ways, 'bout halfway down the fence, then he put his head down and commence to eatin' and we just stands there a little time and then Mr. Taylor says, 'Well, let's go, boys; looks like that's it.' "

Thus Ogden Phipps' bay colt by Tom Fool—Busanda, which left Claiborne three years ago, raced 31 times, won 25, and earned $1,462,014, came home.

Nine miles down the road from the main entrance to Claiborne Farm is 1,600-acre Xalapa Farm, which Hancock leased four years ago. There John Sosby has charge of breaking 78 yearlings on the track Dan Midkiff built for Ed Simms in 1929.

Sosby was putting away a set of nine colts in the 28-stall stone training barn. Riders were throwing tack in a Claiborne truck to move on to a filly barn, where another set would be taken to the track.

"Mr. Charles Engelhard is here this morning and we're getting out all his yearlings so he can see them gallop," Sosby said.

Engelhard is a pleasant, congenial man who likes horses. His control of the world's supply of platinum is said to be such that he can wake in the morning and decide whether an ounce will sell for $1.09 or $1.10. He bears this burden easily. Last summer he bought 21 yearlings at Keeneland and Saratoga for $1,086,000.

Sosby brought out six Engelhard fillies and three owned by Hancock and lined them up on the track. Hancock drove over to the rail from the clocker's stand in the middle of the infield and Engelhard and his trainer, Mackenzie Miller, got out of the station wagon to inspect the fillies.

"This is the Sir Gaylord filly," Hancock said, pointing to a $66,000 daughter of Queen's Gamble.

"She's one going to England, isn't that right, Mac?" asked Engelhard.

"Yessir. Nice-looking filly. Now, this one, this one's out of Leallah," smiled Miller, who trained Leallah for Charlton Clay when she was voted champion 2-year-old filly of 1956. "What price did we have to pay for her?"

"Sixty thousand, I believe," said Hancock, who handled the dispersal of the Clay horses upon the death of his uncle last year.

"Mac and I were talking about that the night we bought her," said Engelhard. "Believe she's the cheapest filly we ever bought."

"Oh, I like her," Miller said. "We must have stolen her. How do you imagine we got her so cheap?"

"Poor salesmanship," said consignor Hancock.

They went down the line, Hancock identifying each: A chestnut Mongo—Decor II, a gray Misty Day—Outsmart ("now, she might act up a little, but she's coming along"), a chestnut Jaipur—Rose O'Neill, a bay My Babu—Tir an Oir. They returned to the clocker's stand, a two-story cupola containing porch chairs, a stove, coffee, and a complete view of the track and the set as the fillies were galloped once around.

"That My Babu on the lead there is an awfully pretty thing, Bull. Who's that bay right behind her?"

"That's one of mine, Charlie, by Tatan. Hated to lose him. I was with him from 6:10 to 11:50 that night...ruptured intestine, nothing we could do for him."

The set was pulled up and walked back to the barn. The move was on to barn 16 at Claiborne, where five colts, two by Sir Gaylord (sire of French Grand Criterium winner Sir Ivor) and others by Ribot, Native Dancer, and

Romulus would be shown before their departure to England for racing next year.

"These are nice training grounds you have here, Bull."

"Well, we have to like it. Six or seven champions, I believe, have come off this track in the last four years." That would be Bold Lad, Queen Empress, Buckpasser, Moccasin, Successor, and Queen of the Stage, with returns still out on Vitriolic, What a Pleasure, Gamely, and some other nice ones.

It is an easy thing to be impressed at Claiborne.


## Bragging Rights

Jorge Velasquez, an 18-year-old Panamanian, won the first six races he rode at Garden State Park Wednesday, then finished third in his last race of the day, an event won by Johnny Sellers.

This put Sellers in much the same position as jockey W. J. O'Brien, who won the first race at old Havre de Grace on Sept. 17, 1919. Earl Sande won the second race on El Mahdi, an 8-1 shot; the third on Wodan at 7-2, the fourth on African Arrow at 2-1, the Bouquet Handicap on Milkmaid at 1-2, the sixth on Sunny Hill at 3-2, and the last on Bathilde at 2-1.

At the end of the day, O'Brien walked into the jocks' room, took off his silks and matter-of-factly announced: "Me and Sande win all them races today."


## Building Blocks

A popular thought is that a man cannot get into the Thoroughbred breeding business quickly and in a first-class way. The cost is prohibitive.

Top broodmares are rare, and, once found, difficult to buy for any sum. Occasionally, of course, an owner can be backed up to a wall and forced to let a good mare go for a price—say the cost of a Saratoga house, a Rolls Royce, a Caribbean island, and two seasons to Bold Ruler.

Consequently, many breeders have resigned themselves to a less expensive—but much slower and less certain—process of racing homebred fillies

291

or buying yearling fillies, testing them on the race course, retiring the best runners to stud, and then culling those which do not prove to be good producers. The late William Woodward Sr. said he spent 25 years building up his Belair Stud broodmare band in this fashion.

It can be done faster. In less than a year and a half, 35-year-old John R. Gaines, a third-generation trotting horse man with enterprise, cash, and intelligence, deliberately set about and accomplished what many have thought improbable if not impossible. Gaines acquired the following:

### STALLION SHARES
Bald Eagle, Crozier (5), Nashua, Sailor, Tom Fool, Tudor Minstrel, and Turn-to (2).

### MARES
BLUE JEANS, b, 1950, by Bull Lea—Blue Grass, by Blue Larkspur. Raced 2 years, 12 starts, 1 win, $3,725, racing index .68. Dam of stakes winners Bluescope and Turf Charger and stakes-placed Natalie. Half-sister to a stakes winner, out of Kentucky Oaks winner. Barren, to be bred to Crozier.

BLUETATION, b, 1953, by Citation—Blue Breeze, by Blue Larkspur. Unraced. Dam of stakes winner Table Mate. Half-sister to two stakes winners, three stakes producers. Slipped, to be bred to Crozier.

COSMAH, b, 1953, by Cosmic Bomb—Almahmoud, by Mahmoud. Raced 3 years, 30 starts, 9 wins, $85,525, racing index 9.56. Won Astarita Stakes, placed in four others. Dam of Tosmah. Half-sister to dam of Northern Dancer. Has Turn-to filly, to be bred to Sailor.

HET'S PET, b, 1958, by All Blue—Aunt Het, by Khaled. Raced 3 years, 23 starts, 9 wins, $50,805, racing index 5.38. Won Hollywood Lassie and Santa Ynez Stakes. Out of stakes winning full sister to four stakes winners, the dams of Candy Spots and Prove It. Maiden, to be bred to Sailor.

LONGFORD, b, 1955, by Menow—Bold Irish, by Fighting Fox. Raced 1 year, 3 starts, no wins, $400, racing index .13. Dam of Castle Forbes. Half-sister to two stakes winners. Barren, to be bred to Crozier.

OIL RICH, br, 1955, by Phalanx—Oil Princess, by Errard. Raced 3 years, 32 starts, 7 wins, $66,732, racing index 7.02. Won Rancocas, Suwanee River, Mary Dyer Stakes, placed in three others. Half-sister to stakes winner Oil Royalty. Has King of the Tudors filly, to be bred to Nashua.

OIL ROYALTY, b, 1958, by Greek Song—Oil Princess, by Errard. Through 1963, raced 4 years, 90 starts, 12 wins, $254,270, racing index 20.12. Won Goose Girl, Firenze, Las Flores, Beldame, Vineland, and placed in 11 other stakes. Still in training.

292

SHEEPSFOOT, ch, 1953, by Count Fleet—Banish, by Count Gallahad. Raced 2 years, 10 starts, 3 wins, $10,280, racing index 1.71. Dam of stakes winner Lamb Chop. Sister to a stakes winner, out of a half-sister to Cosmic Bomb, Fleet Rings, and dam of Prince John and Rulership. Slipped, to be bred to Bold Ruler.

SMALL FAVOR, b, 1951, by Priam II—Little Saint, by St. Germans. Raced 3 years, 30 starts, 4 wins, $58,310, racing index 6.51. Won Selima Stakes. Half-sister to stakes winner, out of half-sister to stakes winner and dam of Silver Spoon. Has Tompion colt, to be bred to Crozier.

SOFARSOGOOD, b, 1952, by Revoked—Apogee, by Pharamond II. Raced 2 years, 12 starts, 1 win, $16,170, racing index 2.76. Won Fashion Stakes. Dam of stakes winner Great Shakes. Half-sister to two stakes winners. Has Turn-to colt, to be bred to Sailor.

TOLUENE, b, 1956, by Hill Prince—Dynamite II, by Dogat. Raced 4 years, 40 starts, 6 wins, $70,068, racing index 5.76. Won Marguerite and Black-Eyed Susan Stakes, placed in three others. Out of a half-sister to The Squaw II, dam of Sequoia, Cherokee Rose, and How (dam of Pocahontas, which produced Chieftain). Has Olympia filly, to be bred to Olympia.

TWO CENT STAMP, b, 1955, by Double Jay—Pelure, by Johnstown. Raced 4 years, 39 starts, 5 wins, $59,394, racing index 4.83. Won Santa Maria Stakes, placed in three others. Out of a half-sister to three stakes winners. Believed in foal to Sailor, to be bred to Crozier.

In recapitulation, Gaines has a dozen stakes-winning or stakes-producing mares which average 10 years in age. The 11 which raced averaged 2.8 years raced, 21 starts, 5.2 wins, $61,425, racing index 5.86; they won 14 stakes and placed in 25 more.

Nine of the mares had produce old enough to race last year. Collectively they produced 28 foals, of which 25 have started, 20 have won, and eight (including champions Lamb Chop, Tosmah, and Castle Forbes) have won or placed in 53 stakes, earning a total of $1,177,525. The mares' progeny Average-Earnings Index for 46 year-starters is 8.12.

Gaines says a man can purchase similar stallion shares and mares for an average $50,000 each. Anyone with a million is qualified to try, but it is suspected here that the project calls for more than just cash.

Although just beginning in the Thoroughbred business, Gaines is not a green man with horses. His indoctrination came at the age of seven while he lived in Sherburne, N. Y. His grandfather, Thomas P. Gaines, who raced two or three Standardbreds each year for more than six decades, took young Gaines to the state fair at Syracuse to see one of his pacers race. This was Hollyrood Sara, 2:01¼, among the best pacing mares in training, and trainer Vic Fleming was of the opinion that the mare had only to be driven onto the track to accept the trophy. She was beaten. Young Gaines was reduced to tears.

"But, granddaddy, you told me she was going to win today. And she didn't!"

Young Gaines' father, Clarence F. Gaines, who originated Gaines dog food, was primarily interested in bird dogs and had more than 100 pointers, show dogs, and field-trial dogs. Late in 1938, however, he purchased a 2-year-old trotting filly by Spencer which had gone undefeated in six races. Named Precise, 2:03½, she was regarded as the champion 3-year-old filly when she finished out of the money only once in 26 heats against good colts. Thereafter Clarence Gaines raced two or three horses each year and in 1944 founded Gainesway Farm near Lexington and began breeding for the yearling market. In 1946, 1947, and 1953, yearling consignments from the 52-mare Gainesway band sold for the highest average in the nation.

Young Gaines received early tutoring from Lao Brosemer, a keen student of animal husbandry who schooled the youngster at the state fair, where they would judge first the chickens, hogs, dogs, show horses, and trotters, then go back and check to see which got the ribbons. Gaines says Brosemer taught him that the most important point of any animal was symmetry of form and balance. Gaines attended Culver Military Academy, which is noted for its equestrian classes, was graduated from Notre Dame with a major in English, then took two years of animal husbandry and genetics at the University of Kentucky while working at Gainesway. After three years of service duty in Air Force intelligence, Gaines returned to Lexington and got his feet wet in the Standardbred business. At the age of 28 he bought his first horse, Demon Hanover, and syndicated him for $500,000. Then he began buying young mares, aiming for a broodmare band of about a dozen young, good performers, but in the process of buying and selling and upgrading his stock would have at times as many as 35 head.

In November of 1961, Gaines began thinking about getting into the Thoroughbred business. At the University of Kentucky library, he spent three weeks reading through all the bound copies of *The Blood-Horse* starting with the issue of May 11, 1929. Gaines says the statistical studies on Thoroughbred breeding confirmed ideas and practices at Gainesway with Standardbreds.

The Gainesway operation was based on the tenet of racing class in the mare, with primary emphasis on soundness. J. A. Estes' statistical studies on Thoroughbreds ratified what had been found to be successful in breeding Standardbreds, that it was important to have broodmares which had raced over a period of time and had proven speed and class.

To acquire a frame of reference in Thoroughbred pedigrees, Gaines studied *The Blood-Horse* annual stakes supplements and began making a list of stakes fillies which met certain standards of racing performance.

He says he was not concerned whether a filly had a fashionable pedigree, only that she had shown speed and class in winning at least one stakes and soundness by racing three years and making 30 or more starts. He would waive racing performance only if he could find a young stakes producer with one or two foals. He determined he wanted a broodmare band of a dozen mares with an average age of 9 or 10, that should cost an average of $50,000.

He stepped into the Thoroughbred world slowly. On April 25, 1962, he bought his first Thoroughbred in partnership with Rigan McKinney, paying $31,000 for a yearling colt by Royal Charger—Marta, by Haltal, from the W. Alton Jones dispersal at Keeneland. The yearling was resold 14 weeks later at Saratoga for $40,000. Gaines thereupon decided he was ready to get into the commercial Thoroughbred breeding business.

Because he planned to buy young mares or racing fillies, thereby excluding older, proven producers, he decided he needed shares in older, proven stallions. In September, he bought seven syndicate shares in Turn-to, Tom Fool, Nashua, Sailor, Tudor Minstrel, and Bald Eagle.

The first filly he bought was Oil Royalty, which had placed in four stakes in 25 starts that season. Gaines hoped to win back some of her $60,000 purchase price and decided to keep her in training. In her first start for Gaines, on Dec. 31, 1962, she won the $20,000-added Los Flores Handicap. In 1963, she upset Lamb Chop in the Beldame and also won the Vineland Handicap, picking up $106,472. So far this year, she has won the $25,000-added Santa Barbara Handicap.

The next mare Gaines bought was Cosmah, in foal to Swaps, with a Ribot weanling at her side. Gaines immediately resold the weanling for $23,000 in the Keeneland fall sale to Anthony Imbesi (who at the time had a Tim Tam yearling filly out of Cosmah which, named Tosmah, was to be voted champion 2-year-old filly of 1963). Cosmah produced a colt by Swaps which had been entered in the 1964 Keeneland summer sale. By its conformation and pedigree, it reasonably may be expected to be one of the highest-priced yearlings ever sold at public auction.

From Elmendorf Farm he bought stakes winner Two Cent Stamp, in foal to Round Table, and her Prince John yearling; stakes winner Toluene, in foal to Nadir; stakes winner Oil Rich, in foal to King of the Tudoes, her Prince John weanling, and Round Table yearling (which was resold privately for $45,000); and stakes winner Small Favor, in foal to Tompion, and

295

her Hasty Road yearling.

He says he tried to buy mares in November, December, and January, because they were near foaling, thus cutting down the chances of their slipping. He bought in lots, with the idea of reselling foals to offset the cost of the mare he wanted to keep.

From Mrs. Reese Kimbrough he bought stakes winner Sofarsogood "on the conformation of her foals alone. She was a big mare, but lacked quality herself, back at the knees, coarse around the head, roomy, and rugged, but not a mare I would have bought if I had not seen her foals, all of which had good symmetry and balance," Gaines says.

From John Eyraud of California he bought stakes winner Het's Pet, from the family of Candy Spots. From Robert E. Hibbert, a Texas horseman, he acquired non-winner Longford, whose daughter, Castle Forbes, beat Tosmah in the Gardenia two months later.

The day after Christmas, he closed a deal with Travis Kerr whereby he obtained Bluetation, dam of Table Mate; Sheepsfoot, dam of Lamb Chop, and Blue Jeans, dam of Bluescope and Turf Charger. That made 12, and it had been 14 months since he had acquired Oil Royalty.

Gaines says he plans to raise yearlings for the market until he gets out on his mare investments. He already has a good return and his entries for the coming Keeneland summer sale give rise to the thought that he will get back his investment sooner than most breeders expect: Swaps—Cosmah colt, Princequillo—Lurline B. colt, Swaps—Most Ardent colt, Round Table—Two Cent Stamp colt, Dedicate—Sofarsogood colt, Nadir—Toluene filly, and a Prince John—Oil Rich filly.

## A Deal

TOP PRICE of Monday's auction at Belmont Park was $46,000 paid by Burt Bacharach for Loyal Ruler, a 4-year-old half-sister to Yorkville consigned by George Widener.

America's most popular music man ("Raindrops Keep Fallin' on My Head," "What the World Needs Now Is Love," "Alfie") explained his zest for horse racing in *Newsweek's* cover story:

"My misfortune was to have my first horse, Battle Royal, win my first race [June 26, 1968]. I had the No. 1 and No. 4 songs in the country and they didn't compare with that feeling. I like the people, too, like Bill Shoemaker and my trainer, Charlie Whittingham. They don't talk about the move they just lost or the record that was a smash in Chicago. It's a no-crap world." Whittingham was quoted, "Burt and I have an agreement. As long as I don't write songs, he won't train horses."

## Too Taxing

COL. CLOYCE TIPPETT was talking about the property tax in California which prompted moving of 36 Llangollen Farm mares out of California to Florida.

"They were going to tax us 25 per cent of 25 per cent of the market value of the mares. Well, if you figure them at, say, $10,000 each as an average, the tax would come to $22,500 just for the privilege of having mares in the state of California. We had a DC-8 leave about 10 days ago with half of them, another plane left last Tuesday—took all our mares to Florida, where they are happy to have the Thoroughbred breeding industry.

"We had a breeding establishment in California worth maybe $1.5 million—probably just have to turn it into real estate. I don't know what they are thinking about out there. Of course, Gov. Reagan is opposed to the thing; he understands how California can lose its breeding industry by this property tax—he's a breeder himself.

"You know what the annual tax would be to stand a million-dollar stallion out there? $62,500. You know what it is in Florida? $50. We just picked up and moved our horses to Florida. If the law is changed, of course, it only takes six hours to fly them back."

## Don't Wait Up For It

OVER the years, Bill Hartack has lodged numerous complaints, nearly all of them offensive, but none frivolous.

A top rider with a sure knowledge of horses and horse racing, Hartack is handicapped by his sporadic displays of conceit, bad manners, and complete

297

lack of tact which irritate nearly everyone. His style of delivery often obscures what might be a valid point.

When the gate was opened to start Saturday's running of the $100,000-added Arlington Classic, Hartack's mount, George Lewis, reared and then bounced along for a quarter-mile before settling into stride, finally getting up to finish third.

Hartack submitted a formal, written protest against the starter. Hartack set out in detail grounds for his believing the starter was remiss in his duties resulting in an unfair break that eliminated George Lewis' chances in the race. He suggested that starters, as well as jockeys, are eligible to be reprimanded for making a mistake.

Hartack was not present at the hearing on the matter. The stewards reviewed video tapes of the race start, found Hartack's complaint without merit, and issued a ruling to that effect with an extraordinary comment: "It is the opinion of this board of stewards that jockey Bill Hartack owes starter James Thomson a public apology."

More than likely that will not be forthcoming.


## The Walking Pole


*The local turfmen are in a terrible mist*
    *About the three-eighths pole being a somnambulist;*
*It showed the talent of a more terrible feat*
    *By walking down the track some forty-four feet.*
*It is believed to have moved in the dead of night*
    *And was probably dreaming of the money in sight.*

*A jockey galloped by on a yearling crack,*
    *But the pole was asleep and it forgot to walk back.*
*The colts came around fine and then broke away,*
    *And here is where that pole came into play.*
*The youngsters were game and well they stood the gaff,*
    *As they sped up the hill in eleven and a half.*

*Coming down the stretch they commenced to tire,*
    *Time—thirty-six and one-quarter from the pole to the wire.*

298

*Then the pole woke up and commenced to look around,*
  *"This really ain't my place, I'm on strange ground,*
*I know not why I moved, but this is sure immense,*
  *I belong at the last panel of the whitewashed fence."*

*The pole pulled himself together and then proved a winner,*
  *He got back in place while the boys were at dinner.*
*To walk in your sleep is no walking disgrace,*
  *But someone caught him while he was out of place.*
*They wondered and agreed as to how it ever walked back,*
  *And now it is gossip at the Lexington track.*

"Micky" Shannon (1901).

Outside the sales pavilion, horsemen gather to inspect yearlings before they are led into the ring. Concommitant with such inspections, there is a good deal of casual, sometimes fascinating, horse talk. At nearly all of these sessions, some hardboot will venture the opinion that they don't sell yearlings right any more, that in the old days yearlings were sold off time trials. Inevitably this leads into the legend of the yearling that was sold off a fast three-eighths work on a short track, and that the late Col. Phil T. Chinn was the man who arranged the sale and the moving of the three-eighths pole.

It is about time to put to rest—again—this canard about the colonel. During more than a half century, Phil T. Chinn bought and sold more horses than any man who ever turned a blade of bluegrass. He dealt primarily in horses negotiable in five figures during an era when a stakes-class horse could be purchased for $2,000. He traded with many people in many countries, and whether the transactions were simple or complicated, the financial arrangements usually were intricate. In this day, *caveat emptor* in horse trading was more widely understood and buyer and seller grappled for the best hold. "In truth," Col. Chinn said shortly before his death in 1962, "I did not always reveal my full knowledge of the animal which was the subject of a transaction."

Col. Chinn did not, however, cause the three-eighths pole at the Kentucky Association track to be moved 44 feet and three inches closer to the finish line on Oct. 24, 1901, according to the findings of an investigating committee made up of the most prominent horsemen in Kentucky.

"We, the committee appointed by a meeting of persons interested in Thoroughbred horses on Oct. 29, 1901, to investigate the report of the attempted fraudulent sale of the [Tevis] Wilkerson and [H. A.] Engman colt [subsequently named Battery, by Wagner—Margaret Jane, by Macduff] and the re-

299

moval of the three-eighths pole on the old Kentucky Association race track, finding that the proposed price of said colt to Mr. [Clarence] Mackay's agent by Dan O'Brien was $5,500 in excess of the price named by his owners to the said O'Brien and that O'Brien is the party who caused the three-eighths pole to be moved." (signed) B. G. Thomas, chairman, Milton Young, F. A. Daingerfield, Thomas J. Carson, Thomas C. McDowell.

O'Brien thereafter elected to amplify, or alter, his original explanation of the matter to the extent of implicating Chinn and several others, and after another hearing a final report was published:

"We, the undersigned members of the continuing committee, for the further investigation of the moving of the three-eighths pole on the old Lexington race track, with the intent to sell upon a false time test the Wagner—Margaret Jane colt do hereby report: That we have diligently investigated all avenues of further information, And we have taken a mass of statements in evidence which we herewith return, And we fail definitely to connect any new parties with the attempted fraud, the evidence connecting the names of others being uncorroborated." (signed) B. G. Thomas, chairman, P. P. Johnston, F. A. Daingerfield, Thomas J. Carson, Thomas W. Moore, Milton Young.

From the published testimony, the facts beneath the legend appear to be:

The Kentucky Association track in Lexington, at which no regular racing meeting had been held since 1898, was being used as a training center in the fall of 1901. From the three-eighths pole to the quarter pole, there was a slight rise which for more than a century sorely tested horses and players. Because of the hill, yearlings usually were tried over the downgrade quarter of a mile to the finish line, Hal Petit Headley testifying that "This was the first yearling I had seen or heard of going three-eighths of a mile this year." For many years, the three-eighths pole had been marked by an old walnut tree, but after the timber had been cut from the centerfield, the distance was marked by a small pole nailed against the fence.

O'Brien, who trained a public stable, was breaking a Wagner colt owned by Wilkerson and Engman. Phil Chinn, then 27, asked O'Brien if he had a good colt. O'Brien worked the colt a quarter in :23½ and informed Chinn that he could be purchased for $10,000. Chinn then told his father, Col. Jack P. Chinn, who informed Clarence Mackay in New York that a good colt in Lexington was available for $10,000. Mackay sent his trainer, C. F. Hill, to inspect the colt.

Hill, in a letter to the investigating committee, said he was met by Jack Chinn at the Phoenix Hotel and they went out to the track. "On walking over the ground from the stand to the three-eighths pole, I thought that the eighth of a mile from the three-eighths pole to the quarter pole would be a very trying eighth of a mile, and the last quarter very fast. To my surprise, the colt ran the first eighth the fastest and this made me feel as though my calculations were all wrong. Dan O'Brien said the colt was priced at $8,000. On my way home, the more I thought of the trial, the more I was puzzled, and on reaching Mr. Mackay's office on Friday, I wired Col. Jack Chinn to make sure that the three-eighths pole was in its proper place."

The yearling had worked over the hill in :11¼ and had swept home in :36¼. The stipulated time necessary for the sale had been :36½.

Col. Jack Chinn was widely known for his courtly manner, his horses (his Leonatus won the 1883 Kentucky Derby), his abilities as a racing starter, judge, and commission chairman; his political acumen (Kentucky's first racing statute was known as the Chinn Act), and his uncommon success in hand-to-hand combat. Immediately after the work, and in the presence of Hill, he ordered his son to have the track measured.

Headley, who also was in the stands with Hill and Chinn clocking the workout, said later that soon after the work, his trainer, L. D. Frazee, advised him that he believed the three-eighths pole had been moved. Later in the morning, Hill "drove to my farm with me and as we drove along I said to Hill, as a rule a man did pretty well to attend to his own business, but that I had noticed something that I thought I ought to tell him. I then told him I thought the pole had been moved."

In his testimony before the second investigating committee, O'Brien said that after Wilkerson and Engman said all they wanted for the colt was $2,500, he advised them to stay away from the track the morning of the workout "because there would have to be a little cheating done."

Q. "The agreement was that you were to get $2,500 for them and as much as you pleased for yourself, by doing a little cheating?"

A. "The balance was to be split between me and Chinn. Phil was the one I was doing business with."

Q. "About the moving of the pole, you say that Phil Chinn knew that you were to do something?"

A. "There is no doubt but that Phil Chinn knew all about it. He knew the pole was moved."

Q. "Will you please tell me who put the pole back?"

A. "Kinnard moved it and put it back [later in the day], at my direction; that is, I told him to do it."

Q. "Who fathered the idea of moving the pole, you or Phil Chinn?"

A. "Well, I believe that Chinn suggested that first; yes, he suggested it first."

Q. "I would like to ask you how young Chinn began the conversation with you about moving this pole?"

A. "He suggested, in an offhand way, that we must get a good move, even if it was necessary to move the pole up a little."

Q. "There was no definite understanding about the division of the money [in excess of $2,500]?"

A. "No, we did not have any understanding, only that it would be split up between Chinn and myself."

Q. "Did Phil Chinn ever suggest to you that anybody else was interested beside you and himself?"

A. "No sir, nobody else."

Dr. R. M. Bryan, a veterinarian who treated many of the horses trained by O'Brien, testified: "I asked O'Brien who suggested the moving of the pole and he said, 'I'm not certain, but I think it was Phil.' I then asked him if both the Chinns knew that the pole had been moved the morning the colt was worked, and he said he knew Phil knew it, and if his father knew, Phil had told him, 'for I did not talk with the old gentleman myself,' but he said Phil knew it. I then asked him if he would come before the committee again and tell the whole business, and he said he would."

Phil Chinn was then called to testify:

Q. "In your conversation with Dan O'Brien, did you say that we can or must make some money for ourselves?"

A. "No sir, not in any way, shape, manner, or form."

Q. "Did you in any way convey that idea to him or to anyone else?"

A. "No, sir. Positively no, sir, not in any particular."

Q. "Did Dan O'Brien say we will have to do a little cheating?"

A. "I was lying in bed the other night and thought of that question about the cheating. When that question was put to me first, I answered it that I did not. I do remember very distinctly that Mr. O'Brien said that he would like to know where he should work the colt, and I said to him to work him where all the horses are worked. And I then said to him to be sure he had a good one, for I did not want my father to bring anyone here from New York unless he absolutely had a good horse. He replied to me that he would get him there in 23 seconds. I then said to him if you can get him there in 23 seconds, he is a good horse. I know he did not say anything about cheating, for I would not have countenanced that for one second."

Q. "You say emphatically you did not understand that there was to be any cheating done?"

A. "Not in any way, shape, manner, or form."

Q. "Did you know or believe from some expressed or implied understand-

302

ing that the three-eighths pole was to be moved up?"

A. "No sir, I had not the slightest idea that the three-eighths pole was to be moved up, nor did I know at that time, the time the colt was worked, that the three-eighths pole had been moved up. My first knowledge of it was after a day had elapsed, here in this hotel, when Mr. Ewing said Jimmie, the boy in the stable, had told him that he was galloping some horses, and the horses shied at the white-wash on the fence."

Q. "Mr. Chinn, please let me ask this question: Did you or did you not expect to receive any part of the money for which this colt was sold?"

A. "I hope I may drop dead this minute if ever I was to receive one copper cent from the sale of this colt."

Q. "Did your father instruct you to survey or measure the track?"

A. "Yes, sir, he did in the presence of Mr. Hill, when we went to the stable to see the colt cool out."

Q. "That is a thought, I presume, that resulted from the exceedingly fast work of the colt?"

A. "Yes, sir. And I think my father timed the horse slower than anyone else."

Q. "State whether or not you first suggested the moving of the three-eighths pole?"

A. "No, sir. I did not. As I have said that I did not know the slightest thing about it. I now reiterate that statement, and I hope I may drop dead this minute if I ever expected to get one cent for the sale of this colt, or if I ever thought there was to be any cheating done."

The testimony of O'Brien then was read to young Chinn, who responded: "In all but a few points—that in no way involved me—that statement is an absolute lie, and is as base a lie as could come out of the foulest man that lives."

Col. Jack Chinn was then called and he testified that at the time of the workout he did not believe the pole had been moved, but suggested that the track be surveyed because the trial was fast and the asking price a big one. After O'Brien's testimony implicating young Phil was read to him, the elder Chinn stated, apparently with some indignation:

"I raised that boy and I do not believe that he would put up a job to rob his father. I have had a great many dealings with that boy from his youth up, and I have never had any trouble with him in any way. He has been my partner in business, had access to my bank account, and I hope, gentlemen, that you will not listen to the statement of that perjurer. Phil knew I wanted a good colt, and I could trust him to find one for me. I have always found that boy to be upright and honest in everything, and I would rather see him

303

dead than to see him in a blotch of this kind. I trust him with my money, as I would with my life, and I have never known him to misrepresent anything to me in any way."

Many other witnesses were called, and at the conclusion a motion was made by Capt. T. J. Clay that, with the exception of O'Brien, all other parties whose names had been connected in any way with the pole-moving be exonerated. The motion carried.

In epilogue, it may be noted that Mackay did not buy the colt. Battery was to race only five times, as a 4-year-old gelding, in Engman's name, trained by J. R. Taylor. His racing career extended over 15 days. In his first race, he finished sixth ("Battery showed speed for three-quarters and is reported very fast"). He finished sixth again, then won his third start, a $400 selling race. He was second in his fourth start, and fifth, beaten by less than a length, in his final start ("Battery was lame when going to the post and quit badly after showing much speed for five-eighths").

## Sounds About Right

WE first encountered Larry Boyce five Belmonts ago when Kauai King was a sentimental betting favorite to win the Triple Crown, but finished out of the money in the Belmont. Boyce was standing next to Kauai King's barn after the race with a glass of champagne in one hand and $10,000 worth of uncashable show tickets on Kauai King in the other.

"I was hoping we would finish in the money," Boyce remarked casually, then wandered off to take a look at Amberoid.

Last October, Boyce's Hark the Lark, which he trains, won his first start at Marlboro, a performance which impressed the owner-trainer to the extent that Hark the Lark was entered in the Garden State Stakes. He finished 11th. In January of this year, Hark the Lark won another race, this time by eight lengths at Liberty Bell, and that left a lasting impression on his owner-trainer.

Hark the Lark has not won a race in his last dozen starts (he finished 15 lengths back in a $25,000 claiming event), but Boyce is getting him ready. He said he entered his horse in the Preakness (he finished 12th) as a prep for the Belmont. In the Belmont paddock, Boyce advised Jean Cruguet that if he rode the horse right (he pushed the pace for a half-mile, then retired to last place, 32 lengths back), he could have the mount back in the English St. Leger.

Nobody ever got to the moon without a lot of preparation.

## The Salesman

The shiny green car bounced over the cattle guard on the bridge and proceeded cautiously through the front field. A mare, long in mane and tooth, one of the oldest expectant dams in Kentucky, viewed the intruder impassively. As if to demonstrate her proprietorship, she caused the car to halt while she slowly walked, with the imperiousness that comes to one of the age and condition, across the roadway.

The car then continued up the hill and stopped at the yard gate. A woolly Saint Bernard lounged on the front porch, raised his head, slightly, and barked twice, his limit for the day. The driver got out of the car and walked up to the yard fence, and we went to meet him.

A big man with ruddy complexion, he was wearing a broad grin and a cap that at first appeared to be made of camouflage material. An Army Reservist, we thought, one who will ask if he can fish in the creek. As we drew closer, we became fascinated. Small green leaves and jonquils that had not yet burst into bloom, were stuck in the band of his hat.

"Howdy." He extended his hand across the fence in warm greeting. "I deal in supplements. Been trying to get by your place before now, but the ice on your bridge stopped me. Figured if I did get across, I would never make it up the hill."

Yes, we have been visited by some real weather this year. Snow and ice came in and just stayed.

The salesman put his foot up on the second plank, the way one does in talking over a fence, and the plank gave way, creaking to the ground.

"Oh, I'm sorry," he said. It was quite all right, we assured him. We had a number of posts we had to replace; just waiting for the weather to get better. That reminded us that we had to repaint this year; really should have done it last year.

We walked up to the tool shed, got a hammer and some nails. He held the plank in place, and we hammered it back. We noticed some locust branches March winds had carried to the ground and together we gathered up these.

305

"Say, I see the creek has shoved some wood up onto your front field there; I'd be glad to help you if you want to clean that up."

Well, this was an introductory offer we were not about to refuse. Together we picked up the flotsam and jetsam of winter that bordered the creek. With a closer view of the land than we had had for months, we noticed bright new blades of green thrusting upward through the beige mass.

We unloaded the driftwood in the sink hole, and the salesman brushed off his hands. With a grin and raised eyebrow, he silently inquired what was next. What kind of supplements was he selling?

"Oh, I'm not *selling* anything. I'm an area distributor." He took off his foliage hat and with it traced the path of the sun.

"I deal in a variety of supplements. They make new foals want to run and kick. They rejuvenate pastures. They stir warm breezes. I work this territory every year about this time."

We were prepared to buy his entire stock.

"You can have 'em," he beamed, "all you want, all you can see and feel. No charge."

If not money, what would he take in trade?

"Doldrums," he said. We promptly gave him all we had on hand and closed the deal.

"Mr. Spring," we said, "it's a pleasure to do business with you." He smiled, tipped his hat, turned and headed North.

# INDEX

308